Thunder from the Right

Thunder from the Right

Ezra Taft Benson
in Mormonism and Politics

Edited by
MATTHEW L. HARRIS

UNIVERSITY OF
ILLINOIS PRESS
Urbana, Chicago, and Springfield

1 2 3 4 5 C P 5 4 3 2 1
Printed and bound in Great Britain by
Marston Book Services Ltd, Oxfordshire
♾ This book is printed on acid-free paper.

Photographs courtesy of the *Salt Lake Tribune*.

Library of Congress Cataloging-in-Publication Data
Names: Harris, Matthew L., editor.
Title: Thunder from the right : Ezra Taft Benson in Mormonism and
     politics / edited by Matthew L. Harris.
Description: [Urbana, Illinois] : [University of Illinois Press], [2019]
     | Photographs courtesy of the Salt Lake Tribune. | Includes
     bibliographical references and index.
Identifiers: LCCN 2018032359| ISBN 9780252042256 (hardcover : alk.
     paper) | ISBN 9780252084010 (pbk. : alk. paper)
Subjects: LCSH: Benson, Ezra Taft—Political activity. | United States—
     Politics and government—1945–1989. | Mormon Church—Political
     activity. | Church of Jesus Christ of Latter-day Saints—Political
     activity.
Classification: LCC BX8695.B38 T48 2019 | DDC 289.3092—dc23
     LC record available at https://lccn.loc.gov/2018032359

E-book ISBN 978-0-252-05108-1

Cover image: Vice President George H. W. Bush with LDS
church president Ezra Taft Benson, Feb. 21, 1986. (Courtesy
of the Salt Lake City Tribune)

Contents

Acknowledgments

My interest in Mormon studies began years ago when I coauthored a book on Mormons and blacks with the distinguished Mormon historian Newell Bringhurst. Newell taught me the "tricks of the trade" as he introduced me to the burgeoning field of Mormon studies. Since our collaboration began nearly a decade ago, Newell has read virtually everything I have written about Mormon history. His keen insights, perceptive criticisms, and gentle encouragement have bolstered my spirits. I value his friendship.

Special thanks also to the numerous archivists and librarians who tracked down obscure documents, located hard-to-find books, and shared materials even when I didn't ask for them. Bill Slaughter, now retired from the LDS Church History Library in Salt Lake City, Utah, is one such archivist. I distinctly recall years ago when I was researching at the Church History Library when, out of the blue, Bill approached me from behind, tapped me on the shoulder, and said, "Matt, you need to see this." With friends like that, you can't go wrong.

Bill's colleagues at the Church History Library have also been a pleasure to work with, as have archivists at Brigham Young University, the University of Utah, Utah State University, and the Utah State Historical Society. To these good folks I must acknowledge the support of my own institution at Colorado State University–Pueblo. Not only has the university provided generous research stipends over the years, but they have funded conference excursions and provided release time from my teaching duties to meet publishing deadlines. None of that compares, though, to the indefatigable Kenneth McKenzie, CSU–Pueblo's interlibrary loan whiz. Kenny has tracked down books and journals with superhuman speed, never complaining about the endless requests I send his way. Thank you, Kenny.

Other friends have aided me along the way. The ever-genial Steve Mayfield sent newspaper clippings, *Ensign* articles, and anything he perceived was related to my work. Greg Prince generously shared his oral histories with me on Ralph Harding and Reed Benson. Gary Bergera patiently read drafts of my work, shared research materials, and offered sound advice. Joe Geisner shared a trove of Benson documents. Bill Morain granted permission for me to use portions of an article I published in *The John Whitmer Historical Association Journal*. The contributing authors deserve a special shout-out as well. Their sensitivity, unflagging honesty, and superb scholarship have carried this book. Thanks, too, to the skilled and efficient staff at the University of Illinois Press, especially to Dawn Durante, the senior acquisitions editor, whose humor and professionalism are unmatched.

And finally, my family. Where to begin? My father and stepmother lent me their "church" (for example, Deseret) books to support my work, and they never hesitated sharing stories or recollections about Ezra Taft Benson. To their support I add my mother, who has been a frequent interlocutor and patient listener as I regaled her with stories about Benson on my long hikes at the Pueblo Reservoir. My brothers and sisters have been stalwarts as well, especially my sister, Trina Hammond, and my brother, Mike Harris. My sister invited me into her home during my research capers in Utah, while my brother has been my intellectual partner for many years on all things Mormon. He and I debate, argue, share stories, and reflect on our shared interest in the Mormon past. Thank you, brother. Thank you, sis.

Last but not least, I end with my wife and children, who make it all possible. Though they didn't help with any of the research, edit any of the prose, or attend any of my presentations, they alone are the indispensable people in my scholarship. They make our home a lively and energetic place to be—one full of love, good nature, and warmth. Courtney, Madison, Taylor, and Jackson: I'm blessed to have you.

Introduction
Breaching the Wall

Ezra Taft Benson on Church and State

MATTHEW L. HARRIS

In the summer of 1989, President George H. W. Bush awarded the Mormon apostle-president Ezra Taft Benson the Presidential Citizen's Medal, the second highest award bestowed by the United States government. Nearly four decades earlier Benson had served as the agricultural secretary in Eisenhower's administration, the first Mormon leader to serve in a presidential cabinet. Benson's dogged advocacy of conservativism and his slashing sermons against communism made him a memorable figure. During his Mormon ministry he gave hundreds of speeches on political themes, fusing his strong political convictions with his religious ones. On at least two occasions he tried to run for the U.S. presidency, vowing to curtail liberal government programs, which he deemed destructive to the republic. Moreover, in sermons and writings he warned about a "communist conspiracy" within the U.S. government, claiming a link between American bureaucrats, civil rights leaders, and Kremlin operatives from the Soviet Union.[1] Perhaps it was fitting, then, that in the commendation citation President Bush recognized Benson's tireless devotion "to the principles of freedom." The Mormon leader, in Bush's judgment, was "one of the most distinguished Americans of his time."[2]

Benson's strong political convictions were formed during a time of intense political conflict between the United States and the Soviet Union. As the Cold War gripped the nation following the chaotic post–World War II years, Benson, like other Americans, promoted Christianity and traditional family values as an antidote to "godless communism."[3] The Mormon apostle frequently discussed "god, family, and country" in his sermons, urging fellow Mormons to join civic groups to fight communism.[4] Benson's own family set the example, energetically embracing the John Birch Society, an extreme anticommunist organization. For more than three decades, Ezra, his wife Flora, and sons Reed and Mark affiliated with this controversial organization, where Reed also served as a regional director and then subsequently as the national director of public relations. The family also associated with other "freedom groups" and was actively involved with the Republican Party, both as consultants and party organizers.[5] Benson viewed his family's civic-mindedness in providential terms: "Certain bloodlines seem to have the spirit of freedom in their veins," the apostle told his children. "Mother and I are grateful that each of our children has that spirit of freedom . . . and have a love for this country and understand its divine destiny."[6]

The apostle's fierce political views were often indistinguishable from his religious ones. During his five decades as an LDS general authority, including forty-two years in the Quorum of the Twelve Apostles (1943–1985) and nine years as LDS church president (1985–1994), Benson promoted a conservative constitutionalism that breached the wall between church and state.[7] Most notably, he criticized the U.S. Supreme Court for striking down school prayer in *Engel v. Vitale* (1962) and balked at other high court rulings, claiming the justices had waged a "weird war" against religion.[8] Indeed, Benson's interpretation of the First Amendment permitted cracks in the proverbial wall between church and state because he believed that political matters were largely spiritual affairs. In his typical blunt fashion, Benson proclaimed that he "never had to separate his religion from his politics" because the two were so closely intertwined. "I think it's all one great big ball of wax," he memorably noted.[9]

Benson similarly linked conservativism with Mormonism. He envisioned a world of free markets, limited government, personal choice, and liberty under law.[10] At the same time, he condemned labor unions, liberalism, and government welfare programs, specifically federal aid to education, Medicaid and Medicare, and Social Security. These programs, he frightfully asserted, not only contravened the basic tenets of Mormonism, but they were neither constitutional nor fiscally sustainable.[11] In his popular Mormon book, *The Red Carpet*, published in 1962, the apostle declared that the welfare state would lead the country down "the royal road to communism."[12] He viewed this as a three-phased process asserting that liberalism would morph into socialism, socialism into communism, and communism into enslavement, thus robbing Americans of free agency and individual initiative. For Benson, then, it was imperative that Latter-day Saints avoid socialism and communism because these "principles run counter to the revealed word of God. . . ."[13]

The apostle's conservative values were forged and nourished growing up on a small family farm in the bucolic agricultural community of Whitney,

Idaho. Benson's rugged individualism and indefatigable work ethic instilled in him an unwavering sense of independence and self-sufficiency that influenced his views of government. Early in his Mormon ministry, for example, he cautioned Latter-day Saints to avoid government assistance, warning them to "stand on [their] own feet" and be resourceful rather that "run to a paternalistic government for help when every problem arises."[14] Later in his ministry Benson was even more direct, instructing Latter-day Saints that if "the individual cannot support himself he should look to his family for assistance. If the family cannot help, the Church may provide necessary sustenance—not as a dole, but in exchange for earned labor."[15]

Benson's Mormon heritage contributed to his conservative values as well. The Mormon church's teachings on self-sufficiency, independence, and hard work influenced his views on government, the welfare state, and public assistance. Benson, moreover, was steeped in American exceptionalism. Since the founding of the Mormon church in 1830, during a time of intense American nationalism after the War of 1812, LDS leaders proclaimed the Constitution "divinely inspired." Mormon prophets and Mormon scripture had foretold the providential destiny of the United States, declaring the fledgling republic a favored nation.[16] Thus, for Benson, the United States was a "choice land" and "the American Constitution . . . an inspired document." The "day will come," he insisted, "when the Constitution will be endangered and hang as it were by a single thread. I was taught that we should study the Constitution, preserve its principles, and defend it against any who would destroy it. To the best of my ability I have always tried to do this."[17]

Benson's conservative views were further solidified during the Great Depression when millions of Americans, crushed by staggering poverty and chronic unemployment, looked to the federal government to help them. In response, President Franklin D. Roosevelt implemented the New Deal, one of the most far-reaching and innovative government programs in the nation's history. Like many conservatives of his generation, Benson viewed it as a form of collectivism that had done irreparable harm to the nation. Especially troubling were Roosevelt's agricultural policies, which the Mormon leader decried for "weakening initiative, destroying character, discouraging industry, breeding waste and dishonesty" and promoting more "government control," which "demoralized people."[18]

Three pivotal moments shaped Benson's Mormon ministry and defined the leader he would become. The first occurred in 1946 when the First Presidency dispatched him to Europe to oversee the church's relief efforts after World War II. To his wife Flora, whom he had left behind along with their six young children, he reflected: "I'm so grateful you and the children can be spared the views of the terrible ravages of war. I fear I'll never be able to erase them from my memory."[19]

Benson traveled with his secretary, Frederick Babbel, visiting Latter-day Saints in Germany and Poland whose lives had been upended by war.[20] When Benson returned home in December 1946, after eleven exhausting months covering nearly sixty-one thousand miles and overseeing some two thousand tons of relief supplies, he was a changed man. He had seen firsthand death, starvation, and poverty. "I have personally witnessed the heart-rending results of the loss of freedom," he dourly noted. "I have seen it with my own eyes." He associated this "godless evil" with totalitarian regimes, which he denounced for usurping free agency and enslaving people. Fellow apostle Gordon B. Hinckley vividly recalled that "the bitter fruit of dictatorship" in war-ravaged Europe instilled in Benson an "almost hatred for communism and socialism."[21]

Six years later another transformative event occurred in Benson's life when he accepted a position to serve as agriculture secretary in president-elect Dwight D. Eisenhower's administration. This was a position for which Benson was well qualified. Prior to his call as an LDS apostle in 1943, he worked as the chairman of the Idaho Department of Economics and Marketing in Boise, where he was employed from 1930 to 1939 overseeing the state's farm policies, and then from 1939 to 1943 when he served as the executive secretary of the National Council of Farm Cooperatives in Washington, D.C., overseeing some five thousand farm cooperatives representing more than two million farmers nationwide.[22] Benson initially resisted the call as the secretary of agriculture. He believed that his ecclesiastical responsibilities as a Mormon apostle were more important than government service. But after LDS church president David O. McKay warmly supported the move, Benson reluctantly acquiesced.[23]

Four factors prompted Benson to accept the call. First, he secured the blessing of President McKay, who granted him a leave of absence from his church responsibilities. Second, Eisenhower convinced him that the nation's agrarian policies were "spiritual matters." Third, Benson came to believe that service in the Eisenhower administration would give him a platform to fight "socialized agriculture," specifically the New Deal, whose policies he abhorred.[24] And fourth, a cabinet appointment gave Benson the opportunity to root out communists in the federal government, particularly the Department of Agriculture, which he alleged had the "first Communist cell."[25]

Benson's tenure in the Eisenhower administration, where he worked from 1953 to 1961, occurred during a time of great uncertainty. He lived in the nation's capital during the rapid expansion of communism around the world compounded by a red scare at home that put Americans on edge. Several international incidences concerned the Mormon apostle. First, the Soviets had gobbled up territory in eastern and central Europe, expanding the borders of their communist empire. Second, the United States failed to unify Korea in a war against communist North Korea and China. And last, Fidel Castro led a revolution in Cuba bringing communism to the tiny sea island ninety miles off the Florida coast. All of these events prompted Benson to write in 1961 that "[n]ever in recorded history has any movement spread its power so far and so fast as has socialistic-communism in the last three decades."[26]

For Benson, these international events were key markers in a communist conspiracy to enslave Americans. The demagogic Wisconsin senator Joseph McCarthy fueled the conspiracy with allegations that communists had infiltrated the U.S. State Department and the U.S. military.[27] J. Edgar Hoover, the powerful, longtime FBI director, also contributed to the frenzy. In his bestselling book *Masters of Deceit*, published in 1958, he asserted that "many persons, including high-ranking statesmen, public officials, educators, ministers of the gospel, professional men, have been duped into helping communism."[28] These allegations alarmed Benson, specifically Hoover's claim that "the gravest danger" in the world was not the spread of communism abroad but the spread of communism from within the United States. For Benson, Hoover's warnings were a call to action.[29] His books were "must reading."[30]

Another pivotal moment in Benson's life occurred in 1961 when he met Robert Welch, the controversial founder of the John Birch Society. The two men became extremely close. They exchanged dozens of letters in the 1960s and 1970s and spent countless hours in person discussing politics and social conditions in the United States.[31] Welch's bold claim that President Eisenhower and members of his cabinet participated in a massive "communist conspiracy" profoundly affected the Mormon apostle.[32]

The turbulent decade of the 1960s brought both men together. Benson and Welch shared a common ideology that the United States was in rapid decline, reflected most vividly by the rise of urban violence, the mismanagement of the Vietnam War, and a promiscuous sexual culture that damaged families, undermined patriotism, and bred "godless atheism." The civil rights movement especially concerned them. They asserted that Dr. Martin Luther King Jr. and his associates were communists and traitors.[33] But most significant, both men vigorously complained that President Lyndon B. Johnson's Great Society programs were destroying the country. They lamented that "no Congress has passed more socialistic legislation recommended by a president than probably any other Congress in the history of our Republic." To that end Benson, with Welch's support, pursued two presidential bids in the 1960s, vowing to roll back Johnson's liberal government programs.[34]

Eisenhower and Johnson were not the only public figures in their cross-hairs. Benson and Welch asserted that environmental activist Rachel Carson, Harvard historian and John F. Kennedy adviser Arthur Schlesinger Jr., musicians Pete Seeger and Woody Guthrie, and various Hollywood producers all leaned red.[35] They also condemned "the communist" Warren Court and supported a movement to impeach Earl Warren, the chief justice of the U.S. Supreme Court.[36]

The apostle and the Birch founder viewed communism in religious terms—as a fight "for the souls and bodies of men." "This world-wide battle," Benson insisted, was "the first of its kind in history, between light and darkness; between freedom and slavery; between the spirit of Christianity and the spirit of the anti-Christ."[37] Moreover, both men asserted that the United States was a Christian nation on the verge of losing its moorings. Though Welch was a Catholic and Benson a Mormon, they shared a common belief that Americans needed a rebirth of Christianity to restore the nation to its religious heritage, which was under siege by "godless communism."[38]

Alarmed by the rapid expansion of communism around the world, Benson looked to the Birch founder to mentor him. "I am most anxious to . . . accurately determine those who are promoting communist purposes," he explained to Welch. "Many of us recognize that you have an uncanny ability to 'sniff-out' the communists and those who are willingly or unwillingly following the communist line."[39] So enamored with the Birch founder, Benson attended Birch events,[40] shared Birch literature with friends and family,[41] and vigorously defended the Birch Society against critics, both inside and outside the LDS church, who condemned it as a subversive organization.[42]

Benson's authoritative position as an LDS apostle, coupled with his warm support of the organization, prompted thousands of Latter-day Saints to join. In the 1960s and 1970s, the John Birch Society established chapters in Utah, Arizona, Idaho, and California, in towns and cities heavily populated by Latter-day Saints. These patriotic Mormons paid monthly dues, attended weekly Birch meetings, and worked tirelessly to spread the Birch line. In ever-increasing numbers, they heeded Benson's call "to participate in non-church meetings that are held to warn people of the threat of Communism."[43] Robert Welch rewarded these earnest Latter-day Saints by dispatching Birch speakers to their neighborhoods, where they gave lectures, did book signings, and provided tips on how to recruit their friends and neighbors into the anticommunist organization.[44]

Although LDS church president David O. McKay rebuffed Benson's request to join the controversial organization or sit on its council, the apostle actively promoted the Birch cause.[45] Francis Gibbons, Benson's secretary and biographer, observed that "thirteen of Elder Benson's eighteen general conference talks" during the 1960s "focused on one aspect or another" of communism. Gibbons further noted that Benson "gave hundreds of other talks, both inside and outside of the Church, in which he dwelled on the perils of communism and the remedies to thwart it."[46] He also published three widely circulated books during this period—*The Red Carpet* (1962), *Title of Liberty* (1964), and *An Enemy Hath Done This* (1969)—each heavily influenced by Birch ideas.[47]

Benson's books fused a militant anticommunism with Christian apocalypticism. His sermons and writings echoed prominent Christian evangelicals, who also warned about communism and "godless atheism."[48] But unlike these evangelicals who used biblical end-times prophecy to understand the Cold War, the apostle turned to Mormon scripture. As the Cold War intensified during the 1960s, Benson quoted extensively from the Book of Mormon, specifically from passages that discussed "secret combinations." Here he postulated that a communist conspiracy existed in the "last days." He was emphatic that the Book of Mormon played a central role in identifying communists because ancient prophets "saw our day."[49] It was therefore imperative for Latter-day Saints to study the book carefully and ponder its message, where they would find a corrective to "many of the current false theories and philosophies of men."[50]

Not surprisingly, the apostle's extreme views polarized the church.[51] Critics scoffed when he blended conservatism, Mormonism, and Birchism. But most troubling, Benson and his son Reed used LDS meetinghouses to promote the Birch message. This drew a sharp response from the First Presidency.[52] Nevertheless, Benson continued his crusade against communism. President McKay, himself an ardent anticommunist, allowed Benson to do so. Though the aging Mormon leader found the Birch Society divisive, he permitted Benson to address anticommunism as long as he refrained from discussing the Birch Society or speaking at Birch events.[53] When Benson crossed the line, McKay's counselors—Henry D. Moyle and Hugh B. Brown—nudged the president to reign him in. "When we pursue any course [of action] which results in numerous letters being written to the Presidency critical of our work, it should be some evidence we should change our course," Moyle explained to an LDS bishop, echoing his frustration with Benson.[54]

The First Presidency, in fact, reprimanded Benson on at least four occasions over the course of two decades. In 1963, President McKay and his counselors issued a statement rejecting the Birch Society after Benson and his son Reed implied that the Mormon president endorsed the controversial organization and its extreme right-wing agenda.[55] Benson ran into more trouble later that year when he delivered an ill-advised speech at the five-year anniversary of the Birch Society. There he expressed support for Welch's claim that Eisenhower and his cabinet were communist sympathizers.[56] After the speech, the First Presidency reprimanded him by dispatching him to Germany, where Benson presided over the European mission from 1964 to 1965. Senior apostle Joseph Fielding Smith quipped that he was "glad to report . . . that it will be some time before we hear anything from Brother Benson," adding, "When he returns I hope his blood will be purified."[57]

In similar fashion, the church hierarchy scolded Benson in 1974 when he told a reporter that the church might endorse political candidates or parties in the near future. Benson also proclaimed that "it would be very hard" to be a "liberal Democrat" and "a good Mormon" if members were "living the gospel and understood it."[58] LDS church president Spencer W. Kimball confided in his journal that a "number of people came in to deplore the things [Benson] said." President Kimball "[c]ounselled Brother Benson that all of the general authorities must speak with one voice," declaring that "we cannot take any partisan position in politics, either candidates or parties."[59] The First Presidency, clearly displeased with the apostle's partisanship, issued a statement of political neutrality to counter him.[60]

Six years later Benson got himself into trouble again when he gave a controversial speech at Brigham Young University. "The prophet may be involved in civic matters," Benson sternly noted. He further added: "Those who would remove prophets from politics would take God out of government."[61] For many Latter-day Saints, the address foreshadowed Benson's rise to the LDS presidency. Dozens of Mormons complained to the First Presidency that Benson, who was next in line to be the church president, might align the church with his right-wing politics. Sterling M. McMurrin, an outspoken and unorthodox Mormon professor at the University of Utah, opined to Kimball that Benson's speech was "extremely divisive within the Church," predicting it would "undo much of the great good that was done by your 1978 revelation" lifting the priesthood ban. Former BYU professor Richard Poll protested that if "Benson tries to put the prophetic imprimatur on this rightist crusade while holding prophetic office, the alienation within the American church will be profound."[62] Even the media outlets commented on the speech. *Newsweek* journalists Kenneth Woodward and Jack Goodman bluntly noted that the Quorum of the Twelve Apostles "will insist that Benson agree to limit his official teachings to spiritual matters before it anoints him as President and Prophet."[63]

Such views concerned President Kimball, who found Benson's politics polarizing. The soft-spoken Mormon president made Benson apologize to the Quorum of the Twelve Apostles after the BYU speech and then again, the following week, to all the general authorities.[64] Benson also drafted a letter of apology to Latter-day Saints, though it is not clear if he delivered it.[65]

Kimball's rebuke ended Benson's public politicking. After Benson became the church president in 1985, the aging Cold Warrior confined his sermons to spiritual matters.[66] Nevertheless, he kept abreast of political affairs. He requested Birch literature for his counselors, Gordon B. Hinckley and Thomas S. Monson, and his secretary, D. Arthur Haycock.[67] He also hosted Birch Society president John F. McManus and other Birch officials at church head-quarters, where Benson asked "many questions about how the Society was progressing." "The whole time we were there was devoted to JBS matters," McManus recalled years later.[68]

When Benson died in 1994, thousands of Latter-day Saints lined the streets from Salt Lake City, Utah, to Whitney, Idaho, to mourn him as his hearse passed along the highway.[69] It was a "solemn moment," recalled one well-wisher. "Our prophet was gone."[70] In the eulogy, delivered before government officials, friends, and family, Gordon B. Hinckley, Benson's colleague for more than thirty years in church leadership, praised the Mormon leader as a "fearless and outspoken enemy of communism, a man who with eloquence and conviction preached the cause of human freedom."[71] With these simple words, Hinckley captured why Latter-day Saints loved Benson—and why they found him polarizing. Simply put, Ezra Taft Benson's intense patriotism and fierce ultraconservatism made him a controversial figure within the Mormon community.

* * *

The essays in this volume probe Ezra Taft Benson's remarkable, though controversial, career as a religious leader, political figure, and anticommunist leader. Each essay is written by an experienced Mormon scholar and is informed by archival material previously underutilized or unavailable to researchers. The essays have been enriched by material from the Robert Welch–Ezra Taft Benson correspondence at the John Birch Society headquarters in Appleton, Wisconsin; the George Wallace Papers at the Alabama Department of Archives and History in Montgomery, Alabama; the William Grede Papers at the Wisconsin Historical Society in Madison, Wisconsin; the Ezra Taft Benson file at the Federal Bureau of Investigation in Washington, D.C.; the Dwight D. Eisenhower Papers at the Eisenhower Presidential Library in Abilene, Kansas; the Richard Nixon Papers at the Nixon Presidential Library in Yorba Linda, California; the Hugh B. Brown Files at Brigham Young University in Provo, Utah; and most importantly the David O. McKay Papers at the University of Utah in Salt Lake City.

The book is divided into two sections, with each essay exploring a critical aspect of Benson's life and career. Part I examines Benson's politics and Cold War anxieties. Brian Cannon evaluates the apostle's tenure as the agricultural secretary in the Eisenhower administration, in particular, how new transformations in technology affected his farm policies and, more critically, how they divided the American public. Gary Bergera critically appraises a statement Benson made about Soviet leader Nikita Khrushchev, in which he argues that Benson deliberately embellished Khrushchev's words to counter critics who found the apostle's public anticommunism polarizing. Robert Goldberg situates Benson within a conservative grassroots movement among Latter-day Saints and argues that Benson was responsible for building a Republican coalition that reshaped Mormon politics. Newell Bringhurst explores Benson's perennial interest in running for the U.S. presidency, an interest stoked by admiring Latter-day Saints who pined to see the Mormon apostle elected. Matthew Harris evaluates Benson's opposition to the civil rights movement—specifically why he believed that Martin Luther King was a communist agent and sympathizer. Harris contends that Benson's anti–civil rights views posed significant challenges for the church when Benson became the church president in 1985.

Part II examines Benson's religious teachings, both as an apostle and as the LDS church president. Matthew Bowman homes in on Benson and "free agency," explaining how the Mormon apostle-president weaved this critical LDS teaching into a larger narrative about freedom, government, and liberty during the Cold War. Andrea Radke-Moss explores Benson's views on women and gender, demonstrating the ways in which the apostle's teachings on these critical topics were similar to and different from his contemporaries. J. B. Haws concludes the volume assessing Benson's church presidency. He discusses Benson's signature teachings on the Book of Mormon, missionary work, and family life, while at the same time acknowledging the many challenges Benson faced during his nine-year tenure as president of the Mormon church.

It is my hope that this book will offer a fresh and stimulating retrospective assessment of Ezra Taft Benson's life and legacy, particularly his considerable accomplishments as a public servant, Cold War figure, and religious leader in the half century after World War II.

Notes

1. Matthew L. Harris "Ezra Taft Benson, Dwight D. Eisenhower, and the Emergence of a Conspiracy Culture Within the Mormon Church," *John Whitmer Historical Association Journal* 37 (Spring/Summer 2017): 51–82; Gregory A. Prince and William Robert Wright,

David O. McKay and the Rise of Modern Mormonism (Salt Lake City: University of Utah Press, 2005), 286–322; D. Michael Quinn, *The Mormon Hierarchy: Extensions of Power* (Salt Lake City: Signature Books, 1997), chap. 3.

2. "Presidential Citizens Medal" Commendation for Ezra Taft Benson, reel 1, Ezra Taft Benson Papers, LDS Church History Library (courtesy of Jay Burrup of the LDS Church History Library). See also "President Benson Awarded Presidential Citizens Medal," *Deseret News*, July 29, 1989.

3. Elaine Tyler May, *Homeward Bound: American Families in the Cold War Era* (New York: Basic Books, 1988; sec. ed., 2008); Kevin M. Kruse, *One Nation Under God: How Corporate America Invented Christian America* (New York: Basic Books, 2015).

4. Benson, "God, Family, and Country," address delivered at the New England rally for God, Family, and Country honor banquet, Boston, Massachusetts, July 4, 1972, in Ezra Taft Benson, *God, Family, Country: Our Three Great Loyalties* (Salt Lake City: Deseret Book, 1974), 401–7.

5. Benson, *Title of Liberty: A Warning Voice*, compiled by Mark A. Benson (Salt Lake City: Deseret Book, 1964), 39. See also David O. McKay journal, October 26, 1962, Box 51, Folder 5, David O. McKay Papers, Special Collections, Marriott Library, University of Utah; Willard Clopton, "Cookies, Talk of Treason Served at Opening of Birch Headquarters," *Washington Post*, September 18, 1965. Besides the Birch Society, Reed and Mark Benson also affiliated the "Utah Forum for the American Idea," the "Freeman Institute," and other anticommunist organizations. See Quinn, *The Mormon Hierarchy*, 71, 111; and John Harrington, "The Freeman Institute," *The Nation* 231 (August 16–23, 1980): 152–53.

6. Ezra Taft Benson to "Our Beloved Children," August 10, 1981, as cited in Sheri L. Dew, *Ezra Taft Benson: A Biography* (Salt Lake City: Deseret Book, 1987), 476. See also Mark Benson to the Benson family, June 29, 1953, reel 2, Ezra Taft Benson Papers, LDS Church History Library; and Reed Benson to the Benson family, December n.d., 1948, ibid. For more on Benson's family, see Andrea Radke-Moss, "Women and Gender" in this volume.

7. Benson was not the only LDS leader to blur the line between church and state. For this point, see J. D. Williams, "The Separation of Church and State in Mormon Theory and Practice," *Dialogue: A Journal of Mormon Thought* 1 (1966): 30–54; Patrick Q. Mason, "God and the People: Theodemocracy in Nineteenth-Century Mormonism," *Journal of Church and State* 53 (September 2011): 349–75; D. Michael Quinn, "Exporting Utah's Theocracy Since 1975: Mormon Organizational Behavior and America's Culture Wars," in Jefferey E. Sells, ed., *God and Country: Politics in Utah* (Salt Lake City: Signature Books, 2005), 129–68; and Randall Balmer and Jana Riess, eds., *Mormonism and American Politics* (New York: Columbia University Press, 2016).

8. For Benson's opposition to the Supreme Court, particularly in regard to the *Engel* decision, see "Godless Forces Threaten Us," *Improvement Era* 72 (December 1969): 69–73 (quote on 70). See also Ezra Taft Benson, *An Enemy Hath Done This* (Salt Lake City: Parliament Publishers, 1969), 31, for a discussion of the "anti-spiritual decisions of the Supreme Court." For criticism of the *Engel* decision in general, see Bruce J. Dierenfield, *The Battle over School Prayer: How Engel v. Vitale Changed America* (Lawrence: University Press of Kansas, 2007).

9. "Support for Candidate Possible Some Day, LDS Apostle Says," *Salt Lake Tribune*, February 22, 1974. See also Benson, *An Enemy Hath Done This*, 306; Benson, *Title of Liberty*, 28; and Reed A. Benson, ed., *The Teachings of Ezra Taft Benson* (Salt Lake City: Bookcraft, 1988), 608–9.

10. Benson's political ideology bears a striking parallel to today's Tea Party. See Jill Lepore, *The Whites of Their Eyes: The Tea Party's Revolution and the Battle over American History* (Princeton, N.J.: Princeton University Press, 2010); Theda Skocpol and Vanessa Williamson, *The Tea Party and the Remaking of Republican Conservatism* (New York: Oxford University Press, 2016).

11. Benson, ed., *Teachings of Ezra Taft Benson*, 627–46, 653–61, 668–74, 679–95.

12. Ezra Taft Benson, *The Red Carpet: Socialism—the Royal Road to Communism* (Salt Lake City: Bookcraft, 1962).

13. Benson BYU devotional address "A Four-Fold Hope" (May 24, 1961), *Brigham Young University Speeches of the Year* (Provo, Utah: BYU Extension Publications, 1961), 10. See also Benson, *Title of Liberty*, 173, 190; and Matthew Bowman, "'The Cold War and the Invention of Free Agency" in this volume.

14. Benson, "Principles of Cooperation," *Improvement Era* 48 (November 1945): 711. See also Ezra Taft Benson, *So Shall Ye Reap: Selected Addresses of Ezra Taft Benson*, compiled by Reed A. Benson (Salt Lake City: Deseret Book, 1960), 187, where Benson wrote that the "God of heaven expects his children to stand on their own feet and not depend on an over-paternalistic government. . . . I know what the God of heaven has said, and he expects us to ask for nothing of the government that we can provide ourselves."

15. Benson, *This Nation Shall Endure* (Salt Lake City: Deseret Book, 1979), 75–76; and Benson, *So Shall Ye Reap*, 331. Here Benson followed the standard church protocol, articulated most vividly in a number of First Presidency statements and church welfare policies. See *Statements of the First Presidency*, compiled by Gary James Bergera (Salt Lake City: Signature Books, 2007), 493–96.

16. Donald Q. Cannon, ed., *Latter-day Prophets and the U.S. Constitution* (Salt Lake City: Bookcraft, 1991); Ray C. Hillam, ed., *"By the Hands of Wise Men": Essays on the U.S. Constitution* (Provo, Utah: Brigham Young University Press, 1979); J. Reuben Clark, *Stand Fast by Our Constitution* (Salt Lake City: Deseret Book, 1962); Noel B. Reynolds, "The Doctrine of an Inspired Constitution," *BYU Studies* 16 (Spring 1976): 315–40.

17. Benson, *Title of Liberty*, 28 (quote), 82, 226; see also Benson, *So Shall Ye Reap*, 223–30; Benson, *This Nation Shall Endure*, chaps. 2–4; Benson, *The Constitution: A Heavenly Banner* (Salt Lake City: Deseret Book, 1986).

18. Benson, *So Shall Ye Reap*, 288; Steve Benson, "Ezra Taft Benson: A Grandson's Remembrance," *Sunstone* (December 1994) 29–37 (quotes at 30–31).

19. No editor listed, *A Labor of Love: The 1946 European Mission of Ezra Taft Benson* (Salt Lake City: Deseret Book, 1989), 188–89. The best treatment of Benson's European mission is Gary James Bergera, "Ezra Taft Benson's 1946 Mission to Europe," *Journal of Mormon History* 34 (Spring 2008): 73–112. See also Dew, *Ezra Taft Benson*, chap. 12; and Francis M. Gibbons, *Ezra Taft Benson: Statesman, Patriot, Prophet of God* (Salt Lake City: Deseret Book, 1996), chap. 10.

20. A seminal account of Benson's European mission is Frederick W. Babbel, *On Wings of Faith* (Salt Lake City: Bookcraft, 1972).

21. Benson, *An Enemy Hath Done This*, 65, 320; Hinckley, "Farewell to a Prophet," *Ensign* (July 1994): https://www.lds.org/ensign/1994/07/farewell-to-a-prophet?lang=eng. See also Gibbons, *Ezra Taft Benson*, 157; and Larry B. Stammer, "Faithful Throngs Remember Benson," *Los Angeles Times*, June 5, 1994.

22. For two biographical sketches of Benson with information on these years, see "Ezra Taft Benson Biographical Sketch" [1966], Box 26, Folder 2, William J. Grede Papers, Wisconsin Historical Society, Madison, Wisconsin; and Benson, *So Shall Ye Reap*, 333–42.

23. Benson recounted his call to Eisenhower's cabinet in several venues. See Benson, *So Shall Ye Reap*, 234–35; Benson, *Cross Fire: The Eight Years with Eisenhower* (Garden City, N.Y.: Doubleday, 1962), 3–12, 345–46; and Reed Benson interview by Greg Prince, September 15, 1999, Box 22, Folder 1, Gregory A. Prince Papers, Special Collections, Marriott Library, University of Utah. See also Prince and Wright, *David O. McKay and the Rise of Modern Mormonism*, 351; Francis M. Gibbons, *David O. McKay: Apostle to the World, Prophet of God* (Salt Lake City: Deseret Book, 1986), 314–15; and Merlo J. Pusey, *Eisenhower, the President* (New York: Macmillan, 1956), 67–68.

24. Benson's anti–New Deal views are discussed in three books he wrote: *Farmers at the Crossroads* (New York: Devin-Adair, 1956); *Freedom to Farm* (Garden City, N.Y.: Doubleday, 1960); and *Cross Fire*. See also Gibbons, *Ezra Taft Benson*, 94–96; and Brian Q. Cannon, "Ezra Taft Benson and the Family Farm" in this volume.

25. On numerous occasions, Benson asserted that the first "communist cell" in government "was organized in the Department of Agriculture in the 1930s." Alger Hiss, a former agricultural official, particularly concerned the Mormon apostle. See Benson, "The Internal Threat to the American Way of Life," talk given at the Shrine Auditorium, Los Angeles, California, December 11, 1961 (Salt Lake City: Bookcraft, 1961), 16; Benson to H. Roland Tietjen, May 22, 1962, Box 7, Folder 3, Alumni Association Records, L. Tom Perry Special Collections, Harold B. Lee Library, Brigham Young University; Benson, "We Must Be Alerted and Informed," address given by Ezra Taft Benson at a Public Patriotic Meeting, Logan, Utah, December 13, 1963, p. 2; "Trade and Treason," talk first given on February 17, 1967, at the Portland Forum for Americanism in the Benson High School Auditorium, Portland, Oregon, reprinted in Benson, *An Enemy Hath Done This*, 65; and Reed Benson interview by Greg Prince, September 15, 1999, Box 22, Folder 1, Gregory A. Prince Papers, Special Collections, Marriott Library, University of Utah. For Alger Hiss's involvement in a communist cell in the Department of Agriculture, go to G. Edward White, *Alger Hiss's Looking-Glass Wars: The Covert Life of a Soviet Spy* (New York: Oxford University Press, 2005).

26. Benson conference address, "The American Heritage of Freedom—A Plan of God," *Improvement Era* 64 (December 1961): 953. Benson's speeches and writings convey his engagement with world affairs in stark terms. See Benson's *So Shall Ye Reap*; *Red Carpet*; *Title of Liberty*; and *An Enemy Hath Done This*. See also Gary James Bergera, "Ezra Taft Benson Meets Nikita Khrushchev, 1959: Memory Embellished" in this volume.

27. The best studies of Cold War hysteria include Ellen Schrecker, *Many are the Crimes: McCarthyism in America* (Boston: Little, Brown, 1998); David M. Oshinsky, *A Conspiracy So Immense: The World of Joe McCarthy* (New York: Oxford University Press, 2005); Richard Gid Powers, *Not Without Honor: The History of American Anticommunism* (New Haven, Conn.: Yale University Press, 1998).

28. Hoover, *Masters of Deceit: The Story of Communism in America and How to Fight It* (New York: Holt, Rinehart, Winston, 1958), 93. Benson frequently quoted Hoover in general conference, at BYU devotionals, and in addresses to civic groups. See Benson, *Red Carpet*, 21, 23, 40, 56, 80–81, 225, 264, 277, 289–90; Benson, *Title of Liberty*, 5, 18, 26–27, 33–34, 39–44, 59, 65–70, 72–73, 111–12, 166, 176; Benson, *An Enemy Hath Done This*, 44, 49, 65, 308, 310.

29. Benson, *An Enemy Hath Done This*, 65.

30. "Race Against Time," *Speeches of the Year* (December 10, 1963) (Provo, Utah: Brigham Young University Extension Services, 1963), 18.

31. Part of this correspondence will be published in Matthew L. Harris, ed., *Ezra Taft Benson and Anticommunism: A Documentary History* (Salt Lake City: University of Utah Press, forthcoming).

32. In *The Politician* (unpublished manuscript, 1958), 267–68, Welch asserted that Eisenhower was a communist. For more on this point, see Harris "Ezra Taft Benson, Dwight D. Eisenhower, and the Emergence of a Conspiracy Culture Within the Mormon Church," 57–59; and Harris, "Martin Luther King, Civil Rights, and Perceptions of a Communist Conspiracy" in this volume.

33. Benson, *An Enemy Hath Done This*, chaps. 1 ("Americans Are Destroying America"), 7 ("The Erosion of America"), 13 ("Civil Rights: Tool of Communist Deception"); Benson, *God, Family, Country*, chap. 25 ("Three Threatening Dangers"). For a critical appraisal of Welch and civil rights, see Benjamin R. Epstein and Arnold Forster, *Report on the John Birch Society, 1966* (New York: Vintage Books, 1966), chap. 2; and Matthew L. Harris, "Martin Luther King, Civil Rights, and Perceptions of a 'Communist Conspiracy'" in this volume.

34. Benson, "The Proper Sphere of Government," *Improvement Era* 71 (December 1968): 51–53; Benson, *An Enemy Hath Done This*, 309. See also Benson to Robert Welch, March 8, 1968, Ezra Taft Benson Correspondence, JBS Headquarters, Appleton, Wisc.; and D. J. Mulloy, *The World of the John Birch Society: Conspiracy, Conservatism, and the Cold War* (Nashville, Tenn.: Vanderbilt University Press, 2014), 99–101, 135, 160–64. For Benson's presidential bids, see Newell G. Bringhurst, "Potomac Fever: Continuing Quest for the U.S. Presidency" in this volume.

35. Benson complained about environmental activist Rachel Carson to President Eisenhower. He wondered why a "spinster was so worried about genetics" and concluded that she was "probably a Communist." In Linda J. Lear, "Rachel Carson's *Silent Spring*," *Environmental History Review* 17 (Summer 1993): 36. To Mormon Tabernacle Choir Director Isaac M. Stewart, Benson expressed dismay that the choir recorded songs by "two hard-core Communists, Woody Guthrie and Pete Seeger." He insisted that the "use of music by these Communist authors will be used to give aid and comfort for the Communists, their fellow-travelers and dupes, and can only bring difficulty to the Church." See Benson to Stewart, November 19, 1965, Richard L. Evans Files CR 605 1, Box 49, Tabernacle-Choir Correspondence File, LDS Church History Library (my thanks to BYU professor Michael Hicks for calling this letter to my attention). For Benson's views on Schlesinger, see Benson to Hugh B. Brown, September 18, 1962, Box 3, Folder 4, Hugh B. Brown Research Files, L. Tom Perry Special Collections, Harold B. Lee Library, BYU; Benson, *Title of Liberty*, 29–30; and Benson, *An Enemy Hath Done This*, 39. Benson and

Welch ruminated on Hollywood producers in a pair of letters they exchanged. See Welch to Benson, November 1, 1965, and Benson to Welch, November 9, 1965, both in Ezra Taft Benson Correspondence, John Birch Society Headquarters, Appleton, Wisc.

36. Benson, *An Enemy Hath Done This*, 31, 68, 101, 104, 308, 332–33, chap. 23 ("The Supreme Court—A Judicial Oligarchy"); and First Presidency Minutes, wherein Benson explained that the Supreme Court issued rulings favorable to communists, Box 61, Folder 4, David O. McKay Papers, Special Collections, Marriott Library, University of Utah. Malloy, *World of the John Birch Society*, 109–17, discusses in some detail the Birchers' attempt to impeach Warren. See also "The Movement to Impeach Earl Warren," *John Birch Society Bulletin* (August 1961): 5; and *John Birch Society Bulletin* (August 1965): 4.

37. Benson, *Title of Liberty*, 59.

38. Benson conveys this sentiment in his books and sermons: see *So Shall Ye Reap*, *Title of Liberty*, *God, Family, Country*, and *This Nation Shall Endure*. For Welch and religion, see *The Blue Book* (1959; reprint, Appleton, Wisc.: Western Islands, 1999). See also Benson to Welch, October 1, 1969, Ezra Taft Benson Correspondence, JBS Headquarters, Appleton, Wisc. Kruse, *One Nation Under God*, chap. 3, discusses other ministers and businessmen who countered communism by invoking Christianity.

39. Benson to Welch, May 17, 1965, Ezra Taft Benson Correspondence, John Birch Society Headquarters, Appleton, Wisc.

40. The correspondence between Ezra Taft Benson and Robert Welch reveals that Benson was active in attending Birch events and sponsoring Birch ideology. See Harris, *Ezra Taft Benson and Anticommunism*.

41. See Ezra Taft Benson to Robert Welch, June 21, 1966, and October 11, 1965, both in Ezra Taft Benson Correspondence, John Birch Society Headquarters, Appleton, Wisc.; and Benson to Spencer W. Kimball, n.d., Box 64, Folder 2, Spencer W. Kimball Papers, LDS Church History Library.

42. Benson defended the Birch Society most vigorously to President Eisenhower and President Nixon. See Benson to Eisenhower, December 9, 1965, Box 20, 1965 Principal File, Dwight D. Eisenhower Presidential Library; Benson to Richard Nixon; December 9, 1965, Box 3, Ezra Taft Benson folder, Wilderness Years: Series I:S; Sub-Series A: 1963–1965, Series 238; Richard Nixon Presidential Library and Museum, Yorba Linda, Calif.

43. Benson, "Protecting Freedom—An Immediate Responsibility," *Improvement Era* 69 (December 1966): 1146.

44. The Birch Society published "coming events" in their magazines, indicating where and when Birchers would speak. Reed Benson and W. Cleon Skousen, a close friend of the apostle, frequently held Birch rallies in LDS communities in Utah, Arizona, California, and Idaho. For other Birch speakers, see *Birch Bulletin* (March 1965): 30–31; (June 1965): 31–32; (July 1965): 32. See also Russell W. Stevenson, *For the Cause of Righteousness: A Global History of Blacks and Mormonism, 1830–2013* (Salt Lake City: Greg Kofford, 2014), 118–19, depicting African American Birchers who spoke in Utah communities.

45. For McKay's denial of Benson's request to join the Birch Society and sit on its board, see McKay journal, August 9, 1963, Box 54, Folder 1, and March 5, 1964, Box 56, Folder 2, in David O. McKay Papers, Special Collections, Marriott Library, University of Utah; and Ezra Taft Benson to William J. Grede, April 19, 1967, Box 26, Folder 2, William J. Grede Papers, Wisconsin Historical Society, Madison, Wisc.

46. Gibbons, *Ezra Taft Benson*, 240.

47. Benson's sermons were also influenced by Birch ideas—so much so that three Utah State University professors accused him of plagiarism. After hearing Benson's sermon in the Logan Tabernacle in December 1963, the professors complained to the First Presidency that the apostle had lifted passages from *The Blue Book*—one of Robert Welch's signature writings. As proof, they sent the First Presidency a copy of the talk, along with passages from the book. See E. Boyd Wennergren, N. Keith Roberts, and B. Delworth Gardner to David O. McKay, January 18, 1964, Box 55, Folder 1, Leonard J. Arrington Papers, Special Collections, Merrill-Cazier Library, Utah State University.

48. Matthew Avery Sutton, *American Apocalypse: A History of Modern Evangelism* (Cambridge, Mass.: Harvard University Press, 2014), chaps. 10–11; Grant Wacker, *America's Pastor: Billy Graham and the Shaping of a Nation* (Cambridge, Mass.: Harvard University Press, 2014); Steven P. Miller, *The Age of Evangelicalism: America's Born-Again Years* (New York: Oxford University Press, 2014); Randall Balmer, *Evangelicalism in America* (Waco, Tex.: Baylor University Press, 2016), chap. 5; Kruse, *One Nation Under God*, chap. 5.

49. Benson, *Conference Report* (October 1986): 5; Benson, *A Witness and a Warning: A Modern-day Prophet Testifies of the Book of Mormon* (Salt Lake City: Deseret Book, 1988), 19–20; Benson, "Book of Mormon Warns America" (BYU devotional, May 21, 1968), *An Enemy Hath Done This*, chap. 29; and Benson, "Book of Mormon is the Word of God," *Ensign* (April 1975): https://www.lds.org/general-conference/1975/04/the-book -of-mormon-is-the-word-of-god?lang=eng.

50. Ezra Taft Benson, "Jesus Christ—Gifts and Expectations" *Ensign* (May 1975): https:// www.lds.org/new-era/1975/05/jesus-christ-gifts-and-expectations?lang=eng. See also Benson, ed., *Teachings of Ezra Taft Benson*, 61. Some scholars aver that Benson's emphasis on reading the Book of Mormon elevated the book to a greater status in the Mormon Church. See Paul C. Gutjahr, *The Book of Mormon: A Biography* (Princeton, N.J.: Princeton University Press, 2012), 108–9; Terryl L. Givens, *By the Hand of Mormon: The American Scripture that Launched a New World Religion* (New York: Oxford University Press, 2002), 241–42; and Patrick Q. Mason, "Ezra Taft Benson and Modern (Book of) Mormon Conservatism," in Patrick Q. Mason and John G. Turner, eds., *Out of Obscurity: Mormonism Since 1945* (New York: Oxford University Press, 2016), 63–80.

51. This point is ably covered in Prince and Wright, *David O. McKay and the Rise of Modern Mormonism*, chap. 12; Gregory A. Prince, "The Red Peril, the Candy Maker, and the Apostle: David O. McKay's Confrontation with Communism," *Dialogue: A Journal of Mormon Thought* 37 (Summer 2004): 37–94; Quinn, *Mormon Hierarchy*, chap. 3: D. Michael Quinn, "Ezra Taft Benson and Mormon Political Conflicts," *Dialogue: A Journal of Mormon Thought* 26 (Summer 1992): 1–87.

52. Hugh B. Brown, "Honor the Priesthood," *Improvement Era* 65 (June 1961): 450; David O. McKay journal, January 23, 1963, Box 52, Folder 4, David O. McKay Papers, Special Collections, Marriott Library, University of Utah. In private letters, the First Presidency warned members to "be wary of such societies." For example, First Presidency (David O. McKay, Hugh B. Brown, N. Eldon Tanner) to Wilson J. Morley, December 12, 1963, Matt Harris files (courtesy of Joe Geisner).

53. McKay told Benson that "it would be best for him not to speak at strictly John Birch Society meetings, but approved of his filling speaking appointments already accepted

which were not associated with this group." In McKay journal, March 23, 1966, Box 62, Folder 1, David O. McKay Papers, Special Collections, Marriott Library, University of Utah; see also Benson to McKay, March 25, 1966. For an astute analysis of McKay's complicated relationship with Benson, see Prince and Wright, *David O. McKay and the Rise of Modern Mormonism*, 300–312.

54. Moyle to J. D. Williams, January 9, 1963, Box 21, Folder 1, J. D. Williams Papers, Special Collections, Marriott Library, University of Utah.

55. The First Presidency statement was printed in several newspapers. See "Church Sets Policy on the Birch Society," *Deseret News*, January 4, 1963; "Birch Tie Flatly Denied by LDS," *Ogden Standard-Examiner*, January 4, 1963; "Mormon Head Clarifies Stand on Birch Society: McKay Lashes at Those Who Try to Align Church With Group's Partisan Views," *Los Angeles Times*, January 4, 1963; "LDS Leaders Reject Any Idea of Link Between Church, Birch Society," *Sacramento Bee*, January 4, 1963. The statement was also published as "Ezra Taft Benson's Support of the John Birch Society is Criticized" (September 25, 1963), in the *Congressional Record, Proceedings and Debates of the 88th Congress, First Session*. For David O. McKay's discussion with Ezra Taft Benson about the statement, see David O. McKay journal, January 23, 1963, Box 52, Folder 4, David O. McKay Papers, Special Collections, Marriott Library, University of Utah.

56. Benson's address, "Let Us Live to Keep Men Free" (September 28, 1963), is republished in Benson, *Title of Liberty*, 1–21. For more on this point, see Harris "Ezra Taft Benson, Dwight D. Eisenhower, and the Emergence of a Conspiracy Culture Within the Mormon Church," 56–59.

57. Smith to Ralph Harding, December 23, 1963, Matt Harris files. Smith complained in his journal that Benson's missionary "farewell meeting was long," a sentiment that underscored Benson's divisiveness. In Smith, "Executive Planner," December 15, 1963, Box 4, Folder 2, Joseph Fielding Smith Papers, LDS Church History Library. Smith kept a journal in his executive planner.

58. For Benson's remarks about political parties and candidates, as well his critique of Democrats, see "Support for Candidate Possible Some Day, LDS Apostle Says," *Salt Lake Tribune*, February 22, 1974. Benson's rhetoric denouncing the Democratic Party has had a lasting effect on Mormon voting patterns, the majority of whom support the Republican Party. For this point, see Robert A. Goldberg, "From New Deal to New Right" in this volume. For data on Mormon voting blocs, see David E. Campbell, John C. Green, and J. Quin Monson, *Seeking the Promised Land: Mormons and American Politics* (New York.: Cambridge University Press, 2014), chap. 4. See also David E. Campbell, Christopher F. Karpowitz, and J. Quin Monson, "A Politically Peculiar People: How Mormons Moved into and Then out of the Political Mainstream," in Balmer and Riess, eds., *Mormonism and American Politics*, chap. 9. For the stigma of being a Democrat in the LDS church, consult Robert D. Putnam and David E. Campbell, *American Grace: How Religion Divides and Unites Us* (New York: Simon and Schuster, 2010), 367–68.

59. For Kimball's anguish over the remarks, see his journal entry, February 22, 1974, and November 5, 1974, both in reel 39, Spencer W. Kimball Journals, LDS Church History Library. Kimball's son writes that "calls flooded the Church phone lines" over Benson's remarks. He also explained that his father "disapproved of political statements by Church leaders as divisive," citing "that statements critical of foreign governments might hamper

missionary work, especially in communist or fascist countries." In Edward L. Kimball, *Lengthen Your Stride: The Presidency of Spencer W. Kimball—Working Draft* (Salt Lake City: Benchmark Books, 2009), 235–36.

60. Kimball immediately reaffirmed the church's neutrality, releasing a public statement indicating that members were free "to make their own choices as to political parties, candidates and issues." See statement to "All Stake and Mission Presidents in the United States," April 1, 1974, copy in Box 55, Folder 1, Leonard J. Arrington Papers, Special Collections, Merrill-Cazier Library, Utah State University. See also "Support for Candidate Possible Some Day, LDS Apostle Says," *Salt Lake Tribune*, February 22, 1974; and John Dart, "Ezra Benson: Will Mormons Go Political," *Los Angeles Times*, April 1, 1976; "LDS Presidency Reaffirms 'Nonpartisan Politics,'" *Salt Lake Tribune*, November 5, 1974; "American Party told, 'Stand Firm,'" *Deseret News*, November 4, 1974; David Briscoe, "Church Says Elder's Speech on Third Party 'Unauthorized,'" *Ogden Standard-Examiner*, November 4, 1974.

61. For Benson's address, see "Fourteen Fundamentals in Following the Prophet" *BYU Speeches of the Year, 1981* (Provo, Utah: BYU Extension Publications, 1981), 26–30. See also Benson, *An Enemy Hath Done This*, 293.

62. McMurrin to Kimball, February 28, 1980, Box 16, Folder 1, George T. Boyd Papers, L. Tom Perry Special Collections, Harold B. Lee Library, Brigham Young University; Poll to David John Buerger, September 19, 1980, Box 46, Box 3, Richard D. Poll Papers, Special Collections, Marriott Library, University of Utah. See also the J. D. Williams Papers, which contains several protest letters from professors at BYU, Utah State and elsewhere. Box 28, Folders 1–3, J. D. Williams Papers.

63. In Kenneth L. Woodward and Jack Goodman, "Thus Saith Ezra Benson," *Newsweek*, October 19, 1981, 109. For media coverage of Benson's controversial address, see "Prophet's Word of 'Law' Benson tells Group," *Ogden Standard-Examiner*, February 26, 1980; "Mormon Professor Says Benson Speech Was Plea Anticipating Rise to LDS Presidency," *Idaho State Journal*, February 28, 1980; "U Teacher Replies to Benson," *Salt Lake Tribune*, February 28, 1980; "Keep Partisan Political Actions Out of Church, Urge LDS," *Salt Lake Tribune*, March 8, 1980; and "No. 2 Mormon Leader Says Leaders' Word is Law," *Los Angeles Times*, March 1, 1980. The church-owned newspaper, the *Deseret News*, downplayed the controversy. See "Pres. Benson Outlines Way to Follow Prophet," *Deseret News*, "Church News," March 1, 1980.

64. Details regarding Benson's apology to general authorities is recounted in Paul Dunn to George T. Boyd, May 30, 1984, Matt Harris files; Leonard Arrington journal, June 17, 1980, Box 34, Folder 6, Leonard J. Arrington Papers, Special Collections, Merrill-Cazier Library, Utah State University; Quinn, *Extensions of Power*, 111, 469, n.353; Kimball, *Working Draft*, 237; Dew, *Ezra Taft Benson*, 469.

65. For Benson's apology to Latter-day Saints, see "Apology" [1980], Ezra Taft and Flora A. Benson file, 1980–1992, LDS Church History Library.

66. J. B. Haws makes this astute point in "The LDS Church Presidency Years, 1985–1994." See his chapter in this volume.

67. Benson to Jeffrey St. John, January 2, 1986, Ezra Taft Benson Correspondence, John Birch Society Headquarters, Appleton, Wisc. St. John was the editor of *The New American* magazine, a Birch publication.

68. John F. McManus, president of the John Birch Society, reflects on Ezra Taft Benson, 2014, Matt Harris files (my thanks to Mr. McManus for his reflections on President Benson).

69. Larry B. Stammer, "Faithful Throngs Remember Benson," *Los Angeles Times*, June 5, 1994; Twila Van Leer, "Church Leader Buried Beside Wife. Cache Pays Tribute As Cortege Passes," *Deseret News*, June 5, 1994.

70. As explained by Pearl Adair, a ninety-six-year-old Mormon Bircher from Mesa, Arizona, April 2017 (in conversation with Matt Harris, her nephew).

71. Gordon B. Hinckley, "Farewell to a Prophet," *Ensign* (July 1994): https://www.lds.org/ensign/1994/07/farewell-to-a-prophet?lang=eng; Gary Avant, "President Benson eulogized," *LDS Church News* (June 11, 1994): http://www.ldschurchnewsarchive.com/articles/24134/President-Benson-eulogized.html.

PART I

Politics and Cold War Anxieties

1 Ezra Taft Benson and the Family Farm

BRIAN Q. CANNON

Ezra Taft Benson ranks among the most controversial secretaries of agriculture in the nation's history. Over Benson's eight-year tenure, American farmers grappled with record surpluses that drove down the price of farm commodities while the costs of farming soared. As millions abandoned agriculture, Benson's political opponents repeatedly blamed his austere fiscal policies for undermining the family farm. Benson, who was reared on a small farm, identified closely with farm families and bristled at the criticism. He justifiably pointed out that far more Americans had abandoned their farms during Harry Truman's presidency than during his tenure as secretary under Eisenhower, and insisted that the exodus from the farm was a harrowing but unavoidable consequence of America's heightened agricultural productivity. Over the course of his administration the secretary argued that most family farmers would benefit in the long run from the administration's policies. Benson believed the family farm was an ideal incubator of virtue and democracy, and he was therefore pleased when struggling farmers were able to stabilize their operations through off-farm income or government-backed repayable loans. But the man who would later become a vocal anti-communist generally combated government efforts to prop up marginal farmers with perpetual grants and subsidies—a New Deal legacy that he derisively dubbed socialized agriculture. The family farm he wanted to perpetuate was large enough to be economically viable in an era of commercial, mechanized agriculture. For marginal farmers Benson proposed a rural development program to boost their options for off-farm employment.

Concerns about the future of family farming had been mounting for decades by the time Benson took office in 1953. Late in the nineteenth century the nation's farm population swelled, rising by nearly 13 percent in the 1880s and 21 percent in the 1890s. The farm population continued to grow, albeit less rapidly, between 1900 and 1916, but then declined during World War I as people moved away to work in industry or joined the military. Some fretted that those who left the farm during the war would never return. "How ya gonna keep 'em down on the farm after they've seen Paree?" asked Sam Lewis and Joe Young in their 1918 hit song. "How ya gonna keep 'em away from Broadway, jazzin' around and paintin' the town?"[1]

Despite the allure of city lights, many wartime migrants returned to the small towns and farms of their childhood after the war ended. Unfortunately for rural Americans, the market for farm products shriveled as farmers in Europe resumed production and as the U.S. military stopped buying food for millions of soldiers. Confronted with bleak economic prospects, rural Americans turned back to the cities, especially as the urban economy improved after 1922. The farm population rebounded somewhat early in the Depression as millions of unemployed Americans moved to the countryside in search of sustenance. But it slipped again in 1935 and plummeted during the Second World War. In the postwar era, the number of out-migrants exceeded the number of births and move-ins in most years; during Truman's presidency, the number of farm residents fell by 8.2 million. Midway through Eisenhower's second term in 1958, fewer than 10 percent of Americans resided on farms, down from close to one-third in 1920. The Census Bureau estimated that well over thirty-one million Americans—approaching one-fifth of the U.S. population—had left the farm since World War I.[2]

The out-migration of farmers did not jeopardize the nation's food supply; America produced far more food than it could consume in the postwar era owing partly to farmers' use of pesticides, chemical fertilizers, and machinery. These trends had been foreseen during the war: in 1944 Roosevelt's secretary of agriculture Claude Wickard anticipated postwar surpluses, warning that agriculture would "offer no large-scale possibilities" for returning soldiers. Indeed, he forecast, "a somewhat smaller, rather than larger, farm labor force will be needed to turn out full farm production."[3]

Notwithstanding America's abundance of food, some Americans worried that a declining farm population would weaken the nation's social fabric. This view drew strength from the widely embraced yeoman ideal famously purveyed by Thomas Jefferson—the view of family farms as the source of national virtue, independence, and a strong work ethic. During the Cold War, politicians touted small farmers as the nation's staunchest bulwark against communism. Historically America had offered abundant, inexpensive land to the rising generation and to immigrants, in marked contrast to the overworked lands of Europe. Many Americans attributed the nation's greatness in part to this heritage of broad-based agricultural opportunity and wanted the government to continue fostering opportunities to farm. To these citizens, policies that perpetuated the family farm seemed inherently good; those that drove small farmers out of business seemed socially irresponsible and politically disastrous.

Having grown up on a small family farm in southeastern Idaho during the heyday of the Country Life Movement, a campaign by President Theodore Roosevelt and the progressives to modernize rural lifestyles and perpetuate America's agricultural identity, Ezra Taft Benson instinctively identified with the yeoman ideal, though he also understood the economic forces driving farmers toward the city. Benson spent his early years in a two-room cabin built by his father. The eighty-acre Benson farmstead furnished much of the family's food. "We ground our own grain or carried grist to a nearby mill. We grew our own vegetables and fruit, made our own bread," he recalled. Benson learned to drive a team of horses and herd cattle, and he worked hard, helping to milk seventeen Holsteins, "digging potatoes and sugar beets, shocking grain, [and] putting up hay." He relished the simple pleasures of an open country boyhood like basketball, baseball, swimming, ice skating, and horseback riding. That some of his farm work was really "half play, like trapping muskrats and rounding up cattle," heightened Benson's nostalgia for his farm boyhood.[4]

The secretary credited farm life with inculcating priceless lessons in "thrift, self-reliance, work, awareness of Providence as evidenced in nature, cooperation, and tolerance." Based upon his own experiences, he was convinced that "country living produces better people. . . . It is a good place to teach the basic virtues that have helped to build this nation." A rock-ribbed opponent of socialism and communism, Benson believed that industrious, independently inclined family farmers were "the strongest bulwark we have against all that is aimed, not only at weakening, but at the very destruction of our American way of life." Thus, family farms were "the best way to produce American citizens."[5]

Although Benson championed the family farm and attributed many virtues to his farm background, educational opportunities ultimately led him, along with many in his generation, away from the farm. His experiences in successfully transitioning to a career in the nation's capital convinced him that with adequate training, rural youth did not need to remain on the farm in order to thrive as adults. In his childhood, Benson recalled, "it was quite an event" when someone left for graduate or professional training. The secretary vividly remembered "the first boy who left our farm community to go East to study dentistry." The boy worked after school at the country store and post office to "earn money to go to college in Chicago . . . in order to begin his professional education." After he left "the ice was broken and a number of them went," including Benson, who traveled to Iowa State in 1926 to study agricultural economics. Benson expected that his university training would make him a better farmer in an era when agriculture was professionalizing. After receiving his master's degree in 1927, he returned to the family farm, which he had purchased with his brother Orval in 1923. Orval soon left the farm to serve as a Mormon missionary in Denmark. Struggling to make mortgage payments on the farm despite low dairy prices, Benson bought more cows and hired another brother to help with bottling and marketing the milk. The Bensons gathered eggs from a flock of 250 chickens and also kept a dozen hogs. They raised alfalfa, sugar beets, and some grain.[6]

Early in 1929 Benson's education opened a professional door. Impressed by his credentials, the county commissioners asked the young farmer's permission to nominate him to serve as Franklin County's agricultural extension agent. Benson assented, received his appointment in March, leased the farm to a neighbor, and moved to town. It turned out to be a fortuitous time to exchange full-time farming for a government job with its consistent salary, just months before the Depression's onset.[7]

Benson relished his work as an extension agent. Like many professionals whose farm backgrounds led them to study agricultural subjects, Benson's career allowed him to keep working in the countryside while enjoying the stability of a monthly paycheck. "Nothing that I have done in agriculture ever gave me more solid satisfaction than working with rural people as a county agent," he reminisced. After working as a county agent for only a year and a half, Benson accepted a promotion and moved to Boise, where he worked as an agricultural economist and marketing specialist for the University of Idaho's Extension Division. In that capacity he helped potato growers, hog farmers, dairy farmers, and poultry producers across the state to organize cooperatives so that they could jointly buy farm machinery at reduced prices and cooperatively market their products at more favorable prices. He helped to found the Idaho Cooperative Council, the second statewide federation of small producers' cooperatives in the nation. Benson was convinced that co-operative marketing was a more effective means of reducing price-depressing agricultural surpluses than the federal government's New Deal program of paying farmers to produce less. As a government-employed marketing specialist, Benson dutifully publicized New Deal programs and assisted those who wanted to sign up, but he regarded the programs as socialistic: as he later recalled, "I never encouraged the farmers to join up."[8]

In 1936 Benson applied for and received a prestigious fellowship to pursue advanced studies at the Giannini Foundation for Agricultural Economics at the University of California in Berkeley. Benson received a nine-month leave from his post in Idaho, not long enough to complete a Ph.D. but nevertheless enough time to study under some of the nation's foremost economists, including Henry Erdman, a "politically progressive" expert in marketing and agricultural co-ops. Benson took advantage of the opportunity to visit nearly "every slaughter and feed yard" in the state as well as numerous avocado, orange, and walnut cooperatives.[9]

Benson's training and success in cooperative marketing attracted the attention of officers in the National Council of Farmer Cooperatives. In 1939 they hired him as executive secretary at the Council's headquarters in Washington, D.C., at the munificent salary of $25,000 a year. As the public face of the council, he lobbied on Capitol Hill and in the executive branch on behalf of the interests of 1.6 million farmers who belonged to 4,600 cooperatives and annually produced commodities valued at $1.3 million. In the process he became acquainted with many of the nation's agricultural experts. Many considered Benson a rising star in farm management circles when he accepted a call to serve full-time as an apostle in the Church of Jesus Christ of Latter-day Saints, a calling with a yearly living allowance of only $6,000. When he resigned from the National Council and moved to Salt Lake City, he expected to spend the rest of his life serving his church, far removed from the world of farming.[10]

After serving as an apostle for nearly a decade, Benson's fortunes changed abruptly when he was summoned to New York City shortly after the 1952 presidential election to meet with the nation's president-elect, Dwight Eisenhower. Ike invited Benson to meet with him at the suggestion of conservative senator and former presidential contender Robert Taft, a powerhouse in the Republican National Committee. Benson drew wide admiration for his visionary advocacy of farmer cooperatives and possessed administrative experience and solid academic training in agricultural economics. Impressed by his credentials, Eisenhower, who did not know Benson personally, invited him to become his secretary of agriculture. Alerted in advance to the possibility of an invitation, Benson had already discussed the possibility with church president David O. McKay, who encouraged him to "accept if it was a clear offer." As Benson conferred with Eisenhower, he recalled, he told the president that he opposed "the New Deal–Fair Deal program for agriculture." When the conservative churchman learned that the president-elect shared his conviction that New Deal–era agricultural subsidies and regulations needed to be rolled back, the challenging prospect of effecting such a shift in policy enthralled him. Benson wondered aloud about his fitness for the position given his religious office, but when Eisenhower dismissed his concerns, Benson accepted the president's invitation. Suddenly, Benson's farm background and his views of agriculture and the family farm became relevant to millions of rural Americans. On January 4, 1953, he began his work from a temporary office in the World Center Building in Washington; just over a week later he met with the rest of the incoming cabinet for the first time.[11]

Benson's intense work ethic served him well in his new post. Arising at 5:30, the secretary worked for an hour at home, often drafting memos for his staff, which they jokingly called "Epistles from an Apostle," and was at the office by 7:30. He ate lunch at his desk and often remained at work until 7 P.M. or later. He expected his associates to keep similar hours. When Benson's new administrative secretary, thirty-six-year-old Arthur Haycock, arrived in Washington on Saturday January 13 after an exhausting train trip from Salt Lake City, he phoned the office, "hoping Bro. Benson would not be in." Unfortunately for Haycock, his boss, who often worked on Saturdays, was there and urged him to hurry on down because of the "telegrams and letters that have been pouring in."[12]

Haycock and Benson's other associates in the Department of Agriculture (USDA) learned that Benson was a man of strong, religiously grounded convictions regarding farming and the Constitution and that these convictions shaped his actions. "Ezra Benson is going to shock Washington," a friend predicted. "He's in the habit of *deciding everything on principle*." Benson's decades of service in prominent church positions, including stints as the president of two stakes and as an apostle, had habituated him to fast and pray frequently for inspiration and to see himself as a divinely called agent. A priesthood blessing given to Benson by President McKay, a fervent anti-communist, before his departure for Washington assured him that "as an apostle of the Lord Jesus Christ [y]ou are entitled to . . . divine guidance which others may not have." McKay blessed him to discern "the enemies who would thwart the freedoms of the individual as vouchsafed by the Constitution" and to "be fearless in the condemnation of those subversive influences, and strong in your defense of the rights and privileges of the Constitution." Benson's agrarian roots, association with politically conservative church leaders, and work with farmer cooperatives in Idaho and Washington, D.C., had convinced him that farmers would be better off in a free market stripped of policies that had been adopted during the Great Depression and Second World War as temporary expedients. He shared McKay's conviction, abetted by Supreme Court rulings and an LDS First Presidency statement in 1936, that elements of the New Deal were unconstitutional. He also shared McKay's distrust of socialism and contempt for communism and believed that "the first Communist cell in our Government was established [in the 1930s] in the Department of Agriculture, including Alger Hiss and some others." Almost certainly these were some of the "subversive influences" that came to Benson's mind when he heard McKay's blessing, although he fit the mold of neither an extremist nor an opportunist of the likes of Joseph McCarthy. Benson never publicly attributed his actions as secretary of agriculture to divine revelation, but Sherman Adams, Eisenhower's special assistant, detected a self-righteous streak in Benson's dogged adherence to principle. Benson's intense religious commitments led him to lobby Eisenhower to open cabinet meetings with prayer. "I really think Ezra is less concerned with his Department than with making sure I open every session with prayer," Eisenhower reportedly quipped.[13]

Many of Benson's fellow Mormons shared the view that his appointment was providential, although some, like apostle and friend J. Reuben Clark, were more circumspect. U.S. senator and former stake president Arthur Watkins expressed gratitude that "a prophet of God was in the cabinet." Fellow apostle Harold B. Lee prophesied in March of that year that Benson's detractors "will be forgotten in the remains of Mother Earth." Benson as an ordained apostle had received "power from Almighty God," and that applied in government as well as church circles. As long as Benson remained faithful "there will be given inspiration and revelation," Lee proclaimed. As was the case with many Mormons who wrote to Benson's office, Carl Burton, president of the church's Great Lakes Mission, felt strongly that Benson's cabinet appointment "was inspired." Charlie Geurts, an accountant in Salt Lake City, rejoiced that "men bearing the Holy Priesthood should have the direction of this most important Government department at a time when the 'Constitution shall hang by a thread.'" With Benson in the cabinet, Geurts expected that the Eisenhower administration would galvanize "a great event in United States history, the turning point for the betterment of all the people."[14]

Benson entered the Department of Agriculture with the verve of a reformer, describing the agency with a $2.1 billion budget as a "swollen bureaucracy." His first major action as secretary was to reorganize the department: he clipped the sails of the pro–New Deal, liberally oriented Production and Marketing Administration and Bureau of Agricultural Economics, where his former Iowa State professor Clarence L. Holmes had finished his career, and warned USDA employees that he expected a full day's work from everyone. His actions appeared autocratic and alienated some staffers. But the shakeup had only begun. In his first press conference the secretary stated that "farmers should not be put in the position of working for government bounty. Too many Americans are already calling on Washington to do for them what they can and should be doing for themselves." Although he did not categorically condemn all federal farm aid, Benson made it clear that he believed many government subsidies to farmers who produced crops that were in oversupply were counterproductive: "price supports should provide insurance against disaster to the farm-producing plant and help to stabilize national food supplies. But price supports which tend to prevent production shifts toward a balanced supply in terms of demand . . . should be avoided."[15]

Price supports in the form of commodity loans administered by the Commodity Credit Corporation (CCC), a subsidiary of the USDA, were a mechanism instituted during the Great Depression to regulate production and prices for key crops and to protect farmers from economic ruin. Farmers who voluntarily entered into marketing agreements to limit production of key commodities to a specified acreage could either sell their crops on the open market or borrow money from the CCC, depositing their crops in government warehouses as collateral. If the price for the crop rose above the loan amount within a year of depositing the crop, the farmer could sell the crop at a profit and repay the loan with interest. If the price remained below the loan level, the farmer could forfeit the crop, which would become government property, and thereby convert the loan into a grant. When Benson took office, most loans went to growers of cotton, corn, and wheat, but the CCC also lent money to producers of butter, cheese, powdered milk, peanuts, cottonseed and linseed oil, wool, tobacco, tung oil, olive oil, rosin, and turpentine. Additionally, the agency supported prices for barley, dry beans, cottonseed meal, flaxseed, rice, sorghum, oats, rye, seeds for hay and pasture, and soybeans.[16]

CCC loan amounts were based upon parity—the concept that farmers should receive a fair return for their labor. In modern history farmers had supposedly enjoyed full parity between 1909 and 1914 when their returns aligned favorably with their expenses. Thus, the USDA adopted those years as its ideal standard. As journalist Jay Richter explained, in determining the justice of farm profits, "if a hog paid for a new suit in 1909–14 . . . today's hog should bring enough to buy an equally good suit." Because they were created as a form of emergency insurance, the CCC's commodity loans were generally pegged at a percentage below full, or 100 percent, parity. The underlying expectation was that in most years supplies would conform to market demand and the going price at some point in the year would exceed the loan amount. When they were introduced in the 1930s loans were pegged at only 52–75 percent of parity, but Congress raised them during the Second World War to 85 percent in 1941 and 90 percent in 1942. To forestall a postwar recession, lawmakers allowed the loan rate to remain at 90 percent of parity for two years beyond the war's end in 1945. In 1948 and 1949 lawmakers approved a gradual reduction in parity rates, but subsequent Congresses postponed those reductions, ostensibly to incentivize farmers to grow more food for troops during the Korean War. By 1953 when Benson took office, vast supplies of surplus crops forfeited by commodity loan recipients clogged government warehouses. Meanwhile the default commodity credit loan level remained at 90 percent, an amount fixed by Congress in 1952 to last through 1954, despite the surpluses the government was withholding from markets in order to prop up market prices. Benson "felt like somebody suddenly asked to take over a train hurtling through the night at 90 miles an hour with the throttle stuck open," he recalled.[17]

Benson, who believed the high loan rate was unjustified given the CCC's immense stockpiles, pledged to honor the 90 percent rate through 1954 as required by law. But he warned that overproduction, falling prices, and farmer dependency would persist as long as the government continued its generous commodity loans, and he promised that in the long term he would work to persuade Congress to reduce the support level. Benson pled with American farmers "to raise our sights beyond the dollar sign, beyond material things. May we have the courage to . . . stand for principle."[18]

Nearly one month into Benson's tenure, hundreds of letters arriving at the USDA headquarters reportedly endorsed his opposition to high price supports and his other policies fifteen to one. "The people are for him, as indicated by the letters and telegrams we receive from around the country," his assistant Arthur Haycock exulted. Wrote one farm couple, "We are 100 percent for any man who has the courage to tell us we are capable of standing on our own feet rather than merely surviving with Government aid." Owing to the fact that commodity loans were unavailable for many of the nation's farm products including fruit, poultry, and beef, many farmers lacked a direct stake in preserving high price supports, and some farmers resented the privileged status of subsidized growers. It was no wonder they were willing to see them go. The nation's dominant farm organization, the American Farm Bureau, which generally promoted the interests of large growers, who tended to have larger profit margins, consistently supported Benson, too. Benson's stand against high subsidies also favored consumers, because commodity loans and government warehouses inflated food prices. One urban letter writer applauded Benson's hostility toward "a policy that has prevailed so long . . . of giving—sometimes quite unfairly—to certain favored groups of our citizenry."[19]

Growers of subsidized commodities, who were concentrated in the corn, wheat, and dairy states of the northern plains and upper Midwest, where relatively small family farms predominated, and their representatives on Capitol Hill (the farm bloc) retorted that 90 percent parity was vital to family farmers. Harriet Oeder, a Minnesotan, bristled at Benson's insinuation that recipients of subsidies were materialistic and greedy. She and her husband, a veteran, labored mightily, saving and investing to improve their farm, and still did not have a furnace, running water, or an indoor bathroom, she wrote. She defied well-heeled bureaucrats like Benson who charged that "we are burden on the taxpayers." Was it fair, she questioned "here in these United States that a hard-working person can't have these [basic amenities]"? On Capitol Hill farm bloc politicians and their allies excoriated the secretary in the name of the small farmer. "Benson is like a man standing on the bank of the river telling a drowning man that all he needs to do is take a deep breath of air," chided Minnesota Representative Eugene McCarthy. Montana senator James Murray accused the secretary of having "no understanding of the measures which brought prosperity to America's farmers." A friendlier tongue-in-cheek letter to Benson published in the *Chicago News* and then reprinted elsewhere quipped: "Dear Ezra: We note that you favor 'letting the Lord handle the farmers' problems.' Their prayers will be for faith, hope and parity." As Benson recalled, Eisenhower privately counseled him following a tumultuous speech in Minnesota, "I believe every word you said in St. Paul. But I'm not sure you should have said it quite so soon."[20]

Benson's supporters condemned the naysayers as selfish and opportunistic. "They don't care about anyone but themselves and the benefits they can derive from it," lamented Claude Petersen. Glen Burt, a Salt Lake City businessman, charged, "There seems to be nothing but selfishness in the minds of most people, with pressure groups seeming to have the upper hand at getting what they want—rather than what might be best for the people of the land."[21]

In April *Time* ran a cover story on the embattled secretary of agriculture. The article quoted Benson's statement that price supports should be sufficiently high to "provide insurance against disaster" but that "no real American wants to be subsidized." The gist of Benson's message, the article reported, was that supports should "not guarantee profits to the inefficient." Whether or not the verbiage was Benson's, the insinuation that farmers living on the edge were inefficient and unpatriotic infuriated some small farmers and their supporters.[22]

Letters to the editor published in response to the *Time* article criticized Benson's stance and defended small farmers. Francis Townsend, whose call for old-age pensions had helped goad the Roosevelt administration into proposing Social Security, defended subsidies as a means of preventing urban poverty and unemployment. "Let us not be afraid," he wrote, "of reasonable subsidies paid to farmers. Let us use these subsidies to keep the little farmers on the land instead of crowding them off and into the big cities where they will become 'surplus.'" Ted Banta, a small wheat farmer and rancher in Geyser, Montana, disputed the charge that farmers in need of assistance were inefficient. "My experience has been that the main difference between efficient and inefficient farmers was merely a matter of weather," he offered. Houston Jones, a son of poor tenant farmers, accused Benson of ignoring "the basic Christian tenet of the brotherhood of all men." Why should the "man who uses his hands" be denied the "bounty of America" when the nation was bestowing "great bounties upon manufacturing and business interests" in contracts, protective tariffs, and tax breaks?[23]

In October, as cattle prices languished, having fallen by one-third since Benson took office, the secretary's opponents plotted to either discredit him or shame him into action. First the House Committee on Agriculture, dominated by defenders of 90 percent parity, enjoined Benson to subsidize cattle prices. Then two weeks later, 350 cattlemen arrived in the nation's capital as part of a widely publicized "cattle caravan" organized by the National Farmers Union (NFU) to lobby for price supports. Considerably smaller than the nation's biggest farm organizations, the NFU billed itself as the champion of low-income "dirt farmers"—the family farmers living on the edge whose plight aroused public sympathy—and employed Benson's Democratic predecessor, Charles Brannan, as its general counsel. The caravan's travels figured prominently on the front pages of newspapers across the nation. In his regular column in *Newsweek*, the conservative political economist Raymond Moley dismissed the caravan as "the hammy show of a small group of cattle raisers." David O. McKay encouraged Benson to stand firm: "Your Agriculture policy is sound. Political demagogues seek to undermine your clear thinking. Loyal citizens are with you. Hold to your standards." Benson met with caravan participants and listened as they complained of having lost staggering sums in the cattle market. He sympathized with their plight, pointed out that the administration was trying to help by purchasing more beef for school lunch programs, and reminded the ranchers that the government's previous attempts to purchase and store perishable commodities, including hogs and potatoes, had been a "dismal failure" and a "fiasco." The secretary pointed out that most cattlemen's organizations, including the American National Cattlemen's Association, opposed price support commodity loans. "I don't say it's not possible for cattle but it would be a terrible thing if we got into this program and found it wouldn't work," he indicated. He promised to keep an open mind and invited the ranchers to respond to his concerns and present a viable new plan the next day. When they returned to merely reiterate their demand for 90 percent of parity, Benson rebuffed them. In explaining his actions, he charged, "They didn't present a plan. They just said put supports on cattle."[24]

The cattle caravan turned out to be a public-relations disaster for the Farmers Union and a triumph for Benson. *Life* magazine gave the secretary a two-page spread to explain his opposition to price supports for cattle, and followed it up with an editorial praising him as a "statesman." *Newsweek* dubbed him a "cool man on the hottest seat in Washington." Benson's forceful, confident handling of the caravan; the fact that the leading cattlemen's associations opposed price supports; and evidence that the caravan included many privileged hobby ranchers claiming to be struggling small-time beef growers, strengthened his clout. "We feel that it was a turning point in our favor," Benson's secretary Haycock wrote.[25]

In his conferences with Eisenhower in 1953, Benson encouraged the president to break with the 1952 Republican Party platform's support for 90 percent parity and instead advocate a sliding scale of price supports that would decrease as surplus commodity stocks rose. Benson believed this step was essential to reduce surpluses and gradually wean farmers from commodity loans. In October Eisenhower at last told Benson he would publicly oppose high, fixed supports, despite the inevitable political fallout of breaking with the Republican platform. He likely decided to take the stance despite the political risk because, as presidential assistant Sherman Adams observed more generally, "the so-called Benson farm policies that everybody indignantly called to Eisenhower's attention were actually Eisenhower's own farm policies." In his farm message to Congress in January 1954 the president urged lawmakers to allow price supports to fluctuate between 75 and 90 percent of parity, depending upon the amount of surplus crops stored in government warehouses. Eisenhower's message ignited protests from members of the farm bloc, many of whom were fighting for reelection. Benson added to the farm bloc's ire when, a few weeks later, he used his discretionary authority under existing legislation on dairy products to reduce dairy price supports from 90 percent to 75 percent.[26]

In his appearances before legislative committees in the first quarter of 1954, Benson argued that, over time, lower price supports would reduce surpluses, incentivize farmers to switch to other crops that would sell more readily, and thereby result in "higher average farm income." Several lawmakers challenged his reasoning. Senator Edward Thye of Minnesota pointed out that surpluses existed for virtually every farm product. Thus, it made little economic sense for a grower to switch from wheat or corn to an unsubsidized crop. North Dakota senator Milton Young claimed that many farmers in his state could not survive on anything less than 90 percent parity because of high production costs. When South Dakota representative Harold Lovre raised the old populist argument that farmers deserved help from the government as much as manufacturers, Benson blandly dismissed the justification, condemning "the trend to more and more Government handouts and subsidies."[27]

In the hearings both Benson and his detractors claimed to speak for small farmers, those culturally potent symbols of America's agrarian ideal. The secretary showed that large producers received a disproportionate share of the commodity loan pie. In Kansas the largest wheat loan issued by the Commodity Credit Corporation in 1953 amounted to $139,237, while the average was only $1,525. In California, the largest cotton loan was just shy of $1.25 million, while the average loan hovered at $1,731. "Present price supports offer very little to the 3,500,000 of our farm operators whose production is so small that price supports mean very few extra dollars," he insisted. For instance, the average Nebraska corn grower who received $2,487 per year under 90 percent parity would have his payment reduced by only $250 under 80 percent parity. When members of the House Committee on Agriculture retorted that the relatively paltry commodity loans were nonetheless vital for small farmers, Benson replied, "I do not deny that the extra dollars which might come to the small farmer through price supports are important. But for every dollar that comes to him, many more dollars come to the big operator and the competitive advantage of the large operator is thereby increased."[28]

Despite Benson's persistent lobbying, the House Committee on Agriculture voted by twenty-one to eight to maintain commodity loans at 90 percent. Benson expected the outcome but was still disappointed. Judging from the remarks of some legislators, he later observed, "one would have thought" that high, rigid price supports were "as inviolable as the Ten Commandments."[29]

The battleground for flexible parity shifted next to the full House. Benson emphasized that the Commodity Credit Corporation was spending $700,000 a day to store surplus crops. Benson's allies insisted that price supports inflated consumer prices, reminding their colleagues that the price of butter had fallen by 25 percent that year after Benson lowered price supports from 90 to 75 percent. They also pointed out that price supports primarily benefited farmers in a handful of states who specialized in supported commodities like corn and wheat. They defended flexible parity as a step toward free enterprise and a step away from "the wreckage of every socialistic system that has come to curse the human race," in the words of Republican Paul Dague of Pennsylvania.[30]

So close was the contest between flexible and fixed parity advocates that the "atmosphere on the floor and in the galleries of the House was electric," recalled Benson. "No one knew for sure who had what votes." When it finally became clear that the administration's proposal for flexible parity rates as low as 70 percent would not pass, House majority leader and Eisenhower ally Charles Halleck shrewdly suggested a compromise to avoid a presidential veto of the entire farm bill: flexibility ranging from 82.5 percent to 90 percent for 1955 for wheat, corn, cotton, rice, and peanuts and 75 to 90 percent for the ensuing years. The House approved the compromise on July 1 and adopted the entire farm bill the next day. After revisiting many of the arguments raised in debates on the floor of the House, the Senate approved a compromise bill setting parity for the first year between 82.5 percent and 90 percent by a vote of forty-nine to forty-four on August 9. Benson was elated when his son Reed, who was monitoring the voting from the Senate gallery, phoned with the news. At least the principle of flexibility and reductions in price supports had been restored, and this promised to whittle away at the size of government payments to farmers. Benson's conviction that he was on a divine errand was reinforced when he received a note from McKay congratulating him on this "outstanding victory." After a House and Senate conference committee ironed out differences in the two bills, Eisenhower signed the compromise bill on August 28.[31]

Comments in the congressional debates demonstrated that small farmers' welfare was tangential to the key objectives of most policymakers in the debates over parity; Benson's overriding objective was reducing farmers' reliance on government payments, while most congressional defenders of high parity were intent upon preventing any further inroads into the New Deal's agricultural legacy. However, a small group of Democrats on Capitol Hill adopted a genuinely populist posture. Among them were Wright Patman of Texas and Barratt O'Hara of Illinois. While Benson used the fact that large farmers were receiving huge subsidies and that subsidies to anyone smacked of socialism as the basis for arguing that subsidies should be abolished, Patman and O'Hara contended that Congress should maintain subsidies but use them exclusively to "guarantee income sufficient to feed, clothe and educate" families on small farms. This could be done by "limit[ing] farm price supports given an individual farmer to a decent family income, and no more." This would save the government a significant amount of money.[32]

Although the president in his 1956 farm message to Congress suggested that lawmakers might consider limiting the amount of money that any farmer could receive in commodity loans, much as Patman and O'Hara had advocated, neither the president nor Benson was willing to directly advocate ceilings on commodity loans, or to specify a particular ceiling that would be appropriate. Both were opposed in principle to any farmer's reliance upon government support. Moreover, they were apparently leery of alienating their support base among relatively large farmers and the Farm Bureau by singling them out for rough treatment. In hearings in 1956 Benson clearly displayed his preference for a certain type of family farm: one that was large enough to be commercially oriented and economically efficient. Pressed by Patman, Benson stated that farmers earning $25,000 in farm income should be as eligible for commodity loans as any other producer, even though barely 4 percent of the nation's full-time commercially oriented farms had sales exceeding $25,000. When Patman inquired if a $75,000 cap would be "too high," Benson replied, "I don't know that it would. Some of these family operations now where they are fully mechanized handle rather sizable volumes." He did concede that $100,000 in income might be close to an appropriate cap.[33]

Seeking to burnish Democrats' credentials as champions of small, economically vulnerable family farms, Harold Cooley, chair of the House Committee on Agriculture, established a nominally bipartisan Subcommittee on Family Farms led by Texas representative Clark Thompson in 1955. The task of the seven Democrats and two Republicans on the subcommittee was to study "ways and means to protect, foster, and promote the family farm as the continuing dominant unit in American agriculture." Thompson candidly alluded to the prospective political benefits of the project as he opened the hearings, quoting from an editorial in a New Orleans newspaper: "Secretary Benson has said that corporation profits and industrial workers' earnings have been going up, while farmers' income has been going down. If that situation isn't corrected, several million farm voters will be after somebody with a pitchfork in 1956." The subcommittee collected political ammunition against Benson in hearings held across the South. L. Y. Ballentine, North Carolina's commissioner of education, told the committee that the average net income for farmers in the Tar Heel state had fallen from $518 in 1951 to $441 in 1954 and blamed Benson's policies. R. J. Howard, a country banker, complained that Benson's attempts to reduce subsidies were "absolutely driving the masses of our farmers into bankruptcy . . . by the multiplied thousands." When bureaucrats including Benson said that struggling small farmers should simply move "to town and get a job," observed Thompson, they overlooked or trivialized the "many years, perhaps a generation or two" that families had invested in improving their farms.[34]

A media-related embarrassment early in 1956 abetted the perception that Benson was hostile to small family farmers. It resulted from a gaffe on the part of a USDA clerk in response to a "vituperative" editorial in the December 1955 issue of *Harper's*. The editorial's author, John Fischer, called farmers "pampered tyrants"; accused both political parties of supporting costly, inefficient farm subsidies in order to woo the farm vote; and credited Benson with "a few gingerly efforts to bring a little sense back into our farm economy." Fischer sent a copy of the article to the USDA, inviting Benson to comment. In his memoirs the secretary wrote that the editorial "did make some good points about the cost of the farm problem" but claimed that the employee who scrawled "This is excellent" across the article had not consulted with him before doing so. Another employee who assumed Benson had written the comment prepared and mailed an endorsement over Benson's name: "I have read the article by John Fischer in the December issue of *Harper's* with a great deal of interest. It is excellent." When the endorsement appeared in the February issue of *Harper's*, reaction on Capitol Hill "rose many decibels too high for comfort," Benson recalled. Opponents branded him as insensitive to small farmers. Standing on the floor of the Senate, Hubert Humphrey roared, "This letter is an insult to every farmer in America. This man should be fired—now—this afternoon!"[35]

Riding a tide of anti-Benson sentiment, Congress in the spring of 1956 passed a bill abrogating key provisions of the 1954 farm bill and restoring 90 percent parity for basic commodities for another year. Against the advice of most of his assistants, who worried about his prospects for reelection, Eisenhower vetoed the bill upon Benson's recommendation. But to the secretary's chagrin the president backpedaled by supporting compromise legislation that maintained price supports between 82.5 percent and 90 percent for another year rather than permitting them to range as low as 75 percent, as the 1954 law had stipulated.[36]

Benson's principled stand against the New Deal legacy suffered a further setback when he acquiesced under pressure from the president and vice president to Eisenhower's proposed soil bank program. To rein in surpluses and boost farm income, the administration asked Congress to pay farmers to retire land from cultivation and place it in a soil bank. North Carolina Democrat Harold Cooley lost no time in pointing out the similarities between the soil bank and the New Deal, which Benson opposed. When Benson denied Cooley's charge that the soil bank was inspired by the New Deal and alleged that "its sources probably go back to Joseph in Egypt," Representative Bob Poage wondered aloud whether Joseph was a Democrat or Republican. Taking the bait, Benson quipped, "He probably was a Republican." Without losing a beat Poage quipped, "Probably so. There was some report for his taking golden vessels from his brethren."[37]

When Benson voiced support for the acreage reserve, he "lost seriously in prestige" among conservatives, according to his informal advisor Karl Butler.

Brigham Young University president Ernest Wilkinson, who denigrated the soil bank as a "complete Federal handout and subsidy," perceived that it was "utterly inconsistent with the feelings" of most LDS church leaders. In mid-1956 Congress approved the soil bank as part of its legislative compromise with Eisenhower.[38]

As the 1956 election approached, Benson campaigned assiduously for Eisenhower. In response to opponents' claims that Benson and Eisenhower were hostile to small farmers, the secretary concentrated increasingly upon the family farm as a theme in his speeches. On September 25 he told the Pennsylvania Millers' and Feed Dealers' Association that the administration was not "ignoring or selling short our family farms." Small farmers were struggling because of the cost-price squeeze: prices of farm commodities were low because supplies exceeded demand, and the problem was exacerbated by the government's stockpiling of surplus crops. As production costs rose owing to mechanization, the best way to pay for the machinery was to farm more land. When some farmers left and their neighbors purchased their land, they enjoyed "a better chance to produce efficiently and live well." The remaining family farmers thereby enhanced their economic security, and this was desirable. Rhetorically he asked, "Would our critics . . . insist that farmers . . . go back to horses and mules, so that adjustments to justify modern equipment would not be necessary?"[39]

In a speech in Illinois Benson accused those who claimed he was hostile to family farms with making "deliberately misleading, careless and irresponsible statements." "We have taken more constructive action for the benefit of the family farm than has any previous Administration in many years," he averred. Some politicians selfishly wanted to enshrine an antiquated form of family farming "the way grandfather did it" by propping up farmers on uneconomical units. This was senseless, Benson argued. He, on the other hand, "want[ed] to see farm families live well—rather than to be held in poverty."[40]

Simply because a farm was large did not make it an industrial operation, Benson indicated. He assured audiences in Missouri and Iowa that 97 percent of the nation's farms were still family operations—the same percentage as thirty years before. They were larger and more efficient than the average farm had been in the 1920s, but "most" of the work was still performed "by the farmer and his family, with perhaps some extra hired labor at harvest time." High price supports primarily benefited agribusiness, and Benson therefore opposed them.[41]

In November Eisenhower was reelected. Thanks in part to rising hog prices, Eisenhower did well in the major hog-producing states. Indeed, he carried every farm state outside the South. Even many counties that were hotbeds of anti-Benson sentiment in Wisconsin, Minnesota, Iowa, and the Dakotas voted solidly for Eisenhower. However, western and midwestern Republican candidates for the House and Senate, who were likely tainted by their partisan link to Benson, lost some of the farm vote.[42]

Although Benson had been one of the most controversial members of Eisenhower's cabinet during his first term in office, Eisenhower retained him as secretary of agriculture. The president reportedly defended his secretary, telling Republicans in Congress who sought his ouster that the only way to secure it was to "ask for my resignation as President." Rumors continued to circulate over the next year, though, that Benson was on the chopping block.[43]

Disillusionment with Benson's policies mounted in Mormon country during Eisenhower's second term, as some Latter-day Saint farmers and ranchers ran aground of the secretary's policies. In a mass meeting in Logan in 1957 Mormon ranchers criticized Benson. A few months later Beth Hovey, a Mormon who operated a dairy farm with her husband Garr, telephoned Apostle J. Reuben Clark complaining that Cache Valley dairy farmers would lose a million dollars over the next year because of cuts in price supports for dairy products. She complained, "With price supports as they are, we can't make a go of it," and wondered if she was duty-bound as a Mormon to support Benson's USDA policies or if she could "dissociate" Benson's government post from his apostolic calling. Clark advised her that a policy disagreement with Benson did not constitute disloyalty to the church. "Don't you know that Church authorities do not always agree [even] on Church doctrines?" he asked.[44]

In September 1957 David O. McKay traveled to Washington to meet with Eisenhower about Benson. He informed the president that the church's First Presidency wanted to call Benson back from Washington to serve as superintendent of the Young Men's Mutual Improvement Association, "if he can be spared from the Government." Church leaders knew that Benson's popularity was waning and had possibly heard rumors that most of Benson's "close advisors" in the USDA believed he should resign. It is unclear whether the presidency genuinely needed Benson, whether they had lost hope that the secretary could realistically make further gains in rolling back the New Deal legacy, or whether they had heard rumors that Eisenhower might shelve Benson and wanted to help him and the church save face. McKay later informed Barry Goldwater that he mentioned the possible church calling to the president "so that he might have an excuse to release Brother Benson if he desired to do so." According to McKay, Ike replied that he valued Benson's service and that he had told Benson a year earlier that "he would be pleased to have him remain, but that he was free to follow his own wishes." Eisenhower told McKay that he had a person in mind who could take Benson's place, provided that the person was willing to do so. McKay then met with Benson. A few days later he told his counselors that he had advised Benson, "We want you to be loyal to your position here, loyal to the government and to the President, but if he can spare you, we would like to use you, and if not, we will do something else." Benson came away from the interchange with the understanding that he should talk the matter over with his wife and with Ike and then "report back by telephone." A few days later Benson phoned to inform McKay that Eisenhower would like him to stay in the cabinet "for at least a year" unless McKay felt that it was "imperative" for Benson to return. McKay advised him to stay. Benson's fellow apostle Harold B. Lee reportedly surmised that Benson was insufficiently humble to accept the call from the First Presidency to "come back and properly take up his work as a member of the Council of the Twelve," but McKay's record suggests that he probably represented service in the Young Men's presidency to Benson ambiguously as a possibility rather than as a calling from the First Presidency.[45]

During Eisenhower's second term, the secretary continued to fight for flexible parity and reductions in parity payments. For instance, early in 1957 Benson squared off against Republican congressman H. Carl Andersen of Minnesota, who introduced a bill that would have guaranteed 90 percent parity to all growers on their first four thousand bushels of corn. Benson and his staff announced that they "unalterably opposed" the bill; they wanted to wean all farmers from high price supports rather than to redirect the benefits to small farmers.[46]

A key contest involving small family farms that embroiled the secretary during the second term surrounded competing plans in Congress and the USDA for rehabilitating the nation's poorest 1.5 million farm families. The congressional approach was packaged in a bill for "preserving the family farm" originally introduced in 1955 by Alabama senator John Sparkman and reintroduced in expanded form by House and Senate Democrats in 1956, 1957, and 1959 as the Family Farm Development Act. The bill authorized the government to assist farmers in as many as five hundred counties with the largest low-income farm populations in the nation and reflected the views of the National Farmers' Union. It authorized county farmer committees, which tended to be bastions of local Democratic patronage, to recommend low-income farmers for assistance and required the USDA to coordinate its efforts with those committees. USDA employees would assist needy farmers in devising "farm and home plans" to boost family income and productivity. Farmers would be eligible for both loans at a maximum interest rate of

4 percent and technical assistance from the USDA. Government agencies would help farmers who desired off-farm employment in identifying job opportunities and would furnish vocational training. The government would also promote industrial development in rural areas and would, if necessary, lend funds to companies for that purpose.[47]

Benson and the USDA rejected the liberal aid provisions of the Democrats' bill and proposed instead a more cautious and less expensive Rural Development Program based upon the agency's internal investigation of low-income farmers' needs. In contrast to the Democrats' call to assist poor farmers in up to five hundred counties, the USDA advocated a minimum of fifty pilot development projects. More research was needed, the USDA claimed, to document the educational and economic needs of low-income farmers before a more comprehensive program could be undertaken. For instance, teenage boys were leaving the countryside in search of work, but it was unclear if they needed additional vocational training to prepare them for urban jobs. The report recommended that the government establish "several experimental and demonstration vocational training programs" in an effort to discover and develop "special lines of instruction adapted to the background and orientation of rural boys." These training programs could be "expanded as experience justifies." The agency recommended allowing federal land banks to consider home value along with farm income in their review of loan applications from part-time farmers—a concrete suggestion that could have helped many low-income rural residents to qualify for assistance—and recommended that the government somehow "encourage" more farm development loans by the private sector, and it generically observed that "Government credit services should be strengthened as needed." The House responded somewhat positively to the USDA's proposal, appropriating $2.6 million for assistance to low-income rural families, but the Senate rejected the package and approved only $350,000 in administrative expenses for a Rural Development Program, although it did allow the Farmers Home Administration to lend more money.[48]

The Rural Development Program's loans for farm expansion would only work if some farm families sold their land to their neighbors and moved away. Jamie Whitten, Benson's nemesis on the Agricultural Appropriations Subcommittee, seized upon this fact as the basis for arguing that the Rural Development Program was advising poor farmers to solve their problems by moving away and "get[ting] a job somewhere else." There was "no question," Benson told a group of senators, that the nation had an "excess" of cropland and farmers. But, he added, the Rural Development Program was not forcing anyone to move. Whitten wanted to permit farmers to remain on hardscrabble farms; Benson thought they should be offered better options off the farm.[49]

The USDA's Rural Development Program hobbled along with minimal funding. It developed by May 1957 to include pilot projects in fifty-seven of the nation's three thousand rural counties. Benson and his colleagues pointed to some successes in inducing industrialists to establish factories in rural areas. In Catawba County, North Carolina, for instance, a new factory with one hundred employees had been established, while Perry County, Indiana, had attracted four new industries. USDA officials showcased a prototypical farm family, Olen and Lessie Carden and their four children, to illustrate the impact of rural development projects. This middle-age couple completed a farm and home management plan with the help of the extension and home demonstration agents. On the basis of that plan they secured a loan from the Farmers Home Administration to purchase a tractor, build a ten-sow farrowing house and a granary, drill a well, and install a bathroom. With help from government employees Mrs. Carden found a temporary job in town and earned money for new curtains, a tile floor, and a reupholstered couch. Under the soil bank program, the Cardens converted eighteen acres of marginal cropland to permanent pasture. Though it was too early in 1957 to know the ultimate financial impact of these developments, the family's situation looked promising.[50]

The Cardens were unquestionably better positioned to succeed as a result of the Rural Development Program, but there were hundreds of thousands of farm families in other counties who also needed help. By the end of 1957 the program had aided only 4,500 families nationwide. Meanwhile, as Georgia senator Richard Russell observed, there were "thousands of poor" farm families "that cannot make but 2 or 3 bales of cotton. That is the only thing they have to sell, and the only way they can make any money." Louisiana senator Allen Ellender acidly remarked that the rural development program "doesn't help [most low-income farmers] now" and that those people would likely lose their farms before the program reached them.[51]

The election of 1958 devastated the Republican contingent on Capitol Hill. Democrats would hold nearly two-thirds of the seats in both the House and the Senate over the next two years. In this condition Benson's prospects of further reforming farm policy in his remaining years in office were limited. "Our job was like trying to move the ball against a team that outweighed us 50 pounds to the man," he recalled. Benson continued to maintain that high price supports harmed small farmers by allowing them to defer tough choices. "They have been discouraged from making the adjustment which is inevitable and which they must make if they are going to get a reasonably good standard of living," he claimed. Georgia senator Herman Talmadge voiced the majority opinion on Capitol Hill, though, when he declared in 1959, "The small farmer does not have any more chance of making a living under the present program than the man in the moon."[52]

With Democrats in control on Capitol Hill it appeared that a significant outpouring of monetary aid to family farmers might be forthcoming, but little changed. In 1960 Democrats introduced twenty-one bills promoting a Family Farm Income Act, with backing from the National Farmers Union. Idaho representative Grace Pfost claimed that the bills were intended to address the needs of "our family farmers" who "have been forced to trade their land for a bus ticket to the city" because they had been "ground to pieces in the cost-price squeeze." The bills sought to redress the cost-price squeeze through marketing quotas designed and approved by growers in referenda. The quotas would be set "at a level low enough to reduce present Government-stored surplus stocks by 10 percent each year." No new surpluses would be purchased by the government, but farmers would be subsidized with payments ranging from $5,000 to $10,000 until the marketing quotas had achieved their purposes. Congress held hearings on the bills between mid-February and mid-March. Benson was convinced that the hearings, which included testimony from seven midwestern Democratic governors, were primarily designed "to dramatize that these strong and true Democratic hearts did indeed bleed for the plight of the farmer" rather than to reform policy. That seems not to have been the case entirely; the bill was defended, amended, and renamed the Farm Surplus Reduction Act, but ultimately it was defeated in the House 236 to 170.[53]

When Benson and the rest of the Eisenhower administration left office early in 1961, flexible parity had become the standard, and wheat and cotton supports had been reduced for the time being from 90 to 75 percent. Benson could take satisfaction that at least the level of supports had been modestly reduced, although he had hoped it would be closer to 60 percent by the end of his time in office in order to wean farmers from commodity loans. During Benson's tenure, close to 28.6 million acres had been removed from cultivation and placed in the conservation reserve, but agricultural productivity was still rising, and overwhelming surpluses remained. Progress had been made in liquidating some of the stored surplus: farm exports had grown by a record $26.6 million over the past seven years—a highly impressive feat attributable in part to congressional support and to Benson's aggressive negotiations and trade missions abroad. Despite Benson's concerns about bloated bureaucracy the USDA remained massive, with more employees than in 1953 and a ballooning budget.[54]

In some respects Benson, along with other conservative opponents of government subsidies and regulations in the 1940s and 1950s, anticipated the stance of neoliberal advocates of free trade, economic deregulation, and budget-balancing in the 1970s like Milton Friedman and Friedrich von Hayek. But Benson's commitments were largely ideological rather than theoretical. Benson's mentors in graduate school favored description over modeling and theory. His professor and friend at Iowa State, C. L. Holmes, favored practical economic education that would assist farmers and focused his research on the organizational and economic practices of farmers. Henry Erdman, Benson's mentor at Berkeley, "avoided involvement with abstract economic theory and preferred realistic description of institutions because he believed that to be more useful." The secretary was fond of paraphrasing economic theorist Adam Smith that producers "are led as if by an invisible hand to benefit the general public." Smith's laissez-faire philosophy harmonized with Benson's views on individual freedom: "Freedom is a God-given, eternal principle vouchsafed to us under the Constitution. . . . It is doubtful if any man can be politically free who depends upon the state for sustenance."[55]

The nation had about a million fewer farms in 1961 than when Benson had been appointed in 1953, a drop of about 20 percent, and the number of small farms with sales of under $2,500 had fallen by nearly 40 percent. But well over 90 percent of the nation's farms remained family-owned enterprises. By working to reduce commodity loan price supports and enforcing acreage allotments in compliance with the law, Benson likely hastened the departure of some struggling farmers. Given the laws of supply and demand, their ultimate exodus was likely inevitable, as Benson believed, but higher subsidies might have enabled some hard-pressed families to hold on for a few more years. Benson could have also assisted small farmers a bit and slightly leveled the playing field by supporting calls in Congress for capping the dollar amount of commodity loans that any farmer could receive; instead he supported a flat percentage rate reduction that fell more onerously upon small farmers than large growers.[56]

Contrary to the criticisms of his political opponents, Benson lobbied for meaningful aid to economically vulnerable family farmers, although it was predicated on the assumption that many would have to quit farming. The secretary and his colleagues proposed a reasonable Rural Development Program that, if properly funded, could have enabled a minority of small farmers to modernize or expand their operations and continue farming. To a limited extent as a pilot program it expanded economic options for some of the remaining marginal farmers by promoting industrial development in rural regions and furnishing training and other resources for rural migrants bound for the city. But it was a cautious, experimental program that would have taken years to mature. Even with solid congressional backing it would have reached many areas too late for the poorest farmers. Historians Edward and Frederick Schapsmeier speculated that Benson's Rural Development Program, properly funded as an experimental program and later expanded, might have "served as a major vehicle for aiding the noncommercial farmers to remain on the land or to retrain them for nonagricultural jobs." The Schapsmeiers likely exaggerated the program's prospects as a "major vehicle" for keeping marginal farmers on the land, given the difficulties of persuading industrialists to relocate in rural regions far removed from markets, but they correctly appreciated the visionary significance of its intent to retrain farmers for jobs off the farm. Modest though it was with the paltry funding Congress furnished, the Rural Development Program undertaken under Benson's watch was the only substantive action taken by USDA in the twentieth century to "help prepare people for displacement" from the farm, as historian Gilbert Fite observed.[57]

The trends Benson viewed as inevitable continued after he left office despite the varied policies of successive administrations. Family-owned farms remained the dominant unit in American agriculture, as Benson predicted. In 2015, the USDA reported that 97 percent of the nation's farms were still family-owned enterprises, roughly the same percentage as when Benson was in office. As Benson had predicted, the exodus from agriculture also continued. In 2015 the total number of farms was 2.1 million, down from 4.8 million farms in 1954.[58]

Notes

1. "How Ya Gonna Keep 'Em Down on the Farm?" National Jukebox, Library of Congress, http://www.loc.gov/jukebox/recordings/detail/id/7001/, accessed August 14, 2015; U.S. Bureau of the Census, *Historical Statistics of the United States, Colonial times to 1970*, Bicentennial Edition, pt. 1 (Washington, D.C.: Government Printing Office [GPO], 1975), 457.

2. Bureau of the Census, *Historical Statistics of the United States*, 457.

3. U.S. Congress, *Post-War Agricultural Policy*, 1233, 1249, 1302, 1413.

4. Ezra Taft Benson, *Freedom to Farm* (Garden City, N.Y.: Doubleday, 1960), 51; Ezra Taft Benson, *Cross Fire: The Eight Years with Eisenhower* (Garden City, N.Y.: Doubleday, 1962), 16. On the Country Life Movement, see Stanford J. Layton, *To No Privileged Class: The Rationalization of Homesteading and Rural Life in the Early Twentieth-Century American West* (Provo, Utah: Charles Redd Center for Western Studies, 1988), 5–20.

5. Address before Darlington County Agricultural Society, Mineral Springs, S.C., September 1, 1953, Ezra Taft Benson Agricultural Speeches, Microfilm no. 1, MS 8462, LDS Church History Library, Salt Lake City; Benson, *Freedom to Farm*, 109; Benson, *Cross Fire*, 15–16;

Edward L. Schapsmeier and Frederick H. Schapsmeier, *Ezra Taft Benson and the Politics of Agriculture: The Eisenhower Years, 1953–1961* (Danville, Ill.: Interstate Printers and Publishers, 1975), 32; Address at Higginsville, Mo., October 10, 1956, Microfilm no. 3, MS 8462.

6. Benson, *Freedom to Farm*, 52–53; Sheri L. Dew, *Ezra Taft Benson: A Biography* (Salt Lake City: Deseret Books, 1987), 89–99, 109–10.

7. Dew, *Ezra Taft* Benson, 100–101; Ezra Taft Benson, *Farmers at the Crossroads* (New York: Devin-Adair, 1956), ix.

8. Benson, *Cross Fire*, 18; Dew, *Ezra Taft Benson*, 101–12; Benson, "Principles of Cooperation," *Conference Report*, October 1945, 159–64. When Benson moved to Boise, his career had carried him so far from the family farm that he sold his half-interest to his brother Orval, who lived on the farm for the rest of his life. Benson, *Freedom to Farm*, 12. Orval's obituary was printed in the *Deseret News*, June 1, 1994.

9. Dew, *Ezra Taft* Benson, 120; Warren E. Johnston, Grace Dote and Alex F. McCalla, "The Giannini Foundation of Agricultural Economics: Origins and Changing Focus over Time," in *A. P. Giannini and the Giannini Foundation of Agricultural Economics*, ed. Warren E. Johnston and Alex F. McCalla (Davis, Calif.: Giannini Foundation, 2009), 30; Sidney S. Hoos, Ewald T. Grether, and Harry R. Wellman, "Henry Ernest Erdman, 1884–1977," in Johnston and McCalla, *A. P. Giannini*, 301.

10. Benson, *Farmers at the Crossroads*, x; "Farm Leaders," *Newsweek*, October 11, 1943, 59; Dew, *Ezra Taft* Benson, 123–25, 143–77; Schapsmeier and Schapsmeier, *Ezra Taft Benson*, 24; Duncan Norton-Taylor, "Mr. Benson's Flexible Flyer," *Fortune*, March 1, 1954, 88; Wesley McCune, *Ezra Taft Benson: Man with a Mission* (Washington, D.C.: Public Affairs Press, 1958), 6–11. Benson's friend and admirer, H. A. Lynn, president of the Sunkist Growers Cooperative, sought to keep Benson involved in agricultural cooperation following his call to the apostleship. In 1948, owing to Lynn's influence, Benson was invited to become a member of the Advisory Board of Consultants for the California Division of Agriculture and Natural Resources. In August 1952 Benson received permission from the First Presidency to accept Lynn's invitation to chair the American Institute of Cooperation. David O. McKay Diaries, August 1 and 5, 1952, Special Collections, Marriott Library, University of Utah.

11. Benson, *Cross Fire*, 3–14, 31–36; "Sketches of the Men in Ike's Official Family," *Newsweek*, December 1, 1952, 18. See also McKay Diaries, November 20, 1952, in which McKay assured Senator Arthur Watkins that he would permit Benson to accept the appointment and Reed Benson, interview by Greg Prince, transcript in author's possession. According to Reed Benson the morning after Watkins's phone call, McKay met Benson in the parking lot at the Church Administration Building on the way in to the office. "President McKay spotted my father and said to him, 'Elder Benson, I received a very important phone call last night, and my mind is clear on this matter. If this job is offered to you in the proper spirit, you are to take it.'"

12. Benson, *Cross Fire*, 31; Dew, *Ezra Taft Benson*, 275; Roul Tunley, "Everybody Picks on Benson," *American Magazine*, June 1954, 108; D. Arthur Haycock to Dear ones at home, January 13, 1953, copy in author's possession, original in D. Arthur Haycock Papers in possession of the Haycock family.

13. Dew, *Ezra Taft Benson*, 228–52, 258–59; Benson, *Cross Fire*, 61; Paul Friggens, "Meet the new Secretary and his family," *Farm Journal*, January 1953, 28; J. Reuben Clark reporting the substance of Benson's comments, Memorandum dated July 1, 1957, Folder 4, Box 387,

Clark Papers, L. Tom Perry Special Collections, Harold B. Lee Library, BYU; Herbert S. Parmet, *Eisenhower and the American Crusades* (New York: MacMillan, 1972), 321; William Bragg Ewald Jr., *Eisenhower the President: Crucial Days, 1951–1960* (Englewood Cliffs, N.J.: Prentice-Hall, 1981), 163; Emmet John Hughes, *The Ordeal of Power: A Political Memoir of the Eisenhower Years* (New York: Athenaeum, 1963), 54.

14. Dew, *Ezra Taft Benson*, 276–77; Schapsmeier and Schapsmeier, *Ezra Taft Benson*, 26; McKay Diaries, November 25, 1952; J. Reuben Clark Office Diary, April 9, 1953, May 11, 1953; Box 18; J. Reuben Clark to Wallace F. Bennett, November 4, 1953, Folder 4, Box 387, Clark Papers; D. Michael Quinn, "Ezra Taft Benson and Mormon Political Conflicts," *Dialogue: A Journal of Mormon Thought* 26 (Summer 1993): 1; D Michael Quinn, *Elder Statesman: A Biography of J. Reuben Clark* (Salt Lake City: Signature Books, 2002), 415; Carl C. Burton to Ezra Taft Benson, June 8, 1953; Charlie Geurts to Art and Maurine [Haycock], November 5, 1953, Haycock Papers, copies in author's possession.

15. Benson, *Cross Fire*, 52–53, 61–62; Jay Richter, "Benson: Prayer, Persuasion and Parity," *New York Times Magazine*, June 14, 1953, 12; "Secretary of Agriculture Ezra Taft Benson," *Life*, February 23, 1953, 42.

16. Congress, Senate, Committee on Agriculture and Forestry, *Commodity Inventories of the Commodity Credit Corporation*, 83rd Cong., 1st sess., February 23, 1953, 3. For concise descriptions of the commodity loan price support program see David B. Danbom, *Born in the Country: A History of Rural America* (Baltimore: Johns Hopkins University Press, 1995), 210–13; and "Benson and Brannan Debate the Farm Issue," in *The Paradox of Plenty: Readings on the Agricultural Surplus Since World War I*, ed. Robert L. Branyan and A. Theodore Brown (Dubuque, Iowa: Wm. C. Brown, 1968), 115–16.

17. Jay Richter, "Benson: Prayer, Persuasion and Parity," *New York Times Magazine*, June 14, 1953, 58; Benson, *Freedom to Farm*, 174–77; Benson, *Farmers at the Crossroads*, 23; "Benson and Brannan Debate the Farm Issue," 102–3; James Daniel, "Secretary Benson's Faith in the American Farmer," *Reader's Digest*, October 1956, 86.

18. Benson, *Cross Fire*, 66; U.S. Congress, Senate, Committee on Agriculture and Forestry, *Agricultural Outlook and the President's Farm Program*, 83rd Cong., 2nd sess., January 18, 1954, 6, 24; "Apostle at Work," *Time*, April 13, 1953, 27.

19. Dew, *Ezra Taft Benson*, 273; D. Arthur Haycock to LaVar H. Whittaker, March 2, 1953, Haycock Papers; "Changing Farm Policy: Interview with Ezra T. Benson," *Newsweek*, March 6, 1953, 31; "Address before the annual meeting of the National Farmers Union in Denver," March 17, 1954, Benson Agricultural Speeches, Microfilm no. 1; Benson, *Cross Fire*, 156; Joseph Anderson to D. Arthur Haycock, March 18, 1953, Haycock Papers.

20. Jon K. Lauck, "George S. McGovern and the Farmer: South Dakota Politics, 1953–1962," *South Dakota History* 32, no. 4 (2002): 337; U.S. Congress, House, Wright Patman of Texas quoting Mrs. Roy (Harriett) Oeder, 83rd Cong., 2nd sess., *Congressional Record* 100, pt. 10 (August 3, 1954): 13176; Dew, *Ezra Taft Benson*, 272; Harold H. Martin, "Elder Benson's Going to Catch It!" *Saturday Evening Post*, March 28, 1953, 112; *Lincoln Star*, March 22, 1953; Benson, *Cross Fire*, 70. On Eisenhower's consistent support of Benson, see Parmet, *Eisenhower and the American Crusades*, 321.

21. Claude Petersen to D. Arthur Haycock, March 2, 1953; Glen S. Burt to Haycock, March 17, 1953, Haycock Papers.

22. "Apostle at Work," *Time*, April 13, 1953, 27.

23. Letters to the editor from Francis Townsend, Ted Banta, and Houston Jones, *Time*, May 4, 1953, 8. Houston G. Jones's background is described in Jeannine D. Whitlow, ed., *The Heritage of Caswell County, North Carolina* (Yanceyville, N.C.: Caswell County Historical Association, 1985), 315–16.

24. Benson, *Cross Fire*, 146–72; McKay Diaries, October 23, 1953; Raymond Moley, "A Show with Two Plots," *Newsweek*, November 9, 1953, 104; Fulton Lewis Jr., "Washington Report," *Reading (Pa.) Eagle*, January 18, 1954; "Cattlemen Caravan Sees Benson; Applauds Speech," *Spokane Daily Chronicle*, October 26, 1953; "Cattlemen to Begin Support Campaign," *Spencer (Iowa) Daily Reporter*, October 28, 1953; "Ezra Benson—On a Spot—Holds Firm to Principles," *U.S. News and World Report*, October 23, 1953, 95.

25. Ezra Taft Benson, "Benson Strikes Back at Critics," *Life*, November 9, 1953, 40, 43; "Respect Comes the Hard Way," *Life*, November 16, 1953, 50; "Cool Man on the Hottest Seat in Washington," *Newsweek*, November 30, 1953, 25; D. Arthur Haycock to Dick Bowen, December 24, 1953; Haycock to Daken K. Broadhead, November 9, 1953, Haycock Papers.

26. Benson, *Cross Fire*, 153, 164–65, 186; Parmet, *Eisenhower and the American Crusades*, 321; Chester J. Pach Jr. and Elmo Richardson, *The Presidency of Dwight D. Eisenhower*, rev. ed. (Lawrence: University Press of Kansas, 1991), 55. U.S. Congress, House, Committee on Agriculture, *Long Range Farm Program*, 83rd Cong., 2nd sess., March 1954, 2575.

27. *Agricultural Outlook and the President's Farm Program* (1954), 6. 15–16. 29–29; U.S. Congress, House, Committee on Agriculture, *Long Range Farm Program*, 83rd Cong., 2nd sess., March 1954, 2535, 2603; Benson, *Cross Fire*, 164.

28. Benson, *Cross Fire*, 180; Address before the annual meeting of the National Farmers Union in Denver; *Long Range Farm Program* (1954), 2539. See also pp. 2592–93.

29. Congress, House, 83rd Cong., 2nd sess., *Congressional Record*, 100, pt. 7 (June 30, 1954): 9384; Benson, *Cross Fire*, 106.

30. Benson, *Cross Fire*, 201; Congress, House, 83rd Cong., 2nd sess., *Congressional Record*, 100, pt. 7 (June 30, 1954): 9371, 9376, and 9380.

31. Benson, *Cross Fire*, 205–6, 211; McKay Diaries, September 7, 1954.

32. U.S. Congress, House, 83rd Cong., 2nd sess., *Congressional Record*, 100, pt. 7 (June 30, 1954): 8777, 8781–82; U.S. Congress, House, Committee on Agriculture, *General Farm Legislation*, 84th Cong., 2nd sess. (February 21, 1956), 8.

33. U.S. Congress, Senate, Committee on Agriculture and Forestry, *Price Support Program*, 84th Cong., 2nd sess., (January 1956), 3298; U.S. Congress, House, Committee on Agriculture, *General Farm Legislation*, 84th Cong., 2nd sess., 158; Congress, House and Senate, Joint Committee on the Economic Report, *January 1956 Economic Report of the President*, 84th Cong., 2nd sess. (January–February 1956), 639, 655–56. Benson's responses two years later to questions from the Senate Committee on Agriculture and Forestry underscored his conviction that the government should not coddle marginal farmers to keep them on the land. "I like farm life and I am grateful that my lot was cast on a farm," Benson stated. But he was unwilling, he added, to "freeze our economy" to perpetuate subsistence farming. In order for a family farm to survive, it needed to be large enough to be economically viable. In some cases this might necessitate making "2 farms out of 3, providing 2 economic units and permitting 1 man to go into factory employment." U.S. Congress, Senate, Committee on Agriculture and Forestry, *Farm Program*, 85th Cong., 2nd sess. (January 1958), 83.

34. Congress, House, Subcommittee on Family Farms, Committee on Agriculture, *Family-Size Farms*, 8th Cong., 2nd sess., (February 1956), 424, 564, 612. After collecting testimony from well over two hundred people, the subcommittee issued its report late in July. U.S. Congress, House, Subcommittee on Family Farms, Committee on Agriculture, *The Family Farm*, 84th Cong., 2nd sess., 1956, Committee Print. The report credited the family farm with "establish[ing] the economic foundation for the liberties and the enterprise, and the national conscience, that are the heritage of the United States" (p. 1). It warned that "in some areas . . . 'the factory in the field' may supplant family farm operations" (p. 10). The committee chair implied that Benson was not "a friendly department head," but did not elaborate.

35. Benson, *Cross Fire*, 202–3; "Signed, But Not Read," *Time*, February 6, 1956, 18; "Man in the Middle," *Newsweek*, February 6, 1956, 23–24.

36. Benson, *Cross Fire*, 315–20; "The Nation," *Time*, April 23, 1956, 25; "Ezra Taft Benson—He Beat the Farm Bloc," *U.S. News and World Report*, April 27, 1956, 74.

37. Benson, *Cross Fire*, 259, 290–91, 323; "Joseph and Ezra," *Time*, March 5, 1956, 19.

38. Ernest L. Wilkinson Diary, September 13, 1957, July 7, 1958, February 12, 1958, Wilkinson Papers, L. Tom Perry Special Collections, Harold B. Lee Library, BYU. In 1955 Butler had warned Benson that his readiness to sell surplus grain to Russia was appalling to conservatives. Butler to Benson, April 8, 1955, Folder 4, Box 387, Clark Papers.

39. For an example of criticism, see Butler to Benson, April 8, 1955, 333. Address before the Pennsylvania Millers' and Feed Dealers' Association, Reading, Pennsylvania, September 25, 1956, Benson Agricultural Speeches, Microfilm no. 3.

40. Address at the dedication of the Thor Research Center, Huntley, Illinois, October 3, 1956, Benson Agricultural Speeches, Microfilm no. 3.

41. Address at Higginsville, Missouri, October 19, 1956; Address at the High School in Spencer, Iowa, October 11, 1956, Benson Agricultural Speeches, Microfilm no. 3.

42. Benson, *Cross Fire*, 334.

43. U.S. Congress, House, Subcommittee on Agricultural Appropriations, Committee on Appropriations, *Present Conditions in Agriculture*, 85th Cong., 1st sess. (February 1957), 144, 145, 149; Senate, Joint Committee on the Economic Report, *January 1956 Economic Report of the President*, 644; Address before Minnesota Bankers' Association, St. Paul, June 12, 1957, Benson Agricultural Speeches, Microfilm no. 3.

44. Clark Diary, October 29, 1957; March 31, 1958; *Deseret News*, October 30, 1957.

45. McKay Diaries, September 5, 1957, September 12, 1957. June 6, 1960; Wilkinson Diary, September 13, 1957, March 7, 1958; Benson, *Cross Fire*, 360; Quinn, "Ezra Taft Benson," 2; Quinn, *Elder Statesman*, 417. Benson recalled that McKay told him, "Now Brother Benson, I left no doubt but that the government and President Eisenhower have first call on your services. We in the Church can make adjustments easier at this time than the government can. We want to support President Eisenhower. He is a noble character, a fine man. In this case our country comes first. But, of course, we also want you to do what you would prefer." After visiting with Eisenhower about the possible church assignment, Benson recalled, Eisenhower instructed him, "I feel Ezra that if you leave now it may mean giving up much of the agricultural program which we've put in operation and are trying to push to completion. I wish very much that you would stay at least one more year. Next fall we can review the situation again. At that time if changes in the Church occur or

other conditions demand that you go back to Utah, I'll no longer stand in your way. But, if not, then I would like you to stay to the bitter end." Benson, *Cross Fire*, 360–61.

46. U.S. Congress, House, Subcommittee on Agricultural Appropriations, Committee on Appropriations, *Present Conditions in Agriculture*, 85th Cong., 1st sess. (February 1957), 144, 145, 149; Senate, Joint Committee on the Economic Report, *January 1956 Economic Report of the President*, 644; Address before Minnesota Bankers' Association, St. Paul, June 12, 1957, Benson Agricultural Speeches, Microfilm no. 3.

47. U.S. Congress, Senate, *A bill to strengthen the nation by preserving the family-size farm*, 84th Cong. 1st sess., S. 1199 (February 23, 1955); McKay Diaries, February 23, 1958.

48. House, Committee on Agriculture, *Development of Agriculture's Human Resources*, 84th Cong., 1st sess., 1955, House Doc. 149; U.S. Congress, Senate, Subcommittee of the Committee on Agriculture and Forestry, *Farmers' Home Administration Operating and Housing Loans*, 84th Cong., 2nd sess., (May 17, 1956), 22; Schapsmeier and Schapsmeier, *Ezra Taft Benson*, 144.

49. U.S. Congress, House, Subcommittee on Agricultural Appropriations, Committee on Appropriations, *Present Conditions in Agriculture*, 48–49; U.S. Congress, Senate, Committee on Agriculture and Forestry, *Farm Program*, 85th Cong., 1st sess. (May 15, 1957), 11.

50. U.S. Congress, House, Subcommittee on Agricultural Appropriations, Committee on Appropriations, *Agricultural Appropriations for 1958*, 85th Cong., 1st sess. (April 30, 1957), 16, 776–77.

51. Ibid., 14, 83–89.

52. Benson, *Cross Fire*, 413, 429; U.S. Congress, Senate, Committee on Agriculture and Forestry, *President's Farm Message, 1959*, 86th Cong., 1st sess., (February 16, 1959), 100; U.S. Congress, House, Subcommittee on Agricultural Appropriations, Committee on Appropriations, *Department of Agriculture Appropriations for 1960*, 86th Cong., 1st sess., (1959), 2505.

53. U.S. Congress, House, Committee on Agriculture, *General Farm Legislation*, 86th Cong., 2nd sess. (February 1960), 288–89; Benson, *Cross Fire*, 521–25.

54. John Osborne, "Ezra Benson's Last Chance," *Fortune*, January 1959, 90–91; John Bird, "The Miseries of Elder Benson," *Life*, December 21, 1957, 19, 58–60; Dew, *Ezra Taft Benson*, 355–56. On marketing of surpluses abroad, see "Two-Way Aid," *Time*, September 10, 1956, 35; "Feeding the World's Hungry: A Cure for U.S. Farm Troubles?" *U.S. News and World Report*, March 14, 1958, 68–72.

55. C. L. Holmes, "Basic Groups in Agricultural Economics" 10 (April 1928): 175; Holmes, "Types of Farming in Iowa," *Iowa Agricultural Experiment Station Bulletin* 22, no. 256 (1928): 116–66; Edward L. Schapsmeier and Frederick H. Schapsmeier, "Eisenhower and Ezra Taft Benson: Farm Policy in the 1950s," in *American Economic Growth: The Historic Challenge*, ed. William F. Donnelly (New York: MSS Information Corporation, 1973), 345.

56. U.S. Bureau of the Census, *Historical Statistics of the United States*, 1:457; U.S. Congress, House, Subcommittee on Family Farms, Committee on Agriculture, *The Family Farm*, 88th Cong., 1st sess. (June 1963), 115; Bowers, Rasmussen and Baker, 22.

57. Schapsmeier, and Schapsmeier, *Ezra Taft Benson*, 144; Gilbert C. Fite, *Cotton Fields No More: Southern Agriculture, 1865–1980* (Lexington: University Press of Kentucky, 1984), 224. In 1955 less than 2 percent of the recipients of wheat loans garnered 17 percent of the

money, and fewer than 15 percent of the recipients received more than half of the wheat loan money. Joint Committee on the Economic Report, *January 1956 Economic Report of the President,* 644.

58. U.S. Department of Agriculture, *2012 Census of Agriculture,* vol. 2, Subject Series, pt. 10, *Farm Typology* (Washington, D.C.: National Agricultural Statistics Service, 2015), http://www.agcensus.usda.gov/Publications/2012/Online_Resources/Typology/typology13 .pdf, accessed August 28, 2015.

2 Ezra Taft Benson Meets Nikita Khrushchev, 1959

Memory Embellished

GARY JAMES BERGERA

Time and memory are true artists; they remould reality nearer to
the heart's desire.
—John Dewey, *Reconstruction in Philosophy*

When in 1959 Ezra Taft Benson, U.S. secretary of agriculture, met briefly
with Nikita Khrushchev, first secretary of the Communist Party of the Soviet
Union, the encounter passed as a relatively minor Cold War public relations
ripple, intended to highlight, on the one side, the superiority of American
agriculture and, on the other, the disarming geniality of the most famous
communist alive. However, seven years later, Benson, who had returned
to his post as a member of the elite Quorum of the Twelve Apostles of the
Church of Jesus Christ of Latter-day Saints, delivered a devotional address
at LDS-owned Brigham Young University and recast the meeting as a near-
mythic confrontation between good and evil. By this time, Benson was beset
by critics, including high-ranking LDS officials, who viewed his public anti-
communism as a distraction to his church work. Benson responded to the
criticisms with a new narrative of his confrontation with Khrushchev that
portrayed the apostle as a crusading American patriot bravely defying naysayers who sought to condemn his defense of individual freedom. Benson's
remembered story of his meeting with Khrushchev highlights the mutability
of memory, especially when placed in the service of a larger personal agenda.

*　*　*

Almost as soon as he stepped down as secretary of agriculture in 1961, an
appointment he had held for eight years,[1] Benson began to position himself
as an outspoken American patriot and Cold Warrior.[2] His fiery speeches

attacking communism's inroads into American life blended the religious and the secular. As one of his church's twelve apostles,[3] Benson enjoyed privileged access to a wide spectrum of forums. Thus when he took the podium, on Thursday morning, October 25, 1966, at BYU in Provo, Utah, as the school's devotional speaker, Benson seized the opportunity to blast communism and to inveigh against American and LDS apathy. His sermon,[4] "Our Immediate Responsibility," recalled the similarly themed talk, "Protecting Freedom—An Immediate Responsibility," he had delivered three weeks earlier at his church's semiannual world general conference.[5]

In his BYU address, Benson referenced his meeting with Khrushchev as the Soviet leader began his twelve-day tour of the United States in September 1959.[6] "I have talked face-to-face with the godless Communist leaders," Benson announced, the memory seemingly still fresh.

> It may surprise you to learn that I was host to Mr. Khrushchev for a half day, when he visited the United States. Not that I'm proud of it—I opposed his coming then and I still feel it was a mistake to welcome this atheistic murderer as a state visitor. But according to President [Dwight D.] Eisenhower, Khrushchev had expressed a desire to learn something of American agriculture, and after seeing Russian agriculture I can understand why.
>
> As we talked face-to-face, he indicated that my grandchildren would live under Communism. After assuring him that I expected to do all in my power to assure that his and all other grandchildren will live under freedom, he arrogantly declared in substance:
>
>> You Americans are so gullible. No, you won't accept Communism outright, but we'll keep feeding you small doses of socialism until you'll finally wake up and find you already have Communism. We won't have to fight you. We'll so weaken your economy until you'll fall like overripe fruit into our hands.[7]

More than a decade later, in 1978, Benson again referred publicly to Khrushchev (now dead):

> Yes, I have stood face to face with tyranny. I was host to Mr. Nikita Khrushchev for a half-day when he visited the United States. I am not proud of this—I had stated my reservation to the President and I still feel it was a mistake to invite this godless despot as a state visitor. To this day, I get an uneasy feeling when I think of that experience.[8]

The next year, Benson employed harsher rhetoric:

> I have stood face to face with Tyranny personified. As Secretary of Agriculture and at the request of President Eisenhower, I was host to Mr. Nikita Khrushchev for a half-day when he visited the United States. I still feel it was a mistake to

invite a godless despot as a state visitor. A despot dedicated, as were his predecessors, to the destruction of our country and the freedom of mankind with a
goal which may be summarized as follows: "First we will take eastern Europe,
then the land masses of Asia, and then we will surround that last bastion of
freedom, the United States of America."

And as Mr. Khruschev [*sic*] said to me face-to-face: "Your grandchildren will
live under Communism." To which I responded, "Mr. Chairman, if I have my
way, your grandchildren and everyone's grandchildren, will live under freedom."
He responded, "Oh, you Americans. You are so gullible. No, you will not accept
Communism outright, but we will keep feeding you small doses of Socialism
until one day you wake up and find you already have Communism. We won't
have to fight you. We will so weaken you until you will fall like overripe fruit
into our hands."[9]

Beginning in 1966 at BYU, Benson's narrative of his encounter with
Khrushchev diverged from his own earlier accounts, which did not link
the Soviet leader's statements regarding communism to the men's 1959 encounter. For example, in *The Red Carpet*, a compilation of Benson's writings
published in April 1962, Benson stated: "They [i.e., Communist subversives]
have made their mark on this land. They march under a variety of political
banners. They work 24 hours a day. They speak glibly of ultimate victory.
Their leader, Khrushchev, said this to an American television audience: 'And
your grandchildren will live under socialism in America.'"[10] Elsewhere in the
volume, Benson reported: "A few months before coming to the United States
[in 1959] Khrushchev is reported to have said: 'We cannot expect the Americans to jump from capitalism to communism, but we can assist their elected
leaders in giving Americans small doses of socialism, until they suddenly
awake to find they have communism.'"[11] In his final paraphrase of statements
attributed to Khrushchev, Benson noted: "Khrushchev tells us to our face
that our grandchildren will be socialists. I do not believe it and neither do
you, my fellow Americans. But that is the challenge."[12]

Six months after *The Red Carpet* appeared, Benson's bulky memoir of
his years as secretary of agriculture, *Cross Fire*, was published nationally.[13]
In it, Benson provided a detailed account of his meeting with Khrushchev.
As the two men and their entourages arrived at the eleven thousand–acre
U.S. government complex in Beltsville, Maryland, on Wednesday morning,
September 16, 1959, Benson gave a brief opening statement on the virtues of
"our *capitalistic free enterprise system*" (italics in original) to which Khrush-
chev "made no response." Then followed an hour-plus tour of the federal
facility accompanied by several hundred journalists and others. At the end,
Khrushchev asked a few questions, turned to the crowd, and, Benson wrote,

"began to show off before the photographers. From the strong, stolid, silent spectator, he became the hearty, blustering, effusive buffoon, joking and wisecracking, even lecturing. He tried very hard for laughs but he did most of the laughing himself." Less than two hours after arriving, Khrushchev returned to Washington, D.C.,[14] for lunch with the National Press Club. The next day, he and his party left for New York City, Los Angeles, San Luis Obispo, San Francisco, Des Moines, Coon Rapids (Iowa), Pittsburgh, and back to Washington, D.C., before departing for Moscow.[15]

*   *   *

The difference between Benson's narratives of his encounter with Khrushchev in 1962 and those beginning in 1966 is apparent. In 1966, Benson asserted that the Soviet leader told him "face-to-face" that his grandchildren would live under communism. Benson objected, and Khrushchev retorted that Americans would be fed "small doses of socialism" until their weakened economy would "fall like overripe fruit into our [the communists'] hands." When he repeated the story in 1979, Benson again stated that the exchange took place "face-to-face." In his 1962 accounts, however, Benson positioned the statements differently. In his autobiography, the statements are entirely absent; his personal journal is equally silent.[16] In fact, at the time of the 1959 event, Benson was specifically asked if "there had been any arguments," to which he answered, "No sir, no arguments in the farm field."[17] Benson's wife added that it "seemed to me they [that is, the Khrushchevs] were all very courteous."[18] In *The Red Carpet*, Benson noted only that the statements attributed to Khrushchev were made "to an American television audience"; that Khrushchev was "reported" to have made the statements "a few months before" his 1959 visit; and that Khrushchev merely "tells us to our face . . ." In 1962, Benson did not source Khrushchev's alleged statements to their 1959 meeting. Four years later, beginning in 1966, Benson explicitly situated them as having occurred during the men's encounter.

Benson was not the first to attribute the ominous-sounding statements to Khrushchev. In his August 1, 1959, speech on Soviet television, following his famous "kitchen debate" with Khrushchev, U.S. vice president Richard M. Nixon (1913–1994) referred to Khrushchev's boast about American grandchildren living under communism:

> I have one final thought to add. Mr. Khrushchev predicted that our grandchildren would live under Communism. He reiterated this to me in our talks last Sunday [July 26, 1959].

Let me say that we do not object to his saying this will happen. We only object if he tries to bring it about.

And this is my answer to him. I do not say that your grandchildren will live under capitalism. We prefer our system. But the very essence of our belief is that we do not and will not try to impose our system on anybody else.[19]

About 1961, if not earlier, Khrushchev's alleged statement regarding "small doses of socialism" began to surface on conservative American forums—sources of much of Benson's own political education—including a July 1961 speech on the floor of the U.S. Senate. (Pressed for a source, the representative of one right-leaning publication said they were told the statement appeared in a speech Khrushchev delivered some four months before his September 1959 trip to the United States but could not produce substantiating documentation.)[20] These early appearances coincided with the publication of Benson's *The Red Carpet*, where the statements also first began to emerge in Benson's own rhetoric. Four years later, in 1966, when Benson explicitly linked "overripe fruit" to "small doses of socialism," he appropriated imagery—"overripe fruit"—that had been previously attributed, not to Khrushchev, but to Vladimir Lenin (1870–1924), first in 1954 in testimony before the U.S. Senate Internal Security Subcommittee, then in 1958 in the ultra-conservative John Birch Society's *Blue Book*.[21] In fact, Benson's use of "overripe fruit" and "small doses" in the same sentence, and his crediting them to Khrushchev, marks the first time in any publication that the two images were linked and then attributed to one speaker.

Almost as soon as the three phrases—"grandchildren living under Communism," "small doses," and "overripe fruit"—appeared in print, questions regarding their authenticity arose. In 1961, Montana senator Lee Metcalfe (1911–1978) stated, "[W]hoever created this quotation, and those who, knowing it to be spurious, nevertheless disseminate it, are cut from the same cloth as Communists and Fascists."[22] The next year, Morris K. Udall (1922–1998), Arizona congressman and LDS church member, asked the Library of Congress about the origin of the "small doses of socialism" statement. The librarians responded: "We have searched the Legislative Reference Service files, checked all the standard reference works on quotations by Khrushchev, and consulted with the Slavic division of the Library of Congress, the Department of State, and the U.S. Information Agency, in an attempt to determine the authenticity of this quotation. From none of these sources were we able to produce evidence that Khrushchev actually made such a statement."[23] Attempts to source the "overripe fruit" statement to Lenin and/or to Khrushchev proved similarly fruitless.[24] Despite repeated efforts, none of the three expressions has ever been authenticated as having originated with either man.

*   *   *

For Benson, the LDS church was "the dominant force in my life,"[25] and its teachings, as he understood them, took precedence over all other "theories, dogmas, hypotheses or relative-truths."[26] Benson believed, as a central tenet of his faith, that God had founded the United States of America as a democratic Christian republic[27] and had inspired the development of a self-regulating economy based on private ownership, individual responsibility, and hard work.[28] As American historian Kenneth S. Davis observed, Benson was "a man whose religion elevate[d] the economic interests of propertied men to the level of universal moral principle."[29] Benson interpreted what he believed to be the whisperings of the Holy Spirit as sanction to speak out on LDS doctrine, including controversial political and social issues, and embraced what he understood his role to be as one of Christ's watchmen on the tower.[30]

At the same time, Benson knew that he sometimes exhibited a rigidity of thought and intemperance of word—what he termed as "resolute resistance"[31]—that impacted his relations with people whose views differed from his. "I had this bad habit . . . ," he explained, "of laying things on the line economically just as hard and cold as I could based on the facts, so they'd register with people, and not give them a lot of soft soap, try and build up good will immediately."[32] Yet even his confession hints at a more controlling personal characteristic: Benson held and voiced strong opinions, which he believed were immutable gospel truth, and did not hesitate to condemn what he believed were doctrines of Satan, even if doing so meant alienating Church members. "Today," he once stated, "you can not effectively fight for freedom and moral principles and not be attacked, and those who think they can are deceiving themselves. While I do not believe in stepping out of the path of duty to pick up a cross I don't need, a man is a coward who refuses to pick up a cross that clearly lies within his path. No cross—no crown, no gall—no glory, no thorns—no throne."[33]

By 1966, Benson's public endorsement of the Birch Society—an organization he would have joined if only the more centrist-oriented LDS president, David O. McKay (1873–1970), had permitted—was proving to be especially problematic for the Church. Despite repeated attempts by several of his colleagues in the Church hierarchy to rein in his activism, Benson remained committed to his interpretation of LDS doctrine, which included a belief in the supremacy of free markets, the private ownership of property, and limited government. While McKay worried about the potentially divisive effects of Benson's hard-line rhetoric, he tended to support Benson's general anti-communist advocacy.[34] McKay tried to accommodate both Benson and his critics without ever fully satisfying either. Benson, who knew he had McKay's ear, was able to benefit from the president's dislike of public controversy.

As Benson prepared in October 1966 to address, first, the LDS general conference and, then, BYU's end-of-the-month devotional assembly, he was more politicized and defensive than ever before. In fact, convinced that neither Republicans nor Democrats were sufficiently hard on the threat of communism, he was entertaining seriously the possibility of running for the U.S. presidency as a third-party candidate.[35] His two October speaking assignments gave him the opportunity to defend his political beliefs and to respond to a growing number of critics. "Should we counsel people, 'Just live your religion. There's no need to get involved in the fight for freedom?'" Benson asked conference visitors on October 2. "No, we should not," he replied, "because our stand for freedom is a most basic part of our religion; this stand helped get us to this earth, and our reaction to freedom in this life will have eternal consequences. Man . . . has no excuse that can compensate for his loss of liberty." Then, to critics, who by this time included several of high-ranking members of the LDS leadership hierarchy,[36] he warned:

> All men are entitled to inspiration, especially men who bear the priesthood, but only one man is the Lord's mouthpiece. Some lesser men have used in the past, and will use in the future, their offices unrighteously. Some will, ignorantly or otherwise, use their office to promote false counsel; some will use it to lead the unwary astray; some will use it to persuade us that all is well in Zion; some will use it to cover and excuse their ignorance.[37]

Three weeks later, at BYU, Benson adopted an even more strident tone, implying that his critics were dupes of the Devil:

> Now Satan is anxious to neutralize the inspired counsel of the Prophet and hence keep the Priesthood off-balance, ineffective and inert in the fight for freedom. He does this through diverse means including the use of perverse reasoning. . . .
>
> Unfortunately some men who do not honor their stewardship may have an adverse effect on many people. Often the greater the man's responsibility the more good or evil he can accomplish. The Lord usually gives the man a long enough rope and sufficient time to determine whether that man wants to pull himself into the presence of God or drop off somewhere below. . . .
>
> Sometimes from behind the pulpit, in our classrooms, in our Council meetings, and in our Church publications we hear, read or witness things that do not square with the truth. This is especially true where freedom is involved.

Now do not let this serve as an excuse for your own wrong-doing. The Lord is letting the wheat and the tares mature before he fully purges the Church. He is also testing you to see if you will be misled. The devil is trying to deceive the very elect.[38]

When, in this BYU devotional speech, Benson highlighted his 1959 meeting with Khrushchev, he turned the episode into a dramatic confrontation regarding the Soviet Union's designs on the West. For Benson, the occasion afforded him the opportunity to portray his brief meeting with the Soviet leader as a major counter-defensive volley that serviced his personal needs as well as his perceptions of a looming communist menace. It also served notice to his critics in the Church that he had no intention of backing down from championing his political views and would not shy away from labeling and name calling. Benson's transformation of memory endowed his activism with a hero's mantle. In the years that followed, Benson would remain the most politically polarizing and divisive member of the LDS hierarchy.

*   *   *

Our memories are not confined to one area of the brain, waiting to be extracted as the contents of a folder from a filing cabinet drawer or from a computer database. Rather, they are composed, puzzle-like, of "fragments of information, stored in different parts of our mind." As we access and assemble the pieces of memory in statements, in conversations with others, in repeated reminiscences, and/or hear others recall their own versions of the same events, our stories "can change as the mind recombines these bits of information."[39] Memory is "malleable," writes Charles V. Ford, a professor of psychiatry at the University of Alabama–Birmingham, "fluid in time and space, and reflective of our current needs. Memories are being continuously reconstructed . . . in terms of our current emotions, experiences, and prejudices . . . [and] also by our relationships with others."[40] Because memory is "reconstructive," researchers Carol Travers and Elliot Aronson add, it is "subject to confabulation—confusing an event that happened to someone else with one that happened to you, or coming to believe that you remember something that never happened at all."[41] Confabulation is neither rare nor difficult to provoke, and what is surprising is the extent to which we become convinced of the factual accuracy of our confabulated memories.[42]

However we may explain Ezra Taft Benson's narratives of his meeting with Nikita Khrushchev, we must keep in mind the following. We cannot know if Benson genuinely misremembered the 1959 encounter and believed he was accurately summarizing the experience. We cannot know, when he recalled the meeting in 1966, if Benson projected backward expressions he believed Khrushchev had made and then represented what he believed had been the gist of their conversations. Nor can we know if Benson intended to embellish some of the specifics of his meeting with Khrushchev to validate and emphasize what he believed was the imminent danger of communism. Because of the reconstructive nature of memory, our speculations about Benson's intentions, however tied they may be to context, source, and fact, are at best educated guesses. As LDS historian Richard D. Poll reminds us: "Who has not discovered the capacity of his own memory to remodel the past?"[43]

Of course, rather than alter the details of his meeting with Khrushchev, Benson could have consulted his 1959 journal and/or his 1962 autobiography, or employed the same rhetoric regarding Khrushchev and communism as he did in *The Red Carpet*. But national and world events since his 1959 encounter had changed, as had relations with some members of his LDS church quorum. Benson may have genuinely misremembered his meeting with Khrushchev. But if so, the needs of October 1966 presented an urgency that, for Benson, required strong action. Benson's confabulated narrative succeeded in protecting and defending a besieged self-image, as well as bolstering a specific political agenda. With repeated tellings—or "warpings"—the new story became part of Benson's identity, larger and "truer" than the factual historical record.[44] One person's embellishment becomes, over time and telling, another person's "truth."[45] Benson's confabulations seem to have resulted from a temptation he simply was unable to resist.

For some readers, the story of Benson's encounter with Khrushchev may be little more than an extended footnote to his biography, especially to his engagement with the anti-communist zeitgeist of the 1950s and 1960s. For others, however, Benson's embellishments may function as a jumping-off point for future explorations of his evolving constructions of self and perceptions of his places on both the American political stage and within the hierarchy of his own church. Additional studies may tackle Benson's confabulations as a gateway into the nature and strategic uses of Benson's political and religious sermonizing as well as of LDS sermonizing more broadly. Benson was not the first high-ranking LDS church official to misstate aspects of his past,[46] but scholarly treatments of his recollections may also shed light on the roles of autobiography when employed to service personal and political agendas as well as on the dangers that result from well-intentioned, if self-serving and ultimately erroneous, misrepresentations of one's history. Finally, what might Benson's confabulations tell us about the processes of personal myth-making, of the specific needs of the myth-maker, and of the expectations and demands of the myth-maker's various audiences?

Notes

Gary James Bergera is the managing director of the Smith-Pettit Foundation, Salt Lake City, Utah. He appreciates the advice and suggestions of Clair V. Barrus, Joseph Geisner, Reid L. Neilson, and especially Ronald O. Barney, Matthew L. Harris, and Patrick Q. Mason. All errors of fact and interpretation are Bergera's own.

Epigraph. John Dewey, *Reconstruction in Philosophy* (New York: Henry Holt, 1920), p. 104.

1. For Benson's years as secretary of agriculture, see Gary James Bergera, "'Rising Above Principle': Ezra Taft Benson as U.S. Secretary of Agriculture, 1953–1961, Part One," *Dialogue: A Journal of Mormon Thought* 41 (Fall 2008): 81–122; and Bergera, "'Weak-Kneed Republicans and Socialist Democrats': Ezra Taft Benson as U.S. Secretary of Agriculture, 1953–1961, Part Two," *Dialogue: A Journal of Mormon Thought* 41 (Winter 2008): 55–95.

2. For Benson's conservative activism, see D. Michael Quinn, *The Mormon Hierarchy: Extensions of Power* (Salt Lake City: Signature Books/Smith Research Associates, 1997), chapter 3. "Ezra Taft Benson: A Study of Inter-Quorum Conflict," pp. 66–115. For Benson's perspective, see Sheri L. Dew, *Ezra Taft Benson: A Biography* (Salt Lake City: Deseret, 1987), chapter 18. "Preaching the Principle of Freedom," pp. 360–82, and chapter 19. "Sounding a Warning," pp. 383–408.

3. For Benson's appointment as LDS church apostle, see Gary James Bergera, ed., "'This Great Thing Which Has Come to Me a Humble, Weak Farmer Boy': Ezra Taft Benson's 1943 Call to the Apostleship," *Mormon Historical Studies* 9 (Fall 2008): 155–64.

4. BYU's president, Ernest L. Wilkinson (1899–1978), who shared Benson's conservatism, recorded of Benson's talk: "He pulled no punches of any kind in carrying on his crusade against Communism. My own feeling was that he was a little extreme in some statements but he may be entirely right. At least he is much more right than the other side" (Wilkinson, Diary, October 25, 1966, Wilkinson Papers, L. Tom Perry Special Collections, Harold B. Lee Library, Brigham Young University, Provo, Utah).

5. See Benson, "Protecting Freedom—An Immediate Responsibility," delivered October 2, 1966, in *Improvement Era* 69 (December 1966): 1144–46; and Benson, "Our Immediate Responsibility," delivered October 25, 1966, printed as *Speeches of the Year* (Provo, Utah: Extension Publications, Division of Continuing Education, Brigham Young University, 1966). The audio version of Benson's BYU speech may be accessed at http://speeches.byu .edu/index.php?act=viewitem&id=1611 (retrieved February 19, 2015). The portion dealing with Khrushchev begins at 40:56.

6. For an informative treatment, see Peter Carlson, *K Blows Top: A Cold War Comic Interlude, Starring Nikita Khrushchev, America's Most Unlikely Tourist* (New York: Public Affairs, 2009).

7. Benson, "Our Immediate Responsibility," p. 16; reprinted in Benson, *An Enemy Hath Done This*, comp. Jerreld L. Newquist (Salt Lake City: Parliament Publishers, 1969), p. 320. See also "Benson Emphasizes Freedom," *BYU Daily Universe*, October 26, 1966, p. 1. Less than four months later, Benson repeated this version in a talk to the Freedom Club

of Los Angeles (see Benson, "Aiding and Abetting the Enemy," an address at the Freedom Club, February 7, 1967, photocopy, Smith-Pettit Foundation, Salt Lake City).

8. Benson, "Some Personal Recollections on the Struggle for Freedom in the 20th Century—Part 1," Remarks to the Church Office Building Employees, Church Office Building Auditorium, Friday, June 2, 1978, 11:30 A.M., p. 5, transcript, Smith-Pettit Foundation.

9. Benson, "The Task Before Us," Flag Raising Ceremony, Washington, D.C., Wednesday, July 4, 1979, p. 2, transcript, Smith-Pettit Foundation. Benson's reminiscence of Khrushchev was reported in "Benson Rakes U.S. 'Subversives,'" *Ogden(Utah) Standard-Examiner*, July 4, 1979, p. 14A. See also "'America Has a Divine Mission,' Says Pres. Benson," *LDS Church News*, July 14, 1979, p. 5. Benson's authorized biographer included Benson's 1966 version of the exchange as fact in her biography; whereas another of Benson's biographers, who served as secretary to four LDS Church First Presidencies, relied instead on the account in Benson's political memoir, *Cross Fire* (see Dew, *Ezra Taft Benson*, pp. 339, 364; and Francis M. Gibbons, *Ezra Taft Benson: Statesman, Patriot, Prophet of God* [Salt Lake City: Deseret, 1996], pp. 224–25).

10. Benson, *The Red Carpet* (Salt Lake City: Bookcraft, 1962), pp. 58–59 (chapter 5. "Communist Threat in America"); paragraphing removed. According to Bookcraft, "Ezra Taft Benson has responded to the urging of the publisher, and of a close circle of friends, to provide the material and direction for the preparation of this book. The words contained herein, largely gleaned from thousands of pages of manuscript and personal correspondence of this courageous public servant, gives Americans the answers to their questions" (p. 6). Bookcraft published books primarily for LDS audiences. For the publication date of *The Red Carpet*, see "Books Treat Communism: Give Patterns for Living," *LDS Church News*, April 7, 1962, p. 13.

11. Benson, *The Red Carpet*, p. 65 (chapter 6. "Creeping Socialism as the Red Carpet").

12. Ibid., p. 126 (chapter 11, "Let's Keep America Strong").

13. See "Elder Benson's New Book Off Press," *LDS Church News*, October 27, 1962, p. 13.

14. Benson, *Cross Fire*, pp. 468–69. Benson's oldest son and fiercest supporter, Reed (1928–2016), returned to Washington, D.C., with members of Khrushchev's party and took the opportunity to debate LDS doctrine with them (see Benson, *Cross Fire*, 470–71; see also Elinor Lee, "K.'s Son-in-Law Asks Benson Son to Proselyte," *Washington Post*, September 17, 1959, p. C20; and "6 Copies [of the Book of Mormon] Given to Khrushchev Family," *LDS Church News*, September 19, 1959, p. 6 [the books were sent to Khrushchev's son-in-law for distribution]).

15. The next month, Benson, accompanied by wife Flora Amussen (1901–1992), daughters Beverly (b. 1937) and Bonnie (b. 1940), and several Department of Agriculture staffers, visited the Soviet Union. "Of all the trade trips," Benson wrote, "this one left the deepest imprint on me . . . because it put before my eyes the pitiful faces of a people enslaved and into my ears the mournful cry of those bemoaning their lost liberty" (*Cross Fire*, p. 472). Benson's most memorable experience occurred when he addressed a Thursday evening meeting of some 1,500 members of Moscow's Central Baptist Church. "I don't remember all that I said," he wrote, "but I recall feeling lifted up, inspired by the rapt faces of these men and women. . . . Never shall I forget this victory of the spirit over tyranny, oppression, and ignorance" (ibid., pp. 487–88). See also Ovid A. Martin, "Benson 'Wins' Soviet Worshipers," *Salt Lake Tribune*, October 4, 1959, p. 8A; "A Church Service in Soviet Russia," *U.S. News & World Report*,

October 26, 1959, p. 76; and especially Reid L. Neilson, "A Light in the Darkness: Apostle Ezra Taft Benson's 1959 Sermon at Moscow's Central Baptist Church," in *The Worldwide Church: Mormonism as a Global Religion*, eds. Michael A. Goodman and Mauro Properzi (Salt Lake City: Deseret, Provo, Utah: Religious Studies Center, Brigham Young University, 2016), pp. 165–84.

16. Benson's journal entry for the encounter reads:

Early in the plans for the visit of Chairman Nikita Khrushchev, the request was made that he visit Beltsville. We had made complete preparations and plans although details of his desires were not available until he arrived in the city yesterday. At 9:45 [A.M.] Mr. Khrushchev arrived with his wife, two daughters, son and son-in-law, and a retinue of [U.S.] secret service men and Russian officials.

I greeted him at the entrance to the Plan Industry building, introduced him to Dr. [Byron] Shaw [director of the Agricultural Research Service], Reed [Benson] and his wife [May (Hinckley) Benson], and Beverly [Benson], who were with me. We then went into the auditorium where I made the following remarks: . . .

[See the paraphrase in Benson, *Cross Fire*, pp. 468–69.]

We then made a presentation on new developments in plant culture, breeding, and weed control. I then, at Mr. Khrushchev's invitation[,] rode with him and [Henry] Cabot Lodge to the dairy buildings. Reed took Mrs. Khrushchev and other members of the family with him in my car. At the dairy building we showed the Chairman breeding and management work in dairy cattle, hog, sheep, and turkeys and demonstrated the method of measuring back fat on hogs developed by our research people. Some 300 newspaper, TV, and radio men were in attendance. I feel good about what we were able to show the Chairman and believe this morning has been a definite plus for us. Probably in no other field is there such a marked difference between the achievement of communists and free enterprise as in the field of agriculture.

At the end of the program, Reed took Mrs. Khrushchev and party to Blair House, Mr. Khrushchev returned in his car and I remained to meet the press and answer questions. . . . (Ezra Taft Benson, Journal, September 16, 1959, electronic scan of holograph, attached to Keith Erekson, email to Gary Bergera, January 27, 2015; the original of Benson's journal is in the LDS Church History Library).

17. Qtd. in Frank K. Hewlett, "Mr. K. Talks Turkey in Benson Visit," *Salt Lake Tribune*, September 17, 1959, p. 1.

18. Qtd. in "Nikita's 'Impressed,' Benson Observes," *Salt Lake Tribune*, September 17, 1959, n.p., photocopy of clipping, Smith-Pettit Foundation.

19. Nixon, "Radio-Television Address from Moscow," in Nixon, *Six Crises* (New York: Simon & Schuster, 1962, 1990), p. 439. Nixon repeated the story the next year at the 1960 Republican Convention, adding: "When Mr. Khrushchev says that our grandchildren will live under communism, let us say his grandchildren will live in freedom" ("The American Presidency Project[;] Richard Nixon[;] Address Accepting the Presidential Nomination at the Republican National Convention in Chicago July 28th, 1960," at www.presidency.ucsb.edu [retrieved June 23, 2007]). For the "kitchen debate," see Stephen E. Ambrose, *Nixon, Volume 1: The Education of a Politician, 1913–1962* (New York: Simon and Schuster, 1987), pp. 509–34.

20. See three early instances of this alleged quote in Morris K. Udall, "Khrushchev Could Have Said It," *New Republic*, May 7, 1962, pp. 14–15; for a fourth, see Ronald Reagan, *A Time for Choosing: The Speeches of Ronald Reagan, 1961–1982* (Washington, D.C.: Regnery, 1983), p. 25. See also Rick Perlstein, *Before the Storm: Barry Goldwater and the Unmaking of the American Consensus* (New York: Hill and Wang, 2001/New York: Nation Books, 2009), pp. 148–49.

21. Available at http://archive.org/stream/TheBlueBook/MicrosoftWord-Document (retrieved January 27, 2015). The fuller quote attributed to Lenin reads: "First, we will take eastern Europe, then the masses of Asia, then we will encircle the United States which will be the last bastion of capitalism. We will not have to attack. It will fall like an overripe fruit into our hands" (qtd. in Paul F. Boller Jr. and John George, *They Never Said It: A Book of Fake Quotes, Misquotes, and Misleading Attributions* [New York: Oxford University Press, 1989], pp. 70).

22. Qtd. in Boller Jr. and George, *They Never Said It*, p. 59.

23. Qtd. in Udall, "Khrushchev Could Have Said It."

24. In 1988, Soviet leader Mikhail Gorbachev (b. 1931) asked U.S. president Ronald Reagan (1911–2004) about his own past use of the disputed quote:

> "Soviet specialists, as far as I know," he [Gorbachev] told the President, "in the American press and workers in the Library of Congress, qualified people, studied all the writings of Lenin and did not find one single similar quotation or something even close. Therefore, I'd like to ask you what you read from the works of Lenin and where did you get the quotations you've used." "Oh, my!" exclaimed the President. "I don't think I could recall and specify here and there. But, I've had a—I'm old enough to have had a great interest in the Soviet Union. And I know that in the things I studied in college, when I was getting my own degree in economics and sociology, that the declarations of Karl Marx, for example—that Karl Marx said your system, Communism, could only succeed when the whole world had become Communist. And so the goal had to be the one-world Communist state. Now, as I say, I can't recall all of the sources from which I gleaned this. And maybe some things have been interested differently in modern versions. But I know that Lenin expounded on that, and said that that must be the goal. . . . For example, here, in our Government, we knew that Lenin had expressed part of the plan that involved Latin America and so forth. And the one line that sounded very ominous to us was when he said that: "The last bastion of capitalism, the United States, would not have to be taken; it would fall into their outstretched hand like overripe fruit" (qtd. in Boller Jr. and George, *They Never Said It*, pp. 71–72).

25. Benson, *Cross Fire*, p. 587.

26. Benson, "Concerning Principles and Standards," Commencement Address, Brigham Young University, June 4, 1947, in *LDS Church News*, June 14, 1947, p. 5.

27. See Benson, *Cross Fire*, p. 578.

28. As early as 1947, Benson defined Communism as "utterly opposed to all we hold dear." See Benson, "Concerning Principles and Standards," p. 5.

29. Davis, qtd. in "New Agricultural Leader Brings Farm 'Co-op' Movement to Front," *LDS Church News*, January 24, 1953, p. 14.

30. Benson's characterization of his conservative, anti-communist political activism as a defense of freedom effectively defined any who disagreed with his views as opponents of freedom.

31. Benson, *Cross Fire*, p. 390.

32. Ezra Taft Benson, Oral History, interviewed by Maclyn Burg, May 21, 1975, pp. 23–24, Dwight D. Eisenhower Presidential Library, Abilene, Kansas.

33. Benson, "Strength for the Battle," address at the Fortieth Anniversary Dinner of the Americanism Educational League, October 17, 1966, p. 8, copy, Smith-Pettit Foundation. The last sentence—rendered as "No pain, no palm; no thorns, no throne; no gall, no glory; no cross, no crown"—has been attributed to early American Quaker William Penn (1644–1718).

34. See David O. McKay, Diary, March 3, 1966, photocopy, Special Collections, J. Willard Marriott Library, University of Utah, Salt Lake City: "I [McKay] said that we would tell Brother Benson not to mention the Birch Society in his remarks, and that I do not think we should mention the Birch Society or have anything to do with it."

35. See David O. McKay, Diary, October 21, 1965. See also Dew, *Ezra Taft Benson*, pp. 383–86. Since late 1954, Benson's name had been floated by various sectors in the Republican Party as a possible presidential candidate (see "Benson Tapped as Possible Top Candidate," *Ithaca (New York) Journal*, November 29, 1954, n.p., photocopy of clipping, Smith-Pettit Foundation. Initially intrigued, McKay eventually decided against exposing the Church to the *sturm und drang* of partisan politics but left Benson free to express his individual opinions. See George Wallace, Letter to McKay, February 12, 1968, and McKay, Letter to Wallace, February 14, 1968, photocopies, Smith-Pettit Foundation; and "Benson Backs Wallace Stand," *Christian Science Monitor*, February 13, 1969, n.p., photocopy of clipping, Smith-Pettit Foundation.

36. By 1966, individuals expressing concern with Benson's political activism included Harold B. Lee (1899–1973), Mark E. Petersen (1900–1984), Joseph Fielding Smith (1876–1972), Hugh B. Brown (1883–1975), and N. Eldon Tanner (1898–1982). All were LDS apostles, the latter three were also First Presidency counselors to David O. McKay. See Quinn, *The Mormon Hierarchy*, pp. 70–79, 86–87, 89–91, 94–96.

37. Benson, "Protecting Freedom—An Immediate Responsibility," p. 1145. The next month, two of McKay's First Presidency counselors (Brown and Tanner) told McKay that "certain parts" of Benson's talk "would give one the impression that Brother Benson and I [McKay] stand alone among the General Authorities [of the Church] on the question of freedom" and that the "talk is wholly objectionable because it does impugn the other Brethren of the Authorities as to their motives when they have advised the people to live their religion and stay away from extremist ideas and philosophies" (McKay, Diary, November 16, 1966). Despite the men's reservations, Benson's talk appeared essentially as delivered in the published proceedings of the conference.

38. Benson, "Our Immediate Responsibility," pp. 10, 13, 15.

39. Tara Parker-Pope, "False Memory vs. Bald Faced Lie," *New York Times*, February 10, 2015, p. D6.

40. Charles V. Ford, *Lies! Lies! Lies! The Psychology of Deceit* (Washington, D.C.: American Psychiatric Press, 1996), p. 176; emphasis in original.

41. Carol Travers and Elliot Aronson, *Mistakes Were Made (but Not by Me): Why We Justify Foolish Beliefs, Bad Decisions, and Hurtful Acts* (New York: Harcourt, 2007), p. 72.

42. See Kathryn Schulz, *Being Wrong: Adventures in the Margin of Error* (New York: Ecco/HarperCollins, 2010), pp. 80–83.

43. Poll, *History and Faith: Reflections of a Mormon Historian* (Salt Lake City: Signature Books, 1989), pp. 126, 127. See also Poll, "Truth, Facts, and Personal Anecdotes," *Sunstone*, September 1991, pp. 54–55.

44. See Travers and Aronson, *Mistakes Were Made,* pp. 76–77.

45. See Ford, *Lies! Lies! Lies!*, pp. 194, 195.

46. For two other instances of confabulation from ranking LDS Church leaders, see Poll, *History and Faith*, pp. 125–27.

3 From New Deal to New Right

ROBERT A. GOLDBERG

In broad outline, scholars and commentators have described the transformation of American political behavior from the 1930s to the 1970s as a shift from class allegiances to loyalties rooted in cultural identities. The national economic emergency of the Great Depression birthed critical elections that moved the mainstream to the Left. In response to the Depression, the Democratic Party proposed a liberal agenda, and an activist federal government shored up the middle and working classes and offered relief to the poor. In the 1960s, activism, war, and social change reawakened submerged racial, gender, religious, ethnic, and regional identities. The Democratic coalition, forged in economic crisis, could not manage the challenge of events and new contenders for influence. In failure, the New Deal liberal consensus unraveled.[1]

This interpretation of liberalism's retreat offers insight, but lacks completeness. The emphasis is on the Democratic Party's inability to adjust the past to the present and respond to disunity within and conflict without. In this scenario, conservatives play secondary roles, benefiting from their adversaries' mistakes in word and deed. Moreover, when conservatives enter history, scholars stake out presidential contenders like Barry Goldwater, Ronald Reagan, and George Wallace for detailed analysis. This makes for disconnect. National campaigns only energized conservatives every four years and revealed little about voters' shifting ideological commitments and the accelerating momentum of the Right at the grassroots. Why did men and women submerge class identities and enlist behind the banner of culture war? What made the conservative message convincing? How did conservatives mobilize their communities?[2]

This essay seeks to flesh out the standard interpretation by focusing on a conservative agent for change, close to the grassroots. In the 1960s and 1970s, Ezra Taft Benson, a leading figure in the hierarchy of the Church of Jesus Christ of Latter-day Saints, persistently hammered at federal programs and a liberalism he defined as "creeping socialism." Using his church authority and grounding his arguments in Mormon scripture and culture, he called his flock to a moral crusade to right America. Benson's efforts, which included embracing the John Birch Society and the movements of the New Right, had effect. He did much to wean Mormons from their Democratic loyalties and firm their support for the Republican Party. Meanwhile, Benson forged alliances with other wings of the conservative cause. His work opened the conservative tent to Mormons and made them key players in the gathering right-wing coalition. Benson's activities thus reveal not only how political change at the grassroots occurs but also that the political is both personal and local.

In political opinion and voting behavior, twenty-first-century members of the Church of Jesus Christ of Latter-day Saints register as both "overwhelmingly conservative" and "predominantly Republican." A recent study concluded that Mormons are staunchly Republican "to the point of peculiarity."[3] Just 6 percent describe themselves as liberal. Ninety-four percent of Mormons believe that the U.S. Constitution is divinely inspired and 73 percent say that woman's place is in the home. Utah vies with Oklahoma as the reddest of states, delivering upward of 60 percent of its vote to Republican presidential candidates and downward of 35 percent to Democrats.[4]

Mormon conservatism has several roots. LDS leaders preach the importance of "free agency," in all things. Choosing the right evokes responsibility—personal, familial, and to the community of saints. Agency shapes attitudes about work, morality, sex, and gender roles. It touches Mormons' understanding of race, with black people in the United States and around the world once condemned to inferior status for poor choices in the preexistence.

Agency is also in tension with government authority. Most Mormon leaders thus reject federal programs for eroding freedom of choice and subverting self-initiative and worth. They claim that Franklin Roosevelt's New Deal weakened the moral fiber of Americans. In their view, minimum wage law, Social Security, and welfare policies sacrificed freedom, while taxes robbed the wealthy of the fruits of their labor. Labor union organizing also posed a threat to agency and many Mormon leaders labeled it un-American.[5]

The New Deal was just the beginning of perceived government encroachment. "The paths we are now following," Mormon Apostle J. Reuben Clark declared, "will inevitably lead us to socialism or communism, and these are like two peas in a pod in their ultimate effect upon our liberties. . . ."[6] In 1942 the Mormon Church's First Presidency warned of continuing threats to the Constitution from "revolutionists" who used "a technique that is as old as the human race—a fervid but false solicitude for the unfortunate over whom they gain mastery, and then enslave them."[7] The message was the same a decade later during the red scare of the 1950s. Church president David O. McKay warned that communism threatened freedom of religion: "Today two mighty forces are battling for the supremacy of the world. The destiny of mankind is in the balance. It is a question of God and liberty, or atheism and slavery."[8] And, he targeted the conspirators at home: "secret, seditious scheming of an enemy within our own ranks, hypocritically professing loyalty to the government, and at the same time plotting against it. . . . It is the enemy from within that is most menacing."[9] Latter-day Saints were expected to heed such counsel and know that it came from God through His prophet. They knew the mantra: The church is true; follow the prophet. He could never lead members astray, for God would not permit it.[10]

Warnings from the pulpit drew added power from the Mormon conviction that the end times were close at hand. In the last days, the world would divide between good and evil with satanic, secret combinations threatening the Lord's people and church. Then, according to Mormon folklore and as church founder Joseph Smith allegedly prophesized, the U.S. Constitution would hang by a thread, government would near collapse, famine would ravage the cities, and racial war would erupt. National salvation was in Mormon hands. Church elders would save America and usher in the second coming of Christ.[11]

Yet, in spite of the messages in their holy books and the preaching of their prophets, Mormons were not reliably conservative in opinion or voting behavior. Some saints saw in the origins of their church the light of egalitarian communalism. They recalled the Book of Mormon's ancient Zion society where "they had all things common among them; therefore there were not rich and poor, bond and free, but they were all made free, and partakers of the heavenly gift."[12] Historian Leonard Arrington wrote of a promise to redistribute wealth and create a new society "characterized by economic equality, socialization of surplus incomes, freedom of enterprise, and group economic self-sufficiency."[13]

Mortal crises also spurred liberal tendencies. During the Great Depression, Utah suffered even more than the rest of the nation when more than a third of its workers were unemployed. Many Mormons broke with their leaders and supported Franklin Roosevelt for president four times. Harry Truman and his Fair Deal also carried the state in 1948.[14]

Right and left politics in Utah subsequently seesawed for almost two more decades. Mormons were aware of their leaders' admonitions and were suspicious of federal encroachment on liberty. Yet, economic concerns about jobs and housing encouraged them to vote for liberals who supported new federal programs in Washington. Alternating between the parties, Utah voters replaced Roosevelt and Truman with Eisenhower. In 1960 Richard Nixon defeated John Kennedy in the state, capturing 55 percent of the vote. Four years later, Lyndon Johnson defeated Barry Goldwater by the same margin. Utah voters elected U.S. senators and House members from both parties, and Democrats and Republicans alternated in winning statewide offices. In 1964 Democrats held both houses of the state legislature. The pattern then broke. Except for isolated cases, the 1960s would be liberalism's last hurrah in Utah for more than half a century.[15]

As context to this transformation, in the late 1950s the power of American conservatism appeared spent. Commentators had written off all threats to "vital center" liberalism with the disgrace of Senator Joseph McCarthy and the end of the red scare. Republican president Dwight Eisenhower had proclaimed "modern Republicanism" and moderated, but did not roll back, New Deal and Fair Deal reforms. Containment of communism and cooperation with the Soviet Union marked the president's foreign policy. With their numbers cut in Congress and lacking academic and media credentials, conservatives could do little more than mount a rear-guard resistance. Even that was a difficult task. Outside the mainstream, conservatives had fractured into loosely structured ideological camps. Traditionalists condemned the twentieth century's rejection of moral absolutes and values and its worship before the new god of relativism. This, they believed, had spawned permissiveness and the decay of family, community, and American institutions. Libertarians summoned men and women to a defense of private property, the free market, and individualism as bulwarks against what they saw as an aggrandizing central government bent on planning America into a regimented state. Anticommunists, tuned to the dangers within and without, rejected containment as appeasement and wanted to know, Why not victory? Although these currents of thought were not mutually exclusive, conservative proponents had yet to coalesce into a cause. No national leader or organization or forum had emerged to mark off the common ground that the three traditions shared or to establish the bases for cooperation. If Mormons could connect with all of these camps, they had yet to find a Moses to lead them.[16]

Timing, opportunity, and desire enabled Ezra Taft Benson to play this role. He had much to offer. Benson was a conservative, a member of the LDS church hierarchy, and a nationally known figure. He burned with ambition to lead America and his church past tribulation. Consistently and persistently, in the face of resistance, he pressed his conservative agenda. His impact on the saints would be felt for generations.

Ezra Taft Benson claimed an exceptional Mormon pedigree. His great grandfather and namesake was called to the Council of Twelve and served Brigham Young as an apostle. Growing up on a farm, Benson internalized his parents' strong allegiance to the Mormon Church and to conservative values. In 1921 he was called to serve a two-year LDS mission to Great Britain. There he met his mission president David O. McKay, to whom he felt a strong affinity. Benson wrote about McKay in his journal: "He is . . . truly a man of God."[17] McKay was impressed as well and entrusted the younger man with added responsibilities. This was the beginning of a life-long friendship. Experiences on his mission confirmed for Benson the truth of the LDS church and his religious calling. He was reluctant to receive his release: "I feel there is so much to do in the field and so few to do it."[18]

Back in the United States, Benson returned to farming but saw the need to further his education. He obtained a bachelor's degree in animal husbandry and later a graduate degree in agricultural economics. During the Great Depression, Benson worked as a county agricultural agent and was assigned to help administer the New Deal's Agricultural Adjustment Act. He openly bridled at provisions of the act that called for plowing crops under to cut production and price supports to secure farmers' incomes. Believing that farm security could best be achieved through the free market, Benson helped organize co-ops that allowed for collective buying and selling. During World War II, Benson worked to mobilize farmers and increase food production. Again, he grew frustrated by federal mandates: "Government controls and regulations have increased almost daily. The morale of the people, laboring under impossible directives, seems to be at low ebb."[19] Benson's expertise and experience, along with party affiliation, led in 1953 to his appointment as secretary of agriculture in the Dwight Eisenhower administration. He held that post for the duration of the Eisenhower presidency.[20]

Paralleling these achievements, Benson rose through the ranks of the LDS church. He served as bishop, stake president, and in 1943 was called as an apostle to the Quorum of the Twelve, at the highest levels of the church. While secretary of agriculture, he was on leave from his church duties.[21]

In the early 1960s, Ezra Taft Benson heard the call to prophecy. He preached an affirmative message to protect and secure the nation, its Constitution, and his church. Juxtaposed with this message were his allegations of a global conspiracy plotted by communists, fellow traveling liberals, and atheists. He positioned himself as a watchman on the tower, charged to warn Americans of threats to their liberties. Benson's national standing and church position gave him authority and legitimacy. They also ensured an attentive media and large audiences. At the time, few in conservative ranks could match his credentials.

While still holding national office, Elder Benson spoke at the LDS church's semi-annual General Conference in April 1960. He titled his talk "My People are Destroyed for Lack of Knowledge," with the theme that Mormons were asleep in Zion and unaware of the dangers posed by communists and their co-conspirators. The enemy, he declared, was insidious and cloaked in many guises. Its goals were to deprive men and women of their agency, weaken the home and family, and deny the existence of God. Mormons, as guardians of the nation's future, must educate themselves and confront the satanic forces that burrowed from within. "Let us stand eternal watch," he preached, "against the accumulation of too much power in government."[22] Six months later, at the October General Conference, he sounded the alarm again, this time focused on the threat from abroad. In the wake of the Cuban Revolution, America must stand firm against further communist expansion and subversion in Latin America.[23]

Benson followed-up these talks in 1961 with new warnings of an enemy closer at hand. Today, he somberly observed, the devil "as a wolf in supposedly a new suit of sheep's clothing is enticing some men, both in and out of the Church, to parrot his line by advocating planned government guaranteed security programs at the expense of our liberties." Benson grounded his concerns in Mormon scripture, observing that socialistic-communism "is amazingly similar to the ancient Book of Mormon record of secret societies such as the Gadiantons." This secret group, he reminded his listeners, had infiltrated established government, murdered its defenders, and secured power to create "ruthless criminal dictatorships." The comparison, Benson insisted, was not of his making. Quoting from the Book of Mormon's Ether 8:25, he related how the prophet Moroni foresaw "a great world-wide secret combination among the gentiles." These verses are intended "so that modern man could recognize this great political conspiracy in the last days."[24] Time was growing short. Benson called on all Mormon priesthood holders to make a stand and resist the satanic conspiracy: "join responsible local groups interested in promoting freedom and free competitive enterprise, in studying political issues." Benson targeted "the communist secret combination" again at an October General Conference session six months later. Referencing LDS theology, he described communism as "the earthly image of the plan which Satan presented in the pre-existence—a program which is essentially a war against God and the plan of salvation."[25]

As an apostle of the LDS church, Ezra Taft Benson knew his audience. His talks were not meant to be theoretical discourses or lectures that marshaled evidence to support an argument. He prefaced his jeremiads by declaring he had not come to "tickle your ears." No opening story or anecdote would detract from the seriousness of his message. He spoke in solemn voice and grave terms. Benson did not use words or phrases that moderated, restrained, or tempered. His was the voice of authority, not open to doubt or challenge. Consistent with his tone, religion became political in short declarative sentences and paragraphs. Chapter and verse quotations from Mormon and biblical scripture were the proof of conspiracy. In this Benson was merely a humble vessel and his church the vehicle to work God's will. Prophets of old, he claimed, had foretold the events of our time. His task was to reveal the truth, connect the prophecies, and rouse men and women of Zion to action.

His were war chants. The nation and church were under siege and hung by threads. Agency and liberty were in retreat. Liberalism was simply creeping socialistic-communism and those who championed its programs were the spawn of Satan, traitors to America and Christianity. Giving his words added weight, LDS church presses like Deseret Books and Bookcraft published his talks, and they appeared in the *Church News* of the Mormon Church–owned *Deseret News*. It was not necessary for members to take a leap of faith to believe that Ezra Taft Benson was the point man of their church.[26]

Benson's efforts had impact. With reference to Benson, members of the LDS First Presidency received letters from concerned saints about a "widespread emotional upsurge of Anti-Communism among members of the Church . . . generally sparked and supported by local Church leadership, which has all but taken precedence over the gospel itself." The letter writer noted that when a General Authority of the Church spoke on such political matters, members take it "as authorization for pursuing their own devious methods." Apostle Hugh B. Brown answered that church leaders "are all very much in sympathy with your viewpoint" and that "word is being sent to bishops and stake presidents to be on guard against 'crackpot' ideas."[27]

Yet, the sense that Benson spoke for his church on matters regarding communism was strengthened when the brethren at the highest levels of the hierarchy echoed his words. Fellow member of the Quorum of the Twelve Spencer Kimball declared at General Conference in October 1961: "While enemies filter into our nation to subvert us and intimidate us and soften us, we continue with our destructive thinking: 'It can't happen here.'"[28] The most liberal church authority, Hugh B. Brown, dismissed extremists in the defense of liberty but wrote in the *Improvement Era*, "Communism is of the devil. . . . Communism started when the devil was cast out of heaven because of his rebelling against the will of his Father that men should have their agency. Satan and his emissaries would rob men of their priceless freedom."[29]

LDS church president David O. McKay also supported Ezra Taft Benson's stand against communism. McKay, in turn, had preached: "The conflict between Communism and freedom is the problem of our times. It overshadows all other problems . . . on the outcome of this conflict depends the future of mankind."[30] Beyond words, McKay sustained the anti-communist movement in deeds. McKay, at Benson's urging, gave permission to Fred Schwarz of the Christian Anti-Communist Crusade to speak at the church's Assembly Hall on Temple Square in downtown Salt Lake City. Meeting privately with Schwarz, McKay "told him of my admiration for anyone who advocates the truth and fights against evil."[31] A follow-up *Deseret News* article quoted McKay referring to Schwarz as "one of these friends fighting the greatest evil in the world."[32] McKay "admonished" members to read W. Cleon Skousen's conspiracy-focused *The Naked Communist*, which claimed extensive subversion of the federal government, schools, media, and churches. McKay described it as an "excellent book" and noted that Skousen's "attitude towards communism is approved."[33] When a concerned LDS stake president in Seattle asked the church's opinion of Ezra Taft Benson's talks, President McKay telephoned him and said, "Brother Benson stands approved fully."[34] If aware of overzealousness on the part of these men, McKay was reluctant to dampen enthusiasm for the anti-communist cause. "We must," he observed, "be careful about condemning any efforts that are anti-Communistic because Communism is a real danger in our country."[35] He only drew the line when enthusiastic patriots attempted to recruit in ward sacrament meetings.[36]

Ezra Taft Benson also proselytized outside Mormon Church auspices. In 1961 he addressed a joint meeting of Salt Lake City's Rotary Club, Kiwanis Club, and Chamber of Commerce on the theme of "world brotherhood." This seemingly humanitarian topic elicited Benson's vitriolic charge that "the pillars of our economic system are being threatened by a strange and unlikely coalition of subversives, do-gooders, and self-servers."[37] Also in 1961, with President McKay's permission, Benson spoke in Los Angeles before the Project Alert School of Anti-Communism. Under the topic the "Internal Threat to the American Way of Life," he described how communists had infiltrated the federal government and were guiding research, preparing memos, drafting laws, and writing speeches for policy makers. Through their efforts, socialism was creeping forward, unnoticed, "gradually using government regulations or government ownership to destroy the basic framework of economic freedom and private production in our own country."[38] President McKay authorized the *Deseret News* to print Benson's speech.[39]

The following year, Benson published *Red Carpet*, a compilation of his speeches, revised to mute Mormonism and appeal to anti-communists outside the LDS community. The communist offensive, he wrote, was well underway, seeking world conquest and enslaving millions of men and women. In America the communist conspirators had penetrated youth groups, radio and television, the press, and both political parties. "Small doses of socialism," or "creeping socialism," he wrote, is "a Red Carpet providing a royal road to communism." High taxes, unbalanced budgets, wasteful spending, welfare programs, and centralized power were plotted means to weaken the nation. "The loss of our liberties," Benson warned, "might easily come about not through the ballot box, but through the death of incentive to work, to earn, and save." America's moral strength was also eroding. Describing the fall of ancient Rome and looking to the future of American conservatism, Benson decried a nation now plagued with the sins of moral decay: the breakdown of the home and family, divorce, sexual excesses, contraception, and abortion. Americans were now on a "slow slide to slavery."[40]

Building on relationships developed in Washington, D.C., Benson's anti-communism talks and publications tied him to a growing conservative movement. His network included activists Fred Schwarz, Stanton Evans, and Clarence Manion and Senators Barry Goldwater of Arizona and Strom Thurmond of South Carolina. Federal Bureau of Investigation director J. Edgar Hoover and Benson connected during the 1950s and maintained a long acquaintance and correspondence.[41]

Of special and growing importance to Benson was his new relationship with Robert Welch, the founder and leader of the John Birch Society. The men had met in 1961 and Benson was very impressed, describing Welch as "a fine Christian gentleman." Benson and his son Reed visited the John Birch Society's original headquarters in Belmont, Massachusetts, and concluded that it was the "most effective organization we have in the country fighting Communism and Socialism." For reassurance, Benson telephoned J. Edgar Hoover to ascertain the FBI director's take on the organization. Hoover was unavailable, so Benson left a message that he had conducted "considerable research" on the Society and "found nothing actually wrong with its activities and purposes." Though Robert Welch had made some "foolish" remarks about President Eisenhower, the Society "had done a lot of good combatting Communism." He also mentioned that Reed had been offered a position as the Society's coordinator for Utah. Had the Bureau, Benson asked, investigated and reached any conclusions? The substance of the message was passed to Hoover, along with the agent's response to Benson: "The FBI has not investigated the John Birch Society as such." Bureau officials gave Hoover plausible deniability, deciding not to have the director respond, but referring Benson to someone who could "discuss" the matter "at length."[42]

A month later, Elder Benson telephoned President David O. McKay to discuss his son's intention of becoming Utah's Birch Society coordinator. Benson explained that he had read Robert Welch's books and believed that his organization was playing a major role in the war against communism. McKay was not receptive: "I have heard about the John Birch Society," he replied, "and everything so far has been negative." Yet, the LDS president would not weigh in on the matter, writing, "*I have nothing whatever to do with it.*" Undeterred, Reed Benson accepted the position and Ezra Taft Benson drew closer to Robert Welch and his organization.[43]

Robert Welch was one of the most determined members of the anticommunist movement. A sixty-year-old candy manufacturer and former member of the National Association of Manufacturers, Welch had founded the secret John Birch Society in December 1958. His organization honored a Baptist missionary killed by Chinese Communists just ten days before the victory over Japan in 1945. In the name of the "first" casualty of the Cold War, he mobilized Americans against a communist conspiracy to dominate the world. It was not the invasion from without that most troubled Welch, but subversion from within. Increasing government control meant the gradual death of capitalism and of the American people's will to resist. Behind this, Welch detected a communist fifth column that had infiltrated the key institutions of American life to brainwash men and women into accepting a hedonistic and immoral creed. Conspiracy-bred permissiveness and disrespect for law and order would mutilate the Constitution, religion, and the family. Once plunged into moral and social chaos, America would be the last domino to fall to the godless communist dictators. Thus, Welch concluded, patriots had to act quickly, for the enemy was within the gates and its timetable was ahead of schedule.[44]

Ezra Taft Benson was not alone in his support of Welch's claims. In general tone and target, conservatives echoed Welch. Hoover declared, the communists had "infiltrated every conceivable sphere of activity; youth groups, radio, television and motion picture industries; church, school, and education groups; the press, nationality minority groups and political units."[45] Ronald Reagan paraphrased Robert Welch when he stated, "One of the foremost authorities in the world today has said we have ten years. Not ten years to make up our minds, but ten years to win or lose—by 1970 the world will be all slave or all free."[46] Meanwhile, Senator Barry Goldwater's books were on the recommended Birch reading list and sold in the Society's chain of American Opinion bookstores.[47]

What set Welch and the John Birch Society apart from other conservatives was his insistence that the conspirators had already breached the highest level of the federal government. Welch's investigation resulted in the publication of *The Politician* and purported to reveal that Franklin Roosevelt and Harry Truman had been under the control of communists. In Dwight Eisenhower, "the Communists have one of their own actually in the presidency. . . . There is only one possible word to describe his purposes and actions. That word is treason."[48] By the end of 1959, the John Birch Society had planted chapters in sixteen states, including California, Massachusetts, New York, Illinois, Florida, and Texas. The Society accelerated its efforts in 1960, organizing active groups in thirty-four states and doubling its membership every four months, reaching eighteen thousand men and women by year's end. Within six months of Reed Benson's appointment as Utah coordinator, the Society had tripled its membership in the state. Among the recruits were Ezra Taft Benson's wife Flora and second son Mark. Only President McKay's resistance kept Benson from enlisting.[49]

Robert Welch's attack on Eisenhower and the rapid expansion of the Birch Society put national conservatives in a quandary. Welch was a liability to the conservative movement, but the growing number of Birch members was crucial to the success of grassroots campaigns. As a national media wave of negative publicity grew in intensity, conservatives Russell Kirk, William Baroody, Barry Goldwater, and William F. Buckley met "as an intellectual council of war" in January 1962 to find resolution.[50] They set a course that they hoped would distance their cause from Welch but hold the allegiance of the Society's members. In follow-up, William F. Buckley's *National Review* lashed Welch for "bearing false witness" and printed Russell Kirk's warning: "Cry wolf often enough and everyone takes you for an imbecile or a knave, when after all there *are* wolves in the world."[51] Barry Goldwater joined in, declaring that Welch was "far removed from reality and common sense." He called on Welch to resign: "We can not allow the emblem of irresponsibility to be attached to the conservative banner."[52] At the same time, Goldwater offered the Birch rank and file an olive branch: "I wish he would step out so the fine responsible people who are members could take charge."[53]

In spite of these efforts, conservatives had not weaned Welch's followers from their leader. They had also underestimated the Society's appeal. When the media siege lifted, Birch organizers took advantage of the surging support for Barry Goldwater's presidential ambitions to pump their membership to sixty thousand men and women in forty-eight states by the end of 1962. In the face of this growing grassroots power, national conservatives tempered their criticism of Welch and his secret society.[54]

As others quieted, Ezra Taft Benson become more vocal in support of the Birch Society. An early endorsement of the organization appeared in Benson's October 1962 General Conference talk. Here he quoted from the Society's *American Opinion* magazine and encouraged the saints to read "a most brilliant discussion."[55] By the fall, with Benson's prodding, Brigham Young University's speakers' forum had hosted members of the John Birch Society National Council. BYU religion professor Glenn Pearson told a multi-stake meeting of students that Elder Benson's support of the Birch Society was "a mission from God."[56] Meanwhile Reed Benson, with his father's knowledge and perhaps consent, was actively recruiting new members in LDS ward houses. Members could also sign petitions in support of the Birch campaign to impeach Supreme Court Chief Justice Earl Warren before and after meetings.[57]

Ezra Taft Benson's anti-communist agitation, and specifically his proselytizing on behalf of the Birchers, caused a rift at the highest levels of the LDS church. He and son Reed were accused of crossing a line in their Birching activities, particularly in using church offices and facilities to recruit. Many expressed deep concern that their politics, never formally endorsed, would be perceived as the official church stance. Several called for disciplinary action to protect the image of the church. President McKay, however, was reluctant to intercede and repudiate the Bensons. During his tenure, the Mormon president had never criticized a General Authority publicly, for he believed all were entitled to exercise their agency without restraint. "Freedom of choice," he declared, is more to be treasured than any possession earth can give. . . . It is a divine gift to every normal being."[58] But, he also realized that "in the minds of the people the General Authorities in their individual capacities cannot be separated from them in their official capacities."[59] Yet, even if the Bensons had embarrassed the church and caused division, McKay was a kindred spirit in the war on communism. Regarding the "freedom battle," McKay had bestowed a formal blessing on Benson when he entered Eisenhower's cabinet in 1953.[60] McKay had said:

> We seal upon you the blessing of . . . sound judgment, clear vision, that you
> might see afar the needs of this country; vision that you might see, too, the

enemies who would thwart the freedoms of the individual as vouchsafed by the Constitution, . . . and may you be fearless in the condemnation of those subversive influences, and strong in your defense of the rights and privileges of the Constitution.[61]

According to son Reed, his father "never shot out on his own," but followed "the marching orders from his captain."[62]

However, this misses the point. McKay's anti-communism did not extend to supporting the Birch message and he explicitly requested that Benson refrain from participating in the Society's events. Here, Ezra Taft Benson ignored his captain and marched to his own beat.

Reluctantly and to protect the church, McKay conceded and recognized the dilemma Benson posed. He and his counselors in the First Presidency issued an official statement in January 1963: "We deplore the presumption of some politicians, especially officers, coordinators and members of the John Birch Society, who undertake to align the Church or its leadership with their political views."[63] A few weeks later, Benson met with McKay and complained, "the statement seemed to be leveled against him and his son, Reed, and also Brother Skousen." McKay confirmed this and reiterated Benson's conflict of interest. Manipulating McKay, Benson then pressed for clarification and asked if "this means that they must never mention Communism." McKay wavered. Communism was the enemy, "an evil thing," and the cause was just. In retreat, the LDS president cautioned Benson not to claim that the church "favors" the Birchers. If members wanted to join, "that is up to them."[64] A few months later, McKay, believing that the official statement went too far, backtracked and responded to saints asking for clarification:

> Members of the Church are free to join anti-Communist organizations if they desire and their membership in the Church is not jeopardized by so doing. The Church is not opposing the John Birch Society or any other organization of like nature; however it is definitely opposed to anyone's using the Church for the purpose of increasing membership for private organizations.[65]

The *Deseret News* published the clarification in March and Benson handed out the statement at a press conference. He assured the ninety-year-old McKay, "I will just put it out as quietly as possible, and not make a big thing of it. . . . This will help to quiet this thing down."[66]

This experience taught all contenders the limits of their influence. McKay sought peace among his apostles and attempted to satisfy the different factions in the hierarchy. With decisions subject to reconsideration, adversaries had to wait on events to gain leverage. The apostles also knew that McKay personalized issues; his physical and mental strength, beliefs, and loyalties were in play in decision-making. Benson, especially, drew clear lessons from this encounter. He had strong ideological and personal bonds to McKay and he would not hesitate to exploit them. McKay could also be flexible and forgive his trespasses. Yet, Benson's support of the Birch Society had put him on the defensive and raised the ire of his fellow apostles. To enhance his credibility with McKay and church members and to deflect criticism, Benson would have to revise his approach and learn to merge the prophet's message with his own.

Rather than being penned, Elder Benson continued his quest. Speaking before a Birch-front organization in Sacramento, California, in March 1963, Benson carefully noted that only President McKay spoke for the church on "matters of policy." Benson's endorsement followed, "The John Birch Society is the most effective non-church organization in our fight against creeping socialism and godless communism."[67] On many occasions, while claiming not to be a member, Benson stressed that he believed "strongly" in the Society's principles and in the "honesty and integrity" of Welch.[68] Wife Flora Benson vouched for the Birch leader as well, telling Mormons "that President McKay is in favor of Mr. Welch."[69] Meanwhile, rumors spread in the Mormon community that McKay's two Democratic counselors had forced the First Presidency's anti-Birch statement upon the aged prophet. As one letter writer observed, "There are too many in the Church who have come to wonder."[70]

Emboldened, Ezra Taft Benson appeared before two thousand people on September 28, 1963, in Los Angeles at a testimonial banquet honoring Robert Welch. Benson prefaced his remarks with a statement that implied the Mormon president's endorsement. Referring to McKay, he declared, "I am here tonight with the knowledge and consent of a great spiritual leader and patriot." Benson strengthened the impression by using quotations from McKay's talks to bracket his own assertions.[71] This tactic not only implied their agreement on issues, but Benson's role as the mouthpiece of the prophet. Benson also parroted the Birch line, observing that Americans have aided the conspiracy "by permitting socialists, communists, and fellow-travelers in high places in government; by giving away vital military secrets . . . by permitting the insidious infiltration of socialistic communist agents and sympathizers into almost every segment of American life." In tribute, he called Welch "one of the greatest patriots in American History."[72] Covering himself in McKay's words certainly enhanced his authority with Latter-day Saints. It surely also infuriated his critics in the church hierarchy.

Benson's offensive continued a few weeks later when he invited Robert Welch to visit President McKay in Salt Lake City. Welch was following up his invitation to have Benson join the National Council of the Birch Society. McKay, however, denied the request, noting that Benson could not serve two masters.[73]

Elder Benson's theme of subversion figured prominently at the October 1963 LDS General Conference in Salt Lake City. This time, Benson warned that the enemy was within the church itself. The apostle began his talk noting that six of the first twelve apostles chosen by Joseph Smith had been excommunicated because of apostasy. Teaching from the Book of Mormon's 2 Nephi 28:20, he reminded his listeners that, "in the last days the devil will 'rage in the hearts of . . . men and stir them up to anger against that which is good.'" And, quoting Joseph Smith, he shall "deceive the very elect." You will know, Benson continued, who the Judases are, for they will assail the divine gift of agency. In line with his new rhetorical approach, Benson recited the skirmishes that he and McKay had fought in "the great struggle against state slavery and the anti-Christ": socialism, communism, unionism, the "tragic decisions of the Supreme Court," and federal aid to education. "Let us not be deceived," he concluded, "in the sifting days ahead. Let us rally together on principle behind the prophet as guided by the promptings of the spirit."[74]

On the back of Benson's support for the Birch Society, the reaction was swift. On October 23, Benson was called to McKay's office and told that he was assigned, effective in January 1964, to preside over the Mormon Church's European mission for two years. McKay denied that this was a rebuke, declaring, "Elder Benson was called by inspiration."[75] Benson loyalists believed he was "being sent to the front lines," for his mission territory abutted the iron curtain.[76] Apostle Joseph Fielding Smith offered a more mundane rationale for Benson's exile: "When he returns I hope his blood will be purified."[77]

Benson remained unbowed. In parting shots, he delivered three farewell talks in December, with a third of the material sourced from the Birch Society's *Blue Book*. These were calls to muster in defense of the nation, and in them his support of the John Birch Society was explicit. At Brigham Young University, Benson referenced Birch Society publications in declaring that America was losing the struggle with communism. The "hour is very late indeed, on the timetable of national survival." We are "plunging headlong down the primrose path toward the inevitable destruction of our great country."[78] Benson provided listeners with the address of the Birch Society to obtain the "terrifying facts."[79] At the Logan, Utah, Tabernacle three days later, he declared that the "so-called 'extreme rightists' . . . in reality are the real patriots in the spirit of Patrick Henry and the founding fathers."[80] Those seeking copies of the speech were directed to write to him directly at the LDS church offices in Salt Lake City. Speaking next in Idaho, and introduced by a local LDS stake president, Benson explained why the warnings of the anti-communists have been ignored: "I am convinced that a major part of the cause can be justly laid at the door of the socialist-communist conspiracy which is led by masters of deceit who deceive the very elect." He mentioned the "tar brush treatment" given the John Birch Society and observed, "I can remember when it was unpopular to defend my own church." Regarding his son's decision to join the Birch Society, Benson said, "I would have given him equal encouragement if he had been considering the FBI."[81] Also in December, the Birch Society's monthly magazine *American Opinion* put Ezra Taft Benson on its cover. In an accompanying article, Benson advised patriots to be on guard against betrayal "by wolves in sheep's garments."[82]

Ezra Taft Benson should not have been discouraged as he made ready to leave for Europe. For three years, he had vigorously served the anti-communist cause. This was particularly true in the LDS community, where he repeatedly pressed his campaign in General Conference sessions and before smaller groups in stakes and wards. Listeners understood a message steeped in Mormon tropes, grounded in scripture, and apparently delivered with the endorsement of their prophet. Passionate and determined, Benson had bred tolerance there for the Birch Society and fashioned it as the vehicle to turn aside the threat to church and country. He had, as well, blurred the line in saints' minds between private and church-sanctioned advocacy. Benson was also secure in President McKay's devout anti-communism. Rarely did McKay accede to Benson's critics. At times, though, Benson's vigorous dedication to his cause led him to take advantage of the prophet-mentor's age, personal affection, and desire for peace among the brethren. His adversaries welcomed Benson's call to Europe as a respite from strife and hoped that his fervor and ambition would cool. Benson, however, was a zealot to his cause. The mission to Europe would slow Ezra Taft Benson's momentum but not break it.

In his father's absence, Reed Benson continued to mobilize the LDS community for the John Birch Society. In support, the Society's *Bulletin* published a letter that President McKay's assistant Clare Middlemiss had sent to a Latter-day Saint asking about the Bensons' standing. Neither Ezra nor Reed Benson, she wrote, has "been rebuked by the church. They, as all members of the church, are at perfect liberty to act according to their own conscience in the matter of safeguarding our way of life and are free to participate in nonchurch meetings which are held to warn people of the threat of communism or another theory . . . which will deprive us of our free agency."[83] The ground was being prepared.

Ezra Taft Benson tended to church business in 1964 and remained out of the limelight. This was in accordance with McKay's strict orders of silence in regard to the Birchers. However, he returned to controversy at the church's General Conference in April 1965. At times, speaking in President McKay's name or directly quoting him to frame issues, Benson asked when would we listen to "the mouthpiece of the Lord [who] keeps constantly and consistently raising his voice of warning about the loss of our freedom?" The devil has "neutralized much of the priesthood. He has reduced them to sleeping giants." If President McKay "has called communism the greatest threat to the Church and it is certainly the greatest moral threat this country has ever faced," when will the saints "wake up?"[84] Stricken on McKay's orders from the printed version, were two of Benson's claims. He had charged that the communists had taken over the civil rights movement to promote the overthrow of the Constitution and government. Also, he warned of traitors in the church who "provide temptations and avenues of apostasy for the unwary and unfaithful."[85] President McKay had set boundaries, but his enforcement was neither consistent nor heartfelt. As Brigham Young University president Ernest Wilkinson wrote in his diary, "Ezra is not going to give up on a cause in which he knows he is right. I know also that he has encouragement from President McKay."[86]

Also occupying Benson while in Europe was a potential run for the presidency of the United States. He informed McKay that he had been approached to head a third-party ticket with segregationist Senator Strom Thurmond in the vice presidential slot. Benson was receptive, for as he wrote "the Republicans were becoming soft toward communism and drifting toward socialism about as badly as the Democrats."[87] Meanwhile, Benson kept up his Bircher work, sending J. Edgar Hoover a copy of Robert Welch's *The Politician* that outlined Dwight Eisenhower's alleged communist connections. Benson told Hoover that the book must be made available cheaply "for maximum distribution."[88] He also wrote to Republican politicians on the importance of holding the allegiance of Birch members. In a letter to former Vice President Richard Nixon, Benson insisted: "In my humble judgment, any attempt to ride these fine Americans out of the Republican party could lead toward political suicide while plumbing the depths of demagoguery."[89]

When mutiny decimated the ranks of the Birch Society, Ezra Taft Benson remained steadfast in support of Robert Welch. Welch provoked uproar when he discovered in 1964 that his focus on communist intrigue was misplaced; communism was merely a subplot of a master conspiracy. Welch now claimed that the real enemy was a secret society called the Illuminati that plotted to destroy all civil and religious authority and abolish marriage, the family, and private property. After fomenting the French Revolution and masterminding the revolutions of 1848, the Illuminati reached for world power. With tentacles in international banking and trade, national political parties, and influential newspapers, the plotters engineered civil unrest, assassination, war, and depression to speed them to global dictatorship. Welch's vision had cleared: financiers, government leaders, socialists, liberals, and communists were merely pawns of a "clique of international gangsters" whose "sole objective" was global "tyrannical rule." Concealed behind their puppets, the identities of these INSIDERS were unknown even to Welch.[90]

Welch followed the conspirators to the United States and found their tracks in Progressive Era legislation like the income tax and Federal Reserve System and in the sinking of the *Lusitania* during World War I. The New Deal brought the intrigue closer to its goal by submerging states' rights under federal authority. During World War II, the INSIDERS controlled the home front with rationing, wage and price controls, and other forms of regimentation. In the postwar period, the pace of conspiracy quickened. Its mark was everywhere: the drug epidemic, a rising divorce rate, birth control, pornography, civil rights activism, Medicare, federal funding of schools, and even the fluoridation of water supplies. The conspirators were close to their endgame, with the United States poised to become a province of what Welch would later call the "New World Order."[91]

Welch understood that his new thesis would startle members, so he broached it "little by little."[92] Still, he underestimated the reaction. Men and women who enlisted to fight a familiar enemy were confused by Welch's claim that the greater peril was posed by secretive INSIDERS who cleverly disguised themselves as both communists and capitalists. This new crusade raised questions about Welch's judgment. In 1965 Ronald Reagan disavowed the Birch Society and suggested that it had been infiltrated by a "kind of lunatic fringe."[93] Perhaps as many as thirty thousand women and men, or one-third of the membership, deserted.[94]

None of this tested Benson upon his return to the United States in 1966, and he quickly immersed himself in a whirlwind of Birch-related activities. In January he endorsed the John Birch Society at an LDS stake conference in Logan, Utah, and at the LDS Institute near Utah State College. Elder Benson did the same at a stake conference in Boise, declaring, "This is a fine group. I know their leaders. I have attended two of their all-day council meetings. I have read their literature."[95] In fact, he recommended that audience members read Welch's *Blue Book* and *The Politician* and subscribe to *American Opinion*. Sticking to his old script, he made no mention of Robert Welch's INSIDERS. In February, Benson organized a speakers' forum in Assembly Hall on Temple Square, with Birch leaders participating. An overflow audience of more than two thousand people attended. In his keynote address, which was billed as given "by express permission"[96] of President McKay, Benson complained that in the two years that he was away, "we have moved a long way and are now moving further and more rapidly down the soul-destroying road of socialism." The centralization of power in Washington had made of state government "virtual federal field offices while weakening individual initiative, enterprise and character."[97] He urged listeners to join the John Birch Society, while reminding them that the LDS church is not opposed to their membership. Wrote one listener, "In this setting, there is a built in endorsement of his statements by the Church."[98] With some modifications, McKay authorized publication of Benson's talk in the *Church News* section of the *Deseret News*. Still, Mormon Church–owned KSL television broadcast the talk and reran it a month later in its entirety. Film of Benson's speech was also shown at ward meetings throughout the Mormon community. According to a Latter-day Saint couple, "feelings run so high in many wards that it behooves one not to mention one is a moderate Republican or liberal Democrat."[99] Benson followed this appearance with talks in Seattle and St. Louis, with another scheduled for Boston in the spring.[100]

In another bid to link the LDS church to the John Birch Society, Benson tried to convince President McKay to allow his portrait to appear on the cover of the April 1966 issue of *American Opinion* magazine. Without mentioning the Birch Society connection, Benson told McKay that this "high-type" magazine had honored Barry Goldwater and J. Edgar Hoover and that the LDS prophet should receive similar recognition.[101] McKay agreed but when informed of the Birch tie, realized that "if my picture is so published, it will certainly look as though the Church is endorsing the John Birch Society."[102] Under Benson's prodding, however, he soon changed his mind, saying that he had already given permission and would not go back on his word. The First Presidency then took up the matter with a confused McKay. Elders N. Eldon Tanner and Mark E. Peterson were emphatic, maintaining that the Birch Society would use you "for their circulation and financial benefit." McKay asked about Benson, "Why is he doing it? What has he in mind[?] He is one of the Twelve."[103] Again, McKay reversed himself and rescinded his permission.[104]

Benson would not be turned from his mission. He invited Robert Welch to a formal dinner in his honor at the church-owned Hotel Utah in Salt Lake City during General Conference week in April. With McKay's permission, Benson would deliver the keynote address. Invitations went out to LDS stake presidents and ward bishops to attend and continue the "education process" with the leader of the Birch Society: "We have been told that our Constitution would some day hang, as it were, by a single thread. Our Constitution has never been in as great a danger as it is today."[105]

Benson's ploy pressed his critics in the church to immediate action. They convinced McKay to withdraw permission for Benson to speak at the Welch dinner. They also persuaded the prophet to sign on to a statement from the First Presidency distancing the church from the Birch Society. In a "Notice to Church Members," the Mormon leadership declared: "The Church is not involved in this dinner in any way, and furthermore . . . the Church has no connection with the John Birch Society whatever."[106] McKay also counseled Benson privately, informing him that it was "best" not to speak at Birch Society events or raise the issue at church meetings.[107]

If Benson's adversaries had thought they had succeeded in convincing the prophet of the Birch danger, they were dismayed by President McKay's talk in the priesthood session of General Conference. Said McKay:

> We wish all of our citizens throughout the land were participating in some type of organized self-education in order that they could better appreciate what is happening and know what they can do about it. Supporting the FBI, the Police, the Congressional Committees investigating Communism, and various organizations that are attempting to awaken the people through educational means is a policy we warmly endorse for all our people.[108]

Such an endorsement overshadowed Apostle Harold B. Lee's condemnation of "false leaders . . . proud and self-vaulting ones, who read by the lamp of their own conceits . . . who become a law unto themselves."[109]

With McKay refusing to repudiate him and convinced of the importance of his anti-communist mission, Elder Benson continued his Birch crusade. He was aware his calling depended on McKay's support. Thus, Benson challenged his critics in the hierarchy while making common cause with the prophet. At the October 1966 General Conference he declared "All men are entitled to inspiration, but only one man is the Lord's mouthpiece." He advised Mormons to "Learn to keep your eye on the Prophet. Let his inspired words be a basis for evaluating the counsel of all lesser authorities."[110] He hit this theme again a few weeks later at Brigham Young University. Beware, he cautioned the students, "The devil is trying to deceive the very elect."[111]

Benson remained wedded to Robert Welch and the John Birch Society in 1967. Curiously, he insisted on formalizing the relationship even though the Society was an outcast nationally. In a nine-page single-spaced letter, Welch wrote to McKay outlining the Society's goals and again asking permission for

Benson to join the Birch National Council. He began by crediting the Society with slowing the communist conspiracy "almost to a standstill" and reviewing the anti-Birch counterattack that "tipped off every crypto-Communist and 'sleeper' who ever climbed out of the woodwork to do everything possible to damage the society." He then outlined his new thrust against "the ruling clique," the INSIDERS. All are "but arms of one octopus-like body, controlled by a central nervous system which serves as a brain." Welch wanted Benson officially on board to be a "weapon of prestige" who would "provide the reinforcements we now need in this battle."[112] It is unclear what McKay thought about this, but he again refused Welch and Benson. A subsequent visit by Welch had no effect.[113]

None of this dampened Benson's anti-communist activism. His endorsement of the Birch Society appeared in television ads. His influence on true believers at the grassroots of the Mormon community remained strong. Writing to Apostle Hugh Brown, one saint described the scene at a ward Sunday school class when a member "stood up and made a statement that he felt that everything an Apostle said must be considered as revelation from God and that if Brother Benson said that Birchism was correct politically, we should be accepting of this."[114] At the October 1967 session of General Conference, Elder Benson, with McKay's blessing, spoke on the topic "Civil Rights—Tool of Communist Deception." Using Birch publications as sources, Benson condemned the "so-called Civil Rights Movement" as a "communist program for revolution in America." He charged that "professional communist agitators" had duped African Americans into being "cannon fodder" in the struggle to overthrow the Constitution and U.S. government. He concluded by quoting McKay that communism was the "greatest Satanical threat to peace, prosperity and the spread of God's work."[115]

Subversion and the war on the Constitution were consistent themes for Benson. But other concerns received increasing attention as social and cultural conflict engulfed the 1960s. In a 1968 General Conference talk titled, "Americans are Destroying America" Elder Benson declared, "We live in a time of crisis. *Never since the period of the Civil War has the nation faced such critical days.*" Drugs, crime, juvenile delinquency, and welfare were symptoms of "our moral erosion." America was not only "decaying, but burning before our eyes."[116] Visible here is Ezra Taft Benson's role in the evolution of American conservatism; in helping move Mormons from the Old Right into the causes of the New.

In all of this, Benson made the Mormon base his priority. He was sure that the saints would defeat the conspiracy and lead the movement to restore American values. This was apparent in his May 1968 address to the student body at Brigham Young University in which he reiterated themes from his many talks. Here his faith is his cause. Once more, he turned to the Book of Mormon, "the word of God," to learn "what is really happening in America." For Benson, the communist war on agency had its origin in the preexistence when Satan challenged God for power. The struggle had continued through time. Citing chapter and verse, he described how God revealed through his prophets the destruction of past civilizations and what would happen to America if their warnings went unheeded. Quotations from David O. McKay and Birch publications bolstered his assertion that "the international, criminal communist conspiracy fits this Book of Mormon description perfectly." Now, with the Constitution "hanging by a thread," Mormons must "wake up" and "follow the prophet." His call to action was Mormon-specific and Birch-themed. He counseled followers to learn the truth by reading *American Opinion*, a "courageous, hard hitting, and truthful magazine." Save America by organizing Birch-front TRAIN (To Restore American Independence Now) committees. The word had been given. For many Mormons, to deny his messenger would be to deny God.[117]

Perhaps it was Benson's attack on the Civil Rights Movement that caught the attention of George Wallace, the segregationist governor of Alabama, as he planned his run for president in 1968. Benson's national standing, membership in the conservative network, and strong credentials with southern leaders also were appealing to Wallace. Benson had picked Strom Thurmond as his running mate for a potential presidential campaign. He counted Senator John McClellan of Arkansas as a friend. Now, Wallace sounded Benson out about joining him on the American Independent Party ticket. Before the Christian evangelical surge into politics, it was not difficult to contemplate such a Mormon-southern strategy. The two men met and agreed on the key issues of states' rights and law and order and were strict Constitutionalists. Wallace wrote to President McKay asking him for his "permission and blessings" and a leave of absence for Benson from his church responsibilities.[118] McKay, who saw little value in third parties, turned Wallace down. Wallace appealed his decision and was again rebuffed. Benson, of course, kept Robert Welch informed of all such matters.[119]

Benson's ambitions beyond the church and accumulating evidence that he still proselytized for the Birch Society spurred his critics at the highest levels of the Mormon Church hierarchy. In February 1969 the First Presidency met to review complaints about Benson and his role in the mobilization of saints in Birch front groups. Apostle N. Eldon Tanner insisted that Benson stop this work "and limit himself to talking about the gospel and its applications."[120] McKay agreed and had Apostle Alvin R. Dyer counsel Benson that "to denounce Governmental Agencies in a Stake Conference" creates "wrong impressions" and raises "controversies among the people."[121] Benson ignored Dyer and in a May talk at Brigham Young University censured President Richard Nixon and members of the U.S. Supreme Court. Apostle Hugh Brown described it as "a very inflammatory speech" that "left the students with the feeling that what Brother Benson said was the church position."[122] In a rebuke to Benson, the First Presidency issued a statement sustaining national leaders and the law. Benson responded by telegram: "You are a great soul, President McKay, as well as the mouthpiece, and if you want me to have complete confidence in our government officials I want to know it and then if the spirit confirms it I will adjust my life accordingly." In the words of one apostle, this was "a disrespectful wire."[123] It was more than that. It was an act of insubordination and a long-delayed moment of reckoning for Elder Benson.

President David O. McKay's death in early 1970 raised up Benson's critics, who restrained his agency to mobilize for the Birch Society. Still, he pressed his listeners to the right, now focusing on concerns that spoke to the times and the core values of his community. Thus, Benson denounced rock music's influence on the young; the devil's "sounds come from the dark world of drugs, immorality, obscenity, and anarchy."[124] He took issue with sex education because it "destroys morals and whetted curiosity."[125] In "A Plea to Strengthen Our Families," his October 1970 General Conference talk, Benson condemned the devil for promoting birth control, evolution, and abortion. Working women drew his ire for seeking to destroy the family by displacing the father as its head. In all of this, he urged Latter-day Saints to seek out allies in the new movements rising to oppose the Equal Rights Amendment, gay rights, and abortion.[126]

Ezra Taft Benson never relinquished belief in the godless global conspiracy. When church leaders' scrutiny relaxed, he resumed his post as a "watchman on the tower." If warnings are not sounded, he declared, "then God will hold us accountable."[127] Again, he drew his jeremiads from the Book of Mormon; its plot-laced prophecies offering the surest guide for the present and future. As Benson said in 1972, "There is no conspiracy theory in the Book of Mormon—it is a conspiracy fact."[128] The alarm had been raised before, but now in this dark hour, country, church, and salvation were on the line. In 1980 Ezra Taft Benson sent copies of his 1962 book *Red Carpet* to all members of Congress. He wrote to Barry Goldwater, "the content is more timely now than it was when first published."[129] When Elder Benson was named president of the LDS church in the 1980s, he admonished members to read the Book of Mormon. He believed that doing so would strengthen their faith. Perhaps, he also hoped that its pages would reveal, before it was too late, the satanic conspiracy that still threatened the saints in the latter days.

The mid-twentieth-century transformation from class to cultural politics swept up the Mormon community. With tendencies toward both conservatism and liberalism, Latter-day Saints had, in the space of a decade, decidedly moved to the right side of the American mainstream. The events of the turbulent 1960s offer context but are not sufficient to explain how or why the shift occurred. Here, Ezra Taft Benson's role is essential. Holding strong national and church credentials, he took up a mission to the saints and aggressively delivered the gospel of anti-communism, fiscal conservatism, and small government to the Mormon grassroots. Also visible in Benson's talks was the path to the New Right and its defense of conventional gender roles, the traditional family, and orthodox moral standards. His message had much salience because it was steeped in the language and imagery of the Book of Mormon and appeared to carry an official church stamp. Opposition, moreover, was sporadic and ineffectual. Benson's adversaries could do little as he embraced the extremist John Birch Society and it burrowed into the ward and stake houses of the Mormon kingdom. There, with family, friends, and neighbors engaged, Birch activism bred tolerance for even a radical conservatism. Benson also midwifed Mormons' acceptance into the national conservative community. His ambition funneled Mormon activists, donors, and voters to the John Birch Society, American Independent Party, and New Right mobilizations against the ERA and abortion. Under Ezra Taft Benson's guidance, the Latter-day flock turned to the right and has not strayed since.

Notes

1. See Allen Matusow, *The Unraveling of America: The History of Liberalism in the 1960s* (New York: Harper and Row, 1984); Todd Gitlin, *The Sixties: Years of Hope, Days of Rage* (New York: Bantam Press, 1993); Jefferson Cowie, *Stayin' Alive: The 1970s and the Last Days of the Working Class* (New York: The New Press, 2012); Daniel Rodgers, *Age of Fracture* (Cambridge, Mass.: Harvard University Press, 2012); Matthew Jacobson, *Roots Too: White Ethnic Revival in Post-Civil Rights America* (Cambridge, Mass.: Harvard University Press, 2008) and *Whiteness of a Different Color: European Immigrants and the Alchemy of Race* (Cambridge, Mass.: Harvard University Press, 1998).

2. See Lisa McGirr, *Suburban Warriors: The Origins of the New American Right* (Princeton, N.J.: Princeton University Press, 2001) for an analysis of grassroots conservatives.

3. David E. Campbell, John C. Green, and J. Quin Monson, *Seeking the Promised Land: Mormons and American Politics* (New York: Cambridge University Press, 2014), 23, 101.

4. Ibid., 78–80, 91–92; *Salt Lake Tribune*, September 16, 2014.

5. Gregory Prince and William Robert Wright, *David O. McKay and the Rise of Modern Mormonism* (Salt Lake City: University of Utah Press, 2009), 325, 328; Nathan Jones, "Restoring the Old-Time Virtues: Mormon Political Thought in the Great Depression and New Deal" (unpublished paper, 2015), 12, 21, 25–26, 29, 42.

6. Quoted in Jerreld L. Newquist, *Prophets, Principles, and National Survival* (Salt Lake City: Publishers Press, 1964), 327.

7. Quoted in Ezra Taft Benson, *An Enemy Hath Done This* (Salt Lake City: Parliament Publishers, 1969), 191.

8. Prince and Wright, *McKay*, 283.

9. Quoted in Newquist, *Prophets*, 229.

10. Church of Jesus Christ of Latter-day Saints, *Doctrine and Covenants*, 1:38.

11. Christopher James Blythe, "Vernacular Mormonism: The Development of Latter-day Saint Apocalyptic—1830–1930" (Ph.D. diss., Florida State University, 2014), 4, 9, 23, 283–84, 327.

12. 4 Nephi 3, Book of Mormon.

13. Leonard Arrington, Feramoaz Y. Fox, and Dean L. May, *Building the City of God: Community and Cooperation Among the Mormons* (Salt Lake City: Deseret Book, 1976), 15.

14. Utah's vote totals cannot be deemed simply as measures of Mormon support for candidates. Political opinion data along demographic variables and exit polling information are unavailable. Still, with members of the Church of Jesus Christ of Latter-day Saints comprising approximately 65–70 percent of Utah's population, these numbers suggest Mormon political preferences. They also indicate the fluid nature of party allegiance from election to election. Note also, the great majority of elected office holders, whether Republicans or Democrats, were active members of the LDS church. www.uen.org/utah_history_encyclopedia/e/ELECTIONS.html, accessed July 6, 2015; May, *Utah*, 177, 180–81; Frank Jonas, "The 1964 Election in Utah," *Western Political Quarterly* 18 (June 1965), 509.

15. Ibid.

16. George H. Nash, *The Conservative Intellectual Movement in America Since 1945* (New York: Basic Books, 1976), xiii–xiv, 3–4, 40–53, 85–91; Jerome Himmelstein, *To the Right: The Transformation of American Conservatism* (Berkeley: University of California Press, 1990), 8, 14, 38–42, 45–46, 49–51, 62; William Rusher, *The Rise of the Right* (New York: William Morrow, 1984), 36; Sidney Blumenthal, *The Rise of the Counter Establishment: From Conservative Ideology to Political Power* (New York: Harper and Row, 1986), 4.

17. Sheri L. Dew, *Ezra Taft Benson, a Biography* (Salt Lake City: Deseret Book, 1987), 60.

18. Ibid., 4–6, 13, 24–25, 49–63 (quote).

19. Ibid., 167.

20. Ibid., 106–11, 147–49, 164–70; Newell Bringhurst and Craig Foster, *The Mormon Quest for the Presidency: From Joseph Smith to Mitt Romney and Jon Huntsman* (Independence, Mo.: John Whitmer Books, 2011), 133–35, 153–54.

21. A ward is the local congregation of the LDS church. A stake is a geographical area encompassing a group of wards. Dew, *Benson*, 106–11, 115–16, 143–44, 156–58, 174–75.

22. Ezra Taft Benson, "My People Are Destroyed for Lack of Knowledge," in *Stand Up For Freedom: Teachings on Liberty* (San Bernardino, Calif.: Ezra Taft Benson Society, 2012), 3.

23. Ibid., 1–4; Ezra Taft Benson, "The Threat of Communism," in *Title of Liberty* (Salt Lake City: Deseret Book, 1964), 158.

24. Ezra Taft Benson, "The American Heritage of Freedom," in *Title of Liberty*, 183, 184, 185, 192.

25. David O. McKay, September 30, 1961, "Diaries," David O. McKay Papers.

26. Prince and Wright, *McKay*, 287–80.

27. George Boyd to Hugh B. Brown, September 22, 1961; Brown to Boyd, October 6, 1961, Harley Hammond to Brown, April 24, 1962, Brown to Hammond, April 25, 1962, "Ezra Taft Benson," Archival Subjects, David O. McKay Papers.

28. Quoted in Newquist, *Prophets*, 66.

29. Hugh B. Brown, "Honor the Priesthood," *Improvement Era* 65 (June 1962): 450.

30. Quoted in D. Michael Quinn, "Ezra Taft Benson and Mormon Political Conflicts," *Dialogue: A Journal of Mormon Thought* 26 (Summer 1993): 68–69. McKay quoted this from the flyleaf of Cleon Skousen's *The Naked Communist* (Salt Lake City: Ensign Publishing, 1961).

31. McKay, December 13, 1961, "Diaries."

32. Ibid.

33. David O. McKay, *Improvement Era* 62 (December 1959): 911; McKay, February 15, 1962, "Diaries."

34. McKay, August 17, 1961, May 18, 1962 (quote), "Diaries."

35. Ibid., August 17, 1961.

36. McKay, December 1, 1961, "Diaries"; Prince and Wright, *McKay*, 287.

37. Ezra Taft Benson, "World Brotherhood," *Title of Liberty*, 147.

38. Ezra Taft Benson, "The Internal Threat to the American Way of Life," *Title of Liberty*, 165, 173 (quote).

39. McKay, December 5, 1961, "Diaries."

40. Ezra Taft Benson, *Red Carpet: Socialism—the Royal Road to Communism* (Salt Lake City: Bookcraft, 1962), 17, 56, 65, 75, 136, 219, 276, 238, 300.

41. Ibid., 204–5; Benson to Barry Goldwater, September 10, 1987, Correspondence, FM MSS-1, Box 2, Folder 7, Barry Goldwater Collection, Arizona State University Archives, Tempe; *Ezra Taft Benson's F.B.I. File* (Salt Lake City: Smith Pettit Foundation, 2008), A. Jones to Cartha DeLoach, "Internal Memorandum," November 9, 1959. According to Reed Benson, Hoover "counseled and helped over the years." Interview with Reed Benson by Gregory Prince, September 15, 1999.

42. Prince and Wright, *McKay*, 286; Benson F.B.I. File, "Memorandum" regarding telephone conversation with Benson, September 18, 1962, A. Jones to Cartha DeLoach, "Memorandum," September 21, 1962.

43. McKay, October 26, 1962, "Diaries."

44. Robert Welch, *The Blue Book of the John Birch Society*, 9th printing (Belmont, Mass.: Western Islands Publishing, 1961), 9, 18–28, 33, 59–64, 104, 141.

45. Jonathan Martin Kolkey, *New Right, 1960–1968: With Epilogue, 1969–1980* (Lanham, Md.: University Press of America, 1983), 82.

46. Ibid., 79.

47. Ibid., 77.

48. Arnold Foster and Benjamin Epstein, *Danger on the Right* (New York: Random House, 1965), 42. Compare quotations in *Danger on the Right* with those toned down in

later editions of *The Politician*. For example, see Robert Welch, *The Politician* (Belmont, Mass.: Belmont Publishing, 1963), 5–6, 277–79.

49. Robert A. Goldberg, *Grassroots Resistance: Social Movements in Twentieth-Century America* (Chicago: Waveland Press, 1996), 116–40. Quinn, "Benson," 8, 14.

50. Russell Kirk, "Sword of Imagination" (unpublished manuscript, 1992), 471.

51. "The Question of Robert Welch," *National Review*, February 13, 1962, 83–88.

52. *National Review*, February 27, 1962, 140.

53. "Newsmakers," *Newsweek*, February 19, 1962, 57.

54. Goldberg, *Grassroots Resistance*, 125–30.

55. Ezra Taft Benson, "It Cannot Happen Here," *Title of Liberty*, 99.

56. Quoted in Quinn, "Benson," 15.

57. Ibid., 19.

58. Quoted in Prince and Wright, *McKay*, 42.

59. McKay, February 6, 1959, "Diaries."

60. Prince, Reed Benson interview.

61. Quoted in Dew, *Benson*, 259.

62. Prince, Reed Benson interview; Quinn, "Benson," 9–12, 16; Prince and Wright, *McKay*, 42, 48–50; 52, 63–64, 279, 282–83, 290.

63. Quoted in Quinn, "Benson," 16.

64. McKay, January 23, 1963, "Diaries."

65. Quinn, "Benson," 16–18; Prince and Wright, *McKay*, 291–92, 298; McKay, January 4, 23, 1963, "Diaries;" *Deseret News*, March 16, 1963.

66. McKay, March 13, 1963, "Diaries."

67. *Deseret News*, March 14, 1963.

68. *Salt Lake Tribune*, March 21, 1963.

69. McKay, March 6, 1963, "Diaries."

70. McKay, June 14, 1963, "Diaries"; Ernest Cook to Hugh Brown, September 25, 1963, "Benson," Archival Subjects, McKay Papers.

71. The Associated Press, CBS News, and United Press International would later report statements by Reed Benson that McKay had assigned his father to speak at the event. See, McKay, November 20, 1963, "Diaries."

72. Ezra Taft Benson, "Let Us Live to Keep Men Free," *Title of Liberty*, 1, 5; Nelson Wadsworth, "Mormon Split over John Birch Society Campaign," *National Observer*, November 4, 1963, in David O. McKay, Scrapbook #69. This line of praise was edited out of the published version of the speech printed in *Title of Liberty*.

73. McKay, August 9, September 24, 1963, "Diaries."

74. Ezra Taft Benson, "Be Not Deceived," *Improvement Era* 66 (December, 1963): 1063–65.

75. *Deseret News*, February 21, 1964.

76. Wadsworth, "Mormon Split."

77. Joseph Fielding Smith to Ralph Harding, December 23, 1963, "Benson," Archival Subjects, McKay Papers.

78. Ezra Taft Benson, "A Race Against Time," *Title of Liberty*, 61.

79. Ibid., 72.

80. Ezra Taft Benson, "We Must Become Alerted and Informed," *Title of* Liberty, II, 47.

81. Ezra Taft Benson, "The Internal Threat Today," *Title of Liberty*, 27, 34, 36, 39.

82. Ezra Taft Benson, "The Christ and the Constitution," *American Opinion* (December 1964), 41; Quinn, "Benson," 26; Prince and Wright, *McKay*, 299; *Logan Herald Journal*, December 15, 1963; Ralph Harding interview with Gregory Prince, October 24, 2000.

83. *John Birch Society Bulletin*, March 1965, in McKay, Scrapbooks, #69.

84. Ezra Taft Benson, "Not Commanded in All Things," in McKay, Scrapbooks, #79.

85. McKay, May 3, 1965, "Diaries"; *Washington Post*, April 13, 1965.

86. Ernest L. Wilkinson, "Diary," April 6, 1965, Brigham Young University Special Collections.

87. McKay, October 21, 1965, "Diaries."

88. Benson to Hoover, May 28, 1965, Benson FBI File.

89. Ezra Taft Benson to Richard M. Nixon, December 9, 1965, Benson, Ezra Taft folder, Box 3, Wilderness Years, Series 1, Correspondence, Sub Series A, Pre Presidential Papers, Richard M. Nixon Presidential Library, Yorba Linda, Calif.

90. Robert H. W. Welch Jr., "The Truth in Time," *American Opinion* 9 (November 1966), 25–27; Robert H. W. Welch Jr., "If You Want it Straight," 8 (December, 1965), 1.

91. Robert H.W. Welch Jr., "Dissent," *American Opinion* 17 (December, 1974): 53; Welch, "Truth in Time," 4–8, 10, 11, 19, 21; Robert H.W. Welch Jr., "In One Generation" (video, 1995); Robert H.W. Welch Jr., "A Touch of Sanity" (video, 1965).

92. G. Edward Griffin, *The Life and Words of Robert Welch, Founder of the John Birch Society* (Thousand Oaks, Calif.: American Media, 1975), 246.

93. Fletcher Knebel, "The GOP Attacks the John Birch Society," *Look* 29 (December 28, 1965): 74.

94. *New York Times*, December 8, 1968, 42.

95. *Salt Lake Tribune*, January 16, 1966.

96. McKay, February 1, 1966, "Diaries."

97. Benson, "Stand Up for Freedom," *Stand Up*, 44.

98. John K. Black to Hugh B. Brown, March 10, 1966, "Benson," Archival Subjects, McKay Papers.

99. Donald and Jane Stromquist to Hugh B. Brown, March 7, 1966, "Benson," Archival Subjects, McKay Papers.

100. Quinn, "Benson," 39–41; *Salt Lake Tribune*, January 16, 1966; McKay, January 7, February 1, 11, 14, 16, March 15, 1966, "Diaries"; Ezra Taft Benson to David O. McKay, "List of Talks in Assembly Hall on Temple Square," February 15, 1966, McKay Scrapbook #84; Benson, "Stand Up," 56–57.

101. McKay, February 19, 1966, "Diaries."

102. Ibid., February 18, 1966.

103. Ibid., March 8, 1966.

104. Ibid., February 9, 18, 19, March 3, 8, 1966.

105. Ibid., March 15, 1966; Prince and Wright, *McKay*, 310.

106. "Notice to Church Members," McKay Scrapbook, #84.

107. McKay, March 8, 25, 1966, "Diaries."

108. Quoted in Prince and Wright, *McKay*, 313.

109. Quoted in Quinn, "Benson," 47.

110. Ibid., 55–57.

111. McKay, May 26, 1966, "Diaries"; Ezra Taft Benson, "Our Immediate Responsibility," *Stand Up*, 143.

112. McKay, February 21, 1967, "Diaries."

113. Ibid., February 24, March 22, April 18, 1967.

114. Dorothy Skinner to Hugh B. Brown, March 24, 1967, "Benson," Archival Subjects, McKay Papers.

115. Gary Rose to Frank Moss, February 4, 1967, MS 146, Box 245, "Birch Letters," Folder 4, Frank Moss Papers, Special Collection, Marriott Library, University of Utah; Prince and Wright, *McKay*, 72; Benson, *Enemy*, 192, 197, 200.

116. Ezra Taft Benson, "Americans are Destroying America," 138th Annual General Conference of the Church of Jesus Christ of Latter-day Saints (Salt Lake City, 1968), 3.

117. Ezra Taft Benson, "The *Book of Mormon* Warns America," May 21, 1968, www .latterdayconservative.com/ezra-taft-benson/the-book-of-Mormon-warns-America/, accessed on May 26, 2015, 1, 4, 5, 9, 14, 18.

118. George Wallace to David O. McKay, February 12, 1968, "E.Z. Benson," Folder, Wallace Family Papers, Alabama Department of Archives and History, Montgomery.

119. McKay, February 13, September 9, 1968, "Diaries"; Matt Harris to Bob Goldberg, March 18, 2015. John McClellan wrote the forward to Benson's book *An Enemy Hath Done This*, published in 1969.

120. McKay, February 2, 1969, "Diaries."

121. Ibid., February 12, 1969.

122. Ibid., May 12, 1969.

123. Ibid., May 20, 1969.

124. Dew, *Benson*, 418.

125. Ibid., 404.

126. Ezra Taft Benson, "A Plea to Strengthen Our Families," *Stand Up*, 5–14.

127. Ezra Taft Benson, "God, Family, Country," *Stand Up*, 198.

128. Ezra Taft Benson, "Civic Standards for the Faithful Saints," *Stand Up*, 87.

129. Ezra Taft Benson to Barry Goldwater, February 18, 1980, Correspondence, MSS-1, Box 2, Folder 7, Barry Goldwater Collection, Arizona State University Archives, Tempe.

4 Potomac Fever

Continuing Quest for the U.S. Presidency

NEWELL G. BRINGHURST

Some four decades before Mitt Romney ran for president, another prominent Mormon, Ezra Taft Benson sought the nation's highest office. Benson's
quest commenced in 1960 and continued into the turbulent decade that followed. Most Latter-day Saints remember Benson as a longtime ecclesiastical
leader, first appointed to the church's elite Quorum of the Twelve in 1943.
He was ultimately elevated to the denomination's highest office, LDS church
president, in 1985, serving until his death in 1994. Concurrently active in the
political arena, he gained national recognition as secretary of agriculture
under President Dwight D. Eisenhower. At the same time, Benson retained
his church position on the Council of Twelve, though granted a leave of
absence. During his eight-year tenure as agriculture secretary from 1953 to
1961, the Mormon apostle interacted with fellow conservatives both within
and outside government.[1]

Benson's 1960 Foray into Presidential Politics

By 1960, with his term as secretary of agriculture ending, Benson's career
reached a critical crossroads. On the one hand, Benson pondered returning
to Utah and resuming his full-time duties as a junior member of the Quorum
of the Twelve. At the same time, he felt the urge to remain politically active,
given the ongoing 1960 presidential campaign.[2] Benson, in fact, envisioned
himself as a candidate. As early as 1954, he earned mention as a presidential
contender. Some four years later, LDS church president David O. McKay
confronted Benson concerning his political aspirations. "I have been hearing
your name mentioned recently, Brother Benson as a possible candidate for the

Vice Presidency and even for the Presidency." Also speculating about Benson's future political ambitions were U.S. Congressman Jamie Whitten of Mississippi; I. Lee Potter, special assistant to the chairman of the Republican Party; Thomas J. Anderson, editor and publisher of *Farm and Ranch* magazine; and Mark Evans, a Washington television personality. Benson discounted such speculation, telling President McKay: "I've said over and over again that I have no political aspirations. All I want to do is serve President Eisenhower [as agriculture secretary] as best I can. . . . Then I want to come home."[3]

Benson's disavowal proved short-lived. The topic of Benson's future political plans surfaced in another meeting with President McKay, this one in March 1960. Also present was the apostle's son, Reed. The younger Benson raised the possibility of his father seeking the Republican presidential nomination—a surprising suggestion given that incumbent Vice President Richard Nixon had, by this time, become the prohibitive favorite. McKay, less than enthusiastic, urged Benson *not* to push himself forward, but "let the political [party] leaders get together and make the suggestion." McKay further added, "do not let it come from you; you may acquiesce, but let them do the suggesting."[4] One month later, Benson met again with President McKay discussing Benson's desire to seek the presidency. McKay reiterated his earlier advice "that the pressure for [his] candidacy must come from outside groups."[5] These discussions took place behind closed doors.[6]

In public, Benson presented a different persona, actively promoting New York Governor Nelson A. Rockefeller as the ideal Republican candidate, even though the governor disavowed all intentions to run.[7] In February 1960, Benson traveled to New York to meet with Rockefeller. Both men expressed doubts about Richard Nixon's prospects for success. They also discussed Rockefeller's dilemma, specifically that while the New York governor could probably win the general election, he could likely not secure the GOP nomination.[8]

Benson persisted in promoting a Rockefeller candidacy, traveling to New York a second time in April 1960. Benson urged Rockefeller to "go to the people and present his views on important issues." "There might still be a chance" for the nomination, Benson told the governor. He further proposed conservative Arizona Senator Barry Goldwater as a running mate, noting that the two men's contrasting ideologies would make for an ideal ticket. At this point, their conversation took a surprising turn, with Rockefeller suggesting: "Much as I like Barry, I would rather have Ezra Taft Benson as my running mate." Benson quickly replied that he "wasn't fishing." The conversation concluded with Benson suggesting that Rockefeller "concentrate on making public appearances in the next few months to see what develops."[9]

Benson continued to promote a belated Rockefeller presidential bid into the summer of 1960. In June Benson expressed pleasure when the New York governor publicly assailed Richard Nixon's views on national defense. The apostle praised Rockefeller for "his forthright challenge," stating that it adds "spirit and interest to the Republican campaign." Benson then mused: "I wondered if Nelson Rockefeller had made a mistake in withdrawing from the campaign for the nomination?"[10]

In late July, on the eve of the Republican National Convention, Benson publicly expressed strong support for Rockefeller. Before doing so, he conferred with President McKay by telephone from Chicago, site of the Convention. Explaining his motives, Benson claimed to be "under considerable pressure to indicate who I think . . . would have the best chance of defeating Senator Kennedy." Benson expressed his desire to make a statement in support of Rockefeller. McKay replied, "I think you are right and I am with you!" Benson then confessed: "I don't know that he [Rockefeller] has much of a chance, but I think there is a long-shot chance he may possibly win the nomination yet."[11]

Their conversation then turned to ongoing efforts to recruit Rockefeller for vice president. Benson claimed Republican Party operatives sought his support "to help persuade" Rockefeller to be Richard Nixon's running mate. McKay quickly replied, "Oh no, I think that would be a mistake." Benson agreed, "I think the best thing to do is try to get him in first place." McKay concurred.

Benson then shared with McKay the statement he intended to issue:

> Having travelled possibly more miles in the United States than any other Republican in the past seven and one-half years, I am convinced the Governor Rockefeller would stand the best chance of defeating Senator Kennedy. The Governor would pull heavily from Republicans, Independents and Democrats, and I strongly believe he would win. Although in some areas I feel Governor Rockefeller may be somewhat too liberal, he is devoted to our basic American concepts, and would make a great president.[12]

Benson, later reflecting on his efforts, mused, "there was perhaps still some faint, forlorn hope that a spark might yet start a Rockefeller-Goldwater conflagration." Or possibly, by getting Rockefeller's name into nomination at the convention, the New York governor could be pressured to be Nixon's running mate, "possibly saving the ticket from defeat." The failure of all such efforts notwithstanding, Benson met with Rockefeller following the convention. Rockefeller "expressed deep gratitude" for Benson's support "of his unannounced candidacy." The Mormon apostle, in turn, confessed admiration for the governor's "deep convictions, his spirituality, and his winning personality."[13]

The obvious question is, what motivated Benson in his persistent, albeit unsuccessful effort to promote Rockefeller over Nixon for the 1960 Republican nomination? There are three possible explanations. First and foremost, Benson was convinced that Rockefeller was the stronger candidate—a view shared by a number of other influential Republicans. Even outgoing President Eisenhower harbored reservations concerning Nixon's suitability to succeed him. Second, there were personal considerations, in that Benson upon meeting and interacting with the New York governor found him both congenial and approachable—such qualities facilitating a close personal friendship. By contrast, Benson's relationship with Richard Nixon was much less congenial—this despite the eight years the two had served together in the Eisenhower administration. Benson characterized Nixon as a man not "easy to get close to."[14] Finally, political ambition clearly drove Benson—the possibility of Benson being selected as Rockefeller's running mate or serving him in some other capacity.

Benson met with Richard Nixon shortly after the convention, pledging support in the upcoming general election campaign. The apostle confessed: "Obviously, I knew I would not be drawing close to him . . . but would be as helpful as I could." He characterized Nixon "a shrewd and effective politician, one who would . . . make a far better President than John Kennedy." Benson then noted his continuing ambivalence toward the Republican nominee in that Nixon "had raised a barrier . . . after the Republican Convention" through his characterization of the agriculture secretary as "a liability." Specifically, Nixon alleged that Benson's highly controversial agricultural policies had harmed residents in the Farm Belt. Nixon did not want Benson campaigning on his behalf in the Midwest given what he termed "the unresolved farm problem." Ultimately, Benson campaigned for the Republican ticket in both the South and Midwest.[15]

In September, however, the Mormon apostle terminated all such activity at the urging of President McKay.[16] McKay's recall of Benson came in the wake of a June 6 meeting between the Mormon leader and U.S. Senator Barry Goldwater. The blunt, plainspoken Goldwater frankly told McKay that "it would be wise to have Brother Benson come home as he fears he [Benson] is going to be embarrassed by both the Republicans and the Democrats."[17] Also expressing concern relative to Benson's political activities were a number of his fellow apostles, who felt that he was "more interested in future political preferment than . . . returning to full-time Church service as a member of the Twelve."[18]

Upon returning to Salt Lake City in late September, Benson dealt with yet another effort to lure him back into the political arena. A committee made up of local Republicans attempted to recruit Benson as a write-in candidate for Utah governor, despite the fact that incumbent Republican Utah governor, George Dewey Clyde, was running for reelection. By early October, mimeographed letters urging a write-in campaign to promote Benson for governor began appearing on automobiles throughout Salt Lake City. Benson quickly discouraged this effort, of which he claimed to be unaware. He announced support for Governor Clyde, along with his intention to resume his full-time duties as an LDS apostle.[19]

Benson, however, betrayed ambivalence about leaving public life and Washington, D.C., confessing: "Having grown to love Washington in the years I had spent there in the 1930s and 1940s, I got a kind of thrill every time I returned in the period that followed; a thrill composed of both nostalgia for the past and a sense of oneness with the life, energy, and hum of accomplishment of this seat of the greatest government ever devised by the ingenuity of man, with the blessings of God."[20]

The Committee of 1976 Drafts Benson for President

Throughout the early 1960s, Benson enhanced his national reputation as a forceful advocate for far-right conservatism through his involvement with the John Birch Society—a militantly anti-communist, anti–civil rights organization. This highly controversial organization founded in 1958 by Massachusetts candy manufacturer Robert W. Welch Jr. attracted a significant following during the turbulent 1960s. The Birch Society at its peak claimed more than 100,000 members.[21] Among the most noteworthy of these were billionaire businessman Fred Koch—a founding member—and his sons, David and Charles.[22] Other prominent members included Texas Oil mogul Nelson Bunker Hunt, radio-television evangelist Billy James Hargis, and three members of the U.S. House of Representatives—Edgar Hiestand, John H. Rousselot, and John G. Schimitz, all from California.[23]

Benson's involvement with the Birch Society commenced in 1961 upon meeting Robert Welch. The two forged a congenial relationship, the Mormon apostle embracing Welch as a mentor and personal friend, although Benson never formally joined the Society.[24] His sons Reed and Mark did join, along with Ezra's wife, Flora. Reed became an important Birch leader, initially as Utah Society coordinator and ultimately as its national director of public relations.[25]

Meanwhile, Ezra Taft Benson asserted himself as an outspoken Birch advocate, vigorously promoting the Society's ideology and agenda at public

gatherings both within and outside the LDS community. Active on the lec-
ture circuit, Benson spoke to audiences not just in Utah, but throughout the
United States. In provocative presentations over the following five years, he
excoriated the civil rights movement as "phony" and "part of the pattern for
the Communist takeover of America."[26] An ardent foe of both an expanding
federal government and the Soviet Union, he extolled the John Birch Society
as "the most effective non-church organization in our fight against creeping
socialism and godless Communism."[27]

Benson's "unrelenting effort to obtain or imply LDS endorsement of the
John Birch Society" created divisions, indeed conflict within the LDS church
hierarchy. In promoting his agenda, Benson found support among at least two
of his fellow apostles, Delbert L. Stapley and Le Grand Richards. More important, the assertive apostle secured the tacit approval of President McKay—by
this time in declining health and diminished mental capacity, convincing the
ailing leader to endorse a number of his controversial statements and related
actions.[28]

By contrast Benson found himself at odds with others in the church hierarchy, apostles Harold B. Lee, Mark E. Peterson, Joseph Fielding Smith,
and Hugh B. Brown—the latter elevated to the First Presidency in 1961.[29]
Lee denounced Benson's "sewing [sic] of the seeds of hatred, suspicion and
contention [as] destructive of the purpose of life and unbecoming to the
children of God." Peterson, even more direct in an editorial carried in the
LDS church–owned and operated Deseret News, proclaimed that the church
"had nothing to do with racists, nothing to do with Birchers, nothing to do
with any slanted group."[30] Brown took direct aim at Benson, urging his BYU
audience to reject "extremists and self-styled patriots who label all those
who disagree with them as Communists." He expressed disdain for those
"individuals [that is, Benson and his surrogates who] ascribe to the Church
personal beliefs which they entertain."[31]

Such attacks notwithstanding, a concerted effort was underway to lure Benson back into the political arena. In late 1965 J. Reese Hunter, a prominent Salt
Lake City optometric physician–businessman and John Birch Society activist,
formed a "Benson for President" committee.[32] Concurrently, Benson met with
President McKay on October 21, 1965, informing him of his political aspirations.
The apostle stated that "a very prominent man who represented a large group
of Americans . . . strongly in favor of freedom and preserving . . . conservative
government" sought "his support [in their] movement to preserve freedom and
to develop a conservative attitude and conservative government in the hopes
we could stem the tide of socialism softness toward communism." Benson
declined to "divulge the name of this man because it was so confidential."[33]

McKay inquired how the movement would promote its agenda. Benson answered that the individual representing this shadowy group wanted the Mormon apostle to contact and enlist the support of anti–civil rights U.S Senator Strom Thurmond of South Carolina. Together the two hard-right conservatives would take their message throughout the United States hoping they could get it into the 1968 Republican Convention. Failing that, they might be compelled "to start a third party." Benson asserted that, "he did not care to get into politics, but he thought the Church should take a stand, that if someone did not do something it would be completely useless." McKay expressed skepticism concerning Benson's possible association with a third party, characterizing any such effort "completely useless." McKay, however, advised Benson "to go ahead and make further inquiry and do what he thought was right."[34]

Benson deliberately concealed from McKay the role of the John Birch Society in this undertaking, which was not surprising given that the Society was perceived as an extremist organization by many Latter-day Saints, as well as certain members of the church's ruling hierarchy.[35] Just two years earlier, in January 1963, the First Presidency proclaimed in an official statement: "We deplore that presumption of some politicians, especially officers, coordinators, and members of the John Birch Society, who undertake to align the Church or its leadership with their political views."[36]

As for Benson's October meeting with McKay, the Mormon apostle gave a somewhat different account in his own written version recorded some six months later. He characterized their earlier discussion as "most important and highly confidential," allegedly telling McKay that he had been "informed by two or three prominent Americans that a movement was under way to set up a non-partisan committee to try and stem the drift toward socialism in this country and to draft Senator Strom Thurmond and me as candidates for the Vice-Presidency and Presidency respectively." Benson claimed that he "expressed serious concern and tried to dissuade them from using my name, but without success. I then tried to get them to put Senator Thurmond first and my name second, also without success. I immediately discussed this with President McKay who said, 'Do not withdraw your name. Let them go ahead and we shall see what develops.'" Benson further stated, "President McKay gave his wholehearted approval to the effort of this bi-partisan Committee."[37]

Six months later in an April 16, 1966, meeting with President McKay, Benson told of his involvement with a just-formed organization—the 1976 Committee, which he characterized as "non-partisan" and designed to "stem the drift towards socialism in this country" by drafting Benson for president and Strom Thurmond for vice president. The Committee

consisted of "prominent men from all over the country."[38] Benson further
noted its Chicago meeting on April 30, where it would urge that "all conservative Americans of both parties demand the immediate nomination and
election of" Benson for president and Thurmond vice president. Benson
then shared with McKay a public statement he intended to issue following
the Committee's Chicago meeting. It stated:

> I approve of [the Committee's] general purpose, as I understand them, and am
> of course complimented and humbled by its specific reference to me. But this
> does not in any way make me a candidate for any public office. So I feel that
> it would be inappropriate and even presumptuous for me to accept any of the
> responsibilities of a candidate. It will be my policy, therefore, not to answer
> questions or to comment on current events and developments, at any time, or
> in any way that my remarks would justifiably be construed as being political
> in nature. If and when, in later months or years, whether because of public
> demands created by The 1976 Committee, or due to other causes, I should
> become a candidate for public office, I shall be glad to accept a candidate's role
> and discuss my views freely and frankly concerning all relevant matters on all
> suitable occasions.[39]

President McKay expressed initial skepticism, commenting, "it would not
be wise to start a third party." The Mormon apostle replied that "he was also
opposed to this," quickly adding that the movement might "result in a re-
alignment between the two [major] parties." Thus reassured, McKay declared
"that this nation is rapidly moving down the road of self-destroying socialism,
and that I hoped and prayed that the efforts of the 1976 Committee would
be successful in stemming the tide . . . I told Elder Benson not to withdraw
his name, to let them [the Committee] go ahead and see what develops." At
Benson's urging, the Mormon leader went a step further—crafting a written
statement of his own in support of Benson, such to be made public at an
"appropriate time." It declared:

> I have been informed of the interest of many prominent Americans in a move-
> ment to draft Ezra Taft Benson for the Presidency. It appears that this is gaining
> momentum and is definitely crystallizing into a formal draft movement. Elder
> Benson has discussed this with me and to whatever extent he may wish to
> become receptive to this movement, his doing so has my full approval.
>   May the Lord bless you in all of your patriotic endeavors to help preserve
> our inspired Constitution and our liberties.[40]

McKay's statement was designed to forestall criticism from those general
authorities, both in the First Presidency and Council of the Twelve, nervous

about Benson's activities with the 1976 Committee and its efforts to draft him for president.[41]

Not disclosed by Benson during his crucial April 16 meeting with McKay was the 1976 Committee's status as a front organization for the John Birch Society. The Committee deliberately played down the Society's direct involvement, stating "every effort should be made to avoid [a John Birch] label."[42] Among the individuals present at that meeting were a number who held positions within the Birch Society, specifically William J. Grede, Fred Koch, Thomas J. Anderson, and Clarence Manion. Grede, a longtime Birch Society stalwart, indeed, one of its founders, became the Committee's permanent chairman.[43] The Committee's effort to conceal Birch involvement proved less than successful. Indeed, the *Deseret News* noted in a May 3, 1966, story shortly after the Committee's formation that half of its organizers claimed membership in the Society.[44]

The 1976 Committee, in a detailed position paper issued shortly after its formation, forcefully outlined its immediate and long-range goals. Its ultimate goal, reflective of its name, involved "A Ten-Year Crusade to Restore the American Republic." The Committee sought to stop the "gradual surrender of American sovereignty into the grasp of a cruel worldwide tyranny," that is, communism. It further promised to lead the charge "to halt and reverse" America's "insidious" movement toward "police-state socialism."[45]

On an immediate level, the Committee sought to fill "the present leadership void" within the conservative movement resulting from conservative Republican Senator Barry Goldwater's overwhelming defeat in the 1964 presidential election.[46] Thus its first task involved restoring "confidence in the Conservative leadership." To accomplish this the Committee looked ahead to the presidential election of 1968. It proposed a "two-man team" consisting of Benson for president and Thurmond for vice president. The Committee expressed confidence that the duo could "be persuaded and drafted into making an active campaign together for the two top positions in the American government—if enough of us make clear our belief that their political leadership offers the one best remaining chance of saving our country . . . from subjugation and enslavement by the worldwide Communist tyranny." Further defining its ambitious goal, the Committee proposed that "all Conservative Americans, of both parties, begin demanding immediately the nomination and election of the Honorable Ezra Taft Benson and Senator Strom Thurmond . . . And that this demand be continued and increased into so mighty roar that, by 1968, this expression of the will of the American people simply cannot be ignored."[47]

Commencing in early May 1966, the 1976 Committee's effort to draft Benson generated extensive media coverage. Through the pages of the *Deseret
News*, Benson claimed to be "shocked" by the committee's proposal—"It's
the first time I've heard of it."[48] To the *Salt Lake Tribune*, Benson was more
forthright. In a formal statement released to the press, Benson endorsed
the Committee's "general principles" and claimed to be "complimented and
humbled" by efforts to unite conservatives "behind him as a presidential
candidate." He further proclaimed, quoting from his previously prepared
statement: "It would be inappropriate and even presumptuous for me to
accept any of the responsibilities [as] a candidate." It continued, "if or when
. . . because of public demand . . . or due to other causes, I should become
a candidate for public office, I shall then be glad to accept a candidate's role
and discuss my views freely and frankly concerning all relevant matters on
all suitable occasions."[49]

The national media also took note of the 1976 Committee's actions. In a
comparatively low-key article the *New York Times*, while noting the Committee's formation, stated that Benson himself "would not comment on a
possible candidacy at this time."[50] The *Wall Street Journal*, in a more in-depth
August 1966 article entitled "Mormons & Politics," characterized Benson a
"dark horse" candidate and potential rival to a fellow Mormon, Michigan
governor George Romney—widely considered a front-runner for the 1968
Republican nomination. The article contrasted the two men's differing ideologies, characterizing Benson as "deeply conservative" standing in stark
contrast to the more moderate Romney.[51] Syndicated conservative newspaper
columnist Dan Smoot gave the fledgling campaign extensive coverage.[52]

Over the next year and a half, Benson briefed President McKay on a regular
basis. He updated the Mormon leader in a May 14, 1966, meeting, immediately following public disclosure of the 1976 Committee's formation, extolling
the "good coverage regarding it."[53] McKay, in turn, indicated his continuing
support, declaring in the wake of a May 28 meeting, "the country needs
strong, conservative, spiritual leadership, as it has never needed it before in
our day."[54]

One month later, on June 24, Benson again met with President McKay,
providing a highly optimistic report concerning the Committee's activities.
He noted that William Grede, its chairman, had received more than five
hundred letters in support, and that the Committee had expanded its operations into two offices—one in Des Plaines, Illinois, and the second in
Holland, Michigan. Benson also informed McKay that Charles R. Sligh Jr., a
successful Grand Rapids, Michigan, furniture manufacturer, agreed to serve
as Committee executive vice chairman. Benson also pressed the Mormon

leader to release his previously drafted statement of support to the press. He went so far as to suggest concurrent publication of it in the LDS "Church News" section of the *Deseret News*. McKay demurred, but did agree to make a copy available to the officers of the 1976 Committee "to reassure them that if the draft movement does develop I would be free to become receptive to the movement . . . and in doing so would have [McKay's] full approval."[55]

Some four months later, on October 31, McKay again met with Benson. Also present were the 1976 Committee's two top leaders, William Grede and Charles Sligh, who had traveled to Salt Lake City. The two presented to McKay "the plan and purpose of the 1976 Committee and their determination to draft Elder Benson for the Presidency of the United States."[56] At the same time, Grede frankly revealed to McKay his dual role as chairman of the executive committee of the John Birch Society.[57] McKay, apparently unfazed by this disclosure, affirmed to Grede and Sligh his continuing support, hoping "their effort to get the country back to the basic concepts embodies in the Constitution would be successful."[58]

Immediately following the October 31 meeting, McKay authorized public release of his supportive statement for the movement to draft Ezra Taft Benson.[59] Sligh promptly wrote the Mormon leader, praising him for "permission to quote" from his statement. He then extolled Benson as "ideally fitted for the Presidency. . . . He is a man of high principles and unquestioned integrity, and is one who can be trusted to follow his conscience in doing his best to serve this great country of ours." Sligh further added, "The 1976 Committee plans to do everything in its power to assure Brother Benson of the nomination for the office of the presidency." He extolled the Mormon leader, "It is especially gratifying to know you join us in recognition of his outstanding qualities which would make his nomination a benefit to the nation."[60] Sligh, in using the term "nomination" to describe their efforts to promote Benson's fledgling candidacy, reassured McKay of the Committee's intent to work within the framework of the Republican Party, thus avoiding formation of a third party.

Committee chairman Grede followed up with his own letter to McKay likewise thanking him, characterizing his statement "as evidence of [McKay's] approval." Grede further described it as "an important step for you to take and we realize that it was done only because of your deep conviction about and your dedication to the principles of your Church and this great nation of ours." He further reminded McKay of his leadership position in the John Birch Society, which he asserted was dedicated to the same principles in fighting Communism as the LDS church.[61]

Benson continued to update McKay on the Committee's activities. In conferring with the Mormon leader on January 6, he described Committee's progress in convening a meeting in Chicago later that month to promote the "Draft Benson" movement. He pointed with pride to the Committee's distribution of automobile bumper stickers with "Benson for President and Thurmond for Vice-President—1968."[62]

In a crucial March 22 meeting, Benson conferred with McKay on two matters. The first involved a further update on his fledgling candidacy. He declared that he was "receiving many hundreds of letters from . . . various parts of the country, and that the Committee is receiving about one hundred per day." Benson also reassured McKay of the Committee's intention to continue working within "the two-party political system."[63]

The second issue involved Benson's request for permission to serve on the council of the John Birch Society. Although Benson had not formally joined the Society, Robert Welch wanted the Mormon apostle on its council. One month earlier Welch, in fact, had written McKay a twelve-page "personal and confidential" letter pleading for permission to allow Benson to serve.[64] After careful consideration, McKay determined that "now was not the appropriate time [for Benson] to become a member of the Council."[65]

This did not end the matter. Benson along with Welch persisted in efforts to secure McKay's approval to allow the Mormon apostle to serve on the Birch council. Welch traveled to Salt Lake City in late April to meet with the Mormon leader. In their April 18 face-to-face meeting, which included Benson, Welch read McKay a lengthy letter in which he articulated the reasons why Benson be allowed to serve. Again, the Mormon leader replied, "It would not be wise for Elder Benson to serve in this capacity."[66]

Meanwhile, Benson continued working closely with the 1976 Committee in promoting his fledgling presidential bid. On April 19 Benson met with both Robert Welch and William Grede to form "policy positions" for Benson's campaign.[67] The Committee distributed some 330,000 copies of its official "1976 Committee Booklet" touting the Benson–Thurmond ticket.[68] The Committee reached out to potential donors both large and small—soliciting funds ranging in amounts from $10 up to $1,000. It sought to expand its original Committee consisting of thirty directors to its announced goal of one hundred, hoping to recruit at least one from each of the fifty states.[69] Benson involved himself in this process, suggesting a number of prominent conservatives for membership.[70] Organizers also sought to organize affiliated groups known as 1976 Clubs and Supporters of the 1976 Committee.[71]

All such activities notwithstanding, the 1976 Committee encountered significant difficulties, leading to its ultimate demise by August 1967. Its most basic problem was a lack of adequate funding. The organization could not raise "sufficient funds to pursue any active program in the political field," such deficiency noted by Benson himself.[72] Committee treasurer Charles M. Sligh Jr. stated that the organization lacked the funds "to obtain needed publicity." By mid-1967 the Committee had an accumulated debt of some $1,500, compelling it to lay off its full-time staff.[73]

Also hurting the cause were persistent questions relative to Benson's viability as a candidate—such reservations expressed both within and outside the LDS community. As early as June 1965, Utah's senior United States senator, Wallace F. Bennett, indicated concern about "unfavorable action [*sic*] within the [LDS] Church in connection with the program of the 1976 Committee."[74]

Expressing greater concern was Hugh B. Brown, first counselor in the First Presidency, doing so during a December 13, 1966, meeting of the First Presidency. Discussion involved a basic question: Did President McKay approve of the 1976 Committee's effort to draft Benson?—this coming to a head as a result of the Mormon leader's recently released statement of support. Brown, "disturbed" about this, directly asked McKay "Whether or not Elder's Benson's proposed candidacy" had McKay's "approval." In response, McKay confessed: "Not remembering at that moment that I had given full permission for Elder Benson to stand ready to enter into this movement should circumstances permit, and said that I had not approved, but later recalled the whole matter and that Elder Benson had talked to me about the whole matter, and that I had given him permission to participate in the movement should it come to a point where he was drafted into it."[75]

Two months later in a February 15, 1967, meeting of the First Presidency, the topic of President McKay's approval of Benson's candidacy was again the focus of discussion. President N. Eldon Tanner, also in the First Presidency, "mentioned that the policy as he understood it [was] that no one of the General Authorities should seek a political nomination without the approval of the President of the Church." President McKay sought to clarify his position on this matter, stating that, "the sentiment was expressed that while I had given Brother Benson permission to become receptive to the nomination, it had not come to the point where any draft movement had been made and that we would meet that when it came."[76]

Further questioning Benson's suitability as a presidential candidate were non-Mormon conservatives, including members of the 1976 Committee. U.S. Congressman Durward G. Hall of Missouri frankly stated, "I seriously question the . . . selection of Ezra Taft Benson to head any ticket."[77] Likewise, William Benton McMillan, a charter 1976 Committee member, was equally blunt. The Mormon apostle generated "little enthusiasm," with McMillan questioning Benson's "stature," thus dismissing his "political significance [as] inadequate."[78] A second Committee member, Howard E. Kershner,

expressed reservations about "an all-out endorsement of Secretary Benson and Senator Thurmond," recommending, instead, Ronald Reagan as
"a much stronger candidate."[79] Charles W. Briggs, a prominent Minnesota
lawyer, pointed to potential problems involving the candidate's LDS faith.
Specifically, he noted the potential for "serious schism" within Mormonism,
given "pronounced differences in political thinking" between conservatives as represented by Benson and moderates who identified with George
Romney.[80] E. J. Presser, a Charlotte, North Carolina, advertising executive, labeled the selection of both Benson and Thurmond as "impractical,"
predicting that "Benson will be smeared by" his son "Reed Benson's John
Birch Society activities" and that "Thurmond will have the segregationist
albatross hung around his neck."[81]

Actually, Strom Thurmond's candidacy caused other unforeseen problems. Thurmond himself proved less than enthusiastic as the Committee's
vice presidential choice. Thurmond's major concern throughout most of
1966 involved his ongoing reelection campaign to the United States Senate,
running for the first time as a Republican. Thurmond had abandoned his
longtime affiliation with the Democratic Party in 1964 to support Republican conservative Barry Goldwater for president and to emphasize his
opposition to the landmark 1964 Civil Rights Act. Thurmond, in fact, had
a history of changing political affiliation, extending back to 1948 when as
South Carolina's segregationist governor, he abandoned the Democratic
Party to run for U.S. president as the nominee of the newly formed states'
rights Democratic "Dixiecrat" Party. Thurmond subsequently switched back
to the Democratic Party, this facilitating his election to the U.S. Senate in
1954.[82]

Thurmond was thus leery about his association with the 1976 Committee,
which fellow South Carolinians could well perceive as an incipient third-
party effort. In May 1967 the *Washington Observer Newsletter* reported that
"Senator Strom Thurmond had cracked down hard on the 1976 Committee,"
forbidding "further use of his name" as their vice presidential choice.[83] A
Committee official attributed Thurmond's actions to his desire to present
himself as "a favorite-son candidate [for president] from the southern states"
at the forthcoming 1968 Republican Convention.[84] By August 1967 Thurmond
had completely disassociated himself from the Committee's efforts. In fact
he declared, albeit inaccurately, "at no time have I ever associated myself"
with the Committee, further adding, "It was impossible for me to disassoci-
ate myself from the 1976 Committee since I was never associated with the
Committee."[85]

Benson also cooled toward his own potential candidacy. In January 1967 he expressed reluctance to declare himself a candidate, wanting to wait "until there is more grass roots pressure for a draft."[86] Benson revealed other concerns. The following month he wrote Chairman Grede, complaining about deficiencies in the Committee's operation. Benson pointed to the "increasing number of letters" he received from potential supporters who failed to receive requested literature and related campaign materials. Benson found perplexing the Committee's lack of response given that these individuals appeared "anxious to work" for and to put "money into the project."[87] Thus Benson continued to hold back from formally declaring his candidacy right up to the time of the Committee's formal demise.[88]

Further contributing to Benson's reluctance "to get into the battle" was the "mixed up . . . political situation" as he described it to President McKay in an August 8 meeting.[89] A myriad of would-be candidates for the nation's highest office were already jockeying for position in anticipation of the 1968 election. Two of these were potential rivals. One was fellow Mormon George W. Romney, whose ongoing presidential campaign placed potential Latter-day Saints backers in a dilemma. President McKay made no secret of his enthusiasm for the Michigan governor. The second was fellow conservative George C. Wallace, Alabama's controversial, segregationist former governor promoting his own candidacy on a self-styled third-party ticket—the American Independent Party.[90] Benson publicly endorsed Wallace immediately following the demise of his own campaign.[91]

Benson Seeks the American Independent Party's Vice Presidential Nomination

George Wallace, within days of formally announcing his candidacy in February 1968, actively sought Benson as his vice-presidential running mate. Benson, in turn, proved eager to accept. At Wallace's request, Benson traveled to Montgomery, Alabama, in February 1968 to meet with the former Alabama governor. Following a three-and-a-half-hour meeting, Benson "became satisfied with Governor Wallace's concepts and determinations concerning the operation of the federal government." Benson, "favorably impressed" with Wallace, informed the governor of his willingness to run, but "only if President McKay would give permission."[92] To facilitate this process, Wallace wrote McKay a personal, confidential letter requesting that the Mormon president grant his "permission and blessings." In it Wallace praised Benson's "many devoted years" of service to "his church and his Nation," labeling the

Mormon apostle "a patriot." Wallace then stated: "My philosophy and that of Mr. Benson are consistent and compatible," concluding that Benson's "service could only lend dignity to a concerted effort to offer the American people a basic choice in 1968."[93]

Benson acted on his own in seeking McKay's approval, preparing a detailed paper outlining "the political viewpoints of George C. Wallace." Benson presented a list of thirteen basic issues on which he and Wallace agreed. Among the most noteworthy were a common antipathy toward communism, opposition to "big government," and support for states' rights. Benson also addressed the critical issue of Wallace's status as a third-party candidate—of particular concern to McKay, who had repeatedly expressed his skepticism about third parties. Benson presented his case, arguing against the existing two-party system. He outlined four major complaints. First, there was nothing in the Constitution "to control or suggest the number or the nature of political parties." Second, there was "nothing in our experience to prove or even indicate that the two-party system is in any way superior to the multi-party of European Parliamentary governments." Third, Benson referred to an alleged prophecy of Joseph Smith in which the Mormon prophet "predicted that following the establishment of the two present parties that an Independent American Party would arise." And finally, Benson restated his basic argument that with "both major parties increasingly embracing more socialist philosophies" and given "the communists' . . . great influence in both present parties . . . patriots in both of these parties are looking for a means where their views can be properly represented," specifically "an independent organization."[94]

Benson also sought the help of First Presidency counselor Alvin R. Dyer in approaching McKay. Dyer, however, expressed both ambivalence and anxiety over Wallace's offer to Benson, admitting that he "did not want to become set against [it] neither did I want to indicate . . . that I favored it." Rather, Dyer urged Benson to go to McKay "with the facts both positive and negative, and in no way attempt to influence him in the decision which Elder Benson sought." But at the same time Dyer manifested some skepticism concerning Benson's basic motives. Dyer pointedly asked Benson if his effort was "simply" the product of a "desire to get back into public life." The Mormon apostle "answered that it was not" and that he was only interested in serving "his country in helping to turn the trend away from Socialism."[95]

On February 13 Dyer arranged a preliminary meeting between himself and McKay just prior to Benson's own scheduled meeting. Dyer told McKay that "Wallace was seeking the office of President . . . on a 3rd party ticket, and that if Elder Benson ran with him it would be on a 3rd party effort. The president almost immediately said he opposed a 3rd party set up." Dyer also outlined other factors mitigating against Benson's candidacy. These included "the Negro situation" and use of a "non-authenticated prophecy" attributed to Joseph Smith "concerning a third party."[96] He also pointed to George Romney's own candidacy for president, expressing concern about the effect "upon the Church" of having Benson as "a member of the Quorum of the Twelve with apparent Church approval" running against a fellow Mormon.[97]

Thus, when Benson met with McKay in early February, the Mormon leader appeared less than enthusiastic. Nevertheless, Benson "spoke of his great desire to serve his country," further declaring "that . . . after meeting with George C. Wallace and questioning him and receiving his views concerning the needs of the Country, he would be willing to accept the invitation of Governor Wallace to run with him . . . but only if it met with President McKay's approval and blessing." After discussing the various pros and cons, Benson asked McKay, "President, what is your decision?" McKay clearly uttered, "You should turn the offer down."[98] As Benson later recalled, McKay told him that such a campaign would be "very lively and controversial" and "felt that my being on the ticket would cause me to be criticized and possibly the Church also."[99] This settled the matter, but only temporarily.

Wallace, denied his first choice, was forced to look elsewhere for a suitable running mate. This task proved much more difficult than expected. Over the next seven months, the Wallace Campaign through its aides approached a number of potential candidates. Among the most prominent was FBI director J. Edger Hoover, who did not "even deign to respond" to Wallace's discreet inquiries. Also considered was Colonel Sanders of Kentucky Fried Chicken fame. In June Wallace surrogates sounded out several conservative U.S. senators and congressmen, none of whom were "even politely interested."[100]

Later the same month, campaign operatives approached A. B. (Happy) Chandler—a one-time Kentucky governor, former U.S. senator, and later Major League Baseball commissioner. Upon initial examination, Chandler appeared an ideal choice, even though his position on various issues, including race, was more moderate than that of Wallace. Nevertheless, Wallace signed off on Chandler in early August. The Kentuckian expressed his willingness to join the ticket. However, when rumors of Chandler's selection reached the press, hard-right activists within the Wallace campaign expressed outrage. Particularly upset were members of the John Birch Society, who had assumed a prominent role in the Wallace campaign. Among the most vocal was Bunker Hunt, who convinced Wallace to drop Chandler. Hunt, in turn, urged Wallace to make a second attempt to convince Ezra Taft Benson to join the ticket.[101]

Thus, in early September 1968, Wallace renewed his offer to Benson. Additional pressure to place Benson on the American Independent Party ballot came from other influential conservative spokesmen. Among the most prominent was Clarence Manion—a key figure in Benson's earlier, unsuccessful presidential effort through his role as a charter member of the 1976 Committee.[102] A number of similar-minded individuals also approached Benson. Wallace asserted that the Mormon apostle was "still [his first] choice." Several states, including Idaho, Arizona, and Nevada, "had arbitrarily placed [Benson's] name on" the American Independent Party ticket as Wallace's running mate, acting on the instructions of American Independent Party conventions in those states.[103]

As before, First Presidency counselor Alvin R. Dyer acted as an intermediary in a hastily called September 9, 1968 meeting with the frail, ailing ninety-five-year-old Mormon leader, who by this time was under the care of a full-time nurse. Benson was not present, with Dyer presenting his case. Dyer indicated to McKay that when the Mormon president had rejected Benson's earlier request to run, George Romney "was still active in seeking the Republican nomination . . . and that this may have had some bearing on" McKay's refusal. By this time, the Michigan governor was no longer a candidate. Dyer further stated that Benson, himself, "was not pressing the issue. He wants only to serve his Country, but over and above all, to be directed by the Prophet of the Lord."[104]

Again, McKay rejected Benson's request. The Mormon president "was quite spontaneous in his decision that he had not changed from his original feeling," according to Dyer. Allowing Benson to run, McKay stated, "could lead to confusion and misunderstanding in the Church." In this, the Mormon leader was clearly alluding to the controversy that a Benson candidacy as George Wallace's running mate was certain to generate among the church's rank-and-file membership. On a practical level, McKay also "expressed himself in saying that Mr. Wallace could not win." He concluded with a rhetorical question: "Where would that leave Elder Benson?"[105]

Benson, when informed of McKay's decision later that same day, reportedly stated: "I feel relieved and will abide by the counsel of the President."[106] The following day, on September 10 at a nationally televised news conference, George C. Wallace announced as his vice-presidential running mate retired United States Air Force general Curtis LeMay. Benson supported the ticket, helping to raise funds, putting Wallace in touch with potential donors, and arranging for the former Alabama governor to campaign in Utah and for his running mate Curtis LeMay to speak at BYU.[107]

LeMay himself proved a less-than-effective candidate, generating controversy of his own. Specifically, the former general supported the use of
tactical nuclear weapons to fight the ongoing Vietnam War. The selection
of Le May, in the words of veteran political observer Theodore H. White,
proved "a turning-point blunder" and "error-in-decision," further facilitating
the failure of Wallace's quest for the presidency.[108] In the 1968 presidential
election, the Wallace–LeMay American Independent Party ticket received
9.9 million votes, representing 13.5 percent of the popular vote and forty-six
electoral votes—the best showing for a third party since the Progressive Party
in 1912.[109]

Some eight years later, extreme right-wing activists tried to coax Benson
back into the political arena. In 1976 a conservative organization known as
Concerned Citizens Party offered the Mormon apostle its nomination for
president. This party was a coalition of former members of George Wallace's
American Independent Party and LDS members of the John Birch Society.
They claimed to be dedicated to "individual rights under the Constitution,"
proposing "to bring God back into government."[110] Benson declined the Concerned Citizens Party offer, with a firm "No to Politics."[111] Shortly thereafter, a
second conservative organization, a "resurrected 1976 Committee," promoted
an effort to run Benson as a vice-presidential candidate on a conservative
party ticket with its proposed presidential candidate John Connolly—a one-
time Texas governor and former U.S. treasury secretary. Again Benson declined, stating, "It is of course, impractical and impossible."[112]

Conclusion

In assessing the significance of Ezra Taft Benson as a presidential contender,
four facts stand out. First, Benson was, without question, the most politically
active Mormon Church president since Joseph Smith. Smith and Benson are
the only two Mormon presidents who also aspired to become president of the
United States. Like the first Mormon prophet, Benson was both interested
and involved in politics throughout his adult life.[113]

Second, Benson, in manifesting a strong conservative position on political
issues, represented a reaction against the more liberal beliefs and practices
manifested within other religious denominations and the larger American
society, particularly during the 1960s. The Mormon Church, in eschewing
the civil rights movement and other forms of protest, stood in sharp contrast
to various other denominations promoting and practicing social activism.
Benson pointed to Mormonism's political and theological conservatism as a

major reason for the church's growth, pointing to a sharp 65 percent increase in membership during the decade from 1956 to 1966.[114]

Third, Benson's strong antipathy toward the civil rights movement brought the Mormon Church increased unwelcome attention relative to its controversial policy of black priesthood denial. By the late 1960s and into the early 1970s, Latter-day Saint officials found themselves under increased pressure to repeal this antiblack practice.[115] This issue, moreover, entered the political arena, as Mormon candidates for state and national office were confronted about this—the most prominent of these George Romney and Morris Udall. Ultimately the 1978 revelation providing for the ordination of "all worthy males" to the Mormon priesthood effectively removed the issue from the political arena.

Finally, Benson, in speaking out on political issues and venturing into the political arena, breached the so-called wall of separation between church and state, considered unassailable by many if not most Americans before 1980. Benson asserted the right, indeed the duty, of the church to speak out on political issues. He stated that "while it might not be popular, a prophet is qualified to speak out on civic affairs. . . . The world prefers prophets that . . . mind their own business" or "want the prophet to be still on politics . . . [but] those who would remove prophets from politics would take God out of government."[116] Benson's statement, while referring directly to the Mormon Church president in using the term "prophet," was undoubtedly also asserting the right of other Mormon Church leaders, including himself, to speak out on political matters. In a larger sense Benson, in defending his own political activism, anticipated the emergence of the Moral Majority and Religious Right, who would vigorously promote their own agenda in the political arena after 1980.

Notes

1. Sheri L. Dew, *Ezra Taft Benson: A Biography* (Salt Lake City: Deseret Book, 1987) and Frances Gibbons, *Ezra Taft Benson: Statesman, Patriot, Prophet of God* (Salt Lake City: Bookcraft, 1996) provide an uncritical perspective on the life and times of the Mormon leader. More critical is D. Michael Quinn in two works, "Ezra Taft Benson and Mormon Political Conflicts," *Dialogue: A Journal of Mormon Thought* 26, no.2 (Summer 1993): 1–87, and in *The Mormon Hierarchy: Extensions of Power* (Salt Lake City: Signature Books, 1997), 66–115. Ezra Taft Benson, *Cross Fire: The Eight Years with Eisenhower* (New York: Doubleday, 1962) provides an autobiographical perspective on Benson's turbulent tenure as secretary of agriculture.

2. Theodore H. White, *The Making of the President, 1960* (New York: Anthenum, 1961) is the classic account of that watershed election campaign.

3. Benson, *Cross Fire*, 407–8.

4. David O McKay journal, March 5, 1960, Bx 45, fd 2, David O. McKay Papers, Special Collections, Marriott Library, University of Utah.

5. David O. McKay journal, April 6, 1960, Bx 45, fd 3, ibid.

6. Benson provided a somewhat different version of his discussions with President McKay, as published in his 1962 memoir, *Cross Fire*, 519. In their March 5 meeting, Benson asserts he "Outlined the political situation as I saw it, including the undertone of doubt and fear that seemed to be growing regarding the Vice President [Nixon] and his leadership; I also mentioned the increasing evidence of support to make myself available for further service in the government, support from individuals as well as groups, usually by word of mouth. I made it plain I had no aspirations, whatever for political office. Following these preliminary remarks Reed [Benson] made an excellent presentation of the entire issue." In response McKay allegedly said, "The country needed more patriots and real statesman. . . . Finally he suggested that we watch this developing groundswell closely for the next few weeks and if we did, we should have the answer by the time of our Church conference in April." In a June 25, 1962 "Memorandum" Benson directed to Clare Middlemiss entitled "Crossfire, The Eight Years with Eisenhower," he provided further details of what was allegedly discussed in his March 5 and subsequent April 6 meetings with McKay. Benson raised the possibility of being the vice presidential nominee on a Rockefeller presidential ticket. Specifically, Benson stated, "On March 5, 1960, Reed and I had a visit with President McKay during which we reviewed the political situation, the increasing evidence of support for me to give further service in the government and to reaffirm the fact that I have no political ambitions." McKay allegedly replied as follows: "If it should come to pass, he [McKay] said, 'Governor Rockefeller and Brother Benson would be a great team. We are all proud of the way you have stood for principle—but then had to do this to be true to your father and grandfather.'" "A month later at the April Conference . . . McKay and I talked again. . . . 'I sincerely hope Brother Benson' he [McKay] said 'That Governor Rockefeller will still be able to get into the race. And I have considered it all carefully and if the opportunity should come unsolicited for you to serve in a higher political post you will have the wholehearted support of all of us.'" Ezra Taft Benson memo to Claire Middlemiss, re: "Crossfire, The Eight Years with Eisenhower," June 25, 1962, David O. McKay journal, Bx 50, fd 3, David O. McKay Papers, Special Collections, Marriott Library, University of Utah.

7. For a discussion of Rockefeller's political activities, see Richard Norton Smith, *On His Own Terms: A Life of Nelson Rockefeller* (New York: Random House, 2014).

8. As recalled by Benson in *Cross Fire*, 518.

9. Ibid., 519–20.

10. Ibid., 520.

11. Telephone conversation between Ezra Taft Benson and David O. McKay, McKay journal, July 22, 1960, bx 45, fd 6, David O. McKay Papers, Special Collections, Marriott Library, University of Utah.

12. Ibid.

13. Benson, *Cross Fire*, 531–33.

14. Ibid., 538.

15. Ibid., 538, 541.

16. David O. McKay journal, September 21, 1960, Bx 46, fd 3, University of Utah.

17. David O. McKay journal, June 6, 1960, Bx 45, fd 5, ibid.

18. Ezra Taft Benson to Henry D. Moyle, November 17, 1960, reel 7, Ezra Taft Benson Papers, LDS Church History Library. In this correspondence, Benson expresses anger, stating "it has disturbed me that this 'widespread gossip' could go on without it being brought to my attention by you or someone else familiar with it. It would be very much appreciated and would help set the record straight by replacing rumor with facts, if you would give me in confidence the names of your principal informers. I'm sure you can understand how deeply it concerns me that among the brethren that I am interested in future political preferment than I am to returning to full-time service as a member of the Twelve. I am sure you can appreciate my earnest desire to clear up this false picture which may have be innocently painted." Two years earlier, fellow apostle Harold B. Lee expressed skepticism concerning Benson's involvement in government service, stating that the agriculture secretary "may be at the end of his rope," adding "that this may be the Lord's way of humbling him so that he could come home and properly take up his work as a member of the Council of the Twelve." Ernest L. Wilkinson journal, March 7, 1958, Bx 99, fd 6, L. Tom Perry Special Collections, Harold B. Lee Library, Brigham Young University. In a second entry later that same year, Wilkinson wrote, "Brother Benson's associates are of the opinion that it was a sad mistake for him to leave his active position as a member of the Council of the Twelve and [leave for] Washington D.C." Ernest L. Wilkinson journal, June 21–12.

19. Benson, *Cross Fire*, 544–45.

20. Ibid., 569.

21. D. J. Mulloy, *The World of the John Birch Society: Conspiracy, Conservatism, and the Cold War* (Nashville, Tenn.: Vanderbilt University Press, 2014) provides an overview of the rise of the John Birch Society during the 1960s and its subsequent decline during the following decades.

22. As noted by Jane Mayer in *Dark Money: The Hidden History of the Billionaires behind the Rise of the Radical Right* (New York: Doubleday, 2016), 38–43.

23. Mulloy, *World of the John Birch Society,* 23–24, 64, 90, 134.

24. Focusing Ezra Taft Benson's involvement with the organization is D. Michael Quinn in two works, "Ezra Taft Benson and Mormon Political Conflicts," *Dialogue: A Journal of Mormon Thought* 26 no. 2 (Summer 1993): 1–87, and *The Mormon Hierarchy: Extension of Power* (Salt Lake City: Signature Books, 1997), 66–115.

25. Quinn, *Mormon Hierarchy*, 68, 71. See also Ezra Taft Benson, *Title of Liberty: A Warning Voice*, compiled by Mark A. Benson (Salt Lake City: Deseret Book, 1964), 39.

26. Ibid., 58.

27. Ibid., 39.

28. Ibid., 66–96.

29. Ibid., 66–115.

30. *April 1966 Conference Report* (Salt Lake City: Church of Jesus Christ of Latter-day Saints, 1966), 64–65, 66, 67, 68; Petersen, "Politics and Religion," *Deseret News*, "Church News," March 26, 1966, 16.

31. As quoted in "Church Leader Rebuffs Self-Styled Patriots," *Ogden Standard-Examiner*, October 26, 1963.

32. As noted in a letter of William J. Grede to Reed A. Benson, July 20, 1967, Wm. J. Grede Papers, Bx 26, fd 2, Wisconsin Historical Society, Madison, Wisconsin. Also noted

in 1976 Committee "Statement to the Press" [n.d.] William. J. Grede Papers. J. Reese Hunter distinguished himself as a stalwart supporter of the John Birch Society over some three decades from the mid-1960s into the mid-1990s. His activities are chronicled in various Utah newspapers. See, for example, *Logan Herald Journal*, July 12, 1966; *Ephraim Enterprise*, March 3, 1967; *Manti Messenger*, March 3, 1967; *Utah Daily Chronicle*, July 7, 1968; and the *Deseret News*, October 22, 1991. A brief overview of Hunter's life and activities is contained in his obituary published in the *Salt Lake Tribune*, November 25, 2000.

33. "Memorandum" by Thorpe B. Isaacson, October 21, 1965, David O. McKay journal, Bx 61, fd 2.

34. Ibid.

35. Ibid.

36. "Church Sets Policy on Birch Society," *Deseret News*, January 4, 1963, B-1.

37. As recalled in Benson's own "Minutes" of a meeting held with President McKay, April 16, 1966, David O. McKay journal, Bx 62, fd 1, David O. McKay Papers.

38. Ibid. Among the "prominent men" listed by Benson were the following: "William Grede, Past President of the National Association of Manufacturers and former national President of the YMCA; the Honorable H. J. Hiestand, Six Term Congressman from California; Lloyd Wright, Past President, American Bar Association, and head of the largest law firm in Los Angeles; Admiral Ben Morell, head of Jones Laughlin Corporation." Not mentioned was involvement with the John Birch Society.

39. David O. McKay journal, April 16, 1966, Bx 62, fd 4, David O. McKay Papers.

40. Ibid.

41. Several senior apostles opposed Benson's candidacy. Joseph Fielding Smith, Benson's superior in the Quorum of the Twelve Apostles, told a reporter, "I want Benson to stay out of it. He has a greater calling in his church position." In Judy Hansen, "Drafted by '1976 Committee': Benson for President in 1968?" *Michigan Journal*, n.d., 1967, Bx 221, fd 1, Sterling M. McMurrin Papers, Special Collections, Marriott Library, University of Utah. When Hugh B. Brown learned that President McKay had supported Benson's desire to run for the presidency, he "was disturbed about this." As recounted in the First Presidency Minutes, December 13, 1966, David O. McKay journal, Bx 64, fd 1, David O. McKay Papers. See also Quinn, *Mormon Hierarchy*, 96–97.

42. "Minutes of the Organization Meeting of the 1976 Committee," Chicago, Illinois, April 10, 1966, Bx 26, fd 1, Wm. Grede Papers, Wisconsin Historical Society. Specifically, they stated: "It was emphasized that the 1976 Committee was a new and independent organization, not associated with any existing group efforts would be made to tag the Committee as another Birch group, or at least Birch dominated," adding that the Committee "make certain a substantial amount of the support of the Committee and its membership should be from non-Birchers."

43. Ibid.

44. "Presidential Draft for Elder Benson," *Deseret News*, May 3, 1966. Affirming the 1976 Committee's close association with the John Birch Society was Mary Welch, the wife of Robert Welch, who in a May 18, 1966 letter to the Mormon apostle warmly stated: "I am glad of this chance to write you to tell you how very much all of us appreciate your association with the 1976 Committee and we only hope that more and more people will come to know that they are being offered a choice other than the lesser of two evils. We

know and appreciate the courage your decision took." Mary Welch to Ezra Taft Benson, May 18, 1966, Ezra Taft Benson Correspondence, John Birch Society Headquarters.

45. "The 1976 Committee Booklet," 1966, Bx 74, fd 3, Wm. J. Grede Papers, Wisconsin Historical Society.

46. Robert Alan Goldberg, *Barry Goldwater* (New Haven, Conn.: Yale University Press, 1995) is the definitive work on the life and times of the conservative U.S. senator.

47. "The 1976 Committee Booklet."

48. "Presidential Draft for Elder Benson," *Deseret News*, May 3, 1966.

49. "Benson Hints Door Open in '68 Race, *Salt Lake Tribune*, May 4, 1966. Also see "Statement By the Honorable Ezra Taft Benson," as contained in David O. McKay journal, April 16, 1966.

50. "Benson is Sought for Ticket in '68," *New York Times*, May 8, 1966, 78.

51. Arlon J. Large, "Mormons and Politics: Benson's Influence Helps Keep Growing Church on Conservative Track," *Wall Street Journal*, August 8, 1966.

52. David O. McKay journal, May 14, 1966, Bx 63, fd 2, David O. McKay Papers.

53. Ibid.

54. "Minutes of a meeting with President McKay by Elder Ezra Taft Benson" as contained in David O. McKay journal, May 28, 1966.

55. "Minutes by Elder Ezra Taft Benson of meeting with David O. McKay" in David O. McKay journal, June 24, 1966, Bx 63, fd 2.

56. "1976 Committee-Visit of Messrs. William J. Grede and Charles R. Sligh, Jr.," as contained in David O. McKay journal, October 31, 1966, Bx 63, fd 6.

57. As noted in letter from William Grede to David O. McKay, November 11, 1966, as contained in David O. McKay journal, October 31, 1966, Bx 63, fd 6, David O. McKay Papers.

58. "1976 Committee-Visit of Messrs. William J. Grede and Charles R. Sligh, Jr.," as contained in David O. McKay journal, October 31, 1966.

59. "Statement by President David O. McKay," as contained in David O. McKay journal, April 16, 1966, and reprinted October 31, 1966.

60. Copy of letter from Charles R. Sligh Jr. to David O. McKay, November 1, 1966, Original in Benson, 1976 file, David O. McKay journal, November 1, 1966, Bx 63, fd 7.

61. Letter from William Grede to David O. McKay, November 11, 1966, as contained in David O. McKay journal, October 31, 1966, Bx 63, fd 6.

62. David O. McKay journal, January 6, 1967, Bx 64, fd 2.

63. David O. McKay journal, March 22, 1967, Bx 64, fd 4.

64. As described in David O. McKay journal, February 24, 1967, Bx 64, fd 3.

65. David O. McKay journal, March 22, 1967, Bx 64, fd 4.

66. David O. McKay journal, April 18, 1967, Bx 65, fd 1.

67. Robert Welch to William J. Grede, April 19, 1967, Box 26, fd 2, Wm. J. Grede Papers, Wisconsin Historical Society.

68. Glen G. Welker to Sam Stillwell, September 16, 1966; William J. Grede to Glen G. Velker, September 21, 1966; "Important Notice," October 11, 1966, Bx 26, fd 2.

69. "The 1976 Committee Booklet," 1966.

70. Charles R. Sligh Jr. to William J. Grede, June 19, 1966, Bx 26 fd 1, Wm J. Grede Papers, Wisconsin Historical Society. Among the individuals Benson suggested were former California U.S. Senator William F. Knowland, economist Milton Friedman, entertainer-

singer Pat Boone, radio personality J. Fulton Lewis, and Harding College president George Benson (no relation to the candidate).

71. "The 1976 Committee Booklet."

72. Ezra Taft Benson to Clare Middlemiss, August 8, 1967 as contained in David O. McKay journal, August 8, 1967, Bx 65, fd 5, David O. McKay Papers.

73. Charles R. Sligh Jr. to Harold F. Falk, August 3, 1967 copy contained in ibid.

74. "Minutes by Ezra Taft Benson of meeting with David O. McKay," June 24, 1966, Bx 63, fd 1.

75. First Presidency Minutes, December 13, 1966, Bx 64, fd 1, ibid. McKay attempted to clear up apparent confusion over the statement, immediately instructing his secretary, Clare Middlemiss, "to strike out of the above minutes the statement that I did not approve, and state that I did not recall at the time that I had given approval Elder Benson permission and had indeed dictated and signed the letter giving my approval to the matter."

76. David O. McKay journal, February 15, 1967, Bx 64, fd 3.

77. Durward G. Hall to Ben McMillan, June 14, 1966, Bx 26, fd 1, Wm. J. Grede Papers, Wisconsin Historical Society. In this same correspondence, Hall went on to suggest, albeit half-jokingly, "I think a ticket of Strom Thurmond for President and Durward Hall for Vice President would be much more apropos at this time."

78. William Benton McMillan to William J. Grede, July 15, 1966, Bx 26, fd 2, Wm. J. Grede Papers, Wisonsin Historical Society.

79. Howard E. Kershner to William J. Grede, July 29, 1966, Bx 26, fd 2.

80. Charles W. Briggs to William J. Grede, August 9, 1966, Bx 26, fd 2.

81. E. J. Presser to William J. Grede, December 27, 1966, Bx 26, fd 2.

82. Joseph Crespino, *Strom Thurmond's America* (New York: Hill and Wang, 2012) provides an overview of the South Carolina conservative's life and career.

83. As noted by William J. Grede to Glen G. Volker, May 31, 1967, Bx 26, fd 1, Wm. J. Grede Papers, Wisconsin Historical Society.

84. William J. Grede to C. Eugene Silver, June 1, 1967, Bx 26, fd 2.

85. Strom Thurmond to Harry Feyer, August 14, 1967.

86. William J. Grede to Bunker Hunt, January 11, 1967, Bx 26, fd 2.

87. Ezra Taft Benson to William J. Grede, February 16, 1967, Bx 26, fd 2.

88. William J. Grede to C. Eugene Silver, June 1, 1967, Bx 26, fd 2.

89. David O. McKay journal, August 8, 1967, Bx 65, fd 5, David O. McKay Papers.

90. Dan T. Carter, *The Politics of Rage: George Wallace, the Origins of the New Conservatism, and the Transformation of American Politics* (New York: Simon & Schuster, 1995) is the definitive work on the life and times of the colorful southerner.

91. "Benson Backs Wallace Stand," *Christian Science Monitor*, February 13, 1968, 3.

92. Benson to Robert Welch of March 8, 1968, Ezra Taft Benson Correspondence, John Birch Society Headquarters; "Journal Record of Alvin R. Dyer," February 13, 1968, copy as contained in David O. McKay journal, February 13, 1968, Bx 67, fd 3, David O. McKay Papers.

93. George C. Wallace to David O. McKay, February 12, 1968, Bx 2, fd 3, George C. Wallace Collection, Alabama Department of Archives and History, Montgomery. Benson requested to Wallace's campaign advisor that Wallace should meet with McKay in person when the governor was in Salt Lake City. Cecil C. Jackson Memo of February 26, 1968.

94. "Paper prepared by Elder Ezra Taft Benson concerning the political viewpoints of George C. Wallace," as contained in David O. McKay journal, February 13, 1968, Bx 67, fd 3, David O. McKay Papers.

95. "Journal Record of Alvin R. Dyer," February 13, 1968.

96. Concerning this so-called "third party prophecy" Dyer stated: "In the discussion which I had with Elder Benson [and his son Reed] I was told Wallace would seek the Presidency on the American Independent Party, a name very similar to that which Joseph Smith is alleged to have said would rise up in America at a time when the Republican and Democratic Parties would be at war with each other. The name of the party which the Prophet is supposed to have used is the *Independent American Party*." Dyer further stated: "It developed that a group in California, calling themselves 'Mormons for Wallace,' used the supposed prophecy to get members of the Church to sign a petition in that State." Dyer then added this: "*Comment*: With regard to the alleged prophecy, the article published in California and other printed material including the quotation is from Duane Crowther's book and the Hancock article—the source is part of this Journal Record. Sufficeth to say, there is very real doubt as to whether the Prophet ever made the statement." "Journal Record of Alvin R. Dyer," February 13, 1968, 2–3.

97. Ibid.

98. Ibid.

99. Ezra Taft Benson journal as quoted by Dew, *Ezra Taft Benson*, 397.

100. Carter, *George Wallace*, 354.

101. Ibid., 355–56.

102. Benson and Manion were friends and exchanged several letters through the years. Their correspondence is located in the Clarence Manion Papers, Bx 60, fd 5, Chicago History Museum, Chicago, Illinois.

103. "Minutes of meeting in Huntsville with President McKay by President Alvin R. Dyer, September 9, 1968," as contained in David O. McKay journal, September 9, 1968, Bx 68, fd 3, David O. McKay Papers.

104. Ibid.

105. Ibid.

106. David O. McKay journal, September 9, 1968.

107. Benson put Wallace campaign chairman Cecil Jackson in touch with a wealthy Mormon donor from Mesa, Arizona. See Benson to Jackson, October 11, 1968, Bx 2, fd 3, George C. Wallace Collection, Alabama Department of Archives and History. See also Benson to Jackson, November 1, 1968, ibid. For Wallace's visit to Utah, see Jackson to Benson, October 15, 1968, ibid. Benson also arranged for General LeMay to speak at BYU, which was advertised in the student newspaper, the *Daily Universe*, November 1, 1968.

108. Theodore H. White, *The Making of the President, 1968* (New York: Atheneum Publishers, 1969), 367.

109. De Gregorio, "Richard Nixon," *The Complete Book of U.S. Presidents*, 589. The most authoritative account of the 1968 election is Michael A. Cohen, *American Maelstrom: The 1968 Election and the Politics of Division* (New York: Oxford University Press, 2016).

110. "Party Qualifies for Utah Ballot," *Salt Lake Tribune*, March 6, 1976, B-5.

111. "LDS Official Says 'No' to Politics," *Salt Lake Tribune*, March 25, 1976, B-4, and "Party Clarifies Stand on Benson Selection," *Salt Lake Tribune*, March 29, 1976, 38.

112. As described and quoted in Dew, *Ezra Taft Benson*, 446.

113. For an exploration of Mormons in politics, see Randall Balmer and Jana Riess, eds., *Mormonism and American Politics* (New York: Columbia University Press, 2016).

114. Large, "Mormons and Politics."

115. Matthew L. Harris and Newell G. Bringhurst, *The Mormon Church and Blacks: A Documentary History* (Urbana: University of Illinois Press, 2015), chs. 5–6.

116. Benson, "Fourteen Fundamentals in Following the Prophet," *BYU Speeches of the Year* (February 26, 1980): https://speeches.byu.edu/talks/ezra-taft-benson_fourteen-fundamentals-following-prophet/.

5 Martin Luther King, Civil Rights, and Perceptions of a "Communist Conspiracy"

MATTHEW L. HARRIS

In the early 1990s members of the Church of Jesus Christ of Latter-day Saints performed sacred temple rituals for acclaimed civil rights leader Martin Luther King Jr. It occurred during the LDS church presidency of Ezra Taft Benson—a remarkable irony considering Benson's decades-long opposition to Dr. King.[1] Dead for nearly twenty-four years at the time of the ritual, the famed civil rights spokesman became the recipient of an important Mormon ordinance allowing for persons to accept or reject the Mormon gospel in an afterlife if they did not encounter while they lived. There is no evidence that King, a southern Baptist minister, had exposure to Mormonism because for much of the nineteenth and twentieth centuries the Mormon Church did not proselytize among black people.[2] In addition, from 1852 to 1978, LDS leaders prohibited persons of African descent from holding the priesthood or participating in sacred temple rituals, bluntly proclaiming they were under a divine curse for sinful conduct in a premortal life.[3]

Mormonism's restrictive racial practices occurred during much of Benson's adult life, which affected how he viewed people of color. Like his fellow apostles, he referred to black people as the "seed of Cain" and actively opposed civil rights during the turbulent decades after World War II. Benson and his colleagues feared that civil rights legislation would break down racial barriers, making it easier for blacks and whites to integrate and thereby marry.[4] But Benson went further than his fellow general authorities in opposing civil rights. Radicalized by right-wing extremism, the apostle came to believe in the 1960s that communists had infiltrated the civil rights movement. He alleged that Dr. King and his allies collaborated with Soviet agents in a secret plot to destroy American democracy and capitalism.

For more than a quarter century Benson's antiblack views influenced how some Latter-day Saints viewed Dr. King and the civil rights movement. This essay examines how Benson developed such views and more importantly, how they polarized the LDS church.

*　*　*

After Ezra Taft Benson finished his government service in 1961 and resumed his duties as a member of the Quorum of the Twelve Apostles, he became more vocal in speaking out against communism. Importantly, he viewed the fledgling civil rights movement as a subplot to a larger communist conspiracy. The apostle's views on civil rights derived from the writings of two non-Mormons whom he admired: J. Edgar Hoover, director of the FBI, and Robert Welch, founder of the John Birch Society, the most extreme anticommunist organization in the United States. Both men impressed upon him that communism and civil rights were inextricably linked and that civil rights leaders were witting agents in a worldwide communist conspiracy to enslave the American people.

Benson met the controversial FBI director in 1952 when he requested a background check after Eisenhower named him to his presidential cabinet.[5] Though the two men were never close, the admiring Mormon apostle extolled Hoover as the "best informed-man in government on the socialist-communist conspiracy" and praised his efforts exposing the aims and tactics of communists.[6] Hoover's 1958 bestselling book, *The Masters of Deceit: The Story of Communism and How to Fight It*, had an enormous impact on Benson, as did Hoover's other principal writing, *A Study of Communism*, published in 1962. Hoover sent him copies of both books when they were published and Benson cherished the gifts as newfound treasures. The books exposed Benson to communist aims and strategies, particularly how they used schools, the media, and the television and radio industries to spread their communist propaganda. "I am most grateful for your exposure of the communist conspiracy and for the wonderful organization you have established in the F.B.I.," he gushed to Hoover in 1965. "I pray that your courage will continue and that your hand will be blessed and prospered in all that you do to preserve our Constitutional Republic."[7]

On several occasions Benson conveyed to Hoover his earnest desire to have the director tutor him on the communist conspiracy. He asked Hoover's permission to reprint his speeches and writings in LDS publications, and on more than one occasion he invited the director to speak in Utah, both at the Mormon Church's annual general conference in Salt Lake City and at a devotional assembly at the church-owned and operated Brigham Young University.[8]

For Benson, Hoover's books were "must reading."[9] In *Masters of Deceit*, a book Benson quoted often, Hoover expressed alarm at how the party had used "the Negro . . . to exploit him and use him as a tool to build a communist America."[10] From Hoover's writings, Benson learned about an alleged long history that communists had with civil rights leaders, in which crafty, enterprising reds tried to infiltrate black organizations and groups, in an effort to pursue social and political equality. But at the same time, Hoover opined, communist leaders did not have much luck because they had a difficult time indoctrinating "any large number of Negroes."[11]

In *A Study of Communism*, Hoover called the civil rights movement a communist-front group, which acted as a "main sphere" for the communist agenda.[12] Hoover asserted that civil rights leaders created chaos with their demands for racial justice, thereby weakening American democracy and laying the foundation for communism. He first advanced this idea before the U.S. Congress in 1958, vigorously affirming that "The Negro situation is . . . being exploited fully and continuously by Communists on a national scale." In 1962, Hoover again warned a congressional committee that communists were using civil rights organizations to advance their nefarious agenda.[13]

In particular, Hoover was concerned that Stanley Levison and Bayard Rustin, both former members of the Communist Party, had joined forces with Martin Luther King. Alarmed, he secured a wiretap from Attorney General Robert Kennedy in 1962 to begin surveilling King and his associates, in a brazen effort to discredit the civil rights leader.[14] Moreover, King's "I Have a Dream" speech, delivered to a quarter million civil rights supporters on the steps at the Lincoln Memorial in 1963, just a short distance from FBI headquarters, further alarmed Hoover. King's enormous popularity, and the influence he had over thousands of civil rights supporters, led the Bureau to call him the "most dangerous and effective Negro leader in the country."[15]

Predictably, King responded to the communist charges with bewilderment and anger. "I'm getting sick and tired of people saying that this movement has been infiltrated by Communists. There are as many Communists in this freedom movement as there are Eskimos in Florida," he angrily explained.[16] There is no credible evidence that King or his associates were communists. The wiretaps reveal that King condemned communism and that Levison, Rustin, and other erstwhile members of the Communist Party were no longer active. Still, Hoover had little regard for the truth. He viewed King as a threat to him, and he spent much of the 1960s trying to besmirch him and undermine the movement he led.[17]

Ezra Taft Benson, of course, had no knowledge of what was going on behind the scenes at FBI headquarters, but he trusted the director's honesty and perspicuity. Years later, when Hoover's crusade against King was exposed,[18] the Mormon apostle brushed it off as the work of critics who embraced "the international Communist conspiracy."[19]

Another formative influence on Benson came from a little-known candy maker named Robert Welch, who founded the John Birch Society in 1958.[20] During the 1960s the Birch founder and the apostle exchanged dozens of letters, met numerous times, and strategized on how best to fight communism and big government.[21] So close and collaborative were the two men that Welch invited Benson to join the Birch Society and serve on its board. However, LDS church president David O. McKay rebuffed both requests, proclaiming the JBS too controversial.[22] Even so, Benson vigorously promoted the Birch Society throughout his life, praising it as "the most effective organization in our fight against creeping socialism and godless communism."[23] Benson was so enamored with the John Birch Society that he invited Welch to relocate the Birch Headquarters to Midway, Utah, next to the cottage that Benson purchased in 1967.[24]

The Mormon apostle eagerly read everything Welch had written. In particular, *The Politician*, Welch's signature work, impressed him, as did the articles in the *American Opinion*, a Birch magazine, and the *Birch Bulletin*, a monthly newsletter. *The Politician*, written in 1958 and ultimately published in 1963, electrified Benson. He found the book "shocking" and "most convincing," asserting that President Eisenhower, "so strong for Christian principles and basic American concepts," could be "so effectively used as a tool to serve the communist conspiracy."[25] Benson studied the work carefully and referred to it repeatedly throughout his ministry. He sent it to his colleagues in the Quorum of the Twelve Apostles, praising it as "essential reading"—"one of the most shocking volumes you have ever read."[26] To FBI director J. Edgar Hoover he called it "a most significant and alarming volume." He ordered copies for the LDS Church History Library, sent it to business executives and friends, and gave dozens of copies away as Christmas gifts.[27]

The Politician became a lightning rod of criticism the moment its pages first leaked to the public in 1958. The Birch founder noted that Eisenhower, the popular five-star general–turned president, was "a dedicated, conscious agent of the communist conspiracy." He further alleged that members of his cabinet were also communists, namely, John Foster Dulles, the secretary of state, Alan Dulles, the CIA director, and Milton Eisenhower, the president's brother, who served as an important adviser. Most astonishing, Welch argued that "Eisenhower and his Communist bosses and their pro-Communist appointees [were] gradually taking over" the United State government, doing so "right under the noses of the American people." In 1962 the Birch founder fearlessly claimed that the United States was "50–70 percent under Communist control."[28]

Just as important, Welch lambasted President Eisenhower for his "role in connection with the segregation storm in the South," alleging in *The Politician* that the president had promoted violence in the region to appease "Communist bosses who planned the whole thing far in advance." Welch specifically contended that

> the whole "civil rights" program and slogan in America today were just as phony as were the "agrarian reform" program and slogan of the Communists in China twenty years ago; and that they were being used by the same people, in the same way, for exactly the same purpose—of creating little flames of civil disorder which could be fanned and coalesced into the huge conflagration of civil war.[29]

He continued:

> The real "activists" and inciters on both sides of the issue don't care anymore about actual Negro "rights" than they do about growing mushrooms on the moon. What they want is the bitterness, strife, and the results of that strife—such as the acceptance of the use of federal troops to put down local "rebellion"—which can be brought about by urging both sides to resistance and violence.[30]

A number of racial incidences in the early 1960s concerned Welch. He decried the federal government's use of force to quell racial unrest with Freedom Riders, who tested court orders that barred segregation in interstate transportation. Similarly, he complained when President Kennedy called in federal troops to ensure that a black man could gain admittance into the University of Mississippi, an all-white school.[31]

Most problematic, however, were the Civil Rights Acts of 1957 and 1964. Welch theorized that President Eisenhower and his successors—John F. Kennedy and Lyndon B. Johnson—were unwitting communist dupes who supported civil rights legislation.[32] The Birch founder articulated these ideas most lucidly in *The Politician* but also in the 1963 issue of the *Birch Bulletin*, just as a civil rights bill was working its way through Congress. This bill, which Welch admonished his followers to reject, would eliminate the last vestiges of discrimination in public accommodations and give all Americans, according to President Kennedy, "the right to be served in facilities which are open to the public."[33] Importantly, the Birch leader warned that civil rights legislation would enlarge the powers of the federal government, hastening the creation of a communist state. By instituting new federal agencies to oversee civil rights and by dispatching federal law enforcement to enforce its provisions, Welch claimed that communist schemers had designed the legislation to gobble up the powers of the state.[34]

The voluble Birch leader found proof of a civil rights conspiracy in the writings of an obscure communist named Joseph Pogany, who wrote under the alias of John Pepper. In Pepper's creative little pamphlet entitled "American Negro Problems," published in 1928, he claimed that the Communist Party in the United States used "white oppression of the Negro masses" as "part of the proletarian revolution in America against capitalism." Pepper further asserted that communists wanted to establish a "Negro Soviet Republic," in which they would achieve these ends through violence and racial strife.[35]

Welch also read the work of communists James W. Ford and James S. Allen, who echoed Pepper's claims. In the "The Negroes in a Soviet America," published in 1935, the authors laid out a carefully crafted plan for a Soviet-backed black republic in the United States. "When the proper time comes," they insisted, "the Communists may either help the Negroes to set up their own Negro Soviet Republic in the Southeast, before the whole United States has been Sovietized; or that the Communist-led Negroes might first help to establish a Soviet central government over the whole United States." The Birch founder read these pamphlets with great zeal and became convinced that the authors' background as members of the Communist Party had given them a unique insight into "the [Kremlin's] plans to establish a Negro Soviet Republic" in the United States.[36]

For Welch, the communists' master plan unfolded in the early 1960s when racial unrest gripped the country. These events provided clear proof that Pepper, Ford, and Allen had accurately predicted communist aims and strategies. Accordingly Welch, like Hoover, went to great lengths to besmirch Martin Luther King, whom the Birch founder claimed belonged to "sixty Communist-front organizations—more than any other Communist in the United States." In the 1963 *Birch Bulletin*, for example, he published a 1957 picture of King at the Highlander Folk School in Tennessee, a school that the Tennessee legislature abolished for "being a subversive organization."[37] Welch asserted that communists ran the school, claiming that the institution's purpose was to bring "tension, disturbance, strife and violence in their advancement of the Communist doctrine of 'racial nationalism.'"[38]

For Birchers and racist southerners, the Highlander School fit the communist profile perfectly. Organized in the 1930s to promote racial equality, its leaders fought discrimination and segregation and supported civil rights legislation. But at the same time scholars have emphatically denied Bircher claims that the Highlander School was something other than what it purported to be: a training center for social justice leadership. Indeed, there is no evidence the Highlander School was led by communists, frequented by communists, or supported by communists, despite being labeled "subversive" by Tennessee legislators and other misguided and agenda-driven segregationists.[39]

Ezra Taft Benson, who had limited exposure to black people growing up in a small, almost entirely white Mormon farming community in Whitney, Idaho, embraced Welch's anti–civil rights agenda uncritically.[40] What is more, the apostle spent much of the 1960s promoting the Birch agenda. A flashpoint occurred in September 1963 when he spoke at a gathering of more than two thousand Birch supporters at the Society's five-year anniversary in Los Angeles. Benson grimly noted that he was not there "to tickle your ears" or "to entertain you. The message I bring is not a happy one." "For thirty years we have aided the cause of the atheistic-socialist conspiracy by permitting socialists, communists, and fellow-travelers in high places in government." Additionally, he decried "the insidious infiltration of socialistic communist agents and sympathizers into almost every segment of American life."[41]

This address marked the first time Benson implied publicly that President Eisenhower allowed communists into the highest echelons of government— and that the president himself was possibly a communist agent. This highly inflammatory address made national headlines when Idaho Congressman Ralph Harding, a fellow Latter-day Saint, "loosed a bitter attack on Ezra Taft Benson on the floor of the House."[42] Harding assailed the apostle for accepting Welch's claim that Eisenhower was a communist and for linking the Birch Society with the LDS church. The speech made it into the *Congressional Record*; the *New York Times* and the *Associated Press* also reported the story.[43]

The unfavorable publicity generated by the Harding affair prompted the First Presidency to call Benson on a mission to Frankfurt, Germany, where they hoped he would tone down his extreme partisanship.[44] But the feisty apostle did not leave quietly. In the weeks leading up to his departure on New Year's Day, 1964, he condemned the civil rights movement. Benson's public denunciation of civil rights marked a sharp contrast with the church, which by the mid-1960s was moving toward a more moderate position with civil rights. In the October 1963 session of general conference, First Presidency counselor Hugh B. Brown, an adamant supporter of racial equality and a vocal critic of the priesthood and temple ban, read a statement in conference expressing support for civil rights, which was a hotly debated issue that fall as civil rights legislation worked its way through Congress.[45] "We would like it to be known," Brown averred, "that there is in this Church no doctrine, belief, or practice, that is intended to deny the enjoyment of full civil rights by any person regardless of race, color, or creed."[46]

Although Brown explained that his statement was not an endorsement of "any stand on any bill,"[47] it came at a propitious time. NAACP officials, who had threatened to protest at the October conference, criticized the church for the state's inaction on civil rights.[48] Nevertheless, the NAACP's sharp criticisms did not temper Benson or bridle his tongue. About two weeks after Brown's general conference address, the apostle told a church gathering in New Orleans that the "federal government should not have sent troops to Little Rock, [Arkansas], and Oxford, Mississippi, in the school integration crisis." Echoing a Birch line, Benson condemned the "integration controversy," asserting that the civil rights movement had "been agitated by radicals" who were "part of the Communist-socialist conspiracy."[49] Furthermore, Benson delivered three hard-hitting speeches in December 1963 to Mormon audiences in Utah and Idaho, claiming that the civil rights movement was part of a "pattern for the Communist takeover of America."[50]

Ironically, Benson's views on civil rights were more in line with Birchers, fundamentalist Christian preachers, and segregationist Dixiecrats than members of his own political party, virtually all of whom rejected the notion that the civil rights movement was tied to communism.[51] Beyond the obvious Birch connection, Benson also sympathized with the Rev. Billy Hargis and the Rev. Bob Jones, two fiery and combative southern ministers who proclaimed that the NAACP was a communist plot. Benson, in fact, spoke at rallies with Hargis and had one of his addresses published in the *Christian Crusade*, Hargis's colorful monthly magazine.[52] The Mormon apostle also sympathized with segregationist Dixiecrats, especially South Carolina Senator Strom Thurmond, Mississippi Senator James Eastland, and Alabama Governor George Wallace, who famously declared that "the Civil Rights Act of 1964 came straight out of the *Communist Manifesto*."[53] Benson, "favorably impressed" with the governor, considered running with him on a third-party presidential ticket. Before Wallace, the apostle considered a presidential run with Strom Thurmond.[54]

But these fringe figures were not the only influence on Benson. The Mormon apostle had much in common with the conservative wing of the Republican Party. Even though the moderates of the party—Nelson Rockefeller, George Romney, Richard Nixon, and Everett Dirksen—supported civil rights, the right-wing of the party did not.[55] Outspoken Arizona Senator Barry Goldwater, the party's nominee in the 1964 presidential election, opposed the Civil Rights Act of 1964, as did controversial South Carolina Senator Strom Thurmond, up-and-coming political newcomer Ronald Reagan, and prominent conservative pundit William F. Buckley Jr., founding editor of the influential *National Review* magazine. These rock-ribbed conservatives believed that racial equality should be voluntary, not compulsory. Added to that, they opposed racial equality on federal principles, citing that the Civil Rights Act of 1964 would enlarge the power of the federal government at the expense of the states.[56] This line of reasoning resonated with Benson. It was consistent with his deep commitment to personal choice but also to states' rights. "I am convinced," he emphatically stated, that the "pending 'civil rights' legislation is . . . about 10% civil rights and about 90% a further extension of socialistic Federal Controls."[57]

Meanwhile, as the apostle denounced civil rights, he disseminated his speeches on official church letterhead.[58] This prompted a sharp response from Utah Senator Frank Moss, a Democrat and practicing Latter-day Saint, who complained that Benson's office had tried to imply institutional support for the apostle's extreme right-wing views. "Apparently whoever is doing this work has mailed copies to all of the people who appear in the Utah Directory in Washington, D.C.," the Senator fumed to First Presidency counselor Hugh B. Brown after receiving one of Benson's speeches.[59]

Benson's Birch support continued unabated while he presided over the European mission in Frankfurt, Germany, where he lived from January 1, 1964 to September 14, 1965. His mission presidency had not quieted his conspiratorial views, nor his willingness to express them publicly. In the April 1965 session of general conference, some nine months after President Lyndon B. Johnson signed the Civil Rights Act into law, Benson delivered another stinging sermon that again drew the ire of the First Presidency. He criticized the civil rights movement, the welfare state, federal aid to education, and labor unions, proclaiming that all were tied to communism. "Before I left for Europe I warned how the communists were using the Civil Rights movement to promote eventual take-over of this country," Benson asserted. "When are we going to wake up? What do you know about the dangerous Civil Rights Agitation in Mississippi? Do you fear the destruction of all vestiges of state government?"[60]

Ernest Wilkinson, Benson's confidante and fellow archconservative, speculated that the "Brethren may have thought [Benson's address] was untactful," adding, "it is apparent that Ezra is not going to give up the cause in which he knows he is right."[61] The First Presidency responded by striking from the record the civil rights portion of the speech, primarily at Hugh Brown's insistence, who candidly explained to the First Presidency "that he had had many unfavorable reactions regarding Brother Benson's remarks." Brown and other senior apostles were upset at the news coverage of the address, in particular Benson's statement on civil rights, which offered a stark counterpoint to Brown's.[62] Indeed, reporters observed that the two men had "sharp and bitter differences . . . on civil rights." They were right. When asked by a reporter whose position on civil rights was correct, Brown "tartly said that Benson 'speaks strictly for himself.' My statement is the official Church position."[63]

The timing of Benson's anti–civil rights sermon was also unfortunate. It came during a contentious legislative session when Utah lawmakers debated whether or not to pass a bill that would outlaw discrimination in public spaces.[64] Frustrated that the church would not support the bill, NAACP activists gathered around Temple Square just days before general conference to protest LDS racial teachings.[65] NAACP president Johnie Driver, the church's most vocal critic, bluntly explained that blacks could not get decent housing or adequate employment in Utah "because of the official L.D.S. Church doctrine of exclusion of Negroes from the priesthood."[66] Driver "asked Church leaders to use their influence to support fair housing and employment in Utah." Church leaders, however, balked. They reasoned that issues like employment and housing were not moral issues and therefore preferred to remain silent.[67]

Benson promptly returned to Germany after his controversial general conference address, where he maintained a vigorous correspondence with Robert Welch.[68] Welch sent him literature that he read voraciously, marking up important passages in red ink.[69] Welch's pamphlet "Two Revolutions at Once" particularly impressed him. Benson underlined nearly every passage, paying close attention to the paragraphs that discussed how "the Communists" would "create bitterness, turmoil, civil disorders" to promote a "civil war" in the country and usher in a "Negro Soviet Republic."[70] He also praised Welch's short essay entitled "What's Wrong with Civil Rights," calling it "excellent." But Benson's favorite reading was the August 1965 *Birch Bulletin*, which he described as "one of the best." He requested "five free copies" to share with his Mormon friends and he effusively praised Welch for his good work.[71]

The August 1965 *Birch Bulletin* struck at the heart of the Birch message: "Fully expose the 'civil rights' fraud and you will break the back of the Communist Conspiracy."[72] Benson heeded the counsel. His sense of urgency to fight civil rights increased during the summer of 1965, as his time in Germany was winding down. A number of factors alarmed him. First, in July 1965 the NAACP passed a unanimous resolution asking various countries "to refuse to grant visas to missionaries and representatives" of the church until LDS officials changed their "doctrine of non-white inferiority" and adopted "a positive policy of support for civil rights."[73] Second, President Johnson signed the Voting Rights Act into law in August 1965, which Benson feared would lead to a Leviathan state. Third, the August 1965 Watts Riots further alarmed him. The riot, which destroyed millions of dollars in property damage and killed thirty-four people, prompted Benson and the Birchers to see the destruction and lawlessness in south central Los Angeles as the opening salvo of the communist revolution.[74]

The apostle asserted that communists "had spent two years in Watts agitating for the uprising."[75] His son Reed concurred, claiming that the racial strife in Los Angeles and the push for racial equality in Utah was ample proof that the "Communist influence" was "growing." Reed was not an impartial observer. He had been serving as regional coordinator for the John Birch Society in Utah since 1962.[76] He responded to the Watts rioting and to Hugh B. Brown's civil rights statement by dispatching a memo in September 1965 to the "Utah Chapters" of the Birch Society. There he instructed members to "begin a whispering campaign and foster rumors that the Civil Rights groups are going to organize demonstrations in Salt Lake City in connection with the forthcoming LDS conference. It will appear logical that such demonstrations are to be made," he averred, "because of the undercurrent of feelings being generated both in and out of the LDS church to champion the cause of Civil Rights." Reed reasoned that a "few well-placed comments will soon mushroom out of control and before the conference begins there will be such a feeling of unrest and distrust that the populace will hardly know who to believe. The news media will play it to the very hilt. No matter what the Civil Rights leaders may try to say to deny it the seed will have been down and again the Civil Rights movement will suffer a telling blow."[77]

The memo was gutsy. It could expose his father to further criticism or it could mobilize opposition against civil rights. Reed's support of the Birch line was already well-known. He had publicly denounced President Eisenhower and President Johnson as communists and had accused "Martin Luther King of hurting the cause of the Negro."[78] Likewise, he assailed the NAACP as a "communist front" group, lamenting that Mormons had joined.[79]

In this highly charged atmosphere, Ezra Taft Benson returned to Utah on September 14, 1965.[80] The apostle came home amid widespread paranoia that black militants would disrupt general conference—a claim that the NAACP emphatically denied—and amid a heightened state of alert from the Utah National Guard.[81]

There is no evidence that Ezra Taft Benson knew about Reed's memo.[82] But at the same time, Reed would not have acted without his father's approval. The two were extremely close. His father urged him to take the job at the Birch Society; moreover, the two were confidantes and committed foes of racial equality.[83] For his part, the elder Benson stayed away from the limelight during the fall of 1965, given the past dust-up from the April 1965 General Conference and the current unrest generated by his son's memo. In private, however, he continued to assail Dr. King. Benson explained to his colleagues in the Quorum of the Twelve Apostles that "we are . . . seeing something being carried out today that was planned by the highest councils of the communist party twenty years ago, and that Martin Luther King is an agent if not a power in the communist party." He further stated that the civil rights movement "is being directed and supported and prompted by agents of the communist party, that the negroes are being used in this whole question of civil rights, integration, etc., and that the NAACP are largely made up of men who are affiliated with . . . one of the communist-front organizations."[84]

The NAACP, meanwhile, grew weary of the "smear tactics" by "Benson and the Birchers." In a 1966 newsletter of the Utah chapter of the NAACP, the writer assailed Robert Welch and Ezra Taft Benson for sponsoring "slides and films trying to link civil rights to communism." Benson, in particular, posed a difficult challenge for the NAACP. His authoritative position as an LDS apostle, coupled with his service in the Eisenhower administration, made him a formidable foe. He not only opposed racial equality, the newsletter bitterly complained, but he actively "smeared" civil rights "in Louisiana . . . and more recently in the Assembly Hall on Temple Square."[85]

From 1966 to 1968 Benson intensified his anti–civil rights stance. The rise of the black power movement particularly frightened him, especially black militants, who couched their rhetoric in violence.[86] Moreover, Benson ignored the mounting pressure against the church to support better jobs and housing for blacks and to lift the priesthood and temple ban.[87] Concurrently, he explored running for the presidency with two ardent segregationists—Strom Thurmond and George Wallace—seemingly oblivious to critics, both within and outside the church, who publicly questioned Mormon racial teachings.[88]

The apostle's opposition to racial equality reached a climax in the fall of 1966 when he attacked King publicly, the first time he had done so. At a devotional assembly at BYU, he excoriated the civil rights leader for lecturing "at a communist training school," soliciting "funds through communist sources," hiring "a communist as a top-level aide," affiliating "with communist fronts," and someone who is "praised in the communist press" and "who unquestionably parallels the communist line." The civil rights leader, Benson continued, "advocates the breaking of the law" and has been described by J. Edgar Hoover as 'the most notorious liar in the country.'"[89] The speech ignited a firestorm on campus. Students debated each other in the student newspaper, questioning whether or not King was a communist. Some agreed with Benson, some rejected the notion, while others remained confused.[90] A BYU professor, angry about the address, limned a one-page letter to Dr. King asking what he could do to confront "such ridiculous charges" linking "questions of Communist involvement with the Civil Rights movement."[91]

Another BYU professor expressed dissatisfaction to Hugh Brown, character-izing Benson's address "to the B.Y.U. student body" as "the most extreme yet." The professor asked if members "of the Quorum of the Twelve have unlimited freedom to present personal biases and prejudices in public assemblies?"[92]

Benson continued his attack on racial equality in the months ahead. Against increasing racial unrest in the United States, and against rumors that armed "Negroes with machine guns and bombs were . . . coming to Salt Lake City" to harm the church,[93] Benson sought the permission of LDS church president David O. McKay to address civil rights at the October 1967 session of General Conference. The aging president consented, not knowing the specifics of Benson's sermon.[94] Benson's "Trust Not the Arm of Flesh" was a devastating indictment of the civil rights movement. Drawing on Robert Welch and J. Edgar Hoover,[95] the apostle criticized black radicals for creating "a Communist program for revolution in America."[96] He explained that the strategy for a communist revolution was three-fold. First, communists would "create hatred." They would "use means to agitate blacks into hating whites and whites into hating blacks" and "play up and exaggerate real grievances," even to the point of manufacturing "false stories and rumors of injustices and brutality." Second, they would "trigger violence." They would "form large mobs."[97] And third, they would seek to "overthrow established government. Once mob violence becomes widespread and commonplace, [communists] would condition those who are emotionally involved to accept violence as the only way to 'settle the score.'" Communists would then "provide leadership and training for guerilla warfare." They would gradually test their training "through sporadic riots and battles with police," then, "at the appointed time, launch an all-out simultaneous offensive in every major city."[98]

Most astonishing, Benson claimed that black radicals would "sabotage . . . water supplies, power grids, main rail road [lines] and highway arteries, communication centers, and government buildings. With fires raging in every . . . part of town, with wanton looting going on in the darkness of a big city without routine police protection, without water to drink, without electrical refrigeration, without transportation or radio or TV, the public will panic, lock its doors in trembling fear, and make it that much easier for the small but assembled and fully disciplined guerrilla bands to capture the power centers of each community." Further, Benson warned, the riots would lead to "more government housing, government welfare, government job training" and "federal control over the police." In short, the civil rights movement was leading to full-blown communism.[99]

The speech was the most comprehensive statement to date of any Mormon leader on the subject of civil rights.[100] Proud of his father's work, Reed sent a copy of the address to Robert Welch. "I thought you might be interested in the approach to, and discussion of, the so-called Civil Rights movement, as my father presented it to our members," Reed explained enthusiastically.[101] Deseret Book, the church-owned and -operated bookstore, published the address the following year as a pamphlet entitled *Civil Rights: A Tool of Communist Deception*. In 1969 it was reprinted in a collection of Benson's sermons entitled *An Enemy Hath Done This*, compiled by Jerreld Newquist, a Mormon Bircher. Neither of Benson's authorized biographies discuss this controversial address.[102]

Benson's speech struck a chord with certain members of the Quorum of the Twelve, especially with apostle Mark Petersen, who also condemned black militants. In a February 1968 address at BYU, he decried the "many vicious elements in this country," theorizing that "they would destroy us if they could." "We're on the verge of another civil war," he explained, echoing Benson. He implored BYU students and faculty to consider "what some of these agitators are now saying in calling upon one great element of the population to arm itself and shoot down the white people because we are not giving them all they think they ought to have."[103] BYU president Ernest Wilkinson was "thrilled at the address." He "could not help think that if Ezra Taft Benson," his close friend, "had given that talk there would have been no end of criticism of him on our campus." Petersen "openly said that it was a fight between the races," but because he did not have the "public image of . . . Benson" there would be "no criticism."[104]

The following spring Benson continued his crusade against the civil rights movement when Martin Luther King was assassinated. Fearful that Americans would make a martyr over the fallen leader, the apostle protested President Lyndon Johnson's executive order to lower flags at half-mast. In April 1968, he sent a memo to the Quorum of the Twelve and First Presidency declaring that "Communists will use Mr. King's death for as much yardage as possible." Much to Hugh Brown's dismay, Benson vilified King as a communist, a liar, and a disreputable person who employed top-level aids as communists.[105]

Also that month Benson wrote a letter to the First Presidency and Quorum of the Twelve, again criticizing King and condemning the civil rights movement. Provocatively titled "Dangers Ahead," the letter represented Benson's growing frustration with the movement, his fear of black militants, and the alarming danger that the communist conspiracy was now in its final stages. Benson did not hold back. He predicted that black Marxists would take to the streets and usher in a revolution, collapse America's financial institutions, and plunge the nation into a "prolonged recession or depression." In language infused with apocalyptic overtones, he ominously noted that black Marxists would lead to the "possible outbreak of World War III."[106]

In May 1968, about a month after he addressed the First Presidency and Quorum of the Twelve, Benson continued his attack on civil rights—this time in another devotional address at BYU. Laced with Birch themes, he condemned secret plottings by black-power advocates, decried "black Marxists" "for burning down America," and excoriated presidential candidates for "buying off those burning . . . cities with more of the federal subsidies."[107]

Benson's warnings were bold, even audacious. They came at a time when the church was under intense scrutiny for its racial teachings. There were rumors that armed black militants would bomb Temple Square during the April 1970 session of General Conference—the third time in five years that such rumors surfaced. "It has come to my attention that some of the less responsible of the Black element may try to disrupt sessions of General Conference," a concerned church member explained to First Presidency counselor Harold B. Lee. Alarmed, church officials held prayer sessions, conducted evacuation exercises, and placed security guards at the entrance of church headquarters.[108]

This daunting threat occurred at the same time the church was already under siege when scores of universities protested BYU's racial policies from 1968 to 1971.[109] Universities refused to play BYU sports teams. Dozens of newspapers and magazines covered the protests.[110] The Western Athletic Conference commissioner and many of the conference schools' presidents discussed "sever[ing] all relations" with BYU until its "discriminatory" policies "are eliminated."[111] Compounding matters further, in the 1960s BYU did not recruit black athletes or black students. There were only three African Americans at BYU in 1968, suggesting to conference officials that black people were neither welcomed nor supported at the church institution.[112] Equally difficult, civil rights investigators from the Department of Health and Human Welfare began exploring whether or not BYU had violated Title VI of the Civil Rights Act of 1964.[113] In addition, critics attacked the Book of Mormon for its alleged racist scriptures.[114]

As before, Benson brushed off the criticism. He felt "no compunction to make the Church popular with liberals, Socialists, or Communists."[115] With Cleon Skousen, his close friend, the apostle opined that the protests were motivated by communists. "Communist-oriented revolutionary groups have been spearheading the wave of protests and violence directed toward Brigham Young University and the Mormon Church," Skousen sneered, quoting Benson's 1967 conference address. What they wanted was to "create resentment and hatred between the races."[116] Benson agreed with Skousen's assessment but he went further, targeting Latter-day Saints, specifically "apostates," whom he assailed for attacking "the church for not being in the forefront of the so-called civil rights movement."[117]

As the BYU protests showed no signs of abating, the apostles decided to meet to discuss ways to burnish the church's "dwindling public image."[118] The meeting took place in New York in February 1970. The apostles convened to discuss "what steps we should take in the direction of public relations to help combat some of the unfavorable publicity that we have been having." They met for two and half hours at the Waldorf Astoria Hotel in midtown New York City. Apostles Harold B. Lee, Spencer W. Kimball, Gordon B. Hinckley, Richard L. Evans, and Ezra Taft Benson attended. J. Willard Marriott and other prominent LDS businessmen from the East also attended the meeting. The group concluded that because "newspapers and other news media seem to be making light and picking on us" that "we should develop a very strong, positive position and program and feed the news media with successful stories."[119]

In the midst of all this, church leaders confronted Benson. They warned him that he was harming the church. Indeed, there is no record of Benson discussing civil rights after the BYU protests ended in 1971. Also important, David O. McKay allowed him to preach his antiblack views, but his successors in the church presidency—Joseph Fielding Smith, Harold B. Lee, and Spencer W. Kimball—did not. After McKay died in 1970, these senior apostles instructed him not to discuss his conspiracy theories in public.[120] Kimball, in particular, reined-in Benson, chastising him on numerous occasions for publicly expressing his extreme right-wing views. The diminutive Mormon president promoted a vision of the church that clashed with Benson's Birch views. Far-sighted and visionary, Kimball embraced an ecumenical vision of Mormonism that expanded missionary work in communist and African nations.[121] More significantly, as church president, Kimball lifted the 126-year-old priesthood and temple ban in 1978.[122] Benson supported Kimball's revelation, but he did not talk about it publicly.[123] He understood the direction President Kimball wanted to take the church and he knew instinctively that he could no longer discuss his antiblack views in public.

Nonetheless, Benson's erstwhile teachings had consequences. When he became the church president in 1985, his Birch past reemerged unexpectedly. During the contentious debate over whether or not to name a federal holiday after Dr. King,[124] some ultraconservative Mormons appealed to Benson's earlier writings to oppose the holiday in Arizona. The matter turned personal when Benson's grandson Steve, a prize-winning cartoonist at the *Arizona Republic*, leaked some letters to an Arizona newspaper that reflected poorly on the church president. The letters, written by Mormons who harbored strong antiblack views, recalled then-apostle Benson's words that King "was a communist and a deceiver, which plainly put him into the category of the anti-Christ."[125]

Recognizing the potential fallout, the LDS public-relations department promptly issued a statement affirming Benson's love for all people regardless of "color, creed or political persuasion."[126] If the Arizona episode was troubling enough, the church also had to deal with the fallout from Utah's refusal to honor Martin Luther King Day, opting instead for the more generic Human Rights Day. Though the aging Mormon president, now in declining health, did not meet with members of the legislature to express opposition to the King holiday, he did not need to. His views about Dr. King were well known.[127]

In 2000, some six years after Benson died, the Utah state legislature renamed the holiday after Dr. King, in what was a *stunning* development considering Benson's public opposition to Dr. King and civil rights.[128] Gordon B. Hinckley promoted the change. As church president, he "lent his support" to rename the holiday after King, while at the same time befriending leaders of the NAACP and promoting LDS outreach in black neighborhoods and communities.[129] Equally significant, he counseled Latter-day Saints to avoid racial slurs and to welcome all people of color within their ranks.[130] Under Hinckley's energetic leadership, he made it clear to the rank-and-file that it was no longer acceptable to demean black people or to deny them basic rights and liberties. More than anyone else in church leadership, Hinckley sought to counteract Benson and usher in a new beginning for Mormon race relations.

Notes

My thanks to Newell G. Bringhurst and Stirling Adams for their insightful critique of this essay. Also, slight portions from the introduction and chapter 5 of this book are drawn from Matthew L. Harris's article "Ezra Taft Benson, Dwight D. Eisenhower and the Emergence of a Conspiracy Culture within the Mormon Church," *John Whitmer Historical Association Society Journal* 37, no. 1 (Spring–Summer 2017): 51–82. I am grateful to William Morain, the editor of the journal, for granting permission to use portions of this work.

1. Dr. King's proxy work was done in the Salt Lake City and Provo Temples in 1991 and 1992, respectively. This included his baptism, endowment, and sealing to his parents. Malcolm X's temple work was done at about the same time. Their "Ordinance Records" are located in the LDS Family History Center, Salt Lake City, Utah.

2. LDS church president Heber J. Grant candidly explained that because of the "penalty of a black skin and exclusion from the exercise of the rights of the priesthood . . . we do not encourage [blacks] to become members of the church." In Grant to L. H. Wilkin, January

28, 1928, in Lester Bush, ed., "Compilation of the Negro in Mormonism" (unpublished compilation, 1972), 228–29, LDS Church History Library; and Bruce R. McConkie, *Mormon Doctrine* (Salt Lake City: Bookcraft, 1958), 477, who explained that the church did not proselytize in black communities, but if worthy blacks requested baptism, missionaries would grant it.

3. Two LDS apostles offered the most vivid expressions of Mormon racial teachings: Joseph Fielding Smith, *The Way to Perfection: Short Discourses on Gospel Themes*, 5th ed. (Salt Lake City: Genealogical Society of Utah, 1945), chaps. 15–16; and McConkie, *Mormon Doctrine*, 102–3, 107–8, 476–77, 553–54. See also Armand L. Mauss, *All Abraham's Children: Changing Mormon Conceptions of Race and Lineage* (Urbana: University of Illinois Press, 2003), chaps. 2, 8.

4. Matthew L. Harris and Newell G. Bringhurst, eds., *The Mormon Church and Blacks: A Documentary History* (Urbana: University of Illinois Press, 2015), 67–83, 109–12. Newell G. Bringhurst, *Saints, Slaves, and Blacks: The Changing Place of Black People Within Mormonism* (Westport, Conn.: Greenwood Press, 1981), chap. 9; Lester E. Bush Jr. and Armand L. Mauss, eds., *Neither White nor Black: Mormon Scholars Confront the Race Issue in a Universal Church* (Midvale, Utah: Signature Books, 1984), 9–30, 86–97. For Benson's depiction of blacks as the "seed of Cain," see "Trust Not the Arm of Flesh," *Improvement Era* 70 (December 1967): 55.

5. FBI background check on Ezra Taft Benson, November 28, 1952, Ezra Taft Benson File (77-54679-21), Federal Bureau of Investigation Files and Records (Freedom of Information Act), Washington, D.C.

6. Ezra Taft Benson, *An Enemy Hath Done This*, compiled by Jerreld L. Newquist (Salt Lake City: Parliament Publishers, 1969), 65.

7. Ezra Taft Benson to J. Edgar Hoover, May 28, 1965, Ezra Taft Benson File (62-104401), Federal Bureau of Investigation Files and Records (Freedom of Information Act), Washington, D.C.

8. For these points, see Matthew L. Harris, *"Watchman on the Tower": Ezra Taft Benson and the Emergence of the Mormon Right* (Salt Lake City: University of Utah Press, forthcoming, 2019).

9. Ezra Taft Benson, *Title of Liberty: A Warning Voice*, compiled by Mark A. Benson (Salt Lake City: Deseret Book, 1964), 83. See also Benson to Hugh B. Brown, September 18, 1962, Box 3, Folder 4, Hugh B. Brown Research Files, L. Tom Perry Special Collections, Harold B. Lee Library, Brigham Young University.

10. J. Edgar Hoover, *Masters of Deceit: The Story of Communism in America and How to Fight It* (New York: Hold, Rinehart, and Winston, 1958), 246. For a trenchant analysis of *Masters of Deceit*, see Richard Gid Powers, *Not Without Honor: The History of American Anticommunism* (New Haven, Conn.: Yale University Press, 1998), 281–82.

11. Hoover, *Masters of Deceit*, 249.

12. J. Edgar Hoover, *A Study of Communism* (New York: Holt, Rinehart, and Winston, 1962), 170. See also J. Edgar Hoover, *On Communism* (New York: Random House, 1969), part 2.

13. *Senate Committee on Commerce, 88th Congress, Civil Rights—Public Accommodations* (Washington, D.C., Government Printing Office, 1963), 68; Taylor Branch, *Parting the Waters: America in the King Years, 1954–63 (New York: Simon and Schuster, 1988), 564.*

14. David J. Garrow, *The FBI and Martin Luther King, Jr.* (New York: Penguin, 1981), chaps. 1–2, remains the best account of Hoover's wiretapping activities. Also useful is Branch, *Parting the Waters*, 568–69; Randall B. Woods, *Prisoners of Hope: Lyndon B. Johnson, the Great Society, and the Limits of Liberalism* (New York: Basic Books, 2016), 161–64; Curt Gentry, *J. Edgar Hoover: The Man and the Secrets* (New York: Penguin, 1991), 502–29; and Kenneth O'Reilly, *Racial Matters: The FBI's Secret File on Black America, 1960–1972* (New York: Free Press, 1989), chap. 4.

15. Garrow, *FBI and Martin Luther King*, 71.

16. King, "Playboy Interview" (1965), in James M. Washington, ed., *The Essential Writings and Speeches of Martin Luther King, Jr.* (New York: Harper One, 1986), 362.

17. Garrow, *FBI and Martin Luther King* makes this point. See also his article, "The FBI and Martin Luther King," *The Atlantic* (July–August 2002): http://www.theatlantic.com/magazine/archive/2002/07/the-fbi-and-martin-luther-king/302537/. Woods, *Prisoners of Hope*, 306, writes that "Hoover and others . . . were determined to establish a link between the forces of internationalism and the civil rights movement."

18. The best treatment detailing Hoover's malfeasance, and his treatment of King, is Betty Medsger, *The Burglary: The Discovery of J. Edgar Hoover's Secret FBI* (New York: Alfred Knopf, 2014). See also Tim Weiner, *Enemies: A History of the FBI* (New York: Random House, 2012), 271, 274.

19. Benson to President Richard Nixon, May 4, 1971, Ezra Taft Benson File (94-38023-66), Federal Bureau of Investigation Files and Records (Freedom of Information Act), Washington, D.C. See also Hoover's admiration for Benson's defense, in a letter to Benson dated May 11, 1971, ibid. As late as 1984, Benson continued to defend Hoover: "I knew Mr. Hoover personally. He was a God-fearing man, and one of the most honorable and able men I have known in government service." In Ezra Taft Benson, "God's Hand in Our Nation's History," Canyon Road Ward sermon, Salt Lake City, Ensign Stake, December 30, 1984, Box 45, folder 10, Duane E. Jeffery Papers, Special Collections, Marriott Library, University of Utah.

20. Three seminal accounts of the Birch Society include D. J. Mulloy, *The World of the John Birch Society: Conspiracy, Conservatism, and the Cold War* (Nashville, Tenn.: Vanderbilt University Press, 2014); Daniel Bell, ed., *The Radical Right: The New American Right*, expanded and updated (New York: Doubleday, 1963), chap. 11; and Jonathan M. Schoenwald, *A Time for Choosing: The Rise of Modern American Conservatism* (New York: Oxford University Press, 2001), chap. 3. For a broader discussion about conspiracy in post–World War II America, see Robert Alan Goldberg, *Enemies Within: The Culture of Conspiracy in Modern America* (New Haven, Conn.: Yale University Press, 2001).

21. Ezra Taft Benson to Robert Welch, May 17, 1965, January 10, 1969, both in Ezra Taft Benson Correspondence, John Birch Society Headquarters, Appleton, Wisc. See also Benson to David O. McKay, April 19, 1967, Box 65, Folder 1, David O. McKay Papers, Special Collections, Marriott Library, University of Utah, extolling Welch as "a great American, a true patriot, and a devoted worker for freedom." For Welch's assessment of Benson, see the "Introductory Remarks" he gave at a speech in Salt Lake, April 7, 1966, Box 2, Folder 3, Hugh B. Brown Research Files.

22. For McKay's rebuff of Benson joining JBS and sitting on its board, see McKay journal, August 9, 1963 (Box 54, Folder 1) and March 5, 1964 (Box 56, Folder 2), David O. McKay Papers.

23. Benson, quoted in "Benson Clarifies Views on Birch Society," *Salt Lake Tribune*, March 21, 1963; see also Benson to David O. McKay, March 25, 1966, Box 62, Folder 2, David O. McKay Papers; and Benson, "The Christ," *American Opinion* 7 (December 1964): 44, where he calls the Birch Society "valiant patriots," who are "courageously acting to bring about 'less government, more individual responsibility and a better world.'"

24. Benson to Welch, November 17, 1967, and Welch's reply politely declining the offer, November 22, 1967, both in Ezra Taft Benson Correspondence, JBS Headquarters.

25. For Benson's assertion that Eisenhower "gave help to the conspiracy," and for his initial reading of *The Politician* in 1961, see Benson to Hoover, May 28, 1965, Ezra Taft Benson File (62-104401).

26. Benson informed senior church official Joseph Fielding Smith that he first read *The Politician* in 1961 in galley form some two years before it was published in 1963. Benson to Smith, July 31, 1963, MSS SC 1260, L. Tom Perry Special Collections, Harold B. Library, Brigham Young University. Also in Box 11, Joseph Fielding Smith Papers, LDS Church History Library. The David O. McKay papers indicate that he sent this letter to each of the apostles.

27. Benson to Hoover, June 15, 1965, Ezra Taft Benson File (94-38023-5), Federal Bureau of Investigation Files and Records (Freedom of Information Act), Washington, D.C. The Benson-Welch papers at the John Birch Society Headquarters in Appleton, Wisconsin, contain receipts and acknowledgements of copies of *The Politician* that Benson ordered.

28. *The Politician* (1958 unpublished manuscript in Matt Harris's files), 267; *The Politician* (Belmont, Mass.: Belmont Publishing, 1964), 221–28, 249. Welch made the initial claim that Eisenhower was a communist in a 1958 unpublished manuscript he circulated among friends. The manuscript, which comprised 302 pages, was eventually titled *The Politician*. When journalists got a hold of it in 1960, they criticized him sharply for his controversial views about Eisenhower. When *The Politician* was officially published in 1963, Welch omitted some of his most controversial claims, including the line that Eisenhower was "a dedicated, conscious agent of the Communist conspiracy." Nevertheless, subsequent editions of *The Politician* affirm Welch's belief that Eisenhower was an unwitting agent of the Communist cause. See *The Politician*, rev. ed. (Appleton, Wisc.: Robert Welch University Press, 2002). Mulloy, *World of the John Birch Society*, 16–22, provides a succinct overview of the evolution of *The Politician* as well as attacks on it. See also David H. Bennett, *The Party of Fear: The American Far Right from Nativism to the Militia Movement*, revised and updated (New York: Vintage, 1995), 318–19.

29. Welch, *The Politician* (1958), 267.

30. Ibid., 267–68. See also Robert Welch, *The Blue Book* (Appleton, Wisc.: Western Islands, orig. pub. 1959; reprint, 1999), 192–93.

31. Mulloy, *World of the John Birch Society*, 117–24. See also Raymond Arsenault, *Freedom Riders: 1961 and the Struggle for Racial Justice* (New York: Oxford University Press, 2006); Henry Hampton and Steve Fayer, *Voices of Freedom: An Oral History of the Civil Rights Movement from the 1950s through the 1980s* (New York: Bantam Books, 1990), 73–96; Robert Dallek, *An Unfinished Life: John F. Kennedy, 1917–1963* (Boston: Little, Brown, 2004), 515–16, 594; Harvard Sitkoff, *The Struggle for Black Equality, 1954–1992*, rev. ed. (New York: Hill and Wang, 1993), 114–15, 129–30.

32. I explore this theme in greater detail in "Ezra Taft Benson, Dwight D. Eisenhower, and the Emergence of a Conspiracy Culture within the Mormon Church," *John Whitmer Historical Association Journal* 37 (Spring/Summer 2017): 59, 70–71.

33. Kennedy "Address on Civil Rights" (June 11, 1963), transcript at the Miller Center, University of Virginia, http://millercenter.org/president/speeches/speech-3375. Welch instructed his followers to "oppose the whole 'civil rights' program" of the Kennedy administration. *Birch Bulletin* (September 1963): 81.

34. Welch's anti–civil rights views are well known in *The Politician*, the *Birch Bulletin*, and the *American Opinion* magazine, but see in particular Welch, *A Letter to the South: On Segregation* (Belmont, Mass.: American Opinion, 1956; 1964); Welch, *To the Negroes of America* (Belmont, Mass.: American Opinion, 1967). Also see Manning Johnson, *Color, Communism, and Common Sense* (Boston: The Alliance, 1958); and Alan Stang, *It's Very Simple: The True Story of Civil Rights* (Boston: Western Islands, 1965). Other influential writings include John Rousselot, "Civil Rights: Communist Betrayal of a Good Cause," *American Opinion* (February 1964): 1–11; Scott Stanley Jr., "Revolution: The Assault on Selma," *American Opinion* (May 1965): 1–9; Gary Allen, "Black Power," *American Opinion* (January 1967): 1–14. See also Benjamin R. Epstein and Arnold Foster, "The War Against Civil Rights," which vividly recounts the Birch Society's opposition to racial equality. In Epstein and Arnold, *Report on the John Birch Society, 1966* (New York: Vintage, 1966), chap. 2.

35. *Birch Bulletin* (September 1963): 70.

36. Ibid., 73–74.

37. *Birch Bulletin* (September 1963): 78. See also Rousselot, "Civil Rights: Communist Betrayal of a Good Cause," 5–6; and Stang, *It's Very Simple*, 103–4, 111–13, 134–35. The best study of the Highlander School is John M. Glen, *Highlander: No Ordinary School, 1932–1962* (Lexington: University Press of Kentucky, 1988).

38. *Birch Bulletin* (September 1963): 78. Glen, *Highlander*, 181–82, details how an undercover photographer infiltrated a meeting at the school with the purpose of exposing it as a communist front group.

39. See, for example, Glen, *Highlander*, chap. 9; Garrow, *FBI and Martin Luther King*, 24–25, 63; Branch, *Parting the Waters*, 853–54.

40. The apostle was born and raised in Whitney, Idaho, in a small, predominantly white Mormon farming community named after LDS apostle Orson F. Whitney. In 1899, the year before Benson was born, the state only had 293 African Americans. By 1940 less than 1 percent of the population in Idaho were African Americans, which limited the apostle's exposure to black people. Arguably, the earliest contact Benson had with African Americans occurred in 1939 when he accepted a position in Washington, D.C., as the Executive Secretary of the National Council of Farm Cooperatives. There he lived among black people in the nation's capital. For Idaho census figures on African Americans, consult Quintard Taylor, *In Search of the Racial Frontier: African Americans in the American West, 1528–1990* (New York: W.W. Norton, 1998), 135, 253. For Benson living among the "colored" population in Washington, D.C., see Benson to David O. McKay, January 17, 1961, reel 7, Ezra Taft Benson Papers, LDS Church History Library.

41. Benson, *Title of Liberty*, 1, 5, 15.

42. So characterized by BYU president Ernest Wilkinson, a close friend of Benson's. In Wilkinson journal, September 27, 1963, Box 101, Folder 3, Ernest Wilkinson Papers, L. Tom Perry Special Collections, Harold B. Lee Library, Brigham Young University.

43. "Ezra Taft Benson's Support of the John Birch Society is Criticized," Proceedings and Debates of the 88th Congress, *Congressional Record* (September 25, 1963): 3–4. Jack Langguth, "Birch Society Aim Hailed by Benson: He Won't Rebut Eisenhower Denunciation by Welch," *New York Times*, September 23, 1963. "Benson Speaker at Testimonial Dinner," *Associated Press*, September 24, 1963. The *Washington Post* reported on the pre-coverage publicity of the event, "Benson to Speak at the John Birch Fete," September 20, 1963. For a succinct explanation of the Harding episode, consult Gregory A. Prince and Wm. Robert Wright, *David O. McKay and the Rise of Modern Mormonism* (Salt Lake City: University of Utah Press, 2005), 296–302; D. Michael Quinn, *The Mormon Hierarchy: Extensions of Power* (Salt Lake City: Signature Books, 1997), 75. For Eisenhower's response to Benson's Birch address, see Harris, "Ezra Taft Benson, Dwight D. Eisenhower, and the Emergence of a Conspiracy Culture within the Mormon Church," 64–69.

44. Smith to Ralph Harding, October 30, 1963, Box 5, Folder 22, David John Buerger Papers, Special Collections, Marriott Library, University of Utah; McKay to Harding, October 18, 1963, ibid. See also Wallace Turner, "Birch Dinner in Salt Lake City Vexes Mormons," *New York Times*, April 8, 1966.

45. Brown tried unsuccessfully to lift the ban in 1962, 1963, and 1969. He did not believe the ban was doctrinal. See Lowell L. Bennion conversation with Brown, February 12, 1962, as recounted by T. Edgar Lyon, scrap of notes, Box 26, Folder 1, T. Edgar Lyon Papers, LDS Church History Library; "'Saint for All Seasons': Interview with Lowell Bennion," *Sunstone* 10 (February 1985): 11; Lowell Bennion oral history with Maureen Ursenbach Beecher, March 9, 1985, LDS History Church Library; Brown to John F. Fitzgerald, March 13, 1962, Box 4, Folder 10, Special Collections, Merrill-Cazier Library, Utah State University. In 1963, Brown told *New York Times* reporter Wallace Turner that "We are in the midst of a survey looking toward the possibility of admitting Negroes." In "Mormons Weigh Stand on Negro," *New York Times*, June 7, 1963; "Negro Issue is Considered by Mormons," *Chicago Tribune*, July 9, 1963; "Mormons Consider Move," *Wall Street Journal*, August 2, 1963. Charlie Brown, the First Presidency counselor's son, emphatically stated that his father had opposed the ban since the 1930s. In Charlie Brown oral history interview with Gregory A. Prince, June 6, 1995, Matt Harris files (courtesy of Greg Prince). See also Edwin B. Firmage, ed., *An Abundant Life: The Memoirs of Hugh B. Brown*, second ed., enlarged (Salt Lake City: Signature Books, 1999), 142.

46. Brown General Conference address, October 4–6, 1963, in *Conference Report* (Salt Lake City: Church of Jesus Christ of Latter-day Saints, 1963), 91; and Brown, "The Fight Between Good and Evil," *Improvement Era* 66 (December 1963): 1058.

47. Brown to John W. Fitzgerald, October 21, 1963, Box 4, Folder 10, John W. Fitzgerald Papers, Special Collections, Merrill-Cazier Library, Utah State University.

48. Even though the NAACP called off its protest at the 1963 General Conference, some NAACP members opined that Brown's statement "wasn't strong enough." Brown did not specifically endorse a public accommodations bill then circulating in the Utah legislature, which frustrated them. As recalled by NAACP member Danny Burnett, in

Burnett oral history interview with Leslie G. Kelen, September 20, 1983, 45, Box 4, Folder 3, Interviews with African Americans in Utah, 1982–1988, Special Collections, Marriott Library, University of Utah.

49. "Benson, Graham Rip Wheat Sale," *Deseret News*, October 28, 1963. See also "Benson Says Black Is Red," *Daily Utah Chronicle* (University of Utah student newspaper), October 29, 1963. See also "Stake Conference Assignments," *Deseret News*, "Church News," October 19, 1963, p. 4.

50. "A Race Against Time" (December 10, 1963; BYU); "We Must Become Alerted and Informed" (December 13, 1963; Logan Tabernacle), "The Internal Threat Today" (December 19, 1963; Boise, Idaho), all in Benson, *Title of Liberty*, 22–41, 42–60, 61–85 (quote on 58).

51. Two exceptions are Republicans J. Edgar Hoover and Ronald Reagan, both of whom depicted racial unrest, urban violence, and black power as communist inspired. For this point, see Woods, *Prisoners of Hope*, 340. Most prominent Republicans rejected the civil rights–communism link and most eschewed the Birch Society. See David Farber, *The Rise and Fall of Modern American Conservatism: A Short History* (Princeton, N.J.: Princeton University Press, 2010), 70–75; Lisa McGirr, *Suburban Warriors: The Origins of the New American Right* (Princeton, N.J.: Princeton University Press, 2001), 218–19, 222–23; Robert Alan Goldberg, *Barry Goldwater* (New Haven, Conn.: Yale University Press, 1995), 137–38; Carol T. Bogus, *Buckley: William F. Buckley, Jr. and the Rise of Modern Conservatism* (New York: Bloomsbury Press, 2011), chap. 4; Schoenwald, *A Time for Choosing*, 98–99.

52. For Hargis's conspiratorial views, see Lee Roy Chapman, "The Strange Love of Dr. Billy James Hargis," *This Land* 3 (November 1, 2012): http://thislandpress.com/2012/11/02/the-strange-love-of-dr-billy-james-hargis/; Bennett, *Party of Fear*, 328–31, 336. Hargis started the Christian Crusade Ministry in 1950 and published a monthly magazine of the same name. Benson published his "Trade and Treason" address in Hargis's magazine *Christian Crusade* 19 (April 1967): 22–24. The pair first met in 1962 when Benson spoke at Hargis's "Anti-Communist Leadership School," along with other anticommunists. For this point, see Powers, *Not Without Honor*, 279; and Hargis to Reed Benson, August 8, 1962, reel 2, Ezra Taft Benson Papers. In 1963 and again in 1967, Benson spoke at rallies with Hargis. See "Ezra Taft Benson Addresses Rally," *Deseret News*, January 7, 1963; Drew Pearson, "Ezra Taft Benson and the Birchers," *Madera Daily Tribune*, January 22, 1963; Hendrik Hertzberg and Michael Lerner, "'Rally for God and Country' Draws 1000 Conservatives, NAACP Pickets," *Harvard Crimson*, January 7, 1963; "This Week! 5 Great Nights of Christian Leadership Training: Christian Crusade Leadership School—Feb. 20–24," advertisement in the *Tulsa Daily World*, February 19, 1967.

53. Woods, *Prisoners of Hope*, 12–13; Dan T. Carter, *The Politics of Rage: George Wallace, the Origins of the New Conservatism, and the Transformation of American Politics* (New York: Simon & Schuster, 1995), 217; George Lewis, "White South, Red Nation: Massive Resistance and the Cold War," in Clive Webb, *Massive Resistance: Southern Opposition to the Second Reconstruction* (New York: Oxford University Press, 2005), 120–29.

54. Benson praised Wallace in a letter to Birch founder Robert Welch of March 8, 1968, Ezra Taft Benson Correspondence, JBS Headquarters. The apostle also characterized Wallace as "a good man." In "Benson Backs Wallace Stand," *Christian Science Monitor*, February 13, 1968. Wallace explained that his philosophy and "that of Mr. Benson are

consistent and compatible." In Wallace to David O. McKay, February 12, 1968, Box 2, Folder 3, George C. Wallace Collection, Alabama Department of Archives and History. Citing Benson's "church responsibilities," McKay rebuffed Wallace's overture to have the Mormon apostle join the ticket. See McKay journal, September 9, 1968, Box 68, Folder 3, David O. McKay Papers; and Carter, *Politics of Rage*, 356.

55. Richard Norton Smith, *On His Own Terms: A Life of Nelson Rockefeller* (New York: Random House, 2014), xx–xxi; Clark R. Mollenhoff, *George Romney: Mormon in Politics* (New York: Meredith Press, 1968), 260–61; Rick Perlstein, *Nixonland: The Rise of a President and the Fracturing of America* (New York: Scribner, 2008), 126–27; Michael A. Cohen, *American Maelstrom: The 1968 Election and the Politics of Division* (New York: Oxford University Press, 2016), 176–77, 186–87, 209; Schoenwald, *A Time for Choosing*, 146–51.

56. Goldberg, *Barry Goldwater*, 174–75, 218–19, 246; Joseph Crespino, *Strom Thurmond's America* (New York: Hill and Wang, 2012), 140–41, 170–76; Farber, *Rise and Fall*, 176, 183, 190–91; McGirr, *Suburban Warriors*, 123, 133, 140; Bogus, *Buckley*, chap. 3. Some of these conservatives were Benson's friends. Apostle Benson and Senator Goldwater, for example, enjoyed a close relationship and exchanged dozens of letters through the years. See Box 41, Folder 20, Ezra Taft Benson Papers; Box 2, Folder 7, Barry Goldwater Papers, Special Collections, Hayden Library, University of Arizona.

57. Benson, *Title of Liberty*, 58 (quote), 62, 76; Benson, *So Shall Ye Reap: Selected Addresses of Ezra Taft Benson*, compiled by Reed A. Benson (Salt Lake City: Deseret Book, 1960), 243–44. Reed Benson also echoed this line, as did Ernest Wilkinson, Benson's close friend. See "Reed Benson Speaks on Birchers; Upholds Civil Rights Battle," *Utah Daily Chronicle*, October 9, 1963; and Wilkinson journal, February 17–22, 1964, Box 101, Folder 4, Ernest L. Wilkinson Papers, L. Tom Perry Special Collections, Harold B. Lee Library, Brigham Young University.

58. "A Race Against Time" (December 10, 1963; BYU); "We Must Become Alerted and Informed" (December 13, 1963; Logan Tabernacle), "The Internal Threat Today" (December 19, 1963; Boise, Idaho), all in Benson, *Title of Liberty*, 22–41, 42–60, 61–85. See also Benson, "Not Commanded in All Things," April 6, 1965, *Improvement Era* 68 (June 1965): 537–39.

59. Moss to Hugh B. Brown, February 19, 1964, Box 122, Folder 3, Frank E. Moss Papers, Special Collections, Marriott Library, University of Utah. Moss also denounced Benson's extreme views on the floor of the U.S. Senate. "Politics of Extremism," Proceedings and Debates of the 89th Congress, *Congressional Record* (July 13, 1966): 5.

60. Ezra Taft Benson general conference address "Not Commanded in All Things," April 6, 1965, unaltered version, David O. McKay Scrapbook #79, David O. McKay Papers. Compare with the published version in *Improvement Era* 68 (June 1965): 537–39. Benson decried federal aid to education some six years earlier when he warned President Eisenhower to reject it. See Benson to Eisenhower, January 19, 1959, reel 6, Ezra Taft Benson Papers.

61. Wilkinson journal, April 6, 1965, Box 101, Folder 5, Ernest L. Wilkinson Papers, L. Tom Perry Special Collections, Harold B. Lee Library, Brigham Young University.

62. First Presidency Minutes, April 23, 1965, Box 59, Folder 5, David O. McKay Papers. For McKay authorizing striking the civil rights portion of Benson's speech from the record,

see First Presidency Minutes, May 3, 1965, ibid. For senior apostle Harold Lee's response to Benson's address, see his BYU devotional address "Be Not Deceived," *Speeches of the Year* (Provo, Utah: Extension Publications, Division of Continuing Education, Brigham Young University, 1965), 9.

63. "Benson Ties Rights Issue to Reds in Mormon Rift," *Washington Post*, April 13, 1965. See also "Mormon 'Fight' over Civil Rights," *San Francisco Chronicle*, April 17, 1965. The *Deseret News*, the church-owned and -operated newspaper, did not discuss the conflict between Benson and Brown. See "Fight Red Influence Church Told," *Deseret News*, April 7, 1965. See also Hugh B. Brown to Sterling M. McMurrin, April 9, 1965, Box 290, Folder 3, Sterling M. McMurrin Papers, Special Collections, Marriott Library, University of Utah, wherein Brown notes that Benson was "still leading[ing] the attack in the opposite direction." Apostle Spencer W. Kimball called Brown's affirmation of civil rights in General Conference "an official statement and the Church's stand with regard to it." In Kimball journal, October 6, 1963, reel 25, Spencer W. Kimball Papers, LDS Church History Library.

64. "An Act to Prohibit Discrimination in Business and Establishments and Places for Public Accommodation and to Provide Civil Remedies for Violation Thereof," 1965, Box 24, Folder 3, J. D. Williams Papers, Special Collections, Marriott Library, University of Utah. Utah's failure to support civil rights legislation was already a concern for civil rights activists. In 1959 and 1961, the United States Commission on Civil Rights issued two reports condemning Utah lawmakers for the state's inaction on civil rights. See "Utah's Advisory Committee," *The National Conference and the Reports of the State Advisory Committees to the U.S. Commission on Civil Rights, 1959* (Washington, D.C.: U.S. Government Printing Press, 1960), 375–83; "1961 Report: Utah Advisory Committee to the United States Commission on Civil Rights," reel 7, part 27 (Utah), Selected Branch Files, *Papers of the National Association for the Advancement of Colored People* (Bethesda, Md.: University Publications of America, 1991).

65. Spencer W. Kimball journal, March 9, 1965, reel 27, Spencer W. Kimball Papers. See also "NAACP Appeals to Church," *Deseret News*, March 8, 1965.

66. Johnie M. Driver, "L.D.S. Church Leaders Should Speak Out for Moral Justice," March 9, 1965, Box 1, Folder 29, Stephen Holbrook Papers, Utah State Historical Society. Albert Fritz, who preceded Driver as the NAACP president, also observed that the "L.D.S. influence" prevented a civil rights bill from passing "because [Mormons] were in control of the legislature." In Fritz oral history interview with Leslie G. Kelen, May 5, 1983, 34, Box 2, Folder 6, Interviews with African Americans in Utah, 1982–1988, Special Collections, Marriott Library, University of Utah. Another NAACP member complained: "We all know that the major cause of discrimination against the Negro in Utah springs from a doctrine of the LDS church which holds that the Negro is cursed and not entitled to the blessings of the Priesthood." In D. H. Oliver, *A Negro on Mormonism* (Salt Lake City: D. H. Oliver, 1963), 14.

67. First Presidency Minutes, March 8, 1965, Box 59, Folder 3, David O. McKay Papers. See also editorial "A Clear Civil Rights Stand," *Deseret News*, March 9, 1965; and "Civil Rights Still Needs Patience," *Deseret News*, February 12, 1964. First Presidency counselor N. Eldon Tanner stated that civil rights "is not a moral question and therefore not a church matter." In Glen W. Davidson, "Mormon Missionaries and the Race Question," *Christian Century* 82 (September 29, 1965): 1185. See also Hugh B. Brown to Sterling M. McMurrin,

April 9, 1965, Box 290, Folder 3, Sterling M. McMurrin Papers, Special Collection, Marriott Library, University of Utah. After resisting civil rights legislation for many years, the Utah State Legislature passed the "Anti-Discrimination Act of 1965," part of which included a public accommodations bill and a fair employment practices bill. In "1965 Session: Bill 62, Legislature House Working Bills, 1896–1989," Box 32, Folder 61, Series 432, Utah State Records and Archives Service, Salt Lake City, Utah.

68. The two men exchanged several letters during Benson's mission assignment. Benson's letters are written on European mission letterhead and are located in the Ezra Taft Benson Correspondence, JBS Headquarters, Appleton, Wisc.

69. My thanks to the Interlibrary Loan Staff at UCLA for lending the originals of Benson's *Birch Bulletin and American Opinion*. Benson wrote "ETB" in the top right-hand corner of these Birch publications.

70. Robert Welch, *Two Revolutions at Once* (Belmont, Mass.: American Opinion, 1965), 6–7.

71. Benson to Welch, August 11, 1965, Ezra Taft Benson Correspondence, JBS Headquarters, Appleton, Wisc. Welch, "What's Wrong with Civil Rights?" (Belmont, Mass.: American Opinion, 1965), n.p.

72. *Birch Bulletin* (August 2, 1965): 4. See also the September issue of the *Birch Bulletin* (September 1965), which also displayed on the front cover the caption: "fully expose the civil rights fraud and you will break the back of the communist conspiracy."

73. "Critical of the Church: NAACP Studies Action," *Deseret News*, July 2, 1965; "NAACP Asks Foreign Bar of Missionaries," *Daily Utah Chronicle*, May 6, 1965.

74. *Birch Bulletin* (September 1965): 23–24; see also Gary Allen and Bill Richardson, "Los Angeles: Hell in the City of Angels," *American Opinion* (September 1965): 1–15; Gary Allen, "The Plan to Burn Los Angeles," *American Opinion* (May 1967): 31–40. The best discussion of the Watts Riots is James T. Patterson, *The Eve of Destruction: How 1965 Transformed America* (New York: Basic Books, 2012), 179–88.

75. Benson, *Enemy Hath Done This*, 69–70.

76. Benson asked President McKay for permission for Reed to join the JBS, but the president told the elder Benson that it was his decision to make. As recounted in David O. McKay journal, October 26, 1962, Box 51, Folder 5, David O. McKay Papers. See also "Reed A. Benson Takes Post in Birch Society," *Deseret News*, October 27, 1962; and Benson, *Title of Liberty*, 39.

77. Reed A. Benson "Memo to the Utah Chapters," September 2, 1965, Ezra Taft Benson Correspondence, JBS Headquarters, Appleton, Wisc.; also in Box 27, Folder 7, J. D. Williams Papers, Special Collection, Marriott Library, University of Utah.

78. "Benson Upholds Bircher Views," *Idaho Free Press*, April 22, 1965; "Bircher Asserts King Injuries Negro's Cause," *Modesto Bee*, July 21, 1965; Doug Bradley, "Reed Benson: Bircher Urges Look at Goals," *Denver Post*, April 24, 1965. See also Willard Clopton, "Cookies, Talk of Treason Served, at Opening of Birch Headquarters," *Washington Post*, September 18, 1965, in which Reed Benson also accused President Johnson of treason.

79. Reed Benson to David O. McKay, January 10, 1963, Matt Harris files (courtesy of Joe Geisner).

80. Neither Francis M. Gibbons, *Ezra Taft Benson: Statesman, Patriot, Prophet of God* (Salt Lake City: Deseret Book, 1996), 244, nor Sheri L. Dew, *Ezra Taft Benson: A Biography*

(Salt Lake City: Deseret Book, 1987), 382, discuss the turmoil surrounding Benson's return from Germany.

81. "NAACP Chapter Claims Riot Report 'Malicious,'" *Ogden Standard-Examiner*, September 28, 1965; "NAACP Assails Rumors of Protest at LDS Meet," *Salt Lake Tribune*, September 29, 1965; "NAACP Says 'Too Fantastic' Rumors of Demonstrations," *Ogden Standard-Examiner*, September 27, 1965; "Race Riots in Utah?" *Daily Utah Chronicle*, September 28, 1965. L. Brent Goates, *Harold B. Lee: Prophet and Seer* (Salt Lake City: Bookcraft, 1985), 378, explained that there were "rumors of blacks invading Salt Lake City to take vengeance upon the Saints and the Church." See also William A. Wilson and Richard C. Poulsen, "The Curse of Cain and Other Stories: Blacks in Mormon Folklore," *Sunstone* 5 (Fall–Winter 1980): 10.

82. In "Memo to the Utah Chapters," Reed explained that Robert Welch had ordered the "whispering campaign."

83. For Benson's support of Reed's employment at the Birch Society, see Benson, *Title of Liberty*, 39; and David O. McKay journal, October 26, 1962, Box 51, Folder 5, David O. McKay Papers.

84. Council of the Twelve Minutes, November 4, 1965, Box 64, Folder 8, Spencer W. Kimball Papers.

85. Salt Lake City NAACP Branch Newsletter, April 1966, reel 7, part 27 (Utah), Selected Branch Files, *Papers of the National Association for the Advancement of Colored People*.

86. Peniel E. Joseph, *Waiting 'Til the Midnight Hour: A Narrative History of Black Power in America* (New York: Henry Holt, 2006); Manning Marable, *Malcolm X: A Life of Reinvention* (New York: Viking, 2011); Peniel E. Joseph, *Stokely: A Life* (New York: Basic Books, 2014); Sitkoff, *Struggle for Black Equality*.

87. Harris and Bringhurst, *Mormon Church and Blacks*, 75–89; Bringhurst, *Saints, Slaves, and Blacks*, 172–73.

88. Two nonpracticing, high-profile Latter-day Saints were the most vocal critics of the priesthood and temple ban: Stewart Udall, secretary of interior in the Kennedy administration, and Sterling McMurrin, commissioner of education in the Kennedy administration and also professor of philosophy at the University of Utah. See Stewart L. Udall, "An Appeal for Full Fellowship of the Negro," *Dialogue: A Journal of Mormon Thought* 2 (Summer 1967): 5–7; Sterling M. McMurrin, "The Negroes Among the Mormons," Address to the Annual Banquet, Salt Lake Chapter NAACP, June 21, 1968, copy in Box 289, Folder 2, Sterling M. McMurrin Papers, Special Collections, Marriott Library, University of Utah. Both critiques made national headlines, prompting a swift response from church authorities. See, for example, "Udall Entreats Mormons on Race," *New York Times*, May 19, 1967; "Udall Urges Mormons to End Negro Bias," *Los Angeles Times*, May 20, 1967; "Udall Prods Mormons to Solve Negro Issue" *Arizona Republic*, May 19, 1967; "Stewart Udall and the Mormon Church," *Arizona Daily Star*, May 20, 1967; "Udall Asks LDS to Reexamine Negro Doctrine," *Salt Lake Tribune*, May 19, 1967; apostle Delbert L. Stapley to Stewart L. Udall, May 26, 1967, Box 209, Folder 5, Stewart L. Udall Papers, Special Collections, University of Arizona Library, University of Arizona; First Presidency Minutes, May 24, 1967, Box 65, Folder 2, David O. McKay Papers; "U Professor Rues LDS Stand Negro Stand," *Salt Lake Tribune*, June 22, 1968; "Mormon Negro Policies Called Harmful to the Church," *Middletown Journal*

(Middletown, Ohio), June 23, 1968; "Race Issue Decried by Mormon," *Arizona Daily Citizen*, June 23, 1968; "Expert Says Racism Hurts Mormon Church," *Bridgeport Post* (Bridgeport, Conn.), June 23, 1968; "Race Policy Change Urged for Mormons," *Fort Lauderdale News-Sun-Sentinel*, June 23, 1968; "Utah Educator Raps Mormon Negro Stand," *Trenton Sunday Times Advertiser* (Trenton, N.J.), June 23, 1968; "Bias Will Drive Out Members, Mormon Warns," *Miami Herald*, June 23, 1968; "Mormon Race Practices Criticized," *Phoenix Gazette*, June 23, 1968; "Ex Commissioner of Education Raps LDS Negro Policy," *Ogden Standard Examiner*, June 22, 1968; David O. McKay journal, June 26, 1968, Box 67, Folder 6, David O. McKay Papers; and Box 14, Folder 30, Joseph Fielding Smith Papers, LDS Church History Library. For an insightful treatment of Benson's presidential aspirations, see Newell G. Bringhurst, "Potomac Fever: Continuing Quest for the U.S. Presidency" in this volume.

89. Benson, *An Enemy Hath Done This*, 310. For the Hoover speech Benson quoted, see "The FBI and Civil Rights—J. Edgar Hoover Speaks Out," *U.S. News and World Report*, November 30, 1964, 56.

90. A number of letters to the editor in the BYU student newspaper the *Daily Universe* illustrates this point. Henry J. Nicholes, October 31, 1966 ("Beliefs"); James S. Olsen, November 29, 1966 ("Poor Judgement"); Brad Larsen, November 29, 1966 ("Lumping"); Cecil Smith, December 1, 1966 ("Answers"); Steven M. Thomas, October 18, 1967 ("Ridiculous"); Jim Hurst, October 20, 1967; Betty J. McDaniel, April 24, 1968 ("Dr. King"); Judy Geissler, April 30, 1969 ("In Memoriam: M.L. King"); Gary L. Olsen, May 6, 1969 ("Geissler's King"); Judy Geissler, May 7, 1969 ("Racial Bigotry: An Open Letter"); Jerry Names, May 12, 1969 ("Disobedience Judy"); May 12, 1969, Michael Vanhille, May 12, 1969 ("King Response").

91. Larry T. Wimmer to Martin Luther King, December 2, 1966, Martin Luther King Papers, King Center, Atlanta, Georgia. Wimmer taught economics at BYU from 1963 to 2006.

92. Gustive O. Larson to Hugh B. Brown, October 26, 1966, Box 1, Folder 5, Hugh B. Brown Research Files, L. Tom Perry Special Collections, Harold B. Lee Library, BYU. Larson taught religion and history at BYU from 1954 to 1972. See also BYU history professors Thomas G. Alexander and Douglas F. Tobler to Ernest L. Wilkinson, November 26, 1969, Box 177, Folder 16, Ernest L. Wilkinson Papers, L. Tom Perry Special Collections, Harold B. Lee Library, Brigham Young University.

93. Hugh B. Brown journal, August 6–12, 1967, Box 52, Folder 14, Richard D. Poll Papers, Special Collections, Marriott Library, University of Utah. See also David O. McKay journal, September 1, 1967, Box 66, Folder 1, David O. McKay Papers.

94. McKay journal, September 22, 1967, Box 66, Folder 2, David O. McKay Papers.

95. Benson, "Trust Not the Arm of Flesh," *Improvement Era* 70 (December 1967): 55–58. Benson referenced Birch writers repeatedly throughout the talk, as well as Hoover's writings.

96. Ibid., 56.

97. Ibid.

98. Ibid., 57.

99. Ibid.

100. For the apostles' views on civil rights, see Harris and Bringhurst, *Mormon Church and Blacks*, 67–68, 74–75; Prince and Wright, *David O. McKay*, chap. 4; Bringhurst, *Saints,*

Slaves, and Blacks, chap. 9; F. Ross Peterson, "'Blindside': Utah on the Eve of *Brown v. Board of Education,*" *Utah Historical Quarterly* 73 (2005): 13–14.

101. Reed Benson to Robert Welch, November 2, 1967, Ezra Taft Benson Correspondence, JBS Headquarters, Appleton, Wisc.

102. Benson, *Civil Rights: A Tool of Communist Deception* (Salt Lake City: Deseret Book, 1968); and published the following year under the same title in Benson, *An Enemy Hath Done This,* 189–200. Remarkably, both of Benson's authorized biographies omit this address. See Dew, *Ezra Taft Benson* and Gibbons, *Ezra Taft Benson. Civil Rights: A Tool of Communist Deception* was widely sold throughout bookstores in Utah, including BYU. See "U.S. Journal: Provo, Utah," *New Yorker,* March 21, 1970, 122.

103. Petersen, "Our Divine Destiny," *BYU Speeches* (February 20, 1968): https://speeches.byu.edu/talks/mark-e-petersen_divine-destiny/. See also his April 1968 conference address, "America and God," *Improvement Era* 71 (June 1968): 76–79; and G. Homer Durham, "The Racial Revolution in America," *Improvement Era* 71 (October 1968): 93–95.

104. Ernest L. Wilkinson memo, "Confidential," to BYU Religion Dean Roy Doxey, February 20, 1968, Box 443, Folder 11, Ernest L. Wilkinson Presidential Papers, L. Tom Perry Special Collections, Harold B. Lee Library, BYU; Wilkinson diary, February 20, 1968, Box 102, Folder 5, Ernest L. Wilkinson Papers.

105. Ezra Taft Benson memo to General Authorities, re: Martin Luther King, April 6, 1968, MS d 4936, LDS Church History Library (my thanks to church archivist William Slaughter for providing a copy); also in Box 63, Folder 1, Spencer W. Kimball Papers. Benson also sent the memo to his close friend, J. Willard Marriott. See Benson to Marriott, May 1, 1969, Box 12, Folder 23, J. Willard Marriott Papers, Special Collections, Marriott Library, University of Utah. Brown's grandson Edwin Firmage recalled that his grandfather was "heartsick" over Benson's memo and believed that the Birch Society was responsible for it. In Edwin B. Firmage oral history interview with Gregory A. Prince, June 6, 1995, Matt Harris files. See also Charlie Brown oral history interview with Gregory A. Prince, Mary 24, 1996. My thanks to Greg Prince for sharing these transcripts with me. Some Latter-day Saints complained that church leaders did not observe President Johnson's "national day of mourning" for Dr. King. See letters to the editor, *Dialogue: A Journal of Mormon Thought* 3 (Summer 1968): 5–7.

106. Benson to the First Presidency and Quorum of the Twelve, April 18, 1968, Box 67, Folder 4, David O. McKay Papers.

107. Benson, "The Book of Mormon Warns America" (May 21, 1968), in *An Enemy Hath Done This,* 334–35. See also Benson, "Americans are Destroying America," *Improvement Era* 71 (June 1968): 68–71.

108. G. Roy Fugal to President Harold B. Lee, March 27, 1970, Box 63, Folder 3, Spencer W. Kimball Papers; Bishop Victor L. Brown memo to General Authorities re: Security during General Conference, April 2, 1970, reel 34, Spencer W. Kimball Papers, ibid.; Spencer W. Kimball journal, April 4–5, 1970, reel 34; L. Brent Goates, *Harold B. Lee: Prophet and Seer* (Salt Lake City: Bookcraft, 1985), 413–14; Heidi S. Swinton, *To the Rescue: The Biography of Thomas S. Monson* (Salt Lake City: Deseret Book, 2010), 365–66; Susan Peterson, "The Great and Dreadful Day: Mormon Folklore of the Apocalypse," in Eric A. Eliason and Tom Mould, eds., *Latter-day Lore: Mormon Folklore Stories* (Salt Lake City: University of Utah Press, 2013), 269.

109. For two seminal accounts of the BYU athletic protests, see J. B. Haws, *The Mormon Image in the American Mind: Fifty Years of Public Perception* (New York: Oxford University Press, 2013), chap. 3; and Gary James Bergera, "'This Time of Crisis': The Race-Based Anti-BYU Athletic Protests of 1968–1971," *Utah Historical Quarterly* 81 (Summer 2013): 204–229. For a broader context to the BYU athletic protests, consult Darron T. Smith, *When Race, Religion, and Sport Collide: Black Athletes at BYU and Beyond* (Lanham, Md.: Rowman and Littlefield, 2016), chap. 4.

110. Bergera, "This Time of Crisis"; Haws, *Mormon Image*; William F. Reed, "The Other Side of 'the Y,'" *Sports Illustrated*, January 26, 1970; *New Yorker* (March 21, 1970): 120–25; "The Angry Black Athlete," *Newsweek*, July 15, 1968; "Trouble in Happy Valley," *Newsweek*, December 1, 1969; "Mormons and the Mark of Cain," *Time*, January 19, 1970 46; "Pigskin Justice and Mormon Theology," *Christian Century* 87 (January 21, 1970): 67. See also stories in the *Los Angeles Times*, August 27, 1967; *Miami Herald*, April 12, 1968; *Arizona Daily Star*, April 14, 1968; *San Francisco Chronicle*, December 20, 1969; *The Mercury*, December 30, 1969; *Seattle Post-Intelligencer*, March 28, 1970; *Honolulu Star-Bulletin*, October 27, 1970.

111. The resolution, proposed by the University of Utah, called for WAC teams to "sever all relations" with BYU until its "discriminatory" policies "are eliminated." In Wilkinson memo to Board of Trustees, re: "Charges of 'Racism' and 'Bigotry' Against the LDS Church," October 29, 1969, 6, MSS 5 C, 1969, "Compiled Information Concerning African Americans, BYU, and the Church," L. Tom Perry Special Collections, Harold B. Lee Library, Brigham Young University.

112. In 1968 and 1970, according to statistics that BYU filed with the U.S. Office for Civil Rights, 0.03 percent of the student body were "Negroes." In Box 42, Folder 11, Robert K. Thomas Papers, L. Tom Perry Special Collections, Harold B. Lee Library, Brigham Young University. WAC officials criticized BYU officials for not recruiting black students or athletes. See Wilkinson memo to Board of Trustees, re: "Charges of 'Racism' and 'Bigotry' Against the LDS Church," October 29, 1969, 8–10.

113. The Ernest L. Wilkinson Presidential Papers contains dozens of letters between his administration and members of the civil rights committee who investigated the alleged civil rights violations. In Box 463, Folders 19–20, Ernest L. Wilkinson Presidential Papers.

114. Wilkinson memo to Board of Trustees, re: "Charges of 'Racism' and 'Bigotry' Against the LDS Church," October 29, 1969, 9. In particular, protestors at the University of Washington criticized the church for its "racist" scriptures. They focused intently on the Book of Mormon. See Ernest L. Wilkinson to Alfred J. Schweppe, June 12, 1970, Box 42, Folder 11, Robert K. Thomas Papers. BYU academic vice president Robert K. Thomas asked BYU Religion dean Daniel H. Ludlow to draft a report outlining the alleged racist scriptures. In Thomas memo to Ludlow, "New Curriculum in the College of Religion," June 8, 1970, Box 27, Folder 8, Register of the Records of the College of Instruction, 1960–1973. Ludlow's report can be found in a memo to BYU President Ernest L. Wilkinson, June 11, 1970, Box 15, Folder 3.

115. Benson to Joseph Fielding Smith, March 3, 1966, reel 6, Ezra Taft Benson Papers, LDS Church History Library.

116. Cleon Skousen, "The Communist Attack on the Mormons," March 1970, in "Special Report by National Research Group," American Fork, Utah, p. 1. Skousen also addressed BYU students, in which he besmirched King and the civil rights movement. See

Skousen, "Know the Truth to Stay Free," speech to BYU students in 1971: http://www
.latterdayconservative.com/articles/know-the-truth-to-stay-free/. Skousen also criticized
King to BYU president Ernest Wilkinson. In Skousen memo to Wilkinson, January 23,
1970, Box 177, Folder 16, Ernest L. Wilkinson Papers, L. Tom Perry Special Collections,
Harold L. Lee Library, Brigham Young University. Benson and Skousen were neighbors
in Midway, Utah, and fellow Birch sympathizers. Though Skousen never joined the Birch
Society, he was sympathetic to their cause. In 1963 he published a twelve-page pamphlet
defending the Society against critics. Cleon Skousen, *The Communist Attack on the John
Birch Society* (Salt Lake City: Ensign Publishing, 1963).

117. Benson, "To the Humble Followers of Christ," *Improvement Era* 72 (June 1969): 43.

118. Goates, *Harold B. Lee*, 433–34; Kimball journal, February 18, 1970, reel 34, Spencer
W. Kimball Papers.

119. Mark E. Petersen asked J. Willard Marriott and other businessmen to attend the
meeting. In Petersen to Marriott, February 5, 1970, Box 52, Folder 14, J. Willard Marriott
Papers, Special Collections, Marriott Library, University of Utah; and Goates, *Harold B.
Lee*, 434.

120. For McKay's support of Benson's anti–civil rights' position, see McKay journal,
September 22, 1967, Box 66, Folder 2, David O. McKay Papers. McKay himself opposed
civil rights, but there is no evidence he believed that communists had infiltrated the civil
rights movement. For McKay and Benson's complicated relationship, and for McKay's
views on civil rights, see Prince and Wright, *David O. McKay*, chap. 4. For McKay's successors cracking down on Benson, see Harris, "Watchman on the Tower"; and D. Michael
Quinn, *The Mormon Hierarchy: Extensions of Power* (Salt Lake City: Signature Books,
1997), 107–8.

121. Kimball recounts several instances in his journal when he called in Benson to
chastise him for publicly expressing his right-wing views. In Kimball journal, February 22,
1974, March 15, 1974, November 5, 1974, all in reel 39, Spencer W. Kimball Papers. Kimball
also scolded Benson for a controversial speech he gave at BYU in 1980. In Leonard J.
Arrington Journal, June 17, 1980, Box 34, Folder 6, Leonard J. Arrington Papers, Special
Collections, Merrill-Cazier Library, Utah State University. For Kimball's universalist vision of the Mormon gospel, see Edward L. Kimball, *Lengthen Your Stride: The Presidency
of Spencer W. Kimball—Working Draft* (Salt Lake City: Benchmark Books, 2009), chaps.
14, 24.

122. This important event is covered in Edward L. Kimball, "Spencer W. Kimball and
the Revelation on Priesthood," *BYU Studies* 47 (Spring 2008): 5–85; Kimball, *Lengthen
Your Stride*, chaps. 21–22; and Harris and Bringhurst, *Mormon Church and Blacks*, 105–9.

123. Benson's biographers, Dew, *Ezra Taft Benson*, 457, and Gibbons, *Ezra Taft Benson*,
282, both explain that his support for the priesthood revelation was warm and genuine.
There is no evidence that Benson discussed the revelation in public, although Benson's
colleagues in church leadership did. See Gordon B. Hinckley, "Priesthood Restoration,"
Ensign 18 (October 1988): 69–72; David B. Haight, "This Work is True," *Ensign* 26 (May
1996): 23; and Bruce R. McConkie, "New Revelation on Priesthood," in *Priesthood* (Salt
Lake City: Deseret Book, 1981), 126–37.

124. David L. Chappell, *Waking from the Dream: The Struggle for Civil Rights in the
Shadow of Martin Luther King, Jr.* (New York: Random House, 2014), 102–5, 110–19. For

Bircher opposition to the proposed MLK holiday, see Hon. Larry McDonald (R-Georgia), "Americans, Stop Thinking Like Communists," June 18, 1980, *Congressional Record: Proceedings and Debates of the 96th Congress*, Second Session, 1–8.

125. "Holiday opponent says King exceeded Lucifer," *Arizona Republic*, October 5, 1989; "Bigotry rides again," *Arizona Republic*, October 6, 1989; "Sanders' letter angers his allies," *Phoenix Gazette*, October 6, 1989. Steve Benson affirmed that he leaked the letters to the Arizona newspaper in an email to Matt Harris, November 6, 2014 (my thanks to Benson for sharing his insights).

126. PR statement quoting Benson in ibid. Benson read this statement when he was first inaugurated as the church president. In Don Searle, "President Ezra Taft Benson Ordained Thirteenth President of the Church," *Ensign* (December 1985): https://www.lds.org/ensign/1985/12/president-ezra-taft-benson-ordained-thirteenth-president-of-the-church?lang=eng.

127. Terry Lee Williams, an African American legislator from Salt Lake City and sponsor of the MLK bill in Utah, explained that his colleagues opposed the King holiday because "King was associated with communists." In Terry Lee Williams oral history with Leslie G. Kelen, April 4, 1986, 62, 67, Box 7, Folder 5, Interviews with Blacks in Utah, 1982–1988, Special Collections, Marriot Library, University of Utah. See also Rev. France A. Davis and Nayra A. Atiya, *France Davis: An American Story Told* (Salt Lake City: University of Utah Press, 2007), 272. Davis is an influential Baptist minister in Salt Lake City and a leading civil rights supporter in the state. He played a pivotal role getting the Utah Legislature to support the King holiday. See John Devilbiss, "Utah, region balks at King holiday," *Ogden Standard-Examiner*, January 11, 1986; and Julie Howard, "Legislator proposes renaming holiday," *Daily Universe*, January 13, 2000. For Mormon complaints about the bill, see Kim Olsen to Gunn McKay, March 2, 1979, Box 450, Folder 4. K. Gunn McKay Papers, Special Collections, Merrill-Cazier Library, Utah State University; and Quinn, *Mormon Hierarchy*, 113, 471 n. 372. One Benson supporter—a prominent Bircher in Utah County—even balked when BYU invited Coretta Scott King, Martin's widow, to campus. Joel Ferguson to Ezra Taft Benson, Brigham Young Board of Trustees, Commissioner Henry D. Eyring, President Jeffery R. Holland, January 17, 1986, Box 15, Folder 6, Paul C. Richards Papers, Special Collections, Marriott Library, University of Utah.

128. Utah was the last state to recognize the King holiday. In Dawn House, "Civil rights speaker questions Utah's history with Martin Luther King, Jr. Day," *Salt Lake Tribune*, January 17, 2012.

129. "The Globe Reacts to Gordon B. Hinckley's Passing," *Salt Lake Tribune*, January 29, 2008; "Tributes to President Hinckley," *Ensign* 38 (March 2008): 4. Hinckley also addressed the NAACP. His sermon can be found in *Discourses of President Gordon B. Hinckley—Volume 1: 1995–1999*, 2 vols. (Salt Lake City: Deseret Book, 2005), 1:532–38. For newspaper coverage of the address, see Peg McEntee, "Families Can Save Us, Hinkley Says," *Salt Lake Tribune*, April 25, 1998; Lois M. Collins, "Bridge Racial Barriers, Hinckley Says," *Deseret News*, April 25, 1998; "Hinckley Speaks at NAACP Meeting," *Ogden Standard Examiner*, April 25, 1998. Hinckley's friendship with members of the NAACP leadership is discussed in "World Mourns Beloved Leader," *Deseret News*, January 28, 2008. Hinckley's outreach to the black community is well chronicled in Haws, *Mormon Image*, 175–81; Mauss, *All Abraham's Children*, 250–51. See also Darius Gray and Margaret Young, in *"Nobody Knows:*

The Untold Story of Black Mormons—Script," *Dialogue: A Journal of Mormon Thought* 42 (Fall 2009): 124–25.

130. Gordon B. Hinckley, "The Need for Greater Kindness," *Ensign* 36 (May 2006): 58–61. See also Hinckley, "This Is the Work of the Master," *Ensign* 25 (May 1995): 69–71; and especially Hinckley, *Standing for Something: 10 Neglected Virtues That Will Heal Our Hearts and Homes* (New York: Times Books, 2000), 47, depicting his racial sensitivity.

Apostles singing: Mark E. Petersen, Matthew Cowley, Spencer W. Kimball, Ezra
Taft Benson, and Harold B. Lee (at the piano).

Ezra Taft Benson and his family, April 7, 1958.

Secretary of Agriculture Ezra Taft Benson, center, introduces his daughter, Barbara, and his granddaughter, to LDS church president David O. McKay, February 1958.

Reed Benson with his father, Ezra Taft Benson, 1958.

Ezra Taft Benson, center, his son Reed Benson, right, and John Birch Society founder Robert Welch, left, at a Birch Society meeting, Salt Lake City, Utah, April 6, 1966.

LDS church president Ezra Taft Benson, center, with his counselors Gordon B. Hinckley, left, and Thomas S. Monson, right, at General Conference, October 1990.

Vice President George H. W. Bush with LDS church president Ezra Taft Benson, LDS church headquarters, Salt Lake City, Utah, February 21, 1986.

PART II

Theology

6   The Cold War and the Invention of Free Agency

MATTHEW BOWMAN

Late in the afternoon of July 26, 1943, Ezra Taft Benson arrived at the summer home of Heber J. Grant, the president of the Church of Jesus Christ of Latter-day Saints. Grant was in his late eighties, frail and resting on his bed when Benson entered, sat down, took Grant's hand, and learned that he had been chosen to join the Quorum of the Twelve Apostles, the second highest body of the Church. Benson was taken aback. "Oh, President Grant, that can't be," he repeated several times, before collecting himself. He and Grant then had an intimate conversation about human frailty and the challenges of running the Church. "We need more cooperation," Grant told Benson. "Bro. Brigham [Young] had the vision of us owning all this intermountain area, and we could have done it thru more cooperation."[1]

Grant was a grown man when Young died in 1877, so Benson believed he knew whereof he spoke. Grant's long life had been somewhat paradoxical; he both excelled at American capitalism and resented it. He had become wealthy in industry while a young man and well known in western business circles. But he also clung to Young's dream of an independent Mormon commonwealth, separate from the ever-expanding capitalism and federal bureaucracy of the United States. For instance, when he became convinced that Salt Lake City's livery companies were reluctant to serve Mormons, he founded his own and operated it at a loss. Grant's notion of freedom was bound into producerism, an ideology common among the independent communities of the American West. Producerists favored independence, hard work, the right to be left alone, and a localist ethos that distrusted large business and large government alike. They believed the health of those communities, from a single church congregation to American democracy itself, depended on a robust, shared morality. All these ideas were congenial to the Mormons.[2]

Like Grant, Ezra Taft Benson was firmly rooted in producerism. He was a lifelong farmer, and made his living organizing agricultural cooperatives, taking pride in the self-reliance that lay at the foundation of the cooperative ideal. When, ten years after his call to the apostleship, new president Dwight Eisenhower offered him a cabinet position, he and his fellow Mormons saw it as an opportunity to strengthen the nation's moral backbone. Then church president David O. McKay instructed Benson to accept Eisenhower's offer in "the proper spirit."[3] But in the twenty years between his conversation with Grant and his departure from Eisenhower's cabinet, Benson wove elements of this moralistic, localist interpretation of freedom into ideas of a larger scale, and in so doing helped to generate a new language of Mormon political theology. It would be harsher and more apocalyptic than Grant's producerism. Before the 1950s, Benson and Grant, like many other American Christians, emphasized the importance of individual morality for the maintenance of a free society. As the Cold War matured, however, Benson traveled to Europe and the Soviet Union and was shaken by what he found there, and through several associates was exposed to the conspiratorial anti-communism of the John Birch Society, a far-right group who warned that communist agents were infiltrating the United States to bring democracy down from within. By the time he left his post in the federal government, Benson's politics had blossomed into a full-blown cosmology, a moralistic libertarianism that amplified producerism's link between liberty and morality. While producerists believed that a firm morality was the bedrock of a robust democracy, Benson came to believe that the lack of political and economic freedom could in turn degrade morality. While earlier Mormons' localism made them suspicious of government, by the 1960s Benson had concluded that government was itself a potential moral hazard.

Free Agency within the Early Mormon Producerist Ideal

The theological pivot on which Benson's transformation turned was the notion of "free agency," a foundational component of Mormon theology. In the new scripture he produced, Joseph Smith rejected original sin, and instead emphasized an expansive notion of human liberty in which all had the ability to choose between good and evil. "Wherefore the Lord God gave unto man that he should act for himself . . . they are free to choose liberty and eternal life through the great mediation of all men, or to choose captivity and death according to the captivity and power of the devil," said the Book of Mormon.[4]

This insistence on the human right to choose developed in a favorable American religious context. In the early nineteenth century American Protestants began abandoning strict Calvinist doctrine that insisted God alone determined human salvation, which was to humankind's benefit, because the human will was utterly depraved from the fall and could not of itself choose goodness. While many American Protestants before the American Revolution—particularly the Puritans—embraced these ideas, during the Second Great Awakening in the early nineteenth century, many more rejected Calvinism and forged a stronger link between salvation and individuals' free moral choice. "Free will implies the power of originating and deciding our own choices, and of exercising our own sovereignty, in every instance of choice upon moral questions," declared the influential revivalist Charley Grandison Finney. "Unless the will is free, man has no freedom; and if he has no freedom he is not a moral agent." For Finney, salvation came only from a free choice to accept Jesus Christ as savior.[5]

Early Mormons intensified these ideas. Years after the production of the Book of Mormon, Joseph Smith dictated a revelation that credited the human ability to choose not to God's gift, as Finney did, but rather to humanity's own eternity. "Man was also in the beginning with God. Intelligence, or the light of truth, was not created or made, neither indeed can be," Joseph Smith said. "Behold, here is the agency of man."[6] This assertion of free agency instilled many Mormon thinkers with an absolute confidence that humanity was not depraved, and therefore, human beings were responsible for their moral choices. One of the most popular Mormon theologians of Benson's youth, James Talmage, explained what this meant: "The free agency of man enables him to choose or reject, to follow the path of life, or the road that leads to destruction; it is but just that he be held to answer for the exercise of his freedom, and that he meet the results of his acts."[7]

Throughout the nineteenth century when Mormon leaders like Talmage invoked the notion of free agency, its boundaries tended to reflect the strict moral demands that also underlay producerism. Mormon leaders emphasized the importance of moral decision making regardless of context, downplaying the importance of political or economic circumstance upon one's ability to choose righteously and instead emphasizing that all individuals had a grave responsibility to choose correctly. "God has given to all men an agency, and has granted to us the privilege to serve Him or serve Him not, to do that which is right or that which is wrong, and this privilege is given to all men irrespective of creed, color or condition. The wealthy have this agency, the poor have this agency, and no man is deprived by any power of God from exercising it in the fullest and in the freest manner," said Joseph F. Smith, future president of the Church, in 1883.[8] Free agency was centered on one's individual choices, and Mormons like Smith expected to exercise it regardless of pressures, needs, or external force.

Such defiance of circumstance dovetailed with the social and political context the Mormons found themselves in in the early twentieth century. In the 1880s and 1890s, through prosecution, court cases, and asset seizure, the federal government drove Mormon leaders to abandon polygamy, and Utah was admitted to the Union. As they cast about in pursuit of a distinct identity, many Mormon leaders came to replace plural marriage with ethical imperatives as key markers of Mormon distinctiveness. Free agency was thus framed as the choice to obey God. Grant, for instance, was a great advocate for the temperance movement, and as he said when he endorsed abstinence from alcohol, "if we shall accomplish anything for the reformation of the world, [we] must accomplish a reformation first in ourselves."[9] Susa Young Gates, a daughter of Brigham Young and the editor of the church's *Relief Society Magazine*, instructed, "There is much talk about freedom, but many forget they are free only insofar as they obey the edicts of Jehovah."[10] As the twentieth century went on, Mormon leaders took pride in a reputation for voluntary moral rigor.

This moral emphasis was matched in Mormon economics, as the church continued to promote producerist ideals. In the 1910s and 1920s, as president of the Utah-Idaho Sugar Company, a church-owned and -operated institution, Grant waged legal warfare with zealous progressives in the U.S. government suspicious of the company's tactics, which included price setting that favored Mormon suppliers and a number of attempts to control the western marketplace. Grant and other church leaders argued, in the words of Susa Young Gates, that the company's "business transaction . . . had for its motive the upbuilding of this state and the people."[11] To the federal government the sugar company represented a monopoly both in religion and economics, the second suspect but the first downright un-American. To these Mormon leaders, on the other hand, the company represented the producerist ethos that had long guided the Mormon settlements.

Given their localist bent, it is no surprise that by the time Grant invited Ezra Taft Benson to his home, both Mormons had developed a suspicion of Franklin Delano Roosevelt and the New Deal. Grant was a lifelong Democrat, but of the moralist, producerist variety that his friend William Jennings Bryan had espoused in his three runs for the presidency decades before.[12]

He feared that Roosevelt's New Deal would sap the nation's moral fervor generally and the ethical rigor of the church in particular. Grant and other Mormons like him built his complaints about the New Deal from a localist reading of Mormon success in the United States. "The hardship of pioneer life thus built into the warp and woof of the grandparents and parents of the present generation the sterling qualities of thrift, industry, honesty, integrity, sobriety, independence, love of liberty, and all the sterling virtues that go to make up a great people. The support of 'home industry' was one of the cardinal principles of the great commonwealth they were founding," read a letter Grant and his counselors sent to the Roosevelt administration in 1941. Because of these values, the letter said, "the Church has not found it possible to follow along the lines of the present general tendency in the matter of property rights, taxes, the curtailment of rights and liberties of the people, nor in general the economic policies of what is termed the 'New Deal.'"[13]

Benson similarly took pride in identifying links between his family's moral backbone, economic status, and loyalty to the LDS church. He often recalled another encounter he had with Grant a few years later, when the two men met on a street corner in Salt Lake City. Grant pointed across the street. "Your great grandfather built the finest home in Salt Lake city on that corner," he told Benson. Until, "Brigham Young called him into the office one day and said 'Brother Benson, we'd like you to go to Cache Valley.'" So Benson's ancestor sold his home and moved to the remote Utah valley to start a flourishing settlement there.[14] The story was instructive. Benson affirmed both his great-grandfather's willingness to sacrifice economic success for the good of the church but at the same time the rugged individualism that rendered him able to found a Mormon community when asked. Indeed, these ideals were the stuff of Benson's career. His lectures from that time detail an understanding of freedom sustained by moral behavior. In 1944 Benson delivered an address on CBS radio called "America Is a Choice Land," which juxtaposed the assertion that "liberty is a gift of heaven" with worry that "few families unite daily in family prayer and the reading of the scriptures. Yet all will agree that this practice in years past contributed much to the strength of this great nation."[15]

Connecting the health of democracy to American piety was not a Mormon innovation; rather, it was a widespread American habit well before the turn of the twentieth century. "Democracy is freedom. . . . The spiritual unification of humanity, the realization of the brotherhood of man all that Christ called the Kingdom of God, is but the further expression of this freedom," declared the young philosopher John Dewey at the University of Michigan in 1894.[16] More, as democracy seemed increasingly imperiled in the rise of

militarist and fascist regimes in the twentieth century, Americans increasingly emphasized that religion's first duty was the propagation of the sort of
moral behavior that could sustain self-government. The professor Alexander
Crawford mourned in the midst of the First World War that "The Germans
have seemed as a people to be devoted to material ends and have had no
interest in the spiritual advantages of free self-government."[17]

Indeed, by the middle twentieth century, the association between faith
and freedom was an article of faith for Dwight Eisenhower, and its language
allowed Benson to translate his Mormon commitments into the argot of
national politics. Nine years after he met with Heber J. Grant, Benson found
himself in a meeting with another president. In November 1952 he flew to
New York to see the freshly elected Eisenhower. On the strength of Benson's
work with the National Council of Farmer Cooperatives, and the fact that
Eisenhower wished to extend an olive branch to Robert Taft, leader of the
conservative wing of the Republican Party whom Benson had supported for
president, Eisenhower picked Benson to serve as secretary of agriculture.
Benson cited his position as a religious leader and his support for Taft to
demur when Eisenhower approached him, but the president-elect was not
having it. "Surely you believe that the job to be done is spiritual. Surely you
know that we have the great responsibility to restore confidence in the minds
of our people in their own government—that we've got to deal with spiritual
matters," responded Eisenhower, as Benson told the story to a Brigham Young
University audience the next month.[18] David O. McKay, then president of
the Church, similarly extoled the spiritual potential of the office in a blessing
he gave to Benson on the eve of Eisenhower's inauguration. "You will have
a responsibility, even greater than your associates in the cabinet . . . because
you go . . . as an apostle of the Lord Jesus Christ," said McKay. "You will have
that divine guidance which others may not have," Benson was promised,
and therefore, his capacity to ensure democracy would flourish would be
greater. "You might see, too, the enemies who would thwart the freedom of
the individual as vouchsafed by the Constitution," McKay exhorted, offering
a foretaste of what was to come in Benson's career.[19]

The Pivot toward Moral Libertarianism: 1940s–1950s

When he spoke there in late 1952, Benson told students at Brigham Young
University the story of Eisenhower to impress upon them the spiritual dimensions of politics but also to interpret the story in Mormon terms, showing
young Mormons that Eisenhower understood the link between free agency
and morality. Benson was at BYU to speak on "our Mormon economics and

philosophy that man shall earn his own living by the sweat of his own brow," as BYU president Ernest Wilkinson introduced his speech, and Benson delivered. More, as had Grant, Benson interpreted preserving freedom in the practical terms of sustaining the Mormon community, spending much of his talk musing on the Mormon struggle for national respect. Benson speculated that God allowed the Mormons to be persecuted in order to build their character, and he drew parallels between that struggle and American capitalism, noting that critics "enjoy pointing out the weaknesses of our free enterprise system—and it has weaknesses; it has weaknesses because it's operated by men and women who are full of weaknesses."[20] Benson's faith in freedom here is conditioned by a tired awareness that the independent, localist ideal is eternally difficult to maintain.

But by the middle of the twentieth century, shaken by the rise of the officially atheist Soviet Union, such weariness seemed a luxury no longer possible. Many American Christians blanched, and many began to conflate religious ideas of freedom with political and economic freedom in ways more explicit than they ever had before. For many Christians the moral rigor demanded of the producerist ideal began to fade in favor of an indictment of the state as a morally degrading force. The New Deal became a particular target. James Fifield, a Congregational minister from Los Angeles, became wealthy and famous by the 1940s arguing that the economic bureaucracy the New Deal created threatened to stifle the spiritual individualism the New Testament as he read it commanded. Fifield was no fundamentalist; indeed some of his backers worried about his stand on the reality of the resurrection. Nonetheless, he asserted that "Christian principle and the spiritual values of liberty and personal responsibility" should hold primacy in politics. For him, Christ's teachings assumed a foundation of individual responsibility essential to carry them out.[21] Similarly, more conservative American Christians read the New Deal through the stitched-together narrative of biblical prophecy fundamentalists had been constructing for forty years. Fearing the official atheism of Communist Russia and the supernatural evil of a soon to come antichrist alike, they saw in Franklin Roosevelt a dangerous figure who might perform the work of Satan in the world and bring about the prophesied apocalypse.[22]

Save for aspects of fundamentalist prophecy, Benson would disagree with none of what these other Christians said about the connections between freedom and religion. Accordingly, during the 1940s and 1950s, he laid groundwork for a transformation of free agency from something sustained through moral exertion into something that stood eternally in peril. More than any other Mormon leader, Benson developed language that linked the religious and moral concerns of Mormon theology to the political and economic status of American society. His experiences in those decades convinced him that while Mormon leaders once referred to free agency as an individual's ability to choose right or wrong in whatever circumstance she found herself, in fact free agency was imperiled and subject to destruction, dependent upon the economic and social circumstances of American society. Thus, the free exercise of religion, and more, the ability to choose, upon which one's eternal fate depends, were dependent upon the state of American politics. Old notions of independent, morally rigorous producerism faded as these new ideas of free agency advanced.

These ideas were mirrored in the work of a group of writers who, in the late 1940s and 1950s, left communism for Christianity and began assailing their former faith in the language of the latter. They laid a foundation for the way of talking about freedom that Benson would later embrace, arguing that large government was not merely an inconvenience or inefficiency, but a genuine spiritual pathology that spiritually sickened humanity and inhibited the possibility of salvation.

Most prominent was the famous author and government witness Whittaker Chambers, who published his self-flagellating memoir *Witness* in 1951. Like Benson would later on, Chambers spoke of the relationship between freedom and Christianity as something of far greater portent than a practical means of enabling people to make righteous choices. Rather, Chambers declared, there were two "irreconcilable faiths of our time—Communism and Freedom." Indeed, in Chambers's telling political liberty was only an immediate manifestation of the soul's eternal condition. Chambers wrote that "Political freedom, as the Western world has known it, is only a political reading of the Bible. Religion and freedom are indivisible. Without freedom the soul dies. Without the soul there is no justification for freedom."[23] In this telling, political liberty was no longer simply the product of Americans' moral effort but a spiritual property whose presence in a society signaled moral righteousness and harmony with God. This way of thinking was reflected in the anti-communist movement more generally; Martin Deis, a congressman from Texas, asserted that American democracy, "the highest order of living" depended on "Faith in Almighty God our Father from whom we derive the blessings of freedom and sustenance [and] confidence that spiritual forces, not material, must rule supreme in the affairs of man."[24]

The notion that communism was less a political philosophy than a pathological way of governing human spirituality was in large part the work of believers like Chambers, but a particularly Mormon spin on the idea derived from the work of Cleon Skousen, variously through the 1940s and 1950s a professor at BYU, a police chief in Salt Lake City, and an FBI agent. He became active in the anti-communist movement in the 1950s, and his writings later influenced Benson. Skousen's 1958 book *The Naked Communist* was particularly popular within the far-right John Birch Society, whose founder had accused Dwight Eisenhower of communist sympathies, and Skousen frequently spoke at Birch Society events. He founded several anti-communist organizations, including one called the All-American Society and one called the Freeman Institute, both of which widely distributed his pamphlets warning of communist infiltration into American culture and agitated for shrinking the size of government.[25] In some ways Skousen was not so different from Chambers or more mainstream anti-communists.[26] Like them, Skousen accused communists of crimes far in excess of the political threat communism posed and all understood communism to be an existential challenge to a divinely ordained way of life.

What made Skousen and other Mormon leaders distinct was their emphasis on the spiritual dangers of state control. They shared Chambers's concern for freedom. Like him, they believed that communism did not merely imprison human beings but denied what was most thoroughly human about them. But Chambers's concern, at least, was that communism perverted true freedom. Like Heber J. Grant, Susa Young Gates, or other Mormon localists, many American Christians traditionally interpreted freedom contextually, as something truly realized through the mediation of tradition, law, and culture passed down from heaven. This was so because human beings were imperfect creatures corrupted by Adam and Eve's fall and thus in need of guidance to truly realize their potential. Communism perverted true freedom by denying that spiritual reality. It promised human beings that they could perfect themselves, it enabled human pride, and led humanity into aggressive self-aggrandizement, which, Chambers warned, always eventually collapsed into despotism. As Chambers argued, communism "is the vision of materialism. . . . Communism restores man to his sovereignty by the simple method of denying God."[27] The issue was less government per se than it was government misused.

Some Mormons concurred. J. Reuben Clark, Grant's counselor in the governing First Presidency of the Church, sounded much like Chambers when he argued that communism promised too much freedom, the "pleasure of a self-chosen few who guide and control a new state—which is to become Deity."[28] But for Mormons like Skousen and later Benson the issue was less a misinterpretation of human freedom than its suffocation. Communism was not a perversion of righteous society; rather, all government was inherently pathological. Thus, Benson and Skousen began the process of reinterpreting free agency in a way that bound Mormon theology to libertarian politics. Skousen began ascribing moral goodness to the American economic system, spiritualizing its methods and finding in them eternal principles. As he said, "Communist leaders have suppressed the natural desires of their people and have tried to motivate them to action through fear." Capitalism, on the other hand, promoted humanity's ability to pursue their natural desires, which Mormons who rejected original sin did not believe were inherently corrupt. Skousen said, "This is one of the greatest blessings of free enterprise capitalism. To a remarkable extent it allows a man to do just about whatever he wants to do."[29]

Benson met Skousen while both were working in Washington, D.C. in the 1940s and followed his work as Skousen published over the next decade and a half. When he returned to Utah, he and Skousen were neighbors. Benson endorsed Skousen's work to the leaders of the church and approved when David O. McKay, Grant's eventual successor, endorsed one of Skousen's books over the pulpit. Later Skousen returned the favor, defending Benson's political activities to McKay.[30] Through Benson's time in Eisenhower's cabinet, signs of his growing sympathy with the anti-communist movement increased. In 1958 Robert Welch, a California candy maker, founded the John Birch Society and Benson soon began associating with its leaders. Neither Skousen nor Benson joined the organization (McKay forbade Benson's request to do so), but Skousen spoke at Birch Society events and published a book defending the group, while Benson took a Birch Society leader with him on a tour of Europe. Soon thereafter, Benson proposed that BYU implement a Birch Society proposal to investigate the possibility of communist sympathizers among the faculty. More, Benson's wife and son Reed became members of the organization. Reed began using Mormon chapels to host events presenting Birch Society ideas and material, and in the early 1960s took a job with the organization.[31]

Benson's Visits to Europe: 1946 and 1959

In the 1940s and 1950s Benson took two trips to Europe. Both were traumatic. Repeatedly over the last thirty years of his life, he told stories of his journeys, invoking what he saw as proof that powerful government destroyed the spiritual potential of a people and demonstrating his attachment to Skousen's ideas about anti-communism. In 1946 Benson spent nearly the entire year shuttling desperately from European city to European city, wrestling bureaucracy, wartime devastation, and the weather as he struggled to establish a supply chain for relief supplies from the United States to the Mormon congregations of Europe.[32] Thirteen years later, in the fall of 1959, he visited the Soviet Union in his official capacity as secretary of agriculture. He visited the famous Bolshoi ballet, toured Soviet collective farms, and one Thursday night more or less dragged his official guides to Moscow's Central Baptist Church, where he delivered an impromptu sermon and heard as he left the building the crowd break into the hymn "God Be With You Till We Meet Again."[33] What Benson saw on these journeys horrified him. "It is difficult for those who did not see it to appreciate how terrible conditions were," he wrote about Europe in 1946. He found the Soviet Union even more distressing—not because he saw overt suffering, but because while there he witnessed a tyranny in operation. "The communist system and its leaders are evil," he concluded, after describing a visit in which he was given false information about the state of the food supply and saw Soviet farms with no electricity or running water, some little better than mud huts.[34]

Benson's visits to Europe convinced him of two things. First, the desolation and backwardness he saw there was not merely economic, but rooted in Soviet spiritual barrenness, which in turn was the direct product of state totalitarianism. "Under their system they cannot equal the over all efficiency and productive ingenuity called forth in a free society," he said of the Soviet farm industry. Likewise, he blamed World War II and the devastation it wrought squarely on the arrogance and overweening power of the totalitarian governments of Germany and Italy. While visiting Germany in 1946, his secretary Frederick Babbel took notes while Benson lamented the destruction the Nazi regime had wrought in a sermon to a Mormon congregation. "No nation can escape the horrors of war unless its people live in accordance with God's word," he told them. "Christ said no man should rule unjustly over his brethren. A violation of this profound truth will always sow the seeds of war and destruction."[35] Benson later remembered how morally wrecked the Nazi regime had left Europe's citizens. "In 1946 I had seen a country still in rubble: military, economic, and spiritual," he said. Not merely was Europe's infrastructure destroyed by the war, but its people were reduced to helplessness. He was told that frequently a driver would encounter a pedestrian "squarely in the path of an approaching automobile, standing there unable to move out of the way. His legs would not obey his brain or perhaps his brain just didn't care anymore whether he lived or died. And so the car would come to a halt, while slowly, pathetically he would shuffle to the curb."[36] The link between physical deprivation, spiritual loss, and the elimination of human agency was here laid bare.

Second, Benson followed Chambers in asserting that tyranny's true tonic was not necessarily democracy, but Christianity, which he believed dispelled political authoritarianism, because true faith necessarily produced political liberty. After visiting Europe in 1946, he not only worried about the devastation he saw, but he repeatedly and roundly asserted that so long as faith persisted, he was sure that freedom would always succeed. He praised the Mormons he visited in Europe, "poorly clad but with the faith of the Gospel written on their faces, a faith that had carried them through the years of torment."[37] More profound was the lesson he took from the Central Baptist Church in Moscow. In the hymn the Baptists sang to him as he departed, he heard "the victory of the spirit over tyranny, oppression, and ignorance. Never can I doubt the ultimate deliverance of the Russian people." He was certain that the two were linked, that because that hymn was sung in that church, the communist regime would not survive. "I came back resolved to tell this story often," he wrote, "because it shows how the spirit of freedom, the spirit of brotherhood, and the spirit of religion live on."[38] He indeed told it often. In 1971 he presented the story to an LDS audience in the church's General Conference. In 1980 he told it to a John Birch Society meeting honoring Robert Welch, the Society's founder. He recounted it in books and on the stage.[39] The story became Benson's touchstone, encapsulating in an anecdote what were becoming his central convictions. In attempting to eliminate freedom political, social, and economic, tyrannical regimes did damage to humanity's spiritual dimensions. However, commitment to maintaining spiritual freedom would in turn liberate human beings from political tyranny.

Retelling the War in Heaven: 1950s–1960s

As Benson pondered what lessons he could draw from his time in Europe, he began developing a new interpretation of the story Mormons call "the war in heaven." Since the reorientation of Mormonism toward ethical behavior after the end of polygamy, Mormons spoke of their salvation as a narrative of progress: the human soul's journey from a preexistent state through earth life to exaltation, the achievement of divinity in eons to come, premised upon the refinement of character through right decision-making. Joseph Smith's scriptures linked this notion of salvation to human free agency. Echoing scattered biblical passages in Isaiah, Revelation, and the Gospels, they described a council in heaven, at which God declared that the purpose of earth life was to test humanity "to see if they will do all things whatsoever the Lord their God shall command them."[40] This meant, of course, that some would not. Satan rose in opposition to God's plan and promised, enigmatically, that he could ensure "one soul shall not be lost." But this was not so nice a deal as it sounded; the narrator of the passage observed his promise required that Satan "destroy the agency of men."[41] Ultimately Satan and his followers were cast from the presence of God. God then decreed Jesus Christ would carry out his plan. The creation went forward with human agency preserved.

Mormon interpretation of this story has varied widely.[42] Joseph Smith himself interpreted it to mean that "Jesus contended that there would be certain souls that would be condemned and the devil said he could save them all—as the grand council gave in for Jesus Christ so the devil fell."[43] He emphasized that all his hearers were at that council, using the story to emphasize that human beings' premortal responsibility for their own salvation required them to live up to that heritage while on earth. Brigham Young and many other nineteenth-century leaders emphasized that the war in heaven taught the need for unity and obedience among the Latter-day Saints. Young mused that the story held lessons for the Civil War generation, remarking that "Party spirit once made its appearance in heaven, but was promptly checked. If our Government had cast out the Seceders, the war would soon have been ended."[44] Many of Young's coterie invoked the story to urge loyalty to Young in the tense few months following the death of Joseph Smith, when it appeared the Mormons would fragment. The apostle Orson Hyde warned that "The power that governs this kingdom is the power of God . . . none can bear rule there except such as are appointed and ordained of God. Lucifer once undertook it, but he with all his adherents, was cast out and thrust down to hell because of an unlawful ambition in aspiring after a station that Heaven was not pleased to give."[45] They did not emphasize agency, but rather, Satan's presumption.

In the early twentieth century, however, shaken by the emergence of totalitarianism in Europe, Mormon leaders began to draw a connection between the rather unclear contours of Satan's plan as presented in Joseph Smith's scripture and political freedom. Rulon Wells, a General Authority of the Church and occasional candidate for state office, made the connection explicit in his blistering attack on the Soviet Union in the Church's General Conference in 1930. "This great struggle for liberty did not begin on this earth. . . . There was war in heaven before the foundations of this earth were laid. And what was that great conflict over? It was a struggle for the liberties of the children of God."[46]

Benson, however, was the primary force driving a reinterpretation of the story as a political allegory in the Cold War, and he defined the term "agency" as a synonym less for the sort of moral responsibility earlier Mormon leaders had emphasized, but instead for political and economic liberty. Indeed, one biographer estimated that at least three-quarters of his General

172 THE COLD WAR AND THE INVENTION OF FREE AGENCY

Conference speeches in the 1960s addressed politics, and many emphasized these themes.[47] While Mormon leaders like Wells had spoken of the war in heaven as a battle over free choice, Benson went further than earlier Mormon leaders in drawing the analogy to contemporary politics, in two key ways. Consistent with his experiences in Europe, Benson interpreted all forms of freedom as of a piece. Deprivation of political or economic freedom was spiritually destructive, and the lack of religious faith would lead invariably to the loss of more temporal freedoms. Thus, Benson argued, the war in heaven was the source of political freedom on earth. Second, more explicitly than any other Mormon leader, Benson attributed the presence of political and economic freedom to active divine influence, and its deprivation to the machinations of Satan. Preaching religion was simply another way to tear down communism, and communism's greatest enemy was Benson's own church.

By the late 1950s Benson was making the case in his General Conference addresses. In October 1958, he explicitly identified free agency with political liberty and rooted both in the war in heaven. He argued that "Since the time of the council in heaven the fight of liberty loving people for freedom has continued . . . it is not only in the moral choice of right and wrong that man is free. Among the relentless quests of human history is the quest for political freedom." Benson asserted that the war in heaven made political freedom possible, but he also did more. In the same talk he argued also that the purpose of Christianity was to preserve political freedom and that its absence was spiritually degrading. "Free agency is an eternal principle vouchsafed to us in the perfect law of liberty—the gospel of Jesus Christ," he said. "Freedom of choice is more to be treasured than any earthly possession."[48]

In October 1961, only months after leaving the cabinet, Benson delivered a speech to the General Conference of the church that took this argument to its logical conclusion. He outlined in full his theory of the war in heaven and the moralistic libertarianism he took it to require. He also added to his spiritual interpretation of political freedom the tone of conflict and conspiracy between religion and communism that would come to characterize his mature moralistic libertarianism. He opened with his thesis: "the American heritage of freedom—a plan of God." He used the word "plan" intentionally, because he explicitly linked American liberty to the "plan" presented by God in the war in heaven, and communism to Satan's opposition to that plan. "The whole program of socialistic-communism is essentially a war against God and the plan of salvation," Benson declared, "the very plan which we fought to uphold during 'the war in heaven.'" For Benson the war in heaven's primary purpose was to guarantee liberty, and it was impossible to separate moral choices from political or economic freedom. Those were the very venues in which moral choices were made, and correct political activity was a sign of correct moral activity. Indeed, Benson lambasted Mormons who supported "planned government guaranteed security programs" for making an improper moral choice. "Latter-day Saints should be reminded how and why they voted as they did in heaven. If some have decided to change their vote they should repent—throw their support on the side of freedom—and cease promoting this subversion."[49]

Just as Benson invested the war in heaven with political ballast it had not held before, he did the same for the Book of Mormon. He seized upon one particular theme of the Book of Mormon: the presence of conspiracies that sought to undermine those civilizations from within. While Mormons had traditionally turned to the Book of Mormon for spiritual guidance, Benson, consonant with his confidence that the political and economic course of any society had spiritual ramifications, read it as a historical map for his own time. In the 1960s he resurrected a Book of Mormon story long neglected. The Gadianton robbers, a "secret combination" sworn to undermine the government of the righteous Nephite civilization, had rarely been discussed in the General Conferences of the church, garnering only one off-hand mention since the nineteenth century.[50] In the 1960s and 1970s, however, Benson invoked the Gadiantons half a dozen times, asserting that their presence in the Book of Mormon showed it offered more than moral lessons. "Realizing that in our time we would be threatened with a similar conspiracy, the Book of Mormon warns" of secret combinations, he declared, counseling that like the Gadiantons communists offered a spiritual as well as a political threat.[51] In so doing Benson combined older producerist language that linked freedom to ethical behavior with a powerful conviction that government itself posed a moral threat to freedom, and a conspiratorial worldview that saw danger omnipresent.

Thus, while previous leaders of the church had argued as did Joseph F. Smith and James Talmage that free agency was an inherent human characteristic that could be exercised in whatever circumstances human beings might find themselves, the dense network of ideas Benson was formulating rendered it more fragile, connected inherently to political and economic circumstance. Increasingly Mormons sympathetic to Benson's ideas began to link government power to the deprivation of free agency, and hence, began to understand salvation as, in some sense, a function of political circumstance. As the apostle Marion G. Romney warned, "God established the Constitution to preserve to men their free agency, because the whole gospel of Jesus Christ presupposes man's untrammeled exercise of free agency. . . . Abridge man's agency, and the whole purpose of his mortality is thwarted."[52] When he delivered his sermons in the early 1960s, Benson's interpretation of free agency had reached full maturity. The moralism and commitment to his church, so evident in the brand of freedom Heber J. Grant had embraced, were still present, but they were now applied to a far larger canvas. Benson's lived experience, the very thing Grant's localism had embraced, had taught him that government possessed vast potential for influence on the spiritual lives of its citizens, and his most visceral experiences with government showed him that that influence was rarely good. His rereading of the war in heaven convinced him that the very nature of humanity required maximal freedom in all possible spheres if human beings were to achieve their full potential, and that efforts to limit that freedom were thus by definition Satanic. Benson's form of Mormonism was suited to a Cold War faith, but it also bore recognizable resemblance to forms of Mormonism that had gone before.

Notes

1. Ezra Taft Benson diary, July 26, 1943, cited in Gary James Bergera, "'This Great Thing Which Has Come to Me a Humble Weak Farmer Boy': Ezra Taft Benson's 1943 Call to the Apostleship," *Mormon Historical Studies* (April 2013): 158. For a survey of Benson's life, see Gary James Bergera, "Ezra Taft Benson's 1921–23 Mission to England," *Journal of Mormon History* 35, no. 4 (Fall 2009): 85–111; Gary James Bergera, "'Rising above Principle': Ezra Taft Benson as U.S. Secretary of Agriculture, 1953–61, Part 1," *Dialogue: A Journal of Mormon Thought* 41, no. 1 (Fall 2008): 81–122, and Gary James Bergera, "'Weak-Kneed Republicans and Socialist Democrats': Ezra Taft Benson as U.S. Secretary of Agriculture, 1953–61, Part 2," *Dialogue : A Journal of Mormon Thought* 41, no. 2 (Winter 2008): 55–95.

2. On Grant's career and tempestuous but successful capitalist commitments, Ronald W. Walker, "Young Heber J. Grant: Entrepreneur Extraordinary," *BYU Studies* 43, no. 1 (2004): 81–113.

3. Ezra Taft Benson, *Cross Fire: The Eight Years with Eisenhower* (Garden City, NY: Doubleday, 1962), 10.

4. 2 Nephi 2:16, 27, Book of Mormon.

5. Charles Grandison Finney, *Lectures on Systematic Theology* (Oberlin, Ohio: James M. Fitch, 1846), 26. On this turn, see E. Brooks Holifield, *Theology in America: Christian Thought from the Age of the Puritans to the Civil War* (New Haven, Conn.: Yale University Press, 2003), 83–87.

6. Doctrine and Covenants 93:29–30. Terryl L. Givens, *Wrestling the Angel: The Foundations of Mormon Thought, Cosmos, God, Humanity* (New York: Oxford University Press, 2015), 194–98.

7. James E. Talmage, *Articles of Faith* (Salt Lake City: Deseret News, 1899), 89–90.

8. "Discourse by President Joseph F. Smith, April 8, 1883," *Journal of Discourses* (Liverpool: George D. Watt, 1854–1886) 24:175. On the differences between "agency" and "liberty"

see Garth Mangum, "Free Agency and Freedom: Some Misconceptions," *Dialogue: A Journal of Mormon Thought* 1, no. 4 (1966): 43–49.

9. Heber J. Grant, "Temperance—Inspirations to Progress," *Young Women's Journal* 20, no. 9 (September 1908): 506. On producerism generally, see Michael Kazin, *The Populist Persuasion* (New York: Basic Books, 1995), 27–49; Lawrence Goodwyn, *The Populist Moment* (New York: Oxford, 1978), 55–95. On Mormon producerism, see Leonard Arrington, *Great Basin Kingdom: An Economic History of the Latter-day Saints, 1830–1900* (1958; Urbana: University of Illinois Press, 2005), 96–131. On the transition from a polygamous Mormonism to a moralist Mormonism, see Matthew Bowman, *The Mormon People: The Making of An American Faith* (New York: Random House, 2012), 152–84.

10. Susa Young Gates, "Obedience," *Young Women's Journal* 20, no. 10 (October 1908): 588.

11. Susa Young Gates, "Susa Young Gates to Mrs. Jane Rockwell," *Relief Society Magazine* 7 (October 1920): 620; see generally Matthew C. Godfrey, *Religion, Politics, and Sugar: The Mormon Church, The Federal Government, and the Utah-Idaho Sugar Company* (Logan: Utah State University Press, 2007), particularly 158–98.

12. On Grant's politics, see Thomas G. Alexander, *Mormonism in Transition: A History of the Latter-day Saints, 1890–1930* (Urbana: University of Illinois Press, 1985), 55–56.

13. Heber J. Grant, J. Reuben Clark, and David O. McKay to William Fitzgibbons, October 11, 1941, Marriner Eccles Papers, Special Collections University of Utah. See also Brian Q. Cannon, "Mormons and the New Deal: The 1936 Election in Utah," *Utah Historical Quarterly* 67, no. 1 (Winter 1999): 4–23. .

14. This story was about Benson's great-grandfather, also named Ezra Taft Benson. When Benson told this story first in "Ezra Taft Benson Remembers," *Idaho Heritage* 9 (August 1977): 16, he identified the subject as his grandfather. Several years later in the Church's magazine *Ensign*, he corrected the error. Ezra Taft Benson, "What I Hope You Will Teach Your Children about the Temple," *Ensign* (August 1985): 5.

15. Ezra Taft Benson, *America Is a Choice Land* (New York: Columbia Broadcasting System, 1944), 1, 4.

16. John Dewey, "Christianity and Democracy" (Ann Arbor: University of Michigan, 1892), 66, 68. Later in his life, Dewey would draw away from this idealist way of speaking about religion and politics, and away from such specifically Christian language as this, but he clung to the notion that societies needed a common faith to survive. Steven C. Rockefeller, *John Dewey, Religious Faith, and Democratic Humanism* (New York: Columbia University Press, 1994), 133–36, 190–95.

17. Alexander Crawford, *Germany's Moral Downfall: The Tragedy of Academic Materialism* (New York: Abingdon Press, 1919), 53. The connections between religion, democracy, and morality that emerged in the age of the American Revolution are discussed in Mark Noll, *America's God: Jonathan Edwards to Abraham Lincoln* (New York: Oxford University Press, 2002), 9–13.

18. Ezra Taft Benson, "The LDS Church and Politics," speech, December 1952 (Provo, Utah: BYU Extension Division), 7. On Eisenhower's cultivation of a public religiosity linked to democracy, see Kevin Kruse, *One Nation Under God: How Corporate America Invented Christian America* (New York: Basic Books, 2015), chapter 2.

19. Sheri Dew, *Ezra Taft Benson: A Biography* (Salt Lake City: Deseret Book, 1987), 259 records the blessing; Bergera, "Rising above Principle," 84–85 discusses it.

20. Benson, "LDS Church and Politics," 9, 8.

21. Kruse, *One Nation under God*, 3–35, quotation from 23.

22. Matthew Avery Sutton, *American Apocalypse: A History of Modern Evangelicalism* (Cambridge, Mass.: Harvard University Press, 2014), 232–63.

23. Whittaker Chambers, *Witness* (1952; New York: Regnary Press, 1987), 4.

24. Martin Deis, *The Trojan Horse in America* (New York: Dodd, Mead, 1940), 238.

25. Skousen's career is discussed in "Roundtable Review: The Naked Capitalist," *Dialogue: A Journal of Mormon Thought* 6, no. 3 (Autumn/Winter 1971), 99–116, and O. Kendell White, "A Review and Commentary on the Prospects of a New Mormon Christian Right Coalition," *Review of Religious Research* 28, no. 2 (December 1986): 182–85.

26. On radical anti-communism in the 1950s and 1960s, helpful are Seymour Martin Lipset and Earl Raab, *The Politics of Unreason* (New York: Harper and Row, 1970), and more recently Lisa McGirr, *Suburban Warriors: The Origin of the New American Right* (Princeton, N.J.: Princeton University Press, 2001), 168–76.

27. Chambers, *Witness*, 10. See also Sam Tanenhaus, *Whittaker Chambers: A Biography* (New York: Random House, 1997), 117–19. Chambers's critique here echoes Roman Catholic notions of freedom, see John McGreevy, *Catholicism and American Freedom* (New York: Norton, 2003), particularly 19–43.

28. David H. Yam, ed., *J. Reuben Clark: Selected Papers on Americanism and National Affairs* (Provo, Utah: Brigham Young University Press, 1987), 57.

29. Skousen, *The Naked Communist*, 31, 32, 36, 51, 327.

30. Dew, *Ezra Taft Benson*, 158. Gregory Prince and William Robert Wright, *David O. McKay and the Rise of Modern Mormonism* (Salt Lake City: University of Utah Press, 2005), 291–92.

31. Skousen's involvement with the John Birch Society is discussed in D. Michael Quinn, *The Mormon Hierarchy: Extensions of Power* (Salt Lake City: Signature Books, 1994), 82–87, 103–4; Benson's in Quinn, "Ezra Taft Benson and Mormon Political Conflicts," *Dialogue: A Journal of Mormon Thought* 26, no. 2 (Summer 1993): 1–87.

32. Gary James Bergera, "Ezra Taft Benson's 1946 Mission to Europe," *Journal of Mormon History* 34, no. 2 (Spring 2008): 4–38.

33. Bergera, "Weak-Kneed Republicans and Socialist Democrats," 69–70. Benson described the event first in his memoir *Cross Fire*.

34. Benson, *Cross Fire*, 264, 482.

35. Frederick W. Babbel, *On Wings of Faith: My Daily Walk with a Prophet* (Springville, Utah: Cedar Fort, 1998), 35.

36. Benson, *Cross Fire*, 265.

37. Ibid., 264.

38. Benson, Ibid., 488.

39. Ezra Taft Benson, "Life Is Eternal," *Ensign* (June 1971): 34; Ezra Taft Benson, "A Moral Challenge," *American Opinion: A Robert Welch Journal* (February 1980): 54.

40. Abraham 3:25, Pearl of Great Price.

41. Moses 4:1, 3, Pearl of Great Price.

42. Boyd Petersen, "'One Soul Shall Not Be Lost': The War in Heaven in Mormon Thought," *Journal of Mormon History* 38, no. 1 (2012): 1–50 explores the narrative from a variety of angles and discusses many of the examples I use below.

43. Andrew Ehat and Lyndon Cook, eds., *The Words of Joseph Smith* (Salt Lake City: Grandin Book, 1991), 343. Abbreviations expanded.

44. "Discourse by Brigham Young, August 3, 1862," *Journal of Discourses* 9, no. 333.

45. Orson Hyde, *Delivered Before the High Priests' Quorum in Nauvoo* (Nauvoo, Utah: Times and Seasons Press, 1845), 4.

46. *Conference Report* (Salt Lake City: Church of Jesus Christ of Latter-day Saints, 1930), 70. On Wells's career, see Alexander, *Mormonism in Transition*, 45–46.

47. As described in Quinn, "Ezra Taft Benson and Mormon Political Conflicts," 16.

48. Ezra Taft Benson, "The Heritage of Freedom, General Conference Address, 1958 October," Ezra Taft Benson Addresses, Box 2 Folder 3, Church History Library, Salt Lake City, Utah.

49. Ezra Taft Benson, "The American Heritage of Freedom—A Plan of God," *Conference Report*, October 1961, 69–75.

50. By Spencer W. Kimball, "Who Is My Neighbor?" *Conference Report*, April 1949, 108. The fading of stories of the Gadianton Robbers is documented in W. Paul Reeve, "As Ugly as Evil and as Wicked as Hell: Gadianton Robbers and the Legend Process among the Mormons," *Journal of Mormon History* 27, no. 2 (Fall 2001): 125–49.

51. Ezra Taft Benson, "The Book of Mormon Warns America," (Provo, Utah: Brigham Young University Press, 1968), 3.

52. Marion G. Romney, "Socialism and the United Order Compared," *Conference Report*, April 1966, 104–5.

7 Women and Gender

ANDREA G. RADKE-MOSS

On February 22, 1987, when he was almost eighty-eight years old, LDS church president Ezra Taft Benson delivered a controversial address at a fireside for Mormon parents, where he declared: "Contrary to conventional wisdom, a mother's place is in the home, not the marketplace."[1] Benson's "To the Mothers in Zion" became a standard reference for Mormons on the roles of women, and was even published as a small, accessible pamphlet for easy distribution to members. Twenty-five years later, the talk is still available and is cited in other church leaders' talks, even while becoming less accessible and somewhat forgotten to younger generations.[2] Benson's talk represented a formalization of ideas about the roles of women that he had collected and articulated for many years.[3] It also showed the influence of his contemporaries in LDS church leadership who had expressed similar views in response to the Equal Rights Amendment and other feminist activism of the 1960s and 1970s. Coming as late as it did within the context of the women's rights move-ment, Benson's directives to women offered a counter-narrative that was not only socially conservative but even reactionary for the late 1980s. In spite of national feminist attention to gendered inequalities in the workforce and education, Church leaders like Benson and his predecessors had remained staunchly resistant to some advancements for women, arguing that those ef-forts would come at the expense of child-bearing and full-time motherhood.

Benson's views on women might be dismissed as simply the old-fashioned vestiges of Mormon patriarchy and generational sexism. Certainly, exclusive motherhood and the redirecting of feminine ambition back toward the home had been a rhetorical line from LDS leaders for many decades, especially in reaction to the gender shifts of two world wars and beyond. Like other anxieties within Mormonism about postwar disruptions in American life, the movement for women's equality—and Church leaders' reactions to it—can best be understood against the backdrop of Cold War fears about the infiltration of communism, atheism, sexual liberation, and anti-authority expressions in American life. Gendered tensions played a significant role in the American–Soviet ideological rivalry. The 1959 "Kitchen Debate" between Vice President Richard Nixon and Soviet Premier Nikita Khrushchev was emblematic of how Americans linked stay-at-home motherhood and the idealization of the American housewife as a hallmark of American capitalist success.[4] Americans feared that a communist industrial society would force women into the dehumanized masses of a Soviet factory system. Benson was certainly informed by these anxieties. For the apostle, Mormonism's emphasis on women's traditional roles and the expectations of idealized motherhood and stable, righteous family life offered a reliable counterinfluence to the social liberalism of the 1960s that brought sexual debauchery, crime, and the degradation of women.

Benson critiqued women working outside the home for the sake of Mormon theological and cultural beliefs on motherhood and family, but he also linked working mothers to a litany of common social ills associated with the liberalism of modern America, including declining marriage and childbirth rates, women's access to birth control and abortion, spiraling numbers of divorces, and the rise of juvenile delinquency. He feared that advancements for women in higher education and military service threatened to masculinize women, pit women against men in the workforce, and deflate male wage-earning power. Benson was not unique in his counsel to LDS women; observers can easily trace his rhetoric back to his own earlier talks and similar discourses by other church leaders. But it was Benson's firm reification of women's traditional domesticity that situated Mormon gender roles as a counterpoint to new definitions of women's sphere in postwar America.

Ezra Taft Benson's views on gender in many ways originated from his Idaho upbringing that was rural, agrarian, conservative, and strongly rooted in Mormon notions about large families and patriarchy in the home. Born the first of eleven children on August 4, 1899, to George and Sarah (Dunkley) Benson, Ezra learned early the strong expectations for a young boy raised on a farm. He emulated his father as a strong patriarch and respected priesthood leader. Ezra learned early on that the outside activities of cultivating, harvesting, and care of livestock were strongly male roles. As Benson's biographer noted, "At an age when most children are scarcely allowed out of their mother's sight, Ezra was an apprentice field hand. As the eldest son, he grew up fast. George Benson relied on his boy to shoulder, in many cases, a man's responsibility."[5] Ezra "idolized his father," and "from the time he could walk, 'T.,' as [he] was nicknamed, was his father's shadow—riding horses, working in the fields, hitching up the horse and buggy for meetings, playing ball and swimming in the creek."[6]

Ezra Taft Benson came of age in the Progressive Era, when reformers warned of the emasculation of the American male. Psychologist and Harvard educator G. Stanley Hall argued that "the key to a powerful manly civilization lay in giving all males free access to the primitive. Parents and educators must encourage boys to relive the evolutionary progress of the race—to be savages and barbarians as boys, so that they would develop the strength to be both virile and civilized as men."[7] Similarly, President Theodore Roosevelt encouraged American youth to embrace the "Strenuous Life," represented by the values of virility, athleticism, militarism, and a return to nature for men who had been effeminized by middle-class American life. The LDS youth of Ezra's generation faced similar modern challenges. According to historian Richard Kimball, "Mormon leaders at the beginning of the twentieth century faced a double dilemma. Not only did they have to construct new distinctions between their religious group and the outside world, they also had to deal with the problems confronting their contemporaries—namely, urbanization, immigration, and industrialization."[8]

To that end, Mormon youth programs and educational institutions began to incorporate the activities necessary for instilling Mormon values and rebuilding frontier skills that leaders feared had been lost to modernization. Ezra was on the cusp of these intensifying and masculinizing expectations for adolescent boys. According to Kimball, "The church program imitated the goals and tactics developed by advocates of 'Muscular Christianity' in the nineteenth century. In effect, 'Muscular Mormonism,' defined as the desire to instill masculinity and the religious tenets of Mormonism, was at the heart of Mormon recreation."[9] Ezra embraced the new physical pursuits offered to youth, like playing basketball at the Oneida Academy with "intensity and enthusiasm."[10] Also, as Scouting took hold in church congregations between 1915 and 1921, Ezra found opportunities for leadership; in 1918, the year that "there were more Scouts in Utah, in proportion to the population, than in any other states," Ezra was called as assistant Scoutmaster to "twenty-four lively, mischievous Scouts."[11] He led the boys in hiking, fishing, camping, and swimming, as well as religious and patriotic instruction.[12] The Boy Scout ethos was embraced by church leadership as a way of building a kind of manhood that was physically robust, patriotic, and righteously minded.

Considering the extent of church and community resources dedicated to the turnout of Mormon boys, Ezra was the beneficiary of a male-centric youth culture that helped shape a strong identity of privileged Mormon boyhood. Ezra was a fan of a 1909 song by Mormon Tabernacle Choir director Evan Stephens, called "I am a Mormon Boy," which highlighted the pull between civilized righteousness and the rough and tumble expectations for exuberant boyhood. "I don't look quite genteel; But, never mind, for I'm a boy that's always full of joy—a rough and ready sort of chap—An honest 'Mormon' boy . . . Yet I'll confess that I am wild, and often do annoy, but that's a fault of many a 'Mormon' boy . . . My father is a 'Mormon' true, And when I am a man, I want to be like him, and do just all the good I can."[13] Later, as church president, Ezra loved to sing this as an anthem to his proud, masculine, religious identity.

With all of the emphasis on "muscular Christianity," reformers did not ignore the roles of women in the "millennial evolutionary ideology of civilization."[14] At a time when population experts worried about the declining birthrate, or "race suicide" for white, middle-class Americans, Theodore Roosevelt contributed to a nationwide encouragement toward childbearing, higher fertility rates, and the idealization of motherhood and traditional domesticity. In raising a large family, the Bensons fulfilled these expectations. To Ezra, his mother always embodied the perfect ideal of domesticity and maternal instinct. As church president, he hearkened back to Sarah Benson as the model of true womanhood for Mormon mothers, which for her, had included frequent and unimpeded childbearing.

> I know the special blessings of a large and happy family, for my dear parents had a quiver full of children. Being the oldest of eleven children, I saw the principles of unselfishness, mutual consideration, loyalty to each other, and a host of other virtues developed in a large and wonderful family with my noble mother as the queen of that home.[15]

Benson's early assumptions about the roles of men and women were informed strongly by the family dynamics of farm life, but mostly by his religious beliefs. Mormonism emphasized stable family life built by supportive, nurturing mothers, and strong, provider fathers. These ideals about family and fatherhood found similar expressions in progressives' emphasis on "man's contributive role with the family . . . [especially] through the family-centered activities and 'domestic masculinity' thought to exist in suburban homes."[16]

When World War I broke out, Benson felt the patriotic duty of serving in the armed forces—a willingness to serve that highlighted how far Mormonism had come in assimilating into the larger American culture of national service and devotion to country. From a young age, Ezra was instilled with a love of country by his father. "George Benson was a patriot. He didn't say much about the war, but his sons knew he looked favorably upon young men who served their country."[17] However, stricken with the flu while still in training, Benson returned home for his recovery, and never had a chance to serve before the war ended.

Coming of age as he did in World War I–era America, Ezra Benson also witnessed the expansion of political, social, and educational roles for women that came with postwar changes in America. While the church academies such as Benson's own hometown Oneida Academy had always embraced coeducation, moving to the Utah Agricultural College gave him a larger experience of engaging with female students and a diversity of activities open to both young men and women in the 1920s. When Ezra met Flora Amussen at the UAC, she represented all that was best about New Womanhood—independent, vivacious, and active—a kind of "Mormon flapper," but without the morally questionable aspects of 1920s sexual liberation.[18]

Ezra and Flora married at a time when Mormon constructs of marriage had shifted from the strongly patriarchal expectations of polygamous marriages to a new, modern emphasis on companionate marriages and complementary gender roles.[19] The turn toward egalitarian marriages still came bound up in patriarchal hierarchy in the home. The notion of male "headship" over wives and children was one that was deeply embedded in the Mormon theology of celestial marriage, and became an important framework for how Ezra and Flora viewed their own marriage, with Ezra as the "head," the leader and ultimate authority to whom all responsibility and final decision-making ultimately fell. Flora, for her part, saw in Ezra the masculine qualities she desired for patriarchal leadership in the home, as well as his great potential as a committed provider.

Ultimately, upon marrying Ezra, Flora threw herself into her role as a supportive and self-sacrificing wife to her husband's educational, professional, and economic ambitions, and his time-consuming requirements of church leadership and professional work. Flora directed her energies toward the support of her husband and beginning a family, and accepted that a wife's primary role was to ensure her husband's success. Later in their marriage, she reflected how that wifely support, even to the subduing of her own interests, had meant "plenty of sacrifice on my part. I have long felt that the woman's role in life was to raise righteous children, to make a haven of love and goodness and to encourage her husband to do well in his church, civic, and professional work."[20]

The sacrifice of females for male success was a principle Flora accepted and promoted to later generations of Mormon women. And while Ezra heralded his wife's supportive nature, it was her strong independence that largely benefited her as a wife and mother, being left alone so often because of her husband's long absences for work and church. Indeed, Flora stepped in to fill the void, and "of necessity, [she] became the anchor in the home."[21] Ironically, those lengthy absences not only prevented Ezra from participating in some of the hands-on fatherly mentoring he had enjoyed from his own father, but they also required that his wife become more independent, not in liberating her from her maternal responsibilities, but in giving her more autonomy within the confines of decision-making for her family. While she rarely complained, she felt the burden of shouldering most of the home responsibilities. According to her son, Reed, "I'm sure she was lonely for Dad, and perhaps worn out from working all day, but she was a natural motivator." Even so, the son remembered that he "sometimes found her crying while she ironed at night."[22]

The Bensons endured the Depression better than most, as Ezra received a stable salary while Flora stayed home and reared their growing family. On this, "Ezra and Flora were particularly united in the view that Flora belonged at home."[23] The economic upheavals of the 1930s had required that some women seek paid labor. However, most of society favored a return to traditional gender arrangements as a way of reaffirming men's economic place in America. In the end, according to historian Elaine Tyler May, "the potential for radically altered gender roles in the family never reached fruition in the 1930s. As the Depression continued, the path toward traditional domestic arrangements appeared to be the one most likely to bring Americans toward the secure homes they desired."[24] And through these years, the Bensons enjoyed both the economic stability of a working father and the domestic security of an at-home mother. Because of Ezra's job in Boise working for the National Council of Farm Cooperatives, the Bensons settled into the successive ownership of two comfortable homes with large yards, and were able to provide their children with toys, clothes, games, sleds, bicycles, and lessons in "piano, voice, organ, art, dance, ice skating, swimming, and sculpture."[25] Ironically, the amenities of middle-class life were among the privileges available to Flora that would have been solidly off-limits to other less advantaged Mormon women who also stayed out of the paid workforce. And yet, as she explained, with unintentional irony: "If I'd gone to work I would have missed so much. You don't need the material things. The Lord will make it up to you in some way."[26] Flora's brand of full-time motherhood came with an expectation of economic self-sacrifice, which Ezra would advocate consistently for Mormon women in his later years of church leadership.

During the years of upheaval owing to the Great Depression and World War II, Benson's fear of socialism, manifest through the liberal New Deal, reinforced his conservative politics and notions of manhood connected to strong economic providers who would not be emasculated by a welfare state and government assistance. As America transitioned from one devastating global war to another, more ideological one, the Bensons clung to the foundations of home and family as a bulwark against rising national insecurities about the spread of communism. According to Elaine Tyler May, "in the early years of the Cold War, amid a world of uncertainties brought about by World War II and its aftermath, the home seemed to offer a secure private nest removed from the dangers of the outside world."[27]

The Cold War gave the Bensons a new backdrop on which to paint their ideals of strict gender role divisions in the home and the values that accompanied secure family life: obedience and loyalty, with a righteous father as head of the home and a supportive and self-sacrificing wife raising virtuous and patriotic children. Indeed, "domestic anticommunism was another manifestation of containment . . . [where] the 'sphere of influence' was the home."[28] And the contributions of women to this cultural retrenchment were key, as "public health professionals argued that inside as well as outside the home, women who challenged traditional roles place the security of the nation at risk."[29] Further, this postwar gender retrenchment received an added boost from psychiatrist Marynia Farnham and sociologist Ferdinand Lundberg, whose publication *Modern Woman: The Lost Sex* (1947) argued that women who pursued work outside the home did so "only at the price of feminine relinquishment."[30] The warnings were dire: "The masculinization of women [came with] enormously dangerous consequences to the home, the children (if any) dependent on it, and to the ability of the woman, as well as her husband, to obtain sexual gratification."[31]

Thus, in spite of some critics' fears that women's expanded work opportunities during the war years would permanently reverse traditional family roles, instead by the late 1940s, "the roles of breadwinner and homemaker were not abandoned, they were embraced."[32] Cold War politics, societal expectations, and modern consumption were linked together "to revive, though with a modern twist, a feminine ideal based in domesticity."[33] At the same time, LDS church leaders were also warning against these "dangerous social forces" associated with the decline of the home and family in postwar America. In 1949, apostle Spencer W. Kimball, who was a colleague to newly called apostle Benson, published a famous marital instruction, "To John and Mary," warning against the pitfalls of women leaving the home for paid labor. To "Mary" he counseled, "It was never intended by the Lord that married women should compete with men in employment." In fact, he cautioned, "You wouldn't want to work outside the home anyway, Mary, for women are expected to earn the living only in emergencies, and *you must know that many are the broken homes resulting when women leave their posts at home.*"[34] Lundberg and Farnham had similarly argued, "Women's rivalry with men today, and the need to 'equal' their accomplishments, engenders all too often anger and resentfulness toward men." They suggested that a working wife had a "profoundly disturbing effect upon her husband . . . [because] he find[s] himself without the satisfactions of a home directed and cared for by a woman happy in providing affection and devotion."[35] Similarly, Kimball predicted the effects of a man coming home to an empty house:

> You see, if both husband and wife are working away from home and come home tired, it is very easy for unpleasantness and misunderstandings to arise. And so, Mary, you will remain at home, making it attractive and heavenly, and when John comes home tired, you will be fresh and pleasant; the house will be orderly; the dinner will be tempting; and life will have real meaning.[36]

Benson found his own uniquely personal celebration of this ideal: "I can't remember a time when I came home and didn't find [Flora] there. She would meet me at the door with a smile and an embrace. It was that love and support that sustained me during my years in Washington when I was constantly under fire."[37]

In many ways, the family values of Mormonism helped to propel the larger nation through its postwar transition from women's factory and government work to the renewed expectations of nuclear families, strong male providers, at-home mothers, and higher rates of reproduction. Mormon women also embraced Cold War ideas about home defense, linking their long-standing practices of pioneer preparedness to new demands for home and national security. The Federal Civil Defense Agency in the early 1950s "devised several campaigns that drew on women's traditional domestic functions to equip them for a nuclear emergency," including "Grandma's Pantries" (bomb shelters), food storage, and home nursing.[38] Like many American women, Mormon women could "draw on their unique domestic expertise to find new roles suited to the Cold War."[39] During these years, Flora's own views on motherhood and homemaking further defined and reinforced her husband's. In this way, the American home became politically significant on a national scale. And through the Bensons, the public face of the Mormon home would play a key role in the diffusion of national domestic ideology.

When Benson became the secretary of agriculture in 1953, the family moved to Washington, D.C., where they were thrown into the social circles of leading politicians and government officials. A new level of economic privilege blessed the Benson family, but Flora shied away from the limelight and the material lifestyles of Washington elites, instead insisting on doing her own housework, hostessing her own gatherings, and shunning Washington social life in favor of being at home and active in the lives of her children. When it was Flora's turn to host the cabinet wives' luncheon in May 1954, she was "determined to . . . prepare everything herself."[40]

Flora, Ezra, and the children exuded such a wholesomeness that in September 1954, they earned a guest appearance on the famous television program, *Person to Person*, hosted by Edward R. Murrow. Besides showcasing the charming and talented children, it became Flora's opportunity to highlight her accomplished homemaking. When Murrow queried, "Do you have any domestic help?" She answered,

> No, we do not have a maid. We feel that we learn by doing. We prepare all of our own meals, and plan them. . . . We play together, sing together. We're a very religious family. We have daily prayer—individual and together—because we feel that a family that prays together stays together. I feel that's true of a nation.[41]

The Benson family consciously chose to set an example as an ideal Mormon family, actively working to promote their values of frugality and wholesome togetherness as *American* family values. Viewer response was overwhelming, and Murrow considered it the "best show he had done to date."[42] Even President Eisenhower complimented Secretary Benson that "it was the best political show you could have put on."[43] Flora's crowning as national "Home Maker of the Year" in 1955 cemented her place as the epitome of American domestic and maternal achievements. Her admiring husband attended the ceremony.

Even in exemplifying the ideal family and traditional gender norms of her life as the agriculture secretary's wife, Flora recognized and felt keenly the pressures and contradictions of her feminine support role. In one uncharacteristic criticism of her wifely duties, she playfully grumbled:

> I was trying to do all the jobs of a good homemaker, cooking, laundress, cleaning woman, nurse, counselor, time with my children, and at the end of the day look rested, posed, relaxed and properly groomed for a formal dinner or social engagement of some kind . . . I was to look like a charming girl, think like a man, work like a dog and act like a lady.[44]

As much as Flora appeared to fit the typical traditional housewife stereotype of the 1950s, she would not have considered herself submissive or passive, but supportive and self-sacrificing. This distinction allowed for an important nuance of agency, pride, and ownership in her domestic role. But her maternal and wifely inclinations also aligned perfectly with both her society's and her religion's expectations for women. Still, she considered herself an equal, by embracing her own version of complementarity. "When we women see things that are wrong, we must not just shake our heads. We must speak up. We are men's helpmates—not just silent partners."[45] In fact, Flora and Ezra insisted upon the egalitarian nature of their marriage. "Ezra has always encouraged me to speak," Flora noted. "For years he has urged me to get up at church affairs and say what's on my mind."[46] Ezra remembered Flora's wifely support:

> I never realized it until later, but I know now that having Flora and the family nearby gave me new confidence in doing my job. I became more decisive, surer of myself, more willing to tackle the tough challenges. For years I had depended on her counsel and wise judgment to supplement my own thinking. In a good marriage that is inevitable. Husband and wife share their thoughts, and their desires, their problems, their joys and sorrows, until their unity is such that it's hard to tell where one person leaves off and the other begins.[47]

While Flora embraced complementary gender roles in marriage, she still found ways to support forms of male patriarchal authority. For example, on April 25, 1950, Ezra was sealed in marriage to his recently deceased cousin, Eva Amanda Benson, who had passed away on August 10, 1946, never having been married. It is most striking that the Bensons chose to participate in theological plural marriage at a time when Mormons were working on their assimilation into postwar American society. Remarkably, the Bensons' polygamous sealing was Flora's idea, and she even acted as proxy for Eva in the ordinance that was performed by apostle Joseph Fielding Smith in the Salt Lake Temple. Here she agreed to "share" her husband with another woman in the afterlife. It is hard to pinpoint Flora's motives for this posthumous polygamous sealing. Perhaps she felt overt concern for the "spinster" cousin's lack of a celestial marriage, which Mormons believe is necessary for the highest level of salvation in the eternities. Or she felt her husband could not obtain the greatest blessings of salvation reserved for men who entered the patriarchal order.[48] Ezra recorded, "I have never witnessed a more unselfish act on the part of any person, and I love Flora all the more because of it. The Lord will richly bless her for this act of unselfish love for Eva and me and the Kingdom. Flora is one of the choicest daughters of our Heavenly Father."[49] While this posthumous sealing would not have directly affected the experience of the Bensons' lived marriage, it demonstrated Flora's willingness to commit to wifely self-sacrifice on behalf of her husband's religious salvation.

By the early 1960s, Benson had begun to link his views on family and gender roles with his strong fears about communist intrusion into American life. The idea that "marriage, home, and family are sacred institutions" rested squarely on biblical notions about male authority, or "that it is not good for man to be alone," and "that woman was created to be a helpmeet for man."[50] In fact, Benson's first public expressions about women's roles had to do with concerns about the decline of the family as the solid foundation of a democratic, free society. "The good home is the rock foundation—the cornerstone of civilization," he affirmed.[51] In one of his first anti-communist publications, *The Red Carpet*, he warned that Marx and Engels considered "the elimination of the family as a social unit" as part of the communist "program to overthrow capitalism." He continued: "To have peace, prosperity, security—all the rewards of freedom, we in America must be prepared to defend our homes against all threats—external and internal."[52]

Benson was particularly concerned that America's youth were not being raised "as self-respecting, law-abiding citizens who truly are worthy of the name American."[53] Designating juvenile delinquency as a serious problem, he echoed larger national anxieties about "teenagers" in postwar America. In the early 1950s, LDS church president David O. McKay had warned against juvenile delinquency, often laying the responsibility with parents for not spending enough time with their children.[54] Benson's own earliest warnings about the decline of the family were reinforced through his associations with staunch anti-communists like Robert Welch of the newly founded John Birch Society (1958), and J. Edgar Hoover, director of the Federal Bureau of Investigation. Benson often cited FBI crime statistics and quoted warnings from Hoover that "the actions of a majority of [juvenile delinquents] were, and are, directly related to the conduct of their parents."[55] Benson also began addressing his concerns for the "ever-increasing divorce rate—the alarming increase in sexual sin—infidelity—yes, even adultery."[56] Indeed, Benson's strong alignment with the John Birch Society significantly escalated his alarmist reactions to social and political changes in 1960s America.[57]

While Benson's early directives about families usually targeted "parents" in general, he began echoing the national indicators that placed the onus of blame for delinquency on mothers, for, only "three out of five delinquent boys said their fathers were indifferent to them," [whereas] a whole "four out of five [said] . . . their mothers were indifferent to them."[58] The role of mothers in building up this ideal of masculinity and male citizenship was key; the accepted sentiment of the day was that "mothers who neglected their children bred criminals; mothers who overindulged their sons turned them into passive, weak, and effeminite 'perverts.'"[59] Benson did not specifically address the "problem that has no name," first articulated by Betty Friedan in 1963 as the feeling of unfulfilled desire in women who had sacrificed everything for their children.[60] But while Friedan encouraged women to find a hobby, part-time employment, business skills, or an educational outlet as a way of supplanting the drudgery of homemaking, Ezra Taft Benson argued that

> There is no satisfactory substitute for mother, and no one can take care of her children like she can. No so-called social obligations, social enticements, or outside interests should impel any mother to neglect the sacred charge which is hers of caring for her own flesh and blood.[61]

Benson later repeated this counsel in a 1974 compilation of his writings, adding that "I feel confident that while civic and social activities may return much good, she will serve her community and her nation best if she first devotes herself to the needs of her own children."[62] As the gender discussions of the 1960s continued, Benson warned again about the pitfalls of absentee mothers. But he continued to find the ultimate maternal ideal in his own wife, Flora, someone who historian Patrick Mason described as "a woman of talent and capability who refused to apply it to herself and found personal development and fulfillment primarily, and perhaps only, through the erasure of self in the service of others, most notably her husband and children."[63]

Benson also emphasized the importance of male authority in the home as a general bulwark against societal decay. He was not alone in the context of the Cold War, for as May has argued, "[f]oreign policy itself rested on well-articulated assumptions about masculine power [and] husbands, especially fathers, wore the badge of 'family man' as a sign of virility and patriotism."[64] Benson remained committed to building up righteous boyhood through the LDS Boy Scout program, which he considered necessary for instilling masculine and patriotic values. Scouting, he believed, was "a tremendous test of leadership, devotion, and courage," for shaping boys into men. "I have faith in the manhood of America; we will not let our boys down. Upon the character of our boys depends America's future. . . . May God bless us in the task of building men, real men."[65]

As much as Flora and Ezra continued to exemplify an idealized form of companionate marriage to members of the church, they were both influenced by a persistently strong view of patriarchy in marriage, in which men "ruled" or "presided over" their wives and children, and women gave loving self-sacrifice and uncomplaining support to their husbands. During one period of Ezra's long absences from home for national farm tours, Flora reflected, "If my husband's services are going to benefit our country, then we can make a contribution by sacrificing his company without complaint."[66]

LDS historian Patrick Mason has defined Flora's deference to patriarchy as a type of anti-feminism that "in some fashion work[ed] to undermine, limit, or halt [feminism's] advance, reckoning it as a danger to the structures of society and the value of true womanhood."[67] Importantly, Flora did not simply limit herself to a positive expression and defense of a woman's agency to find fulfillment in the home and family. Instead, she "went beyond that to articulate and defend male privilege, [and] assert a woman's duty to buttress that privilege."[68] Even in the task of raising children, Flora Benson appeared to preference the raising of sons for long-term societal success. In an address at the March 1969 Ricks College Women's Week, Flora directed her comments to the largely female audience about the importance of supporting men and boys.

> What a privilege it is for [a woman] to raise her children within the Church and soon, as her sons reach the age of 12, a new generation in the priesthood begins all over again. . . . We women should encourage and help our menfolk in their line of duty, for we cannot advance fully without them.[69]

She continued. "Mothers have a great responsibility and a sacred obligation. *Mothers are the builders of men.*"[70]

Mormon encouragement for male supremacy in the home reached its apex in the early 1970s with alarming rhetoric. For example, Southern Illinois University professor Brent Barlow, in a 1973 *Ensign* article, strongly warned against the modern "transition from patriarchal to a democratic or even matriarchal type of family."[71] Lamenting the loss of respect for male authority in the home, Barlow quoted President Joseph F. Smith, who had argued that "It is not merely a question of who is perhaps the best qualified. Neither it is wholly a question of who is living the most worthy life. It is a question largely of law and order, and its importance seen often from the fact that the authority remains and is respected long after a man is really unworthy to exercise it." In other words, a wife's submission to her husband's authority was not as much contingent upon his moral behavior as it was upon his maleness. Barlow furthermore compared wives' position in their families to that of children. "When a wife challenges the right of her husband to officiate in the home, is it not a logical consequence that the children will challenge that right also?"[72] Though it is impossible to know whether Benson had read or even approved of these attitudes, he was part of a larger Mormon effort to buttress male authority in the home as a reaction to changing gender norms in America.

For Benson, the importance of male authority evolved to a full articulation in his 1974 compilation, *God, Family, Country*, with a chapter titled,

"Putting Father at the Head of the Family." Benson declared "[t]he father is the presiding authority in the home. He is the patriarch or head of the family. The mother is the helpmate, the counselor. You cannot talk about father without talking about the role of the mother—they are one, sealed for time and all eternity."[73] Benson was contributing to a new negotiation of rhetoric for Mormon men's and women's roles in marriage, one that conceded a form of equality and unity between husbands and wives, while also leaving space for male headship "over" their wives and children. Mormon leaders like Benson employed this language as a nod to egalitarian marriages, while also simultaneously holding onto a Mormon theology of patriarchy in the home. Known as "soft patriarchy," Benson emphasized that men should love their wives and treat them well, while assuming the responsibility for the bulk of salvific duties in the home. Over time, he modified his rhetoric about familial patriarchy, stating that to "preside" means to set a "righteous example" in the home.[74] Or, not as "power over women," but as "men being involved and present in the lives of others."[75] And yet, Benson's legacy is alive and well through what Caroline Kline has described as the "pro-egalitarian rhetoric of certain Mormon General Authorities, who strongly emphasize the importance of equal partnership of spouses, while simultaneously sustaining men's presiding role."[76]

Much of this emphasis on male authority in the home was strengthened by a broader church context of the Correlation movement. Begun as a way of modernizing church programs, auxiliaries, and curriculum into an efficient whole, Correlation received energetic attention after World War II from President McKay and apostle Harold B. Lee. The purpose of Correlation was to bring all of the church auxiliaries under the authority of the Quorum of the Twelve, by consolidating programs and streamlining materials in more-efficient ways.[77] Correlation was necessary for responding to the growth of an expanding international church, but it came at great cost. One of its major results was the loss in autonomy of finances, publications, and curriculum for the female Relief Society, which had previously functioned with more independence.

Another major intent of Correlation was to strengthen the family unit by taking the church directly into Latter-day Saint homes. General Young Women president Ruth Hardy Funk noted in 1972 that Correlation was a response to "Lee's fear of modern society and its impact on the members. He had," she said, "this sense of social breakdown. . . . He saw the breakdown of the nuclear family."[78] Lee believed, as Benson did, that "[t]he father, the husband, must be considered the representative of the priesthood in the home, and through that relationship church attitudes, policies, and doctrines could be reinforced."[79] Through revitalized Family Home Evening programs, family prayer, scripture study, and home teaching (wherein male priesthood leaders visited assigned families once a month in their homes), church leadership could assure proper functioning of church programs and authority on the most intimate and personal level of the family. "'Placing the priesthood as the Lord intended, at the center of the Kingdom of God,' Lee told one group of church leaders, '[includes] a greater emphasis on the fathers in the homes as Priesthood bearer in strengthening the family unit."'[80] The Correlation movement also "paralleled the Mormon counterattack about the role and definition of women in society . . . [that] stressed the power of the priesthood and women's roles as homemakers."[81] As Correlation effectively buttressed male authority in the institutional church and the home, it simultaneously eroded female authority, even as the expansion of women's rights was gaining ground in American society.

Whereas the Cold War had provided Benson an early political framework for articulating his views on gender roles, the feminist movement of the 1960s further intensified his reactions to widespread and rapid changes for women, like the Pill and equal pay. Benson and other cultural conservatives strongly resisted these changes, and increasingly linked women's rights with other social identity movements as part of a larger effort to undermine American exceptionalism, tradition, and freedom.[82] In 1969 Benson warned against contraception:

> The world teaches birth control. Tragically, many of our sisters subscribe to its pills and practices when they could easily provide earthly tabernacles for more of our Father's children. . . . God [will] glorify that husband and wife who have a large posterity and who have tried to raise them up in righteousness.[83]

Of particular concern was the 1973 Supreme Court decision, *Roe vs. Wade.* While considered a major victory for women's rights to reproductive choice, the ruling added a new threat to traditional Mormon views on unimpeded reproduction. *Roe* was a galvanizing moment for the larger community of Christian conservatives in America, whose traditional views on gender, reproduction, and women's roles increasingly stood out against the broader movement for women's rights. These included those expanded rights that Mormons were particularly uncomfortable with—abortion, birth control, and gay rights. And although women's liberation included a range of voices, approaches, and solutions to gender discrimination in America, it was the radical voices within the movement that reinforced Americans' perceptions that feminists were hostile to traditional marriage and motherhood. To that, LDS church leaders responded most forcefully. In one strident example,

N. Eldon Tanner of the First Presidency spoke in 1973 "on what he saw as a connection between women's liberation and the devil."[84]

> We hear so much about emancipation, independence, sexual liberation, birth control, abortion, and other insidious propaganda belittling the role of motherhood, all of which is Satan's way of destroying women, the home, and the family—the basic unit of society.[85]

By drawing such rigid lines in the sand, "Tanner's rhetoric created an adversarial relationship between traditional Mormon women and proponents of women's rights, leaving no middle ground."[86]

Ultimately, the divide between traditionalists and feminists proved to be the most disastrous to the fate of the Equal Rights Amendment (ERA), the constitutional amendment for women's equality. Building on the momentum of 1960s second-wave feminism, the ERA had finally passed both houses of Congress in 1972 and was on its way through the states for ratification. Even as the pro-ERA movement gained widespread support and came close to ratification, it was doomed to defeat by the collective efforts of right-wing groups, anti-communists, and traditional, conservative religious groups like Catholics and Mormons. As LDS historian Claudia Bushman has noted, "the feminist movement collided with the church's emphasis on motherhood, [which] collision played out nationally with official opposition to the proposed Equal Rights Amendments to legalize gender equality."[87] Similarly, historian J. B. Haws has shown how the church consciously constructed a public image centered on the family, just as "political trends in the 1970s seemed to threaten the very family model the Latter-day Saints preached." So, "for Latter-day Saint officials, the decision to speak out against the E.R.A. was part and parcel with their pro-family agenda. It was an identity they sought to cultivate."[88]

The LDS church entered the national debate with vocal opposition to ERA, which led to very heated divides within the church between women who supported ERA and those who opposed it. The First Presidency took a formal stance against ERA on October 22, 1976, asserting that ERA presented a significant "moral" issue to which the church must respond, and warning that it would "undoubtedly lead to further interpretations that could 'demean women rather than ennoble them, and that would threaten the stability of the family which is a creation of God.'"[89] Although statements like these were couched in very ambiguous terms, some church leaders made very specific warnings that ERA would lead to unisex bathrooms, a military draft requirement for women, lack of legal protections against domestic violence, no-fault divorce laws, a widespread acceptance of gender fluidity, and ultimately legal rights for LGBTQ individuals.[90] Using these ideas, the First Presidency reaffirmed its opposition in 1978 and then issued a formal statement in 1980, which was distributed to women all over the church, warning against the "encouragement of those who seek a unisex society, an increase in the practice of homosexual and lesbian activities, and other concepts which could alter the natural, God-given relationship of men and women."[91]

As newly called president of the Quorum of Twelve Apostles in 1973, Benson gained an added influence articulating Mormon rhetoric on gender, and took an active role in trying to stop the ratification of the ERA. Influenced by LDS teachings on families, Benson's anti-ERA stance was also partly informed by his allegiance to the John Birch Society, since its "dislike of big government and willingness to fight moral issues on a political stage brought its objectives in line with those of the Mormon Church."[92] Although the Birch Society was not a religious organization, historian Martha Bradley described how its "rhetorical arguments against ERA matched closely those used by other conservative religious groups," including Mormons. One Bircher, Dan Smoot, reminded followers that "the idealizing of women—honoring them, especially mothers, as if on a pedestal—has always been an obvious fact of American life . . . [that] has profoundly influenced our moral codes, our laws, our customs, all of our institutions, and even our taste."[93] Opposition to ERA was necessary to preserve women's "special status which they do not enjoy elsewhere."[94] Through new threats to families like abortion on demand, promiscuous sexuality, and gay rights, the Birch Society "saw the amendment as a threat to the Constitution and a part of the 'Socialist-Communist menace." Smoot had also "reminded readers that men were legally heads of families" and worried that ERA would upend this important family position.[95] Apostle Benson felt a similar anxiety, and argued that "Men are dominant . . . because 'someone must be in charge and take leadership.'" The church's official position had always been that the ERA "threatened the family," but one of Benson's overriding fears was that "he felt the amendment would 'weaken men.'"[96]

Much of this action culminated in the important International Women's Year celebrations of 1977. Salt Lake City prepared to host Utah's state IWY meeting, which was meant to be a gathering of men and women across the political and ideological spectrum, for "discussing positions on a variety of social, political, and legal questions facing women today."[97] Although active LDS women were involved in the planning of the conference, Mormon leadership reacted with alarm, fearing that the IWY was a front for ERA activism, and particularly for advocating abortion and reproductive freedom. Indeed, "the national and local Equal Rights Amendment battle was an inseparable context for the IWY conferences."[98] Mormon women had worried that their voices would not be represented fairly at the conference, especially in the context of the recent IWY conferences in Colorado and Benson's own home state of Idaho, where Mormon women had, in fact, been marginalized and mocked by secular feminists.[99]

Leading up to the conference, church leadership worked to rally Mormon women to attend the meeting, even if they had no previous interest in the issues. For the few months prior to the meeting, General Relief Society president Barbara B. Smith "met weekly" with Ezra Taft Benson and "other male church leaders, although the men would not take part in the ongoing controversy in a visible way."[100] Benson's anti-ERA work was mostly behind the scenes, like when he sent a letter to stake presidents encouraging them to speak against the amendment in their localities. By early June, Benson called for each Utah ward to send ten women to the IWY conference, "and hopefully many more," with instructions to educate themselves on procedure, voting, and the nominating process.[101] Under Benson's direction, attendance at the conference swelled from the expected three thousand to more than 13,800 participants. One of the attendees "understood that they were 'to vote no on practically everything' even though some had not received proper education on vital issues. . . . Some attendees even resorted to boos, hisses, shouting, and interrupting speakers."[102] The vocal opposition must be understood as a legitimate response to fears Mormon women felt of being marginalized on significant moral issues. Still, the disruptions of the IWY meeting came to characterize many discussions of women's rights, in which Mormons became further divided along ideological lines of feminism versus anti-feminism.

Apostle Benson issued a defining theological blow to the Equal Rights Amendment and philosophical feminism with his October 1981 General Conference address to the women (and men) of the church. The talk became the church's last formal jab at ERA before the amendment's final defeat in June 1982, but more importantly, it became the longest-lasting rhetorical instrument used by LDS leaders for reifying traditional gender roles. Benson once again articulated a form of idealized motherhood, an emphasis for Benson that had remained consistent for years, but that now was being used especially as a counter to the perception of anti-motherhood in the feminist movement. "God placed woman in a companion role with the priesthood . . . [thus], [w]oman was given to man as an helpmeet."[103] The secondary, or accessory relationship of woman is clear, in that she is "given to man," and never the other way around.

Still, just as he had done in earlier discourses, Benson articulated a "complementary association" between husbands and wives that suggested gender equality, while also holding onto the supremacy of the husband's authority in the home: "Support, encourage, and strengthen your husband in his responsibility as patriarch in the home. You are partners with him. A woman's role in a man's life is to lift him, to help him uphold lofty standards, and to prepare through righteous living to be his queen for all eternity." Even those activities for which a mother must take an involved role, like family home evening and scripture study, she should do under her "husband's direction." Once again, he found in his wife, Flora, the epitome of all that he expected of Mormon women: stay-at-home motherhood, deference to male authority, and perfected homemaking skills. He seemed most proud that in "losing herself in service to her husband and children, she has shown a courageous determination to magnify what she knows is the divine and glorious calling of being a worthy wife and mother."[104]

Benson took his expectation of self-sacrificing motherhood to a new level by suggesting that women should even eschew higher education and outside interests in the name of appropriate motherhood. "It is a misguided idea that a woman should leave the home, where there is a husband and children, to prepare educationally and financially for an unforeseen eventuality." He saw women's desires for outside ambition as a result of recent feminist awakenings: "Too often, I fear, even women in the Church use the world as their standard for success and basis for self-worth." To that end, he warned against limiting family size, especially if it meant seeking "personal goals and self-fulfillment."[105]

Benson's warnings against women working outside the home were dire. "Now can you see why Satan wants to destroy the home through having the mother leave the care of her children to others?"[106] Harkening back to the gender anxieties he first expressed in the 1960s, Benson laid the blame of juvenile delinquency and divorce at the feet of working moms. While not naming delinquency specifically, he hinted that "all of us are aware of instances of active Latter-day Saint families who are experiencing difficulties with their children because mother is not where she ought to be—in the home." Then, he warned, "[t]he seeds of divorce are often sown and the problems of children begin when mother works outside the home. You mothers should carefully count the cost before you decide to share breadwinning responsibilities with your husbands." Benson expressed concerns about families outsourcing the raising of children to the state or private institutions. "It is a fundamental truth that the responsibilities of motherhood cannot be successfully delegated. No, not to day-care-centers, not to schools, not to nurseries, not to babysitters." He even disparaged the idea of "preschool training outside the home" which only "places young children in an environment away from the mother's influence."[107] Perhaps Benson's fears about public education informed his insistence on present, hands-on mothering: children should literally have no time away from their mothers.[108]

Embedded within Benson's emphasis on old-fashioned family values were many useful and encouraging ideas about family togetherness and raising children: teaching children to work, eating dinner together, honest family communication, and attending cultural arts events. However, this also came with carefully outlined expectations for women's domestic roles. For women who embraced the exclusivity of motherhood, this address was a positive reinforcement of their life's choices. But for others, it felt like Benson was setting forth a one-size-fits-all formula that was limiting and proscriptive, especially as a reaction to calls for women to find self-fulfillment outside the home. Indeed, women who rejected motherhood did so at their own eternal peril. "You were elected by God to be wives and mothers in Zion. Exaltation in the celestial kingdom is predicated on faithfulness to that calling."[109] Characterizing Benson's talk, historian Martha Bradley suggests "[t]he cult of true womanhood never had a more eloquent spokesman than in this twentieth-century prophet."[110]

Coming when it did from the president of the Quorum of Twelve Apostles, "The Honored Place of Woman" was a clear answer to the Equal Rights Amendment and the feared intrusion of feminist impulses into LDS life. In fact, Bradley called this one of the nine defining Mormon documents used to push back against the ratification of ERA. But the legacy Benson left on gender roles for Mormon women was complicated: he successfully worked to elevate motherhood as an acceptable and honored role for women, at a time when more American women were postponing or rejecting pregnancy and childrearing.[111] But his parameters for acceptable maternity represented not only a push back, but a full step back. In many ways, it locked Mormonism into an anti-feminist narrative that it has at once both clung to and struggled to discard in recent years. Between 1981 and 1992, Benson repeated the themes of his original talk in other talks, firesides, and pamphlets for women.

In 1985, at age eighty-six, Benson became the president and prophet of the church upon the death of his predecessor, Spencer W. Kimball. In spite of some members' fears that Benson's right-wing politics would define the tone of his tenure as church president, instead he mostly backed off from political commentary.[112] However, he stuck to his conservative views on gender, re-packaging them for new audiences. Most famously, in 1987, Benson presented a fireside for mothers that received wide attention and became an essential treatise for defining church leaders' expectations for Mormon women.[113] Benson reiterated his main themes with an official stamp of revelatory authority:

1) that motherhood is a noble calling and that women's chief responsibility in life is "to conceive, to nourish, to love and to train" children; 2) that fathers should act as the presiding authority in the home "to provide, to love, to teach and to direct," and that family prayers should be done under the "direction of the father" or with a "husband presiding"; 3) that couples should not postpone having children for any reason, including education, home ownership, or waiting out poverty, but especially for materialistic reasons. "Do not," he warned, "curtail the number of . . . children for personal or selfish reasons," and "Have your children and have them early." The only allowance for limiting reproduction was a brief caution he gave to husbands to "always be considerate of your wives in the bearing of children."[114] And 4) that mothers should not work outside the home for any reason, except in dire emergencies, divorce, or widowhood. "Contrary to conventional wisdom," he counseled, "a mother's calling is in the home, not in the market place." To emphasize this point, Benson quoted from Kimball's almost forty-year-old instructions from 1949: "Wives, come home from the typewriter, the laundry, the nursing, come home from the factory, the café."[115]

Reaction to the fireside was swift and polarizing. Many felt that the talk was a much-needed reaffirmation of the importance of motherhood; it was printed, after all, as a "pink pamphlet" for wide distribution to wards and stakes in the weeks following, giving it an added air of authoritative importance. But others resisted Benson's proscriptive and reactionary tone, which made it "possible to hear it as also accusatory."[116] Few women would have disagreed with Benson "that child-rearing was not supremely important." As Lavina Anderson acknowledged, "Certainly the counsel in this list [Benson's list of ten guidelines for effective mothering] is good. I know no mother, including myself, who does not enjoy spending time with their children and who does not try to do most of the things on this list."[117] Still, many women seemed "concerned with the sweeping nature of his instructions, which did not adequately acknowledge the diversity of women and their circumstances."[118] One observer remarked with frustration that "President Benson lays down the law. A woman's place is in the home, he says, whether the family needs the money or not. Furthermore, women must bear many children regardless of their economic means."[119]

To encourage LDS women in 1987 to leave their employment at a time when women made up 50 percent of the paid workforce represented a perceptibly reactionary directive, especially after decades of expanding educational and professional opportunities for women and changing economic realities in America and globally. *Dialogue* editor Karen Shepherd noted, "[Benson] did not suggest what Utah would do if it were to lose 44 percent of its entire work force." Indeed, a 1981 survey showed that "Fifty-one percent of LDS women were either working or looking for work in 1981, compared to a national average of 52 percent." For women with young children under six, "the figure drops to 36.5 percent but climbs to 57 percent of mothers with children between six and seventeen."[120] Indeed, rather than instances of mothers working being the "exception, not the rule," as Benson stated, Mormon feminist Claudia Bushman in 1987 argued that even for Mormon women, "[t]he luxury of being a full-time mother is only for those who can afford it."[121]

The talk prompted other responses. Some mothers lamented that Benson's talk privileged the conceiving and bearing of children over women who acquired their children through adoption or were childless altogether. Anderson pointed out the seeming contradiction: "the physical processes of conception, pregnancy, and birthing are not 'quality' operations, like loving and training. In fact they are virtually involuntary operations."[122] And the results could be ambiguous at best: Some veteran mothers expressed "agony" that, in spite of practicing the devoted, selfless, hands-on mothering of Benson's formula, their children still turned out "deviant" by the Church's standards. One mother cried,

> I stayed home, I never worked, I was always there when they got home from school, I made cookies, I read to them, I prayed with them. I always had hot meals for them, and I loved them. Tell me, what more could I have done? I did everything on this list and it still didn't work.[123]

In total, the mixed and controversial response to Benson's talk was probably its strongest legacy. Certainly, the talk could be celebrated for its "strong statements about the centrality and value of family life." But the overall message to women who already struggled in balancing maternity and professional work was clear: "Mothering is not only a woman's most important responsibility but that it is also her *only* responsibility and that it is *only* her responsibility."[124]

Benson's final "address" to women was published in 1992, as *Elect Women of God*, a brief booklet-compilation of his writings on women, probably ghost-written and edited by his son Reed because of the prophet's failing health. Whereas Benson's 1987 fireside had included the warning that "numerous divorces can be traced directly to the day when the wife left the home," *Elect Women* only stuck to the injunctions against working women, but without directly blaming working women for society's ills.[125]

When Benson died in 1994, just two years after Flora, the church was in the midst of experiencing important transitions regarding the place of women.[126] In 1985, the very year that Benson ascended to the church presidency, and two years prior to the "Mothers of Zion" fireside, apostle James E. Faust had spoken strongly about the real problem of female poverty. While the purpose of his talk was to warn Mormon women against "having it all," and to encourage righteous motherhood, his tone was expansive, and he made a clear nod to the importance of women's education and work skills.

> It is unfortunate that it is taking so long to bring full economic justice to women. The feminization of poverty is both real and tragic. That is why you should work very hard to prepare for your future by gaining some marketable skills. The struggle to improve the place of women in society has been a noble cause, and I sincerely hope the day will come when women with equal skills will be fully equal with men in the marketplace.[127]

In comparison to Faust's realistic and nuanced approach, Benson's directives of 1987 seemed all that more regressive and reactive. Indeed, by the 1990s, other general authorities had begun to retreat from the punitive language directed to working women. In 2001 Gordon B. Hinckley, one of Benson's successors in the LDS church presidency, offered a counterpoint to Benson's stricter views on women's sphere.

> Find purpose in your life. Choose the things you would like to do, and educate yourselves to be effective in their pursuit. For most it is very difficult to settle on a vocation. . . . In this day and time, a girl needs an education. She needs the means and skills by which to earn a living should she find herself in a situation where it becomes necessary to do so.[128]

In 1995 the Church formally released "The Family: A Proclamation to the World" as an edict about the importance of heterosexual marriage and wholesome childrearing in a moral and uplifting environment. The Proclamation was a formal codification of the traditional gender roles espoused by Benson and many of his generation, but it came with modifications of more strident language directed to women, especially working women. Still, the instruction on gender roles remains insistent that "By divine design, fathers are to preside over their families in love and righteousness," and women are "primarily responsible for the nurture of their children." Even so, the Proclamation has conceded a gendered sharing that probably would have surprised those of Benson's generation, in that "Fathers and Mothers are obligated to assist one another as equal partners."[129]

The Proclamation represented the culmination of a long trajectory of church leaders' post–World War II concerns about the breakdown of the family because of consumerism, affluence, and immorality. These worries had informed Benson's early reactions to the counterculture in general, and women's rights as a large part of that shifting social movement, but now found their way into a major church directive on family roles and relationships. Today's Mormon rhetoric and prescriptions for women carry the hallmarks of Ezra Taft Benson. His influence on gender role rhetoric might be buried underneath his much more pronounced super-patriotism, anti-communism, and teachings on the Book of Mormon and pride. However, it is not difficult to trace a connection between Benson's early language on male authority in the home and the Proclamation's emphasis on men's responsibilities to "preside, provide, and protect." Although the impetus for the Proclamation in 1995 came as a response to the legalization of same-sex marriage, Benson's interest in the traditional family as a bulwark of righteous American civilization reflected his persistent response to the breakdown of traditional family as he knew it. While not formally canonized as scripture, the Proclamation enjoys a quasi-canonical status, keeping Benson's ideas of gender and family alive and well. Perhaps his most indelible stamp is the fundamentally unresolved tension between whether the church will hold onto its gender hierarchies, or whether it will someday make space for full female equality in marriage, families, and religious practice.

Notes

1. Ezra Taft Benson, "To the Mothers in Zion," February 22, 1987, copy of the pamphlet at the LDS Church History Library, Salt Lake City, Utah.

2. The talk can be referenced through online sites, as well as appearing in some Church Education System materials, like other notable talks by LDS leaders.

3. One early iteration was "The Honored Place of Woman," delivered at General Conference in October 1981 (https://www.lds.org/general-conference/1981/10/the-honored-place-of-woman?lang=eng).

4. Elaine Tyler May, *Homeward Bound: American Families in the Cold War Era* (New York: Basic Books, 1988), 16–20.

5. Sheri L. Dew, *Ezra Taft Benson: A Biography* (Salt Lake City: Deseret Book, 1987), 16. At age twelve, Benson's position as "man of the house" was cemented when his father was called on a mission.

6. Ibid., 14.

7. Gail Bederman, *Manliness and Civilization: A Cultural History of Gender and Race in the United States, 1880–1917* (Chicago and London: University of Chicago Press, 1995), 43.

8. Richard Ian Kimball, *Sports in Zion: Mormon Recreation, 1890–1940* (Urbana and Chicago: University of Illinois Press, 2003), 3.

9. Kimball, *Sports in Zion*, 4. See Clifford Putney, *Muscular Christianity: Manhood and Sports in Protestant America, 1880–1920* (Cambridge, Mass.: Harvard University Press, 2001), 53.

10. Dew, *Ezra Taft Benson*, 38.

11. Kimball, *Sports in Zion*, 142. In 1918, "3,705 boys had registered with official BSA troops, while another 2,162 participated in LDS scouting activities beyond BSA recognition." Also, Dew, *Ezra Taft Benson*, 43.

12. Benson later recalled, "What a challenge it was to work with and to lead twenty-four boys in the first Scout troop in this little rural community. Talk about rewards for effort!" Ezra Taft Benson, *God, Family, Country: Our Three Great Loyalties* (Salt Lake City: Deseret Book, 1974), 207.

13. Evan Stephens, "The 'Mormon' Boy," Hymn No. 269, *Deseret Sunday School Songs* (Salt Lake City: Deseret Sunday School Union, 1909).

14. Bederman, *Manliness and Civilization*, 44.

15. Benson, "To the Mothers in Israel."

16. Howard P. Chudacoff, *The Age of the Bachelor: Creating an American Subculture* (Princeton, N.J.: Princeton University Press, 2000), 17.

17. Dew, *Ezra Taft Benson*, 44.

18. Ibid., 75–76. For more on Ezra's and Flora's early courtship, see John P. Livingstone, "Profiles of the Prophets: Ezra Taft Benson," *Religious Educator: Perspectives on the Restored Gospel* 9, no. 1 (2008): http://scholarsarchive.byu.edu/cgi/viewcontent.cgi?article=1305&context=re.

19. Kathryn Shirts, "'Priesthood and Womanhood': Leah Widtsoe's Role in Defining an Identity for Latter-day Saint Women of the Twentieth Century." Paper presented at the Mormon History Association Conference, San Antonio, Texas, June 6, 2014. Copy in possession of the author.

20. "'What I Admire Most in My Husband,' Mrs. Ezra Taft Benson [Flora Amussen Benson], as told to Leonard J. Snyder," *Capper's Farmer*, June 1955, 47 and 54; quoted in Gary James Bergera, "Weak-Kneed Republicans," *Dialogue: A Journal of Mormon Thought* 41, no. 4 (Winter 2008): 59.

21. Dew, *Ezra Taft Benson*, 130.

22. Ibid., 133.

23. Ibid., 130.

24. May, *Homeward Bound*, 57.

25. Dew, *Ezra Taft Benson*, 136–37.

26. Ibid., 130.

27. May, *Homeward Bound*, 3.

28. Ibid., 14.

29. Ibid., 99.

30. Ferdinand Lundberg and Marynia F. Farnham, *Modern Woman: The Lost Sex* (New York: HarperCollins, 1947), reprinted in *Major Problems in American Women's History*, 5th ed., edited by Sharon Block, Ruth M. Alexander, and Mary Beth Norton (Boston: Cengage Learning, 2014), 437.

31. Lundberg and Farnham, *Modern Woman*, quoted in *Major Problems*, 437.

32. May, *Homeward Bound*, 5. Whereas women went to work during the war in military industries and government services, that transition was temporary. After the war, women's employment shifted to "pink-collar" jobs like secretarial work and teaching.

33. Block, Anderson, and Norton, *Major Problems*, 435.

34. Elder Spencer W. Kimball, "An Apostle Speaks about Marriage to John and Mary," *Improvement Era* 52, no. 2 (February 1949): 74–75. Emphasis mine.

35. Lundberg and Farnham, *Modern Woman*, quoted in *Major Problems*, p. 437.

36. Kimball, "An Apostle Speaks about Marriage to John and Mary," 74–75.

37. Derin Head Rodriguez, "Flora Amussen Benson: Handmaiden of the Lord, Helpmeet of a Prophet, Mother in Zion," *Ensign* (March 1987), https://www.lds.org/ensign/1987/03/flora-amussen-benson-handmaiden-of-the-lord-helpmeet-of-a-prophet-mother-in-zion?lang=eng. In reference to Flora, the word "support" is mentioned four times in the *Ensign* article and interview with the Bensons.

38. May, *Homeward Bound*, 104–5. For Mormon Relief Societies (the Church's organization for women), activities like home canning and homemaking classes gained renewed popularity after the war.

39. Ibid., 104.

40. Dew, *Ezra Taft Benson*, 300–301; Bergera, "Weak-Kneed Republicans," 58.

41. Dew, *Ezra Taft Benson*, 298.

42. Bergera, "Weak-Kneed Republicans," 58.

43. Ibid., and Dew, 298.

44. "Talk by Flora Amussen Benson, May 1962," quoted in Bergera, "Weak-Kneed Republicans," 60.

45. Dorothy McCardle, "Mrs. Truman Puts the Kettle On," *Washington Post and Times Herald*, August 21, 1955, quoted in Gary Bergera, "Weak-Kneed Republicans," 59 n. 6.

46. McCardle, quoted in Bergera, "Weak-Kneed Republicans," 84 n. 30.

47. Ezra Taft Benson, *Cross Fire: The Eight Years with Eisenhower* (Garden City, N.Y.: Doubleday, 1962), 143.

48. When Mormons announced the end of plural marriage in 1890 and then again in 1904, that cessation had driven plural marriage underground, or into fundamentalist sects, or, in cases like the Bensons, toward the practice of sealing posthumously to deceased women. For this point, see Newell G. Bringhurst and Craig L. Foster, eds., *The Persistence of Polygamy, Vol. 3: Fundamentalist Mormon Polygamy from 1890 to the Present* (Independence, Mo.: John Whitmer Books, 2015).

49. Ezra Taft Benson diary, April 25, 1950, copy in possession of the Smith-Petit Foundation, quoted in Bergera, "Weak-Kneed Republicans," 83.

50. Ezra Taft Benson, *The Red Carpet* (Salt Lake City: Bookcraft, 1962), 275.

51. Ibid., 274.

52. Ibid.

53. Ibid., 277.

54. Robert Gottlieb & Peter Wiley, *America's Saints: The Rise of Mormon Power* (New York: G.P. Putnam's Sons, 1984), 194.

55. Benson, *God, Family, Country*, 169.

56. Ezra Taft Benson, *Title of Liberty*, comp. by Mark A. Benson (Salt Lake City: Deseret Book, 1964), 105.

57. For a thorough discussion of Benson's affiliation with the John Birch Society, see D. Michael Quinn, "Ezra Taft Benson and Mormon Political Conflicts," in *Dialogue: A Journal of Mormon Thought* 26, no. 2 (Summer 1993): 1–87. "Although Benson was never a member of record, his wife Flora and sons Reed and Mark all joined the Birch Society"

(8). The Birch Society was "the most significant grass-roots organization to express the 'Great Fear' of Communist triumphs internationally and of Communist subversion in America after World War II" (4). Benson himself called it the "most effective non-church organization in our fight against creeping socialism and godless communism" (5). See also Gregory A. Prince and Wm. Robert Wright, *David O. McKay and the Rise of Modern Mormonism* (Salt Lake City: University of Utah Press, 2005), chap. 12; Robert Goldberg, "From New Deal to New Right"; and Matthew L. Harris, "Martin Luther King, Civil Rights, and Perceptions of a 'Communist Conspiracy.'" The Goldberg and Harris essays are published in this volume.

58. Benson, *The Red Carpet*, 277.

59. May, *Homeward Bound*, 96.

60. Betty Friedan, *The Feminine Mystique* (New York: W.W. Norton, 1963; Norton paperback, 2001). "The only problems now are those that might disturb her adjustment as a housewife. So career is a problem, education is a problem, political interest, even the very admission of women's intelligence and individuality is a problem. And finally, there is the problem that has no name, a vague undefined wish for 'something more' than washing dishes, ironing, punishing and praising the children" (61).

61. Benson, *The Red Carpet*, 278.

62. Benson, *God, Family, Country*, 170.

63. Patrick Q. Mason, "Flora Benson and the Problem of Female Anti-Feminism," 5; paper presented for the Mormon Women's History Initiative Symposium, August 9, 2014, Utah Valley University.

64. May, *Homeward Bound*, 98.

65. Benson, *God, Family, Country*, 215.

66. Dew, *Ezra Taft Benson*, 286.

67. Mason, "Flora Benson and the Problem of Female Anti-Feminism," 3.

68. Ibid.

69. Flora Benson, speech given at Ricks College, March 25, 1969, in "Featured Speeches of the Year" (Rexburg, Id.: Ricks College, 1969), 1.

70. Ibid.

71. Brent Barlow, "Strengthening the Patriarchal Order in the Home," *Ensign* (February 1973): https://www.lds.org/ensign/1973/02/strengthening-the-patriarchal-order-in-the-home?lang=eng.

72. Barlow, "Strengthening the Patriarchal Order in the Home."

73. Benson, *God, Family, Country*, 183.

74. Ibid., 118.

75. Caroline Kline, "Patriarchy," in Claudia L. Bushman and Caroline Kline, eds., *Mormon Women Have Their Say: Essays from the Claremont Oral History Collection* (Salt Lake City: Greg Kofford Books, 2013), 215–34.

76. Kline, "Patriarchy," 218 n. 5. For further examination of Mormon expectations of male patriarchy in equal marriages, see Kline, "Patriarchy," in Bushman and Kline, eds., *Mormon Women Have Their Say*, 215–34; Kristy Money and Rolf Straubhaar, "Egalitarian Marriage in a Patriarchal Church," in Gordon Shepherd, Lavina Fielding Anderson, and Gary Shepherd, *Voices for Equality: Ordain Women and Resurgent Mormon Feminism* (Salt Lake City: Greg Kofford Books, 2015), 103–15; and Kynthia Taylor, "The Trouble with

Chicken Patriarchy," November 20, 2007, Zelophehad's Daughters, at http://zelophehads daughters.com/2007/11/30/the-trouble-with-chicken-patriarchy/ (accessed August 12, 2016); and April Young Bennet, "The Evolving Mormon Definition of Preside," October 18, 2012, Exponent II at http://www.the-exponent.com/the-evolving-mormon-definition-of -preside/ (accessed August 12, 2016).

77. For a discussion of the history and development of Correlation, see Prince and Wright, "Correlation and Church Administration," in Prince and Wright, *David O. McKay* 139–58; see also Gottlieb and Wiley, *America's Saints*.

78. Martha Sonntag Bradley, *Pedestals and Podiums: Utah Women, Religious Authority & Equal Rights* (Salt Lake City: Signature Books, 2005), 113.

79. Gottlieb and Wiley, *America's Saints*, 195.

80. Ibid., 195.

81. Ibid., 198.

82. In 1964, conservative lawyer and activist, Phyllis Schlafly published *A Choice Not an Echo*, which brought her into right-wing circles, especially the John Birch Society. But it was her anti-feminist rhetoric that propelled her to the forefront of the larger conservative retrenchment against women's rights in the 1970s.

83. Elder Ezra Taft Benson, "To the Humble Followers of Christ," *Conference Report* (April 1969): 10–15; found at http://scriptures.byu.edu/gettalk.php?ID=1669.

84. Bradley, *Pedestals and Podiums*, 72.

85. N. Eldon Tanner, "No Greater Calling: The Woman's Role," October 1973 General Conference address, quoted in ibid., 72.

86. Ibid.

87. Claudia Bushman, *Contemporary Mormonism: Latter-day Saints in Modern America* (Westport, Conn. and London: Praeger, 2008), 118.

88. J. B. Haws, *The Mormon Image in the American Mind: Fifty Years of Public Perception* (Oxford and New York: Oxford University Press, 2013), 74.

89. Bradley, *Pedestals and Podiums*, p. 81, 99.

90. For a detailed examination of the history of the battle over the Equal Rights Amendment within a Mormon context, see Bradley, *Pedestals and Podiums*. See also Sonia Johnson's autobiographical approach to ERA and her ultimate excommunication in 1982 for opposing Church leadership on the issue of ERA support. *From Housewife to Heretic: One Woman's Spiritual Awakening and Her Excommunication from the Mormon Church* (Garden City, N.Y.: Doubleday, 1981); for a collection of key writings related to Mormon feminists' responses to the ERA and women's religious participation in general, see Joanna Brooks, Rachel Hunt Steenblik, and Hannah Wheelwright, eds., *Mormon Feminism: Essential Writings* (Oxford and New York: Oxford University Press, 2016).

91. "The Church and the Proposed Equal Rights Amendment: A Moral Issue," *Ensign* (March 1980): https://www.lds.org/ensign/1980/03/the-church-and-the-proposed-equal -rights-amendment-a-moral-issue?lang=eng.

92. Bradley, *Pedestals and Podiums*, 117.

93. Dan Smoot, "The Dan Smoot Report—Reject or Rescind the E.R.A.," *Review of the News*, March 13, 1974, 31–38, quoted in Bradley, *Pedestals and Podiums*, 117, also 537 n. 72.

94. Bradley, *Pedestals and Podiums*, 117.

95. Ibid., 118.

96. Kay Mills, "Those Aren't Prayer Meetings They Hold on Sunday, Those are Precinct Meetings," *Daily Breakthrough*, November 19, 1977, 3, quoted in Bradley, 273, also 563 n. 44.

97. Bradley, *Pedestals and Podiums*, 155.

98. Ibid., 161.

99. Ibid., 175.

100. Bradley, *Pedestals and Podiums*, 160.

101. Ibid., 169, 175–76.

102. Ibid., 190, 198–201.

103. Ezra Taft Benson, "The Honored Place of Woman," *Ensign* (October 1981): https://www.lds.org/general-conference/1981/10/the-honored-place-of-woman?lang=eng.

104. Ibid.

105. Ibid.

106. Ibid.

107. Ibid.

108. Benson's son, Reed, and his wife, May, had homeschooled all of their nine children, and Reed advocated for homeschooling, even writing his 1981 Ed.D. dissertation on the homeschool movement. In general, father and son viewed public education with an eye of suspicion for its supposed associations with socialism, rational science, and secularism. Reed Amussen Benson, "The development of a home school," Brigham Young University, Ed.D., 1981.

109. Benson, "The Honored Place of Woman."

110. Bradley, *Pedestals and Podiums*, 111.

111. See William D. Mosher, Ph.D., Jo Jones, Ph.D., and Joyce C. Abma, Ph.D., Division of Vital Statistics, "Intended and Unintended Births in the United States, 1982–2010," National Health Statistics Report, No. 55 (July 24, 2012), found at https://www.cdc.gov/nchs/data/nhsr/nhsr055.pdf#x2013;2010 [PDF - 416 KB]; see also Population Reference Bureau, "World Population Data Sheet, 2012," found at http://www.prb.org/publications/datasheets/2012/world-population-data-sheet/fact-sheet-us-population.aspx

112. Haws, *Mormon Image in the American Mind*, 154.

113. Benson, "To the Mothers in Zion." Benson also gave a similar talk to the men of the church called "To the Fathers in Israel" at the October 1987 priesthood session of General Conference (https://www.lds.org/general-conference/1987/10/to-the-fathers-in-israel?lang=eng).

114. Benson, "To the Mothers in Zion." This caution might have been a reminder of Ezra's and Flora's own heartaches, when Flora's health deteriorated after the birth of their last daughter. Eventually, Flora had a hysterectomy and was never able to fulfill her dream of twelve children. The Church's stance on the use of birth control to limit the numbers of children had evolved alongside other changes for women. See Melissa Proctor, "Bodies, Babies, and Birth Control," *Dialogue: A Journal of Mormon Thought* 36, no. 3 (Fall 2003): 159–75.

115. Kimball, "An Apostle Speaks about Marriage to John and Mary," quoted in Benson, "To the Mothers in Zion."

116. Lavina Fielding Anderson, "A Voice From the Past: The Benson Instructions for Parents," *Dialogue: A Journal of Mormon Thought* 21, no. 2 (1988): 106.

117. Ibid., 110.

118. Ibid., 104.

119. *Dialogue* editor Karen Shepherd, quoted in ibid., 103–4.

120. These statistics on female employment and wages in 1980s Utah were taken from Kristen L. Goodman and Tim B. Heaton, "LDS Church Members in the United States and Canada: A Demographic Profile," *AMCAP Journal* 12, no. 1 (1986): 88–107; quoted in Anderson, "A Voice From the Past," 107–8.

121. Claudia L. Bushman, "From the Daughters of Zion," review of *Sisters in Spirit: Mormon Women in Historical Perspective*, eds. Maureen Ursenbach Beecher and Lavina Fielding Anderson, *Sunstone* 11, no. 6 (November 1987): 37–39, quoted in Anderson, "A Voice From the Past," 108.

122. Anderson, "A Voice From the Past," 107.

123. Ibid., 106.

124. Ibid., 109, 112.

125. Benson, "To the Mothers in Zion." While Benson's quotes against working mothers can still be found in some CES curricula, the original text to the fireside is somewhat elusive to internet search, except for an occasional blog reproduction. And the more strident parts have been left out entirely from the Relief Society and Priesthood Sunday instruction manual on Ezra Taft Benson.

126. The years between 1992 and 1994 saw the release of the following Mormon feminist publications: Maxine Hanks, ed., *Women and Authority: Re-emerging Mormon Feminism* (Salt Lake City: Signature Books, 1992); Linda King Newell, and Valeen Tippetts Avery, *Mormon Enigma: Emma Hale Smith* (Champaign: University of Illinois Press, 1994); and Jill Mulvay Derr, Janath Russell Cannon, and Maureen Ursenbach Beecher, *Women of Covenant: The Story of Relief Society* (Salt Lake City: Deseret Book, 1992).

127. James E. Faust, "A Message to my Granddaughters: Become 'Great Women,'" BYU Devotional Address (February 12, 1985): https://www.lds.org/ensign/1986/09/a-message-to-my-granddaughters-becoming-great-women?lang=eng.

128. Gordon B. Hinckley, "How Can I Become the Woman of Whom I Dream?" *Ensign* (May 2001): https://www.lds.org/ensign/2001/05/how-can-i-become-the-woman-of-whom-i-dream?lang=eng.

129. The First Presidency and the Council of the Twelve Apostles of the Church of Jesus Christ of Latter-day Saints, "The Family: a Proclamation to the World," at https://www.lds.org/topics/family-proclamation?lang=eng&old=true.

8 LDS Church Presidency Years, 1985–1994

J. B. HAWS

On Monday, November 11, 1985, at a press conference that everyone in Salt Lake City expected, Ezra Taft Benson stood before reporters as the newly appointed president of the Church of Jesus Christ of Latter-day Saints. Only one of his predecessors—ninety-three-year-old Joseph Fielding Smith in 1970—had come to this position of church leadership older than the eighty-six-year-old Benson. And none of his predecessors had come to the position with the kind of national renown that Benson already had; as the *Salt Lake Tribune* said it well, "in Ezra Taft Benson, the LDS Church has . . . a new president with a name instantly recognizable outside Utah and well beyond Mormonism."[1]

That renown was, in many ways, the undertone playing beneath the statement that President Benson read to the assembled press conference crowd. "Some have expectantly inquired," he said, "about the direction the church will take in the future."[2] The expectancy that Benson acknowledged was more like anxiety in some quarters. The refrain that had begun to echo among interested parties across the nation, really, as the health of Spencer W. Kimball (Benson's immediate predecessor in the Church's top leadership spot) steadily declined was whether or not the LDS church would take a sharp right turn if Ezra Taft Benson were to become the Mormon leader. Even the judiciously worded authorized biography of Ezra Taft Benson, published by church-owned Deseret Book Company, observed that while news coverage of the "imminent appointment of Ezra Taft Benson as the Church's new spiritual leader . . . wasn't necessarily more extensive for President Benson than his predecessors, . . . much of it was distinctive in tone and approach."[3] Distinctive, indeed—the prospect of Mormonism's most politically outspoken and controversial apostle assuming the prophetic mantle made some observers, both inside and outside the church, nervous.[4]

Some saw portents of a strong new direction, building like thunderheads in the distance, in several of Benson's addresses as an apostle. After all, Benson was well known for his staunch anti-communism and right-wing conservatism, even in his church discourses; his years of support of the John Birch Society became the symbolic shorthand, in virtually every biographical sketch, to describe his political leanings.[5] And in 1980, as the second in seniority in the church's hierarchy, Benson had delivered a memorable speech in which he had affirmed the church prophet's unique right to speak on all matters political and social. Both progressive Mormons with long memories and journalists who had done their research referenced that speech in the build-up to President Benson's appointment.[6]

Thus the implications of Benson's first public statement were not lost on reporters when he said, "My heart has been filled with an overwhelming love and compassion for all members of the church and our Heavenly Father's children everywhere. I love all our Father's children of every color, creed and political persuasion." His opening statement did indeed take a conservative tack, but *conservative* in the broader sense, in the sense of moderation over innovation, more continuity than change. Benson affirmed that he expected to move forward in the trajectory set by his predecessor: "May we suggest that the Lord, through President Kimball, has sharply focused on the threefold mission of the Church: to preach the gospel, to perfect the Saints, and to redeem the dead. We shall continue every effort to carry out this mission."[7]

These opening remarks commend themselves as a good starting place here for reasons that go beyond simple chronology. They point to ways that Benson's public ministry as church president in the 1980s would be different in tone, in approach, and in focus than his ministry as an apostle in the 1960s and 1970s. Changes were already discernible in the years just preceding Benson's appointment as church president. His expressed desire, in that initial press conference, to continue President Kimball's work must be understood as more than just a polite, perfunctory nod to a recently deceased predecessor. It would miss the mark to discuss the tenor of Benson's presidency without starting with Spencer Kimball. The two men were named Mormon apostles on the same day in 1943; Kimball had hierarchical seniority because he was four years older than Benson. That seniority—and a mutual esteem—meant that Kimball's repeated pleas that Benson drop his divisive politics would carry special weight.

For example, Kimball had called in Benson to account for a statement he made in early 1974 that a good Mormon could not be a Democrat; Benson

apologized for the embarrassment caused to the church, and Kimball "reminded him that as president of the Council of the Twelve he should avoid
involvement in politically sensitive and potentially divisive matters." Nine
months later, though—and just before election day—Benson publicly endorsed the American Party. The First Presidency quickly issued a statement
reaffirming the church's partisan neutrality, and that "any person who makes
representations to the contrary does so without authorization." Kimball and
his counselors met with Benson to discuss the remarks that Kimball called
"unfortunate," and told Benson that "all General Authorities must speak with
one voice and . . . [not] take any partisan position in politics as to candidates
or parties." Finally, in 1980, Kimball expressed strong reservations about the
very "Fourteen Fundamentals in Following a Prophet" speech mentioned
earlier, where Benson advocated for the prophet's prerogative to speak on
political and social matters. Another First Presidency statement followed to
"reaffirm that we take no partisan stand as to candidates or political parties,
and exercise no constraint on the freedom of individuals to make their own
choices in these matters." In all of this, Kimball prevailed upon Benson to
focus on the universality of the gospel message, especially considering the
diverse political contexts in which church members and church missionaries
found themselves.[8] It was this universality—this attention, as Benson had
said, to people of "every color, creed and political persuasion"—that stood
out in the November 1985 press conference. Considering his past reputation,
all of those words mattered.

In the days before Benson was named president of the church, news
reports had several observers noting a "mellowing" in Ezra Taft Benson;
that was the word Mormon educator Sterling McMurrin used with the *New
York Times* when he predicted the transition to Benson's leadership would
not "make more than a ripple."[9] L. Jackson Newell, editor of the Mormon
journal *Dialogue*, likewise noted that "there are a lot of liberals around
me expressing great alarm over this but I generally don't panic until I see
a reason to. . . . [T]here's a different point of view when one speaks within
an organization—or for the entire organization."[10] McMurrin and Newell
proved to be prophetic. Benson's presidency stands out, in retrospect, for
the ways in which it did *not* go as many expected.[11]

The Benson Presidency: Juxtapositions

This is not to say, however, that there were no controversies. While Benson
himself largely was noncontroversial as church president—and that, again,
was for some a surprise—the years of his presidency marked a tumultuous

time for Mormonism. In fact, the secretary to the church's First Presidency later remembered that a still-unfolding controversy—the investigation into the Mark Hofmann bombings, only one month old at that point—was a primary reason why reporters were not given time for questions at Benson's introductory press conference.[12] It was a decade of milestone-type highs, especially in the LDS church's international expansion, but it was also a decade where tensions within strains of American Mormonism came to the foreground in ways that became national news. It seemed almost providentially fitting that the Mormon apostle who spoke most consistently and persistently against communism presided over the church during the years in which the Soviet bloc crumbled—and yet he said very little about communism as church president. This widely-recognized American patriot was church president when the United States celebrated the bicentennial of the Constitution, and yet, near the end of his church presidency, self-proclaimed patriots who saw Ezra Taft Benson as their ultraconservative champion faced church discipline for views that church general authorities deemed too radical. His presidency was bookended by two related controversies that centered on Mormon history: the first, the Mark Hofmann tragedy mentioned above, marked by what some saw as a church that was too trusting; the second, the September Six excommunications, marked by what some saw as a church that was too suspicious.

Even the very years of his presidency call for this kind of juxtaposing, since any discussion of Benson's administration essentially becomes a discussion of *two* administrative periods: the first three years, when Ezra Taft Benson was active in traveling and speaking in a variety of church settings; and the final five-plus years, when health challenges severely limited his day-to-day involvement in church leadership. This is not an uncommon story in the history of the Latter-day Saints, but it was a story with different overtones this time around.

With all of this in mind, this essay proposes to consider the years of Ezra Taft Benson's tenure by considering in turn some of these tensions, these juxtapositions, before coming back to the one aspect of his leadership for which he is best remembered, now more than two decades later: his advocacy of the Book of Mormon's centrality to Latter-day Saint religious life. Taking this tack in this essay means that the discussion will not proceed precisely chronologically, but will instead mostly consider the last two-thirds of his presidency first, when Benson was generally absent from the public's eye and day-to-day church operations. Then, the central story of the first third of his presidency is where the essay will end, since that seems in retrospect the most significant for what it says about Benson as president—and, more broadly, about Mormonism theologically and culturally.

A Changing Global Map for Mormonism

Just five months before Ezra Taft Benson became its new prophet/president, the LDS church had dedicated a temple in Freiberg, Germany. The early 1980s had seen an unprecedented run of Mormon temple building, from Tahiti to Taiwan to Texas. The church dedicated a dozen new temples in 1983 and 1984 alone. But Freiberg stood out among all of the others. Freiberg was in communist East Germany, such that this temple spoke to looming changes in the geopolitical map, and the opening of new fields for Latter-day Saint evangelizing. No voice in the LDS hierarchy had been as clear—or controversial—as Benson's in decrying the threat of the Soviet Union, and now he would be the president of the church at the time when Mormon missionaries first entered (or reentered, in some cases, for the first time since pre–World War II days) East Berlin, or St. Petersburg, or Budapest.[13] Yet it is worth noting again that his anti-communism rhetoric had been one of those features of his earlier ministry that he had noticeably moderated. Of course, by the mid-1980s, signs of Soviet communism's demise were everywhere, and the conservative credentials and leadership of U.S. president Ronald Reagan meant that the world of the mid-1980s felt much different than the world of the 1950s or 1960s.[14] Still, in a 1986 speech at church-owned Brigham Young University to launch the yearlong celebration for the bicentennial of the U.S. Constitution, Benson did not even mention the word "communism"; the "crisis of our constitution," he warned, was internal, a declining morality at home.[15]

Even if communism was still on his mind, his administration's *public* direction envisioned the solution to that threat as spiritual rather than political in nature. Russell M. Nelson, one of the junior apostles in 1985—Nelson had only been an apostle for a year at the time—remembered that the assignment he received from President Benson and his counselors in that first round of meetings with the new president came with these words: "Elder Nelson, you are responsible for the affairs of the Church in Africa and Europe, with the specific assignment to open the doors in Europe that are now under the yoke of Communism."[16] Thomas S. Monson, the apostle that Benson had chosen as his second counselor in the three-member First Presidency, had previously had the portfolio for East Germany, and the gains the church had made under his direction had been unexpected, to say the least. German Democratic Republic officials had recently invited the LDS church to build the temple in Freiberg (near Dresden) that could serve the four thousand Latter-day

Saints living in East Germany. That temple had been finished in the summer of 1985, and sent strong signals about the level of trust that Mormon leaders had cultivated with government personnel. That trust would pave the way for another landmark moment in Mormon missionary history that came during the Benson years: GDR officials opened the way for foreign Mormon missionaries to enter that country in the spring of 1989, eight months before the fall of the Berlin Wall.[17]

The map of global LDS missions changed rapidly after that. By the time of President Benson's death, the church had congregations in all of the former Soviet bloc nations—including in Moscow, Russia, home in 1959 to the Central Baptist Church, where Benson had briefly preached (and drawn the attention of the American media corps by doing so) when he was in the Soviet Union on a Department of Agriculture trip.[18]

Just as unexpected as this dramatic turn in geopolitics might have been LDS church developments in Africa, when considered from the vantage point of a decade earlier, at least in terms of the map of Mormon global membership. It was during President Benson's administration that the first stake (analogous to a diocese, in Mormon parlance) outside South Africa was organized on that continent—in Aba, Nigeria, in 1988. Official church missionary work in west Africa only began in 1978, when Benson's predecessor announced a revelation that ended a long-standing policy that had restricted black Mormon men from ordination to the church's priesthood and barred black Mormon men and women from participating in the church's highest temple rites. Benson had been part of the apostolic gathering in June 1978 that had experienced that revelation, something that he and all of his colleagues later described in superlative terms. Benson said that he "had never experienced anything of such spiritual power and magnitude."[19] Church growth in Africa took on a lively pace after the policy change. By the time LDS missionaries arrived in 1978, hundreds of Nigerians and Ghanaians were waiting for them. These groups had already encountered the Book of Mormon and other church literature, and had even in some cases incorporated in their nations with handwritten "The Church of Jesus Christ of Latter-day Saints" signs.[20]

Here is another juxtaposition to consider. Ezra Taft Benson himself was often remembered for his strong statements about the Soviet communist backing behind civil rights causes and groups in the 1960s—even if, in his view, civil rights activists were most often unwitting communist pawns.[21] These provocative assertions were squarely in the mix when observers expressed concerns about Benson's archconservative politics of earlier decades.[22]

It is not insignificant, therefore, that true to the spirit of Ezra Taft Benson's opening press conference statement, the LDS church made concerted overtures to people "of all creed and color" during the Benson years. It was during Benson's administration that Helvecio Martins became the first black Mormon called as a mission president (in 1987) and church general authority (in 1990).[23] Both callings were First Presidency appointments.

During the Benson years new missions were also established in Zaire (now Democratic Republic of the Congo), Zimbabwe, Liberia, Kenya, Cameroon, and Ivory Coast.[24] The organization of the church stake in Nigeria in 1988 signaled something significant about the maturity and depth of the converts there, since in Mormonism all of the church leadership in stakes must be local—and stakes have a degree of autonomy and authority that mission branches do not.

The recognized reality was that Mormon growth in the 1980s among African Americans was slower—more fraught with historical tension—than was Mormon growth in Africa. Still, other Mormon initiatives that became African American community traditions saw their inception in the years of Benson's presidency. *Ebony Rose*, an independent black Mormon periodical, covered the "First Annual EBONY ROSE Black History Conference" held in Salt Lake City in February 1987.[25] That gathering became an initial installment in church genealogy projects designed with black families specifically in mind.[26] Mormon congregations took an active role in subsequent Black History Month celebrations in the early 1990s in places like Washington, D.C., and Oakland, California, hosting community gatherings in large LDS church meeting halls.[27] And in 1990, a church employee suggested that the LDS Family History Department start a project to create a digital database of the almost 500,000 names in the Freedman's Bank records at the U.S. National Archives. The church released the completed searchable database in 2001 after eleven years of work.[28]

Also during the Benson administration, church efforts—including "caravans" of Mormon cars carrying relief supplies and cleanup volunteers—in the aftermath of the 1992 Los Angeles riots (sparked by the acquittal of police officers accused of beating motorist Rodney King) forged a special relationship with local black community leaders. This was, for example, AME Zion pastor Cecil Murray's first interaction with Mormons, and he subsequently came to the LDS church's aid in working with L.A. mayor Tom Bradley to remove some zoning hurdles that were blocking a planned Mormon stake center.[29] Other signals about this new attention to the universality of the Mormon message were subtle but nonetheless visible. A *Chicago Tribune* feature in 1988—the year that marked the ten-year anniversary of the revelation that opened the priesthood and temple to black Mormons—described a Mormon congregation in that city that had "seen striking growth, led by an influx of new black members since 1978. The church at 54th Street and University Avenue in Hyde Park has grown from 85 members, including a few blacks, to a congregation of 400, nearly half of whom are black. . . . Since Kimball's revelation, the Hyde Park congregation has quadrupled and become one of the most integrated in the city."[30]

Old prejudices and insensitivities can be difficult to dispel, though, and long-standing theological justifications for the racially based priesthood and temple restrictions in the Mormon past persisted in quasi-official publications and in local-level church discourse. But there were important, prominent hierarchical voices during the early years of Benson's presidency that sought to put to rest those justifications—voices that would grow into a chorus over the next few decades.[31] Church apostle Dallin H. Oaks, for example, was interviewed by the Associated Press in 1988. Oaks strongly disavowed statements, "even by [Mormon] general authorities," that implied blacks had been "less valiant" in a premortal existence and hence had been barred from full church participation for a time. When a reporter asked Oaks about these types of explanations for the priesthood ban, Oaks forcefully called such reasoning "spectacularly wrong."[32]

When historian Newell Bringhurst surveyed in 1992 the issues of the LDS *Church News* (a weekly supplement to the church-owned *Deseret News*) from the 1980s, he concluded that the reporting on "Mormon activity in black areas throughout the world . . ., a practice inconceivable just a few years earlier," meant that the "growth clearly projected in the pages of the *Church News*" showed "a capacity to outgrow old prejudices and manifest a greater awareness and sensitivity." In Bringhurst's evaluation, too, Mormon "blacks [were] significant motivators of . . . geographic growth"; this was true in Africa, but also in places like Brazil, Colombia, Venezuela, and the Caribbean.[33]

Growth, in general, really was the story of global Mormonism during Ezra Taft Benson's presidency. Church membership grew by 42 percent from year-end 1985 to year-end 1994, from 5.9 million to 9 million members. The number of missionaries—always a focus for missionary-minded prophets like Spencer Kimball and Ezra Taft Benson—grew by 62 percent over those same years, from 29,000 to 47,000.[34] Just two years after Ezra Taft Benson's death, the church announced that more Latter-day Saints lived outside the United States than within.

These growth numbers, impressive as they are, do not tell the full story, though. When Benson's first counselor, Gordon B. Hinckley, became church president in 1995, "retention" of converts became a watchword. High rates of convert baptisms did not always translate into strong congregations or committed, lifelong members. The seriousness of the retention concern came to the fore when Hinckley in 2002 assigned two apostles, Dallin H. Oaks and Jeffrey R. Holland, to move to two of the countries that had experienced meteoric growth—the Philippines and Chile, respectively—in order to "[meet] the challenges," the church press release said, "that the church has faced for years in many developing areas: rapid church growth and the need to train leadership and to help new members assimilate into the church and attend the temple."[35]

This account of Mormonism's global growth—successes and setbacks—during the years of Benson's presidency only speaks again to the complexity and contraries in this story, and, as with so much that happened during those years, how that story defies simplistic narratives. Such was also the case as the church attempted what Jan Shipps—a well-known historian of Mormonism, though not a Mormon herself—called "a middle course" in its handling of internal criticisms. Shipps told *Time* magazine, at the time of Ezra Taft Benson's death, that the church was "steering" that course in its disciplinary actions against members deemed too far to the right or to the left.[36] But the middle course was a fraught path.

Domestic Discontent

All of the LDS church's presidents (Benson was the thirteenth in that line that began with church founder Joseph Smith) have continued in their posts until their deaths. This has meant that a number of church presidents have been debilitated at the close of their lives and church ministry; that had been the case for President Benson's immediate predecessor, Spencer Kimball, too. Benson's appointed first counselor in the First Presidency, apostle Gordon B. Hinckley, had also been a First Presidency counselor to Kimball. In that role, Hinckley had already been the de facto day-to-day administrative head of the church since 1981 because of Kimball's poor health and the poor health of Kimball's other counselors. Hinckley would assume that responsibility again during the last two-thirds of Benson's presidency. In 1992 Hinckley outlined the approach he and his colleagues were taking: "As it was during the time when President Kimball was ill, we have moved without hesitation when there is well-established policy. Where there is not firmly established policy, we have talked with the President and received his approval before taking action. Let it never be said that there has been any disposition to assume authority or to do anything or say anything or teach anything which might be at variance with the wishes of him who has been put in his place by the Lord. . . . We simply desire to do that which needs to be done, when it needs to be done, and according to policies on which the President has expressed himself."[37]

But the apostles' assurances of their adherence to that administrative philosophy did not satisfy everyone when the prophet was not publicly speaking
for himself. In the early 1990s, Latter-day Saints on both the right and the left
of the conservative-liberal spectrum felt that the church's disciplinary crack-
down in those years bore the fingerprints of individual apostles who operated
without the constraints that a vibrant church president might have imposed.
At the center of this internal controversy that bubbled into American national
media consciousness in the early 1990s was an LDS church committee called
"Strengthening Church Members." While such a title seemed innocuous
enough, critics felt it took on an Orwellian cast as they leveled charges against
the committee's actions, including keeping files on the activities of members
who were deemed suspect.

So widespread did reporting about this church committee become that
LDS leaders took the unusual step of releasing a statement explaining the
purpose of, and the names of the people on, the committee. The church did
not deny that the committee did keep tabs on members and movements that
it found worrying—and the church's statement listed scriptural support for
the committee's raison d'etre: Doctrine and Covenants 123:1–5.[38] The 1980s
had witnessed a resurgence in fundamentalist polygamy at the edges of Mormonism. While the church had not officially sanctioned polygamy for more
than eight decades by the time Ezra Taft Benson became church president, a
number of break-off groups over the years had continued that practice. And
those groups were in the news with surprising frequency in the 1980s, and
often for horrific intrafamily violence (or for violence that spilled over the
boundaries of the family-based sects, too), so that names like Lebaron and
Lafferty and Singer-Swapp made repeated headlines. Plus, the 1990s saw new
break-off groups advocating polygamy—most notably Jim Harmston's "True
and Living Church of Jesus Christ of Saints of The Last Days" that settled in
Manti, Utah. It was in response to this threat of fundamentalist polygamy
that the Strengthening Church Members Committee was formed. Church
leaders did not want closet polygamists infiltrating church congregations—
nor, as media observers saw it, distorting the public's perception of modern
Mormonism.[39]

But other groups at the time also drew the displeasure of church authorities. On the right—the far right—were Mormons who saw themselves as
patriots and survivalists preparing for the imminent apocalypse. Talk of a
United Nations–led "new world order" in the 1990s spurred groups who
worried about the demise of the United States. Bo Gritz became something
of a gravitational and symbolic center for this movement. He was a decorated

army Green Beret, an adult convert to Mormonism, and in 1992 a candidate for the U.S. presidency.[40]

Church leaders' worries about some of the more radical rhetoric coming from these camps—including the refusal to pay income taxes—found expression in regional meetings that discussed creeping apostasy. Lists of warning signs began to circulate among some stake presidents in Utah who collaborated informally with each other to identify trends that they found troubling. Prominent on one such list was "John Birch [Society] membership or leanings." Given Ezra Taft Benson's long affinity for the society (though he never joined),[41] it was perhaps only natural that John Birch loyalists felt betrayed by the church that was headed, at the time, by someone who they were sure would be highly sympathetic to their cause—and only natural that conspiracy theories would arise about the silencing or "sedating" of Benson by church underlings.[42] Gritz said in December 1992, "There are a lot of people who wonder because he [President Benson] has been quiet lately if church leaders need to put words in his mouth. . . . He's been a gentleman and a true patriot and he has never varied from the views he talked about as an apostle. He hasn't stood up and said to anyone, 'Forget what I said before.'"[43] Bo Gritz was not disciplined by the church, though others were. Gritz instead resigned his membership in 1994.[44]

In the end, these conspiracy theories fell flat because they seemed uninformed and out of step with other current realities. That may be the important point—these ultra-conservatives did not appreciate how much their church's prophet had both expanded his focus and narrowed his message in the preceding years—and how much the geopolitical world had turned since then. Plus, those close to Benson knew that no "silencing" strategies were in place; this was simply encroaching mortality. Benson did not speak again at a church conference after the fall of 1988 because a stroke limited his ability to communicate thereafter. And after other health challenges in late 1990 and early 1991, he was mostly confined to his apartment, where his counselors would visit him to discuss church business.[45]

But it was precisely this type of incapacity that Steve Benson cited in his public departure from Mormonism in 1993. He was a Pulitzer Prize–winning cartoonist for the *Arizona Republic*, and he was Ezra Taft Benson's grandson. Steve Benson said that he felt it was the course of "intellectual honesty" for him to resign his church membership because of the church's "loss of vision." He told *Christianity Today*, "I believe that in many respects the modern church has lost the sense of its original destiny and spiritual vitality that encouraged individuals to seek out a personal and profoundly intimate relationship with the divine." Steve Benson was particularly disturbed by what he saw as church attempts to "portray [his grandfather] as a functioning executive"—to keep up appearances, in his view, that the prophet had an active hand and voice in guiding the church. The younger Benson said he knew, firsthand, how frail his grandfather—the prophet—actually was, telling the Associated Press in July 1993, "The last time I saw him, he said virtually nothing to me."[46]

Steve Benson's high-profile renunciation of his faith came at a time when national media outlets were reporting other casualties among those that they characterized as progressive Mormons. This was the other camp in Mormonism—the other "extreme," as some saw it—that in the 1990s complained about church disciplinary practices. And it was the excommunication of members deemed left of center, more than that of those on the right, that really generated the controversy as Benson's presidency years drew to a close.

Six Mormon intellectuals—three men and three women—were disciplined in September 1993. There were a variety of issues involved: advocacy for women's ordination to the priesthood, worship of a "Mother in Heaven," challenges to the accuracy of the church's traditional historical narrative, even the correct way to interpret apocalyptic scripture. Though general church leaders denied that the disciplinary actions were coordinated (disciplinary action in Mormonism takes place on the local, stake level), these denials did not convince disgruntled Mormons or reporters who picked up the story. Journalists saw the "September Six" as victims of a "purge."[47]

This would mean that, from one point of view, Benson's presidency would be book-ended by two not-unrelated controversies. As mentioned earlier, he acceded to the office in late November 1985, one month after historical documents dealer Mark Hofmann had killed two fellow Latter-day Saints with bombs to cover up what was not yet suspected at the time: the documents he sold were forgeries. That dark episode was a still-developing story when Benson was named church president, but even in the earliest reports about the bombings, the church did not fare well. In those days before Hofmann's "finds" were confirmed to be fakes, media outlets and historians and religionists who worried about Mormon heterodoxy roundly criticized the LDS church for hiding documents that painted its history in an unfavorable light, and for interfering with the police investigation in order to protect its own interests.[48]

The Hofmann saga put a discernible chill on church support for the academic study of Mormon history. Some vocal scholars accused the church of settling into a bunker mentality where free inquiry and investigation were suppressed.[49] As complaints from these quarters increased, the church responded by warning members, in 1991, about participating in "symposia"

that "ridicule[d] sacred things or injur[ed] the Church." Mormon intellectuals responded by documenting—and publicizing—instances of what they
described as "ecclesiastical abuse."[50]

President Benson's incapacity at the time complicated the matter. Steve
Benson's accusations fit with other charges that the church was taking pains
to maintain a façade, taking pains to maintain a charade that Ezra Taft Benson still played an active role in church governance. And a number of critics
focused attention especially on the outspokenness of apostle Boyd K. Packer.
Yet even though Benson's voice was not being heard on these issues, it seems
difficult to assert that the church's leadership was out of step philosophically
with the course Benson had—or would have—charted.[51] After all, Benson
himself, while still second in apostolic seniority in the church, had delivered
a cautionary address to LDS educators in 1976 with this central thesis about
academic history in the church: "We hope that if you feel you must write
for the scholarly journals, you always defend the faith," so as to avoid the
tendency to "inordinately humanize the prophets of God so that their human
frailties become more apparent than their spiritual qualities."[52] This address
and Packer's 1981 address, "The Mantle Is Far, Far Greater than the Intellect,"
were often paired together for their philosophical resonance.[53]

And as president of the church, Ezra Taft Benson delivered "To the Mothers in Zion," an address in February 1987 that was broadcast on the church's
satellite system. Benson was unequivocal in his determination that the place
of mothers was in the home: "Contrary to conventional wisdom, a mother's
calling is in the home, not in the market place."[54] Apostle Packer explicitly
referred to this "Mothers in Zion" address in a May 1993 talk to the All-
Church Coordinating Committee, an important church curriculum review
body. Precedent was very important for Elder Packer; he noted that "if you
read [President Benson's] talk carefully, it was, for the most part, simply a
compilation of quotations on the subject from the prophets who have preceded him." This compilation of quotes dictated, for Packer, the approach
that church leaders should take on this subject: "Some mothers must work
out of the home. There is no other way. And in this they are justified and
for this they should not be criticized. We cannot, however, because of their
discomfort over their plight, abandon a position that has been taught by the
prophets from the beginning of this dispensation. The question then is, 'How
can we give solace to those who are justified without giving license to those
who are not?'"[55]

Here again was evidence of the tensions, the opposing impulses, that were
so often at play during the Benson presidency. From one perspective, the
church had made some important strides during Benson's administration

that were widely seen as benefiting its female members. In February 1986, for example, church leaders made a policy change that allowed a woman to receive temple rites even if her husband was not a Latter-day Saint—a move that was widely celebrated.[56] Four years later, the *New York Times* reported that other modifications in the Church's temple endowment rite had "both church members and non-Mormon scholars [saying] the changes reflected a new sensitivity toward women in the church and an evolution of Mormonism away from its stormy origins in 19th-century America to a multicultural world religion." In that same 1990 *New York Times* article, Lavina Fielding Anderson—who would become one of the September Six three years later—said that the modification "gives me hope and renewed faith that changes will occur in the future as they have in the past"; Anderson went on to say that "the temple and what it means is extremely important in my spiritual life. . . . I do not find the secrecy inappropriate. In an age of so much communications, there may be some value in having something you only think about and share in a special place."[57]

But at the same time, the "To the Mothers in Zion" address, and the sentiment behind it, caused both heartache and heartburn, and both emotions surfaced in news reports and intra-Mormon dialogue—and surfaced in the wave of Mormon feminist writings that had precipitated a number of the September 1993 disciplinary decisions.[58]

Looking back on these contraries a quarter of a century later, the advantage of hindsight can give the era a different cast. Defining boundaries—and the right way to maintain those boundaries—was not always a clear-cut process. *Salt Lake Tribune* religion writer Peggy Fletcher Stack composed a retrospective reflection on the September Six excommunications in 2013. She quoted Utah State University's Philip Barlow, who saw missteps on both sides: "A couple of [the September Six] had grown so animated by their (sometimes legitimate) issues and activism that they struck me as having lost the spirit of good will, humility and good judgment; I empathized with the church's concern. In other instances, I thought we as Mormon people and leaders shared responsibility for letting things get to the stage of confrontation without more lovingly, thoughtfully and patiently addressing issues of real importance that have come back to hurt the church."[59]

This sense of lessons learned—part prescription, part description—should not be missed. In the decades since 1993, two of the September Six rejoined the church. The LDS church as an institution has made an emphatic turn toward historical transparency, with new publication initiatives like the Joseph Smith Papers project; the posting of online "Gospel Topics Essays" that confront head-on complex historical issues like the origins of polygamy or

the translation of the Book of Mormon or race and priesthood/temple participation; and the release of important documentary histories on the first
fifty years of the Relief Society and the almost-mythical Council of Fifty. In
2016 apostle M. Russell Ballard told the church's educators that, in looking
back to this earlier era, "our curriculum, though well-meaning at the time,
did not prepare students for today—a day when students have instant access
to virtually everything about the Church from every possible point of view."[60]
Church historian Marlin K. Jensen, appointed as a general authority during
the Benson administration (in 1989), told the Mormon History Association
in 2012, at the end of his general authority tenure, "I'm also pleased that we
have labored diligently to be completely open and honest about the Church's
past. After all, it is of truth that the Holy Ghost testifies. The internet almost
mandates transparency as the order of the day, but it is also the right way to
do our historical business."[61]

In 1994 this type of sentiment seemed a long way off for John Brooke.
In the closing chapter of his 1994 book, *The Refiner's Fire: The Making of
Mormon Cosmology*, Brooke worried that Mormon leaders were betray-
ing the theological inheritance that was theirs by closing their archives
and restricting inquiry.[62] Yet even by 1994, already there were portents of
the historical openness that would fully flower a decade later—and these
initiatives complicate any simplistic narrative about Mormon hierarchical
attitudes about intellectual inquiry in the early 1990s. For example, church
leaders gave managing director of the Church History Department Richard Turley remarkable access to write a detailed account of the church's
involvement with Mark Hofmann, a book that became *Victims*, published
by the University of Illinois Press in 1992. Also in 1992, in celebration of the
Relief Society's sesquicentennial, church-owned Deseret Book published an
officially sponsored history, *Women of Covenant*, that dealt with historical
issues that were at the heart of Mormon feminist conversations, including
female ministrations to their sisters in times of childbirth and illness.[63]
Finally, in that same year, Deseret Book released a second edition of *The
Story of the Latter-day Saints*, a one-volume history of Mormonism that
had made Ezra Taft Benson uncomfortable when it first appeared in 1976,
because it struck Benson and others as symptomatic of a naturalistic approach to history that did not give enough attention to divine providence.[64]

Knowing, too, what twenty-first-century readers know of Gordon B.
Hinckley's subsequent time as church president, it seems only natural that
observers looking back would infer his involvement in these portents of
a new attitude, of the church's letting its guard down—especially considering Hinckley's leadership role during the years when Ezra Taft Benson

was confined to his home because of declining health. Hinckley had spent his career writing for the church, preparing missionary materials and radio broadcasts and displays for world's fair pavilions. His instincts were in the direction of openness and public relations. After some bruising news-making controversies in the 1980s and early 1990s, the LDS church's First Presidency, under the de facto leadership of first counselor Hinckley, commissioned a "Communications Futures Committee" in January 1993 to give recommendations. In so doing, the church's hierarchy sought input from "thirty-five of the Church's top media professionals" from "all over the country" who over the course of a year "gathered in brain-storming sessions and committees to review these issues."[65] Moves like these gave the sense, at the end of President Benson's administration, that the church was opting for more proactivity in its public posture and in improving lines of communication and cooperation with its neighbors, especially in its North American context.

All of the complexity and competing impulses of this era in Mormonism figured into a lengthy feature piece that Jeffrey Sheler and Betsy Wagner wrote for *U.S. News and World Report*, after they had checked in on the Mormons in 1992. The article was titled—not surprisingly, considering all that was in the air—"Latter-day Struggles." But then the journalists concluded their report by noting that "whatever its present problems, there are few pessimists in the Mormon kingdom, and, according to insiders, relatively few dissatisfied members." That was because, as apostle Neal Maxwell was quoted as saying, "We ask a lot of our people, but we give them a lot in terms of Scriptures and temples and covenants." Even Elbert Peck, editor of *Sunstone*—one of the venues implicitly targeted by the church's warning about questionable symposia—added that "the typical Mormon loves the church because 'it provides community, allows people to experience God and helps them raise families and cultivate values. These are much more important than the troublesome issues.'" Sheler and Wagner sounded this final note: "In a church where turmoil is no stranger, that, more than anything else, bodes well for its future."[66]

Their article appeared in September 1992, more than three years since Ezra Taft Benson had last spoken in a church meeting, yet there was no mention of Benson's incapacity—or, for that matter, Benson at all—in the article. That seems to be a subtle, but significant, reflection of the journalists' perception of just how thoroughly mundane leadership in the modern LDS church had become. "As an organization," Sheler and Wagner wrote, "[the LDS church] has become much more centralized and bureaucratized. Unlike the charismatic icons of the past—such as Joseph Smith and Brigham Young—today's Mormon leaders function more like corporate executives."[67] In many ways, such an assessment fits the administration of Ezra Taft Benson. He presided over a church making expected moves in the world of the late 1980s and 1990s: digitizing vast amounts of data, simplifying budget procedures, streamlining the church's hierarchy. This is true. But something that becomes clearest in hindsight is that President Benson's imprint on the modern church reminds observers that even in a "more centralized and bureaucratized" Mormonism, charisma cannot be discounted. In the totality of his tenure, then, Ezra Taft Benson becomes a case study in the place of the prophet in the contemporary LDS church, as both "corporate executive" *and* "charismatic icon"—a final juxtaposition worth considering.

The First Three Years: A Case Study in Prophetic Charisma

It is for the wielding of charismatic authority, and a recourse to a revealed message, that Ezra Taft Benson's presidency is best remembered—especially the first three years of his presidency—now more than two decades later. The central theme of that revealed message was a new prominence for the Book of Mormon in LDS religious life—and Benson wasted no time in introducing that theme. He made it the focus of his remarks at his first local church conference in January 1986.[68] By the account of the secretary to the First Presidency, he also asked all church general authorities to make the Book of Mormon a top priority when preparing their addresses for the upcoming April 1986 General Conference.[69]

At first glance, outside observers of contemporary Mormonism might find it unexpected that a church president in the 1980s would need to emphasize the Book of Mormon. After all, this was the scripture that launched the movement and that gave the movement and its people their most recognizable moniker. But the book's history within Mormonism is more complex.[70]

For much of the church's first century and a half, the Book of Mormon figured most prominently as a sign of Joseph Smith's prophetic call.[71] The book always was a key feature in church proselytizing efforts, since Latter-day Saints saw its existence as the chief evidence that God had once more opened the heavens and given new revelation. But the contents of the book itself had not been utilized in church sermons and lesson manuals to the degree that the Bible, or even the story of the church's pioneering past, had been. It seems important that this benign neglect of the Book of Mormon not be overstated, since the church printed and distributed thousands of copies of the book each year, and even by 1972 church Sunday School curriculum devoted one year in its four-year cycle of study to the Book of Mormon.[72] So while the text's status as scripture had never been in doubt in the LDS church, for much of the church's history there was a demonstrable statistical gap in the frequency with which church leaders cited and taught from the Bible as opposed to the frequency with which they cited and taught from the Book of Mormon.[73]

Ezra Taft Benson, among others in church leadership, had long been an exception. As an apostle, he had quoted from the Book of Mormon again and again in his discourses at the church's semiannual General Conferences.[74] Ever a missionary for his faith since his days preaching in England, Benson had given copies of the Book of Mormon to business associates, government colleagues, U.S. presidents—even Soviet officials.[75] Benson's son Reed remembered an occasion in the 1940s when he asked his father about some of the books Reed had planned to read while working as a farmhand during his summer break. His father's response: "Take only the Book of Mormon."[76]

Historian Patrick Mason has offered an important reading of Ezra Taft Benson's lifelong Book of Mormon advocacy, a reading that sees his early advocacy as lining up well with Benson's political and theological worldview—and a reading that only underscores again the subtle shifts in focus and tone and approach of Benson-as-church-president. In the 1960s and 1970s, Benson often used the Book of Mormon to emphasize America's chosen-land status, to expose "secret combination" conspiracies, or to encourage the vigilant defense of individual freedoms in the face of creeping tyranny. But "in the 1970s and 1980s," Mason writes, "Benson steadily moved beyond his three themes of America, freedom, and secret combinations when he preached from or about the Book of Mormon. He increasingly emphasized that the Book of Mormon was first and foremost a testimony of Jesus Christ. This would constitute the core of his message, particularly in the 1980s." As church president, Benson still spoke of the Book of Mormon's value in its unmasking of the "enemies of Christ," but his Book of Mormon discourses as president brought other themes to the theological fore: Christ's unique ability to save fallen humanity; spiritual rebirth; conquering pride.[77]

The year before becoming the church's president, Benson intimated to the church's membership that he had felt divinely directed to preach more widespread Book of Mormon usage. He opened his address at the October 1984 conference—one year before Spencer W. Kimball's death—on a sober note: "My beloved brethren and sisters, for some years now I have been deeply concerned that we are not using the Book of Mormon as God intends." He then related, "As I participated in the Mexico City Temple dedication"—in December 1983—"I received the distinct impression that God is not pleased with our neglect of the Book of Mormon." It was underappreciation more than disdain of the book that troubled Benson.[78]

The directness of that message was undeniably pointed. But the way this message took on new momentum after Benson became church president offers a telling snapshot into Mormonism, both culturally and theologically. It was one thing to have an apostle—even a senior apostle—encourage Book of Mormon study; it was quite another to have the church's prophet, seer, and revelator do so.[79]

The unique influence that a prophet exercises was on display at the April 1986 church General Conference, the first conference over which Benson presided in his new role. Francis Gibbons, secretary to the First Presidency of the Church, noted in his diary five months earlier that at the first meeting Benson, as church president, held with the Twelve Apostles in that first week after his ordination, he set out four areas that he hoped would "be given special emphasis at the coming April General Conference." First among those priorities was the Book of Mormon. Benson asked all church general authorities to reread the book in advance of the conference.[80] The response was dramatic.

Richard Galbraith's statistical survey of Book of Mormon usage in LDS general conferences showed that in the years preceding Benson's 1986 inaugural address, Book of Mormon citations comprised 12 percent of scriptural references made by conference speakers. For the three years after 1986, they comprised 40 percent—and then stayed in the 25–35 percent range in the years thereafter.[81] As church apostle L. Tom Perry noted in his conference address in April 1987, after a succession of speakers had centered their remarks on the Book of Mormon, "President, I'm starting to receive the distinct impression that we've been listening to you. I, too, will take my text from the Book of Mormon."[82]

In 1986 the total number of copies of the Book of Mormon that the LDS church distributed, through its missionaries and members, exceeded three million. More copies of the Book of Mormon in English were distributed in 1986 than the number of English copies distributed in 1982, 1983, and 1984 combined.[83] In 1990 more than 6.5 million copies were distributed.[84] More than ever, Book of Mormon distribution became the universal rallying cry of missionaries worldwide—and more missionaries than ever before were rallying.

It is worth repeating that the story of this dramatic uptick in Book of Mormon attention is significant—indeed, probably the most significant story of Benson's presidency—not just for the impact that Book of Mormon study has had on contemporary Mormonism, although more will be said about that below. It is also significant because of the way a worldwide institution moved, almost immediately, at the urging of its new helmsman. This is the persistence of charismatic authority in Mormonism—and represents Latter-day Saints' readiness to respond to what they see as prophetic revelation.

In a pre-April 1986 conference meeting with top church leaders, Ezra Taft Benson used a historical precedent to capture what he was feeling about the Book of Mormon, and the prescience of the analogy is evident in hindsight. He compared his sense of urgency in preaching the Book of Mormon to the anxiety Lorenzo Snow—the church's fifth president—felt about the need to reemphasize the payment of tithes.[85] Benson repeated the analogy to the full church membership at his first General Conference in April 1986: "The Lord inspired His servant Lorenzo Snow to reemphasize the principle of tithing to redeem the Church from financial bondage. . . . Now, in our day, the Lord has revealed the need to reemphasize the Book of Mormon."[86]

The Snow comparison was a potent one. Lorenzo Snow made tithing his watchword during a tour of Mormon congregations throughout Utah in 1899, and his priesthood subordinates took their cues from him. Tithing, long part of Mormon religious practice, became the focal point of subsequent general conferences for the first several years of the twentieth century. Eight years after that initial tour, Snow's successor Joseph F. Smith announced that the church was finally debt free, as tithing receipts soared. It is for this initiative that Lorenzo Snow is best remembered in the Latter-day Saint collective consciousness.

The parallels with Ezra Taft Benson and the Book of Mormon are apt. Lorenzo Snow's tenure was a brief one—only three years, from 1898 to 1901. But his legacy was remarkably memorable for its focus and effect. Similarly, President Benson's ill health effectively truncated his public visibility after three years in the president's office, but his legacy has likewise been marked in its lasting effect.

That is undoubtedly because Ezra Taft Benson–inspired attention to the Book of Mormon extended far beyond conference pulpits. Benson called for more than simply reading the Book of Mormon. He challenged artists and musicians and filmmakers to promulgate Book of Mormon themes in innovative ways. He invited families to make it the centerpiece of their devotional practices. And he invited Mormon thinkers to make the Book of Mormon the subject of their most robust writing and teaching.[87]

One result of this is rich with theological irony. President Benson assumed his post in the midst of a campaign that has been called "a new wave in counter-Mormonism."[88] Strong LDS growth in the 1960s and 1970s meant that new Mormon congregations were popping up throughout the United States, and

LDS church–sponsored "Homefront" public service commercials during that same period introduced Mormonism's family friendliness to a nation of media consumers. At the same time, evangelical Christians rocketed into national prominence with the election of Jimmy Carter, a self-proclaimed evangelical, in 1976, and even more so at the election of Ronald Reagan in 1980, when pundits across the country credited the new "Christian Right" as being the difference makers at the polls. This coincidence of Mormon ascendancy and evangelical ascendancy meant that a "turf war" was almost inevitable, in the competition for winning souls.[89] The LDS church announced new temples— sure signs of a growing Mormon presence—in Dallas and Atlanta in the early 1980s. Many suspicious Christians responded by embracing *The God Makers*, a 1982 film made by Ex-Mormons for Jesus that depicted Mormonism as a potentially Satanic counterfeit of Christianity. By the time Benson was named president of the LDS church three years later, millions of Americans had already viewed the film with their church congregations.

In 1982, and in the midst of reenergized claims that Mormons weren't Christians, LDS church leaders added a subtitle to the Book of Mormon: "Another Testament of Jesus Christ." For those who disputed Mormonism's Christian credentials, the Book of Mormon had always appeared high on the list of offenses. It flew in the face of "sola scriptura" orthodoxy. Yet the new subtitle represented a Mormon line of thinking that became central to President Benson's preaching about the book: it was thoroughly Christocentric. As Latter-day Saints read and taught and quoted and did more sophisticated exegetical work from the Book of Mormon in response to their prophet's invitation, the overall tenor of the church's theological outlook changed. BYU religion professor Robert Millet suggested that readers of the Book of Mormon could not help but be immersed in redemptive theology, in commentary about human fallenness and utter dependence on the merits and mercies and grace of a Savior. Thus, this theological turn was not prompted by outside, cultural influences as much as internal, scriptural ones.[90]

Even evangelical Christians who find Mormonism dubious on any number of counts have agreed that the Book of Mormon promotes the kind of Christ-centered theology that they doubted existed in Mormonism. And therein lies the irony. The Book of Mormon, the very symbol of the Mormon fallacy in the eyes of so many religionists, shifted Mormon discourse, at the end of the twentieth century, in a direction that many evangelicals would agree is more orthodox and, frankly, Christian.[91] This should not be taken to mean that Latter-day Saints have renounced other unique aspects of their theology, but that the tenets of Book of Mormon Christology have come to the foreground while other themes have receded into a softened background.[92] *Newsweek* asked historian and astute Mormon-watcher Jan Shipps if the fact that "Mormon rhetoric [was] becoming more overtly evangelical" signaled that "the Mormons [were] going mainstream." "Not at all" was how she responded. "After a century of cultivating their separate identity as a religious people, Mormons now want to stress their affinities with traditional Christianity yet highlight their uniqueness."[93]

It does not seem an exaggeration to say that the recent, serious interfaith work that has taken place on a number of levels between Mormon academics and church leaders and their counterparts from other faith groups—especially conservative Christian faith groups—since the early 2000s might not have happened without the common ground laid, and laid bare, by the Latter-day Saints' increased conversancy with the text and themes of the Book of Mormon.[94]

Conclusion

In the end, returning to Jan Shipps's "middle course" assessment seems a fair way to assess President Benson's own presidential ministry, too.[95] He personally reflected something of that "middle course," as his prophetic rhetoric showed a moderation of his own strongly conservative politics in favor of a broadly conservative morality. The causes the church embraced during his tenure fit with that retrenchment mentality: anti-pornography, anti-gambling, traditional family roles.[96]

There were a number of signals, in the early years of Benson's tenure, that he was presiding over a church that was simply continuing its transition into a new modern age. The church's Genealogical Society (renamed the Family History Department during the Benson years) celebrated the conversion of all of its cards to computer files in July 1987—a project that took an estimated one million worker hours. In April 1988, the church released a searchable computerized database of the Mormon canon. Satellite broadcasts became the norm to commemorate significant events, like the bicentennial of the U.S. Constitution or the sesquicentennial celebration of the founding of the church's women's auxiliary, the Relief Society. Organizationally, several church initiatives planted earlier came to fruition under President Benson's direction, including an expansion of the number of third-tier general authority "seventies" that could help administer an increasingly global faith.[97]

All of this fits with the idea, framed in that 1992 *U.S. News and World Report* article cited above, of the Mormon-leader-as-corporate-executive, as one who directs an organization that is moving forward on a well-marked trajectory, shaped as much by long-standing organizational philosophy as by any one leader's vision. This view of Mormonism goes a long way toward explaining the tone of media reports at the close of Ezra Taft Benson's life: the sense that recent controversies notwithstanding, Mormonism was growing unabated, moving forward steadily almost out of sheer institutional—and traditional—inertia.

But then Ezra Taft Benson's legacy reminds observers that what should not be missed is the persistence of charismatic authority in Mormonism, the existence of forces that can, almost immediately, change the religion's course. This meant that while Ezra Taft Benson's voice was not heard for the final few years of his tenure as the Mormon prophet, the clarion call of the first few years of his tenure reverberated so long and loudly that three decades later, the echoes are still distinguishable. And that clarion call centered on one innovation, one contribution, that he did not hint at in his initial press conference. It was a singular focus on the Book of Mormon, presented as divine direction. The impact of that directive suggests that practicing Latter-day Saints really did retain deep respect for the prophetic office. Modern Mormons at their core still held to a view of God's living oracles that set them apart, in the American religious landscape, as a peculiar people. As much as anything else, Ezra Taft Benson personifies, and stands as a reminder of, that.

Notes

1. "New LDS Leadership Indicates No Drastic Change," *Salt Lake Tribune*, November 12, 1985, A14.

2. "Ezra Taft Benson Is LDS Leader," *Salt Lake Tribune*, November 12, 1985, A1. For the full text of Benson's statement at the press conference, see "Pres. Benson Expresses Feelings on First Presidency Reorganization," *Church News* (a weekly *Deseret News* insert), November 17, 1985, 3, 7.

3. Sheri L. Dew, *Ezra Taft Benson: A Biography* (Salt Lake City: Deseret Book, 1987), 481.

4. See, for example, "Mormons Split on Outspoken Benson: Ex-Agriculture Secretary's Archconservative Views Upset Some Liberals," *Orlando Sentinel*, November 10, 1985, A19.

5. For two thorough treatments of this, see "Confrontation with Communism," chapter 12 of Gregory A. Prince and Wm. Robert Wright, *David O. McKay and the Rise of Modern Mormonism* (Salt Lake City: University of Utah Press, 2005), 279–322; and "Ezra Taft Benson: A Study of Inter-Quorum Conflict," chapter 3 of D. Michael Quinn, *The Mormon Hierarchy: Extensions of Power* (Salt Lake City: Signature Books, 1997), 66–115.

6. See "Man in the News: Ezra Taft Benson: New Chief of Mormons," *New York Times*, November 12, 1985, A16; Dawn Tracy, "LDS Liberals Fear a Swing to Far Right," *Salt Lake Tribune*, November 7, 1985, A5. The address, "Fourteen Fundamentals in Following the Prophet," was delivered at Brigham Young University on February 26, 1980, and reprinted in the church's June 1981 *Ensign* magazine.

7. "Pres. Benson Expresses Feelings on First Presidency Reorganization," 3, 7. See also Rodd G. Wagner, "Conservative LDS Leader Reaches Out to Liberals," *Salt Lake Tribune*, November 12, 1985, 2A.

8. Edward L. Kimball, *Lengthen Your Stride: The Presidency of Spencer W. Kimball*, working draft, chapter 16, 12–14. The working draft was included on a CD that accompanied Kimball's *Lengthen Your Stride* (Salt Lake City: Deseret Book, 2005).

9. Sterling McMurrin was quoted in Wallace Turner, "For Benson, the Wait Is Nearly Over," *New York Times*, November 8, 1985, A22: "I don't think the transition of power to Benson is going to make more than a ripple. His advanced years, his bad health, and his mellowing will keep things from getting out of hand. Besides, Mormon presidents need support from their colleagues and those fellows by and large are a sensible bunch now. . . . However, if he had become president 10 years ago, it would have been a different story."

10. Tracy, "LDS Liberals Fear a Swing to Far Right," A5.

11. See Kimball, *Lengthen Your Stride*, 161, note 16.

12. See Gibbons, *Ezra Taft Benson*, 296.

13. For an overview of LDS missionary developments in eastern Europe, see Khalile B. Mehr, *Mormon Missionaries Enter Eastern Europe* (Provo, Utah: Brigham Young University Press, and Salt Lake City: Deseret Book, 2002), especially chapter 5: "The Curtain Rises, 1985–1991."

14. See Kimball, *Lengthen Your Stride*, 161, note 16.

15. Ezra Taft Benson, "The Constitution—A Heavenly Banner," address at Brigham Young University, September 16, 1986, https://speeches.byu.edu/talks/ezra-taft-benson_constitution-heavenly-banner/.

16. Heidi L. Swinton, *To the Rescue: The Biography of Thomas S. Monson* (Salt Lake City: Deseret Book, 2010), 428.

17. See Mehr, *Mormon Missionaries Enter Eastern Europe*, 173–74. For a personal retelling of these events, see Thomas S. Monson, *Faith Rewarded: A Personal Account of Prophetic Promises to East German Saints from the Journal of Thomas S. Monson* (Salt Lake City: Deseret Book, 1996), 132–39.

18. See the account by Grant Salisbury, "A Church Service in Soviet Russia," *U.S. News and World Report*, October 26, 1959, 76.

19. Quoted in Edward L. Kimball, "Spencer W. Kimball and the Revelation on the Priesthood," *BYU Studies* 47, no. 2 (2008): 58. Benson wrote in his journal about the experience, "Following the prayer [offered by Spencer Kimball about the policy change], we experienced the sweetest spirit of unity and conviction that I have ever experienced" (Dew, *Ezra Taft Benson*, 457).

20. See Russell Stevenson, *For the Cause of Righteousness: A Global History of Blacks and Mormonism, 1830–2013* (Salt Lake City: Greg Kofford Books, 2014), especially chapters 4 and 6. See also Kimball, "Spencer Kimball and the Revelation on Priesthood," 23–25; and Prince and Wright, *David O. McKay and the Rise of Modern Mormonism*, 81–94.

21. See Ezra Taft Benson, "Trust Not in the Arm of Flesh," address at the October 1967 LDS Church General Conference, in *Conference Report: October 1967*, 34–39. Compare also Ezra Taft Benson's comments at the time that the LDS church was considering, in 1965, the possibilities of church missionary work in Nigeria, as quoted in Prince and Wright, *David O. McKay*, 92–93.

22. See, for example, Turner, "For Benson, the Wait Is Nearly Over," A22; Richard N. Ostling, "Awaiting the 13th Prophet," *Time*, November 18, 1985.

23. For an overview of Helvecio Martins's life and church career, see Mark L. Grover, "Helvecio Martins: First Black General Authority," *Journal of Mormon History* 36, no. 3 (Summer 2010): 27–53. Grover notes that few media outlets—National Public Radio was the one exception—made significant note of Elder Martins's race when he was called—and that Martins is still relatively unknown for many contemporary Mormons (46–49). *Ebony Rose*, No. 23 (January 1987), 2, notes that Bishop Helvecio Martins was called as the first black mission president. Issues of *Ebony Rose*, which ran from 1983 until July 1988, are held in Special Collections, Marriott Library, University of Utah. For a biographical sketch of Helvecio Martins published at the time of his appointment as a general authority, see "Elder Helvecio Martins of the Seventy," *Ensign*, May 1990, https://www.lds.org/ensign/1990/05/news-of-the-church/elder-helvcio-martins-of-the -seventy?lang=eng. It is worth noting that while Helvecio Martins's appointment as a general authority came in the years when President Benson was less involved in day-to-day church operations, Martins's appointment as a mission president came in November 1986, in the first year of Ezra Taft Benson's presidency. The actual call to serve as a mission president was delivered by Benson's first counselor, Gordon B. Hinckley. Martins remembered that Hinckley said, "I am calling you, in the name of the prophet, to be a mission president." The call to serve as a general authority was delivered by Benson's second counselor, Thomas S. Monson. See Helvecio Martins, with Mark Grover, *The Autobiography of Helvecio Martins* (Salt Lake City: Aspen Books, 1994), 96, 112–13.

24. *Deseret News 1999–2000 Church Almanac*, 430–34.

25. See "Black History Conference a Success," *Ebony Rose*, March 1987, 1, 4.

26. For an example of another genealogy project intended to involve a larger black community and add to church repositories, see information on the participation of LDS missionaries at the 1993 "Black Family Reunion" in Cincinnati, Ohio, found in Kentucky Louisville Mission, box 2, folder 3, LR 2422 32, LDS Church History Library, Salt Lake City, Utah.

27. See Armand L. Mauss, *All Abraham's Children: Changing Conceptions of Race and Lineage* (Urbana and Chicago: University of Illinois Press, 2003), 247–48.

28. See "Freedman's Bank Records Offer Priceless Family History Tool," *Ensign,* May 2001, https://www.lds.org/ensign/2001/05/news-of-the-church/freedmans-bank-records -offer-priceless-family-history-tool?lang=eng. See also Armand L. Mauss, "Casting Off the 'Curse of Cain,'" in Newell G. Bringhurst and Darron T. Smith, eds., *Black and Mormon* (Urbana and Chicago: University of Illinois Press, 2004), 93.

29. Mauss, *All Abraham's Children*, 246–47.

30. Michael Hirsley, "Blacks Flocking to Mormon Life," *Chicago Tribune*, June 10, 1988, B7 (also published as "Mormons: A Decade of Difference," in *Fort Lauderdale Sun Sentinel*, June 18, 1988, 5D). In that same month, civil rights leader and presidential candidate Jesse Jackson "paid a courtesy visit to leaders of the Mormon Church, which until 1978 banned blacks from its priesthood. Jackson said he discussed such concerns as drug abuse and strengthening families" ("Jackson Hails Platform Work," *New York Times*, June 15 1988, B6).

31. For analysis that offers important historical framing of Dallin H. Oaks's comments, see Matthew L. Harris and Newell G. Bringhurst, *The Mormon Church and Blacks: A Documentary History* (Urbana and Chicago: University of Illinois Press, 2015), 133–35.

32. "Apostles Talk about Reasons for Lifting Ban," *Provo Daily Herald*, June 5, 1988, 21, as cited in Juan Henderson, "A Time for Healing: Official Declaration 2," in *Out of Obscurity: The LDS Church in the Twentieth Century* (Salt Lake City: Deseret Book, 2000), 156.

33. Newell G. Bringhurst, "The Image of Blacks within Mormonism as Presented in the *Church News* (1978–1988)," *American Periodicals* 2 (Fall 1992): 121–23.

34. See church statistics in Deseret News 1999–2000 Church Almanac (Salt Lake City: Deseret News, 1998), 552–54; also "Statistical Report, 1985," in the April 1986 LDS Church General Conference, https://www.lds.org/general-conference/1986/04/statistical-report-1985 ?lang=eng; and "Statistical Report, 1994," in the April 1995 LDS General Conference, https://www.lds.org/general-conference/1995/04/statistical-report-1994?lang=eng.

35. Carrie A. Moore, "2 Apostles Assigned to Live outside U.S.," *Deseret News*, April 10, 2002, https://www.deseretnews.com/article/906937/2-apostles-assigned-to-live-outside -US.html.

36. In Sophia Scott Gregory, "Saints Preserve Us," 66.

37. Gordon B. Hinckley, "The Church Is on Course," address at the October 1992 semi-annual General Conference of the LDS Church, https://www.lds.org/general-conference/1992/10/the-church-is-on-course?lang=eng.

38. See Lavina Fielding Anderson, "The LDS Intellectual Community and Church Leadership: A Contemporary Chronology," *Dialogue: A Journal of Mormon Thought* 26, no. 1 (Spring 1993): 7- 64. See also, for example, "Mormon Secret Files," *The Christian Century*, September 9–16, 1992, 800; Sheler, "Latter-day Struggles," 77; "Media Coverage Spurs LDS Leaders to Address Criticism," *Deseret News*, August 14, 1992, B1. For the letter that came from the First Presidency explaining the rationale for the committee, see "First Presidency Statement Cites Scriptural Mandate for Church Committee," *Church News*, August 22, 1992, 7.

39. See Sheler, "Latter-day Struggles," 77. See also J. B. Haws, *The Mormon Image in the American Mind: Fifty Years of Public Perception* (New York and Oxford: Oxford University Press, 2013), 149–50.

40. For an overview of Bo Gritz's career, see chapter 9 of Newell G. Bringhurst and Craig L. Foster, *The Mormon Quest for the Presidency* (Independence, Mo.: John Whitmer Books, 2008), 208–25. See also Quinn, *The Mormon Hierarchy*, 114–15. See, for example, Christopher Smith, "Ultraconservative Gritz Remains as Bold as Ever," *Salt Lake Tribune*, December 7, 1992, B1-B2. Significantly, LDS church spokesman Don LeFevre issued a statement that same week that denied church leaders had been "sedating" Benson. See "Survivalist Views Need to Be Balanced," *The (Brigham Young University) Daily Universe*, December 3, 1992, 4; also Anderson, "The LDS Intellectual Community and Church Leadership: A Contemporary Chronology," 59.

41. It is important to note that church president David O. McKay specifically forbade Benson's participation on the John Birch Society board, saying to Birch Society founder Robert Welch that Benson "cannot be a member of that Board and be a member of the Quorum of the Twelve Apostles." In Prince and Wright, *David O. McKay*, 295.

42. Anderson, "The Intellectual Community and Church Leadership," 54, 59.

43. Quoted in Smith, "Ultraconservative Gritz Remains as Bold as Ever," *Salt Lake Tribune*, December 7, 1992, B1-B2. Church general authority Malcolm Jeppsen described an encounter he had with a Mormon who worried that Benson was being silenced: "At one of my stake conferences in the Manti area one of the priesthood leaders came to me after my priesthood leadership meeting and told me this wild tale. He said he had it on good authority that President Benson had come to the Manti temple and upon getting inside fell down on his knees and offered prayer of thanks for letting him get away from his counselors who were keeping him quiet and not letting him speak at conferences. He asked if I could believe his counselors were that cruel. I replied that no I could not believe it, because nothing could be farther from the truth. They visited the President on a daily basis, and passed everything that he could possibly understand by him. They loved President Benson dearly. They looked at me as if I must not know what was going on for sure." Malcom S. Jeppsen, *Up Close and Personal: The Life History of Malcolm Seth and Marian Jeppsen* (2013), 429, copy in possession of author.

44. See Bringhurst and Foster, *The Mormon Quest for the Presidency*, 220; also see Christopher Smith, "Hero-Turned-Heretic? Gritz May Be Leading LDS Flock into Wilderness," *Salt Lake Tribune*, November 29, 1992, A2; "Speaking Their Peace: Survivalists Sound Off: LDS Zealots Muzzling Outspoken to Protect Tax Status, Gritz Says," *Salt Lake Tribune*, January 22, 1993, B1; Christopher Smith, "Bo Gritz Blasts His Fair-Weather Friends," *Salt Lake Tribune*, December 24, 1994, C2.

45. See Gibbons, *Ezra Taft Benson*, 315–20. One of Benson's most influential general conference addresses was "Beware of Pride," read by his counselor Gordon Hinckley in the April 1989 conference. Although Benson did not deliver the talk, a recent study, based on access to Benson's extensive personal files on the topic, demonstrates Benson's close participation in the preparation of the sermon. See Sharon Black, Brad Wilcox, and Spencer Olsen, "'Beware of Pride': Prophetic Preparation for a Classic Address," *Religious Educator* 16, no. 3 (2015): 159–83.

46. Mark A. Kellner, "Latter-day Saints: Prophet's Grandson Quits Church in Public Protest," *Christianity Today*, November 22, 1993, 46; "Mormon President's Health Raises Questions : Succession: Famed Grandson Says Church Hierarchy Is Presenting a Misleading Image of Ezra Taft Benson, Who Serves as the Faith's Prophet for Life," *Los Angeles Times*, July 31, 1993, http://articles.latimes.com/1993-07-31/local/me-18763_1_ezra-taft -benson.

47. See "Mormons Penalize Dissident Members," *New York Times*, September 19, 1993, section 1, page 31. Also Dirk Johnson, "As Mormon Church Grows, So Does Dissent from Feminists and Scholars," *New York Times*, October 2, 1993, section 1, page 7; "Mormon Leaders Back Acts of Discipline," *Washington Times*, October 23, 1993, D4. See Jeppsen, *Up Close and Personal*, 423–37, for Jeppsen's role, as president of the church's Utah South Area, in coordinating with congregational leaders about dissident members. Jeppsen describes directing stake presidents to interview members whose activities had made church superiors nervous, and recommending disciplinary action if local leaders were not satisfied that the members in question had renounced troubling tendencies.

48. See Haws, *The Mormon Image*, 132–48.

49. See Anderson, "The LDS Intellectual Community and the Church," 18, 29, 35, 49.

50. Anderson, "The LDS Intellectual Community and the Church," 35, 36, 62.

51. Michael Quinn has argued that Benson's past involvement with a "spy ring" at BYU in the 1970s fit philosophically with the establishment of the "Strengthening Church Members Committee"—but Quinn also saw Benson's apostolic colleagues' more moderate political views figuring into church wariness about ultraconservatives in the 1990s. See Quinn, *The Mormon Hierarchy*, 113–15.

52. Ezra Taft Benson, "The Gospel Teacher and His Message," Address to Church Educational System Religious Educators, September 17, 1976, 5–6. For Ezra Taft Benson's concerns about the initiatives of the church's historians during Leonard Arrington's tenure as church historian—a period of professionalization and publications in the 1970s and early 1980s—see Leonard J. Arrington, *Adventures of a Church Historian* (Urbana and Chicago: University of Illinois Press, 1998), 148, 216–17.

53. See Gregory A. Prince, *Leonard Arrington and the Writing of Mormon History* (Salt Lake City: University of Utah Press, 2016), 412–13.

54. Ezra Taft Benson, "To the Mothers in Zion," February 22, 1987.

55. Boyd K. Packer, "Talk to the All-Church Coordinating Council," May 18, 1993, reprint available at http://www.zionsbest.com/face.html.

56. See "Significant Highlights in Prophet's Ministry," *Church News*, June 4, 1994, 12; also Susan Buhler Taber, *Mormon Lives: A Year in the Elkton Ward* (Urbana and Chicago: University of Illinois Press, 1993), 6.

57. Peter Steinfels, "Mormons Drop Rites Opposed by Women," *New York Times*, May 3, 1990, http://www.nytimes.com/1990/05/03/us/mormons-drop-rites-opposed-by-women .html.

58. See Dew, *Ezra Taft Benson*, 505–7, for a discussion of the reaction to the address; also Lavina Fielding Anderson, "A Voice from the Past: The Benson Instructions for Parents," *Dialogue: A Journal of Mormon Thought* 21, no. 4 (Winter 1988): 103–13. For an important sampling of Mormon feminist writing in the early 1990s, see Maxine Hanks, ed., *Women and Authority: Re-emerging Mormon Feminism* (Salt Lake City: Signature Books, 1992). For the way Benson's talk, "To the Mothers in Zion," still reverberates, see the anthology *Mormon Feminism: Essential Writings*, ed. Joanna Brooks, Rachel Hunt Steenblik, and Hannah Wheelwright (New York and Oxford: Oxford University Press, 2016), 14, 117, 157, and 239.

59. Peggy Fletcher Stack, "Healthy or Hurtful? Twenty Years Later, Mormon 'Purge' Still Debated," *Salt Lake Tribune*, October 1, 1993, http://archive.sltrib.com/article.php ?id=56920802&itype=CMSID.

60. M. Russell Ballard, "The Opportunities and Responsibilities of CES Teachers in the 21st Century," Address to CES (Church Educational System) Religious Educators, February 26, 2016, https://www.lds.org/broadcasts/article/evening-with-a-general-authority/ 2016/02/the-opportunities-and-responsibilities-of-ces-teachers-in-the-21st-century ?lang=eng. Importantly, the talk was also reprinted in the church's magazine, the *Ensign*, in December 2016.

61. Marlin K. Jensen, "Minding the House of Church History: Reflections of a Church Historian at the End of His Time," *Journal of Mormon History* 39, no. 2 (Spring 2013): 89.

62. John L. Brooke, *The Refiner's Fire: The Making of Mormon Cosmology, 1644–1844* (New York and Cambridge, U.K.: Cambridge University Press, 1994), 304–5.

63. See Jill Mulvay Derr, Janath Russell Cannon, and Maureen Ursenbach Beecher, *Women of Covenant: The Story of Relief Society* (Salt Lake City: Deseret Book, 1992), 220.

64. For a thorough account of the back and forth discussion when the book was released, see Prince, *Leonard Arrington and the Writing of Mormon History*, 276–92.

65. Report of the Communications Futures Committee, internal document, Public Affairs Department, The Church of Jesus Christ of Latter-day Saints, 4, 15, 46. The committee was chaired by apostle David B. Haight, and included apostles James E. Faust and M. Russell Ballard, prominent political pollster Dr. Richard B. Wirthlin, and Bruce Olsen, managing director of LDS Public Affairs. See Haws, *The Mormon Image*, 165.

66. Jeffrey L. Sheler, with Betsy Wagner, "Latter-day Struggles," *U.S. News and World Report*, September 28, 1992, 78.

67. Sheler and Wagner, "Latter-day Struggles," 77.

68. This was a stake (analogous to a diocese) conference in Annandale, Virginia. See Dew, *Ezra Taft Benson*, 489.

69. Francis M. Gibbons, *Ezra Taft Benson: Statesman, Patriot, Prophet of God* (Salt Lake City: Deseret Book, 1996), 304. Gibbons was secretary to the church's governing First Presidency from 1980 until the spring of 1986, when he began a five-year term of service as a church general authority in the quorums of Seventy.

70. For detailed discussion of the changing place of the Book of Mormon in Mormon thought and discourse, see Grant Underwood, *The Millenarian World of Early Mormonism* (Urbana and Chicago: University of Illinois Press, 1993), 76–96; Noel Reynolds, "The Coming Forth of the Book of Mormon in the Twentieth Century," *BYU Studies* 38, no. 2 (1999), 7–47; Terryl Givens, *By the Hand of Mormon: The American Scripture that Launched a New World Religion* (New York and Oxford: Oxford University Press, 2002), 62–71; and Casey Paul Griffiths, "The Book of Mormon among the Saints: Evolving Use of the Keystone Scripture," in *The Coming Forth of the Book of Mormon* (Provo, Utah: Religious Studies Center, and Salt Lake City: Deseret Book, 2015), 199–226.

71. See Underwood, *The Millenarian World of Early Mormonism*, 91–94.

72. See Reynolds, "The Coming Forth of the Book of Mormon in the Twentieth Century," 19, 32. For the first decade of this Sunday School plan, the rotation was on an eight-year basis, and two years were devoted to the Book of Mormon.

73. See Philip L. Barlow, *Mormons and the Bible: The Place of the Latter-day Saints in American Religion*, updated edition (New York and Oxford: Oxford University Press, 2013), 47: "Mormon periodicals in the 1830s cited the Bible nineteen times as often as the Book of Mormon, and in the 173 discourses given in Nauvoo, Illinois, for which contemporary records exist, Smith paraphrased the Book of Mormon only twenty-three times but quoted or paraphrased the Bible more than six hundred times."

74. See Dew, *Ezra Taft Benson*, 492.

75. Ibid., 292, 339, 350; Gibbons, *Ezra Taft Benson*, 301.

76. Dew, *Ezra Taft Benson*, 195.

77. Patrick Q. Mason, "Ezra Taft Benson and Modern (Book of) Mormon Conservatism," in Mason and John G. Turner, eds., *Out of Obscurity: Mormonism since 1945* (New York and Oxford: Oxford University Press, 2016), 74. For Mason's insightful assessment of the impact of Ezra Taft Benson's Book of Mormon advocacy, see this passage on page 79: "Mormons picked up the Book of Mormon and started reading it regularly and seriously in large part because of Ezra Taft Benson. That has changed the face of modern Mormonism, most dramatically by helping usher in a new age of Mormon Christocen-

trism. Benson may have originally intended for readers to discover 'America, freedom, and secret combinations' in their study of the Book of Mormon, but when they opened the book they found a lot more than those three themes. Empowering people to read scripture has always had unintended consequences." For examples of Benson's later use of the Book of Mormon to emphasize Christ-centered Mormon soteriology, see Ezra Taft Benson, *A Witness and a Warning* (Salt Lake City: Deseret Book, 1988), 33; "Born of God," address at the October 1985 LDS General Conference, https://www.lds.org/general -conference/1985/10/born-of-god?lang=eng; "Cleansing the Inner Vessel," address at the April 1986 LDS General Conference, https://www.lds.org/general-conference/1986/04/ cleansing-the-inner-vessel?lang=eng; "A Mighty Change of Heart," *Ensign*, October 1989, https://www.lds.org/ensign/1989/10/a-mighty-change-of-heart?lang=eng.

78. Ezra Taft Benson, "A New Witness for Christ," address at the October 1984 LDS Semiannual General Conference, https://www.lds.org/general-conference/1984/10/a-new -witness-for-christ?lang=eng.

79. See Reynolds, "The Coming Forth of the Book of Mormon in the Twentieth Century," 30.

80. Gibbons, *Ezra Taft Benson*, 297, 304.

81. Cited in Reynolds, "The Coming Forth of the Book of Mormon in the Twentieth Century," 10.

82. L. Tom Perry, "United in Building the Kingdom of God," address at the April 1987 LDS General Conference, https://www.lds.org/general-conference/1987/04/united-in-building -the-kingdom-of-god?lang=eng. See also Dew, *Ezra Taft Benson*, 496.

83. Dew, *Ezra Taft Benson*, 495.

84. See the chart in *Church News*, June 4, 1994, 6.

85. Dew, *Ezra Taft Benson*, 493.

86. Benson, "A Sacred Responsibility," address at the April 1986 annual LDS general conference, https://www.lds.org/general-conference/1986/04/a-sacred-responsibility?lang=eng.

87. Two examples of this are worth mentioning. Prominent Mormon intellectual Eugene England published a collection of testimonials about the Book of Mormon from dozens of Latter-day Saints of all walks of life as *Converted to Christ through the Book of Mormon* (Salt Lake City: Deseret Book, 1989). England dedicated the book to Ezra Taft Benson, "Our Book of Mormon Prophet." In 1987 the church began production on a feature-length film, *How Rare a Possession*. See Janet Thomas, "How Rare a Possession: The Making of a New Church Film," *New Era*, November 1987, https://www.lds.org/new-era/1987/11/ how-rare-a-possession?lang=eng).

88. Massimo Introvigne, "The Devil Makers: Contemporary Evangelical Fundamentalist Anti-Mormonism," *Dialogue* 27, no. 1 (Spring 1994): 154; see also Massimo Introvigne, "Old Wine in New Bottles: The Story Behind Fundamentalist Anti-Mormonism," *BYU Studies* 35, no. 3 (1995–1996): 45. Daniel C. Peterson advanced a similar analysis. See his "A Modern 'Malleus maleficarum,'" in *Review of Books on the Book of Mormon* 3 (Provo, Utah: FARMS, 1991): 231–60, cited by Introvigne, "The Devil Makers," 154.

89. Kenneth L. Woodward and Barbara Bugower, "Bible-Belt Confrontation," *Newsweek*, March 4, 1985, 65.

90. See Robert L. Millet, "Joseph Smith and Modern Mormonism: Orthodoxy, Neoorthodoxy, Tension, and Tradition," *BYU Studies* 29, no. 3 (1989): 66. Compare O. Kendall

White Jr., *Mormon Neo-Orthodoxy: A Crisis Theology* (Salt Lake City: Signature Books, 1987); and Klaus Hansen, "Review of *Mormon Neo-Orthodoxy: A Crisis Theology by O. Kendall White, Jr.*," *Church History* 58, no. 3 (September 1989): 415. See also Terryl Givens's thoughtful analysis of several of the Book of Mormon's additional theological contributions and innovations in his *By the Hand of Mormon*, especially chapter 7 ("'Plain and Precious Truths': The Book of Mormon as New Theology, Part 1—The Encounter with Biblical Christianity") and chapter 8 ("'Plain and Precious Truths': The Book of Mormon as New Theology, Part 2—Dialogic Revelation"). Givens writes, "By 1988, it was clear that Benson had launched the church into a new era in which the Book of Mormon received unprecedented attention and respect" (241).

91. See Carl Mosser, "And the Saints Go Marching On: The New Mormon Challenge for World Missions, Apologetics, and Theology," chapter 2 of Francis Beckwith, Carl Mosser, and Paul Owen, eds., *The New Mormon Challenge: Responding to the Latest Defenses of a Fast-Growing Movement* (Grand Rapids, Mich.: Zondervan, 2002), 79–80: "As anyone who has read the Book of Mormon knows, its theology is largely orthodox in nature. . . . I am not fully convinced that this movement [in Mormon theology] is primarily a reaction to the crisis of secularization as White claims Mormon neo-orthodoxy is. Rather, it seems to be a natural by-product of the LDS church's emphasis of the last twenty-five years on the Book of Mormon and its teachings."

92. See, for example, Richard J. Mouw, *Talking with Mormons: An Invitation to Evangelicals* (Grand Rapids, Mich.: William B. Eerdmans Publishing, 2012), 92–96.

93. Kenneth L. Woodward, "A Mormon Moment," *Newsweek*, September 10, 2001, 48. LDS historian Richard Bushman raised essentially the same point in a discussion with journalists and academics at the Pew Forum's biannual Faith Angle Conference, May 14, 2007. Bushman was the forum's guest speaker, and *Newsweek*'s Kenneth Woodward asked about the place of grace in Mormon theology. Bushman responded: "In dialogues with evangelical Christians, Mormons are recovering their own grace theology, which is plentifully presented in the Book of Mormon. And they are recovering it not just at the high level of discussion between BYU faculty and Baylor faculty, but right down in the congregation" ("Mormonism and Democratic Politics: Are They Compatible?" 16; transcript accessible at http://pewforum.org/Politics-and-Elections/Mormonism-and-Politics-Are-They-Compatible.aspx).

94. For two examples of that dialogue, see Craig L. Blomberg and Stephen E. Robinson, *How Wide the Divide? A Mormon and an Evangelical in Conversation* (Downer's Grove, Ill.: Intervarsity Press, 1997), and Richard J. Mouw and Robert L. Millet, eds., *Talking Doctrine: Mormons and Evangelicals in Conversation* (Downer's Grove, Ill.: IVP Academic, 2015).

95. In Gregory, "Saints Preserve Us," 66.

96. See, for example, a First Presidency statement against "the legalization and government sponsorship of lotteries," in *Church News*, October 5, 1986, 4.

97. For a brief detailing of these events, see the timeline in *Deseret News 1989–1990 Church Almanac* (Salt Lake City: Deseret News, 1988), 306–22; "Significant Highlights in Prophet's Ministry," *Church News*, June 4, 1994, 12.

Contributors

GARY JAMES BERGERA is managing director of the Smith-Pettit Foundation, Salt Lake City, Utah. He is author of *Conflict in the Quorum: Orson Pratt, Joseph Smith, Brigham Young*; co-author of *Brigham Young University: A House of Faith*; editor of *Line Upon Line: Essays on Mormon Doctrine*, *The Autobiography of B. H. Roberts*, and *Statements of the LDS First Presidency: A Topical Compendium*; and co-editor of *Joseph Smith's Quorum of the Anointed: A Documentary History, 1842–1845*, and *The Nauvoo Endowment Companies: A Documentary History, 1845–1846*. His publications have received awards from the Dialogue Foundation, the Mormon History Association, and the Utah Historical Society. He currently serves on the editorial boards of the *Journal of Mormon History* and the *John Whitmer Historical Association Journal*; and previously was managing editor of *Dialogue: A Journal of Mormon Thought*; director of publishing, Signature Books, Inc.; and a member of the Board of Directors of the Mormon History Association.

MATTHEW BOWMAN is associate professor of history at Henderson State University and the author of *The Mormon People: The Making of an American Faith* (Random House, 2012) and *The Urban Pulpit: New York City and the Fate of Liberal Evangelicalism* (Oxford University Press, 2014). He is also co-editor of *Women and Mormonism: Historical and Contemporary Perspectives* (with Kate Holbrook; University of Utah Press, 2016).

NEWELL G. BRINGHURST is an independent scholar and Professor Emeritus of History and Political Science at College of the Sequoias in Visalia, California. He is the author/editor of thirteen books published since 1981. His most recent are *The Mormon Quest of the Presidency: Eleven Mormons Who Ran for*

President from 1844 to 2012 (2008, original ed., 2011, enlarged, expanded ed.), co-authored with Craig L. Foster; and, as co-editor (with Craig L. Foster), a trilogy under the title *The Persistence of Polygamy*. The three books of the trilogy are *Joseph Smith and the Origins of Mormon Polygamy* (2010), *From Joseph Smith's Martyrdom to the First Manifesto* (2013), and *Fundamentalist Mormon Polygamy from 1890 to the Present* (2015). Also published in 2015 was *The Mormon Church and Blacks: A Documentary History*, co-edited with Matthew L. Harris. Bringhurst is a longtime member of the Mormon History Association, having served as its president in 1999–2000. He is also a member of the John Whitmer Historical Association, of which he served as president from 2005 to 2006.

BRIAN Q. CANNON is professor of history and director of the Charles Redd Center at Brigham Young University. He is president of the Mormon History Association and past president of the Agricultural History Society. Cannon is the author of three books, the co-editor of two volumes, and the author of more than two dozen scholarly articles on facets of western American, rural, Utah, and Mormon history.

ROBERT A. GOLDBERG is professor of history and director of the Tanner Humanities Center at the University of Utah. He is the author of eight books, with his last two, *Barry Goldwater* and *Enemies Within: The Culture of Conspiracy in Modern America,* published by Yale University Press. He has won twelve teaching honors, including the Distinguished Honors Professor Award, Presidential Teaching Scholar Award, and University of Utah Distinguished Teaching Award. In 2003 he held the Fulbright Distinguished Chair in American Studies at the Swedish Institute for North American Studies, Uppsala University. Goldberg organized the Mormon Studies Initiative at the University of Utah in 2010. He has also received the Rosenblatt Prize for Excellence, the University of Utah's most prestigious award.

MATTHEW L. HARRIS is a professor of history at Colorado State University–Pueblo. He is the author and/or editor of three books, including *The Mormon Church and Blacks: A Documentary History*, published by the University of Illinois Press in 2015. With Newell Bringhurst, he has edited a volume of essays entitled *The Mormon Church and Its Gospel Topics Essays: The Scholarly Community Responds*, to be published by the University of Utah Press in 2019. In addition, his book *"Watchman on the Tower": Ezra Taft Benson and the Emergence of the Mormon Right* will be published by the University of Utah Press in 2019. He has won the Provost's Award for Teaching Excellence at Colorado State University–Pueblo, the Student's Choice Award, and two awards for scholarly and creative excellence.

J. B. Haws is an assistant professor of church history and doctrine at Brigham Young University. His PhD in American history is from the University of Utah. He is interested in the place of Mormonism on the twentieth- and twenty-first-century religious landscape of America, and is the author of *The Mormon Image in the American Mind: Fifty Years of Public Perception* (Oxford University Press, 2013) and articles in the *Journal of Mormon History*, the *Journal of Book of Mormon Studies*, and several essays in Mormon anthologies.

Andrea G. Radke-Moss is a professor of history at Brigham Young University–Idaho, where she teaches courses in American history, particularly U.S. women's history and the history of the American West. She currently serves as the associate dean of faculty development for the College of Language and Letters at BYU-Idaho. Her book, *Bright Epoch: Women and Coeducation in the American West*, was published by the University of Nebraska Press in 2008. Her research interests and publications include women and higher education, rural women of the Great Plains, women and suffrage in the West, women's experiences at the World's Columbian Exposition (Chicago World's Fair) of 1893, and a range of topics on the history of Mormon women. Currently, Radke-Moss is researching a history of western women's activism and participation at the Chicago World's Fair, and Mormon women's experiences in the Mormon-Missouri War of 1838.

Index

Eisenhower, Milton, 127
Elect Women of God, 199
Ellender, Allen, 43
Enemy Hath Done This, An, 7, 137
Equal Rights Amendment, 90, 91, 178,
    193–95, 197
Erdman, Henry, 45
Europe, 3–5, 24, 65n21, 83, 84, 132, 160,
    168–72, 212
Evans, Richard L., 139
Evans, Stanton, 76

Fair Deal, 71
Family: A Proclamation to the World, 200,
    201
Family Farm Development Act, 41, 44
Family History Department, 214, 229
Faust, James E., 200
Federal Bureau of Investigation, 5, 9, 76–77,
    83, 86, 87, 113, 125–27, 167, 188
First Amendment, 2
First Presidency of the LDS Church, 132
Florida, 5, 78
Ford, James W., 129
free agency, 10, 69, 82, 160–62
freedom, 1, 2, 4, 6, 9, 10, 45, 53, 66n30,
    66n37, 69, 70, 79, 84, 102, 136, 159–67,
    170–74, 188, 192, 210, 225
Freedom Club, 63n7
Freedom Riders, 128
free market, 2, 28, 45, 58, 71, 72
Freiberg, Germany, 212
Friedman, Milton, 45
fundamentalist polygamy, 217

Gadianton Robbers, 73, 173, 177n50
gay rights, 90, 192, 194
German Democratic Republic. *See* Ger-
    many
Germany, 4, 8, 133, 169, 212, 213
Gibbons, Francis, 6–7
Goldwater, Barry, 40, 68, 71, 76, 78, 86, 90,
    98, 99, 105, 110, 131
Goodman, Jack, 8
Gorbachev, Mikhail, 65n24
Grand Rapids, Michigan, 106
Grant, Heber J., 140n2, 159, 160, 162
Great Britain, 72
Great Depression, 3, 28, 30, 68, 70, 72
Great Society, 5
Grede, William J., 105–8, 111, 119n38

Gritz, Bo, 217–18
Guthrie, Woody, 6, 14n35

Halleck, Charles, 36
Harding, Ralph 130
Hargis, Billy James, 101, 131
Haycock, D. Arthur, 9, 28, 31, 34
Henry, Patrick, 82
Highlander Folk School, 129, 130
Hinckley, Gordon B., 9, 139, 140, 200, 215,
    216, 222–23
Hiss, Alger, 13n25, 29
Hofmann, Mark, 211, 219, 222
Holland, Jeffrey R., 216
Holland, Michigan, 106
Holmes, Clarence L., 29, 45
Hoover, J. Edgar, 5, 76, 77, 84, 86, 113, 125,
    127, 135, 136, 142n19
House Committee on Agriculture, 33, 35, 37
Hunt, Nelson Bunker, 101
Hunter, J. Reese, 102, 119n32

Idaho, 6, 28, 83, 114, 144n40, 195
Idaho Cooperative Council, 26
Idaho Department of Economics and Mar-
    keting, 4
Illinois, 39, 78
Illuminati, 84–85
Iowa State University, 26, 29, 45

Jefferson, Thomas, 24
Jensen, Marlin K., 222
John Birch Society, 1, 5–9, 15n44, 57, 58,
    66n34, 69, 76–91, 101–3, 105, 110, 125, 127,
    130, 134, 160, 194, 209, 218
Johnson, Lyndon B., 5, 6, 71, 115, 128, 132–34,
    137
Jones, Bob, 131

Kennedy, John F., 6, 71, 128
Kennedy, Robert, 126
Kimball, Spencer W., 8, 75, 139, 148n63; 197,
    208, 209, 215, 216, 225
King, Martin Luther, 5, 10, 124–26, 129,
    134–40, 155n127
Kirk, Russell, 78
kitchen debate, 56, 64n16, 179
Koch, Fred, 101, 105
Korean War, 31
Krushchev, Nikita, 10, 53–57, 60–61, 63n14,
    64n16

Republican National Committee, 27
Richards, LeGrand, 102
right-wing, 7, 8, 209
Rockefeller, Nelson A., 98–100, 117n6, 131
Romney, George W., 106, 110, 111, 114, 116, 131
Romney, Mitt, 97
Roosevelt, Franklin D., 3, 24, 69, 71, 78, 162, 163
Rural Development Program, 42, 43, 45, 46
Rustin, Bayard, 126

Sacramento, California, 81
Salt Lake City, Utah, 9, 27, 81–83, 101, 102, 107, 108, 136, 159, 163, 194, 208, 214
Salt Lake Tribune, 106, 208, 221
Schlesinger, Arthur, Jr., 6
school integration, 131
Schwartz, Fred, 75, 76
secret combinations, 7, 70, 173, 225, 236–37n77
segregation, 128
Seeger, Pete, 6, 14n35
September Six, 211, 219, 221
Shaw, Byron, 64n16
Skousen, W. Cleon, 15n44, 75, 138
Sligh, Edward R., Jr., 106, 107, 109
Smith, Adam, 45
Smith, Barbara B., 195
Smith, Joseph, 70, 82, 112, 115, 160, 161, 223, 224
Smith, Joseph F., 162, 173, 190, 227
Smith, Joseph Fielding, 8, 66n36, 82, 102, 119n41, 139, 208
Snow, Lorenzo, 227
socialism, 4, 26, 55, 57, 68–70, 76, 81, 82, 86, 102, 104
socialist, 35, 130, 138
Soviets, 5, 60, 213
Soviet Union, 1, 53, 60, 63n15, 71, 160, 211, 213
Strengthening Church Members Committee, 217
Study of Communism, A, 125, 126

Talmage, James E., 161, 173
Tanner, Nathan E., 66n36, 86, 89, 109, 148n67, 192–93
Texas, 78
Thompson, Clark, 37

Thurmond, Strom, 76, 84, 89, 103, 105, 108, 110, 131, 135
Title of Liberty, 7
Townsend, Francis, 32
Truman, Harry S., 23, 71, 78

Udall, Morris K., 57, 116
United States, 5, 54, 65n21, 72, 84, 85; Christian nation, 6, 58
University of California Berkeley, 27
University of Mississippi, 128
University of Utah, 8, 153n111
U.S. Constitution, 3, 28, 45, 69, 73, 77, 79, 87, 88, 104, 107, 112, 115, 164, 173, 194, 211, 212, 229; hanging by a thread, 29, 70, 89
U.S. Supreme Court, 2, 28, 79, 82, 90
Utah, 6, 69–71, 77, 92n14, 97, 101, 102, 135, 140, 162

Vietnam War, 5, 115
Von Hayek, Friedrich, 45
Voting Rights Act, 133

Wallace, George C., 9, 68, 89, 111–15, 131, 135, 146n54
Warren, Earl, 79
Washington, D.C., 27, 28, 56, 63n14, 76, 101, 118n18, 144n40, 214
Watkins, Arthur, 29, 47n11
Watts Riots, 133
Welch, Mary, 119n44
Welch, Robert W., Jr., 5, 6, 8, 76–78, 81–89, 101, 108, 119n44, 125–28, 133–36, 143n28
Western Athletic Conference, 138, 153n111
Whitney, Idaho, 2–3, 9, 144n40
Whitney, Orson F., 144n40
Whitten, Jamie, 42, 98
Wickard, Claude, 24
Wilkinson, Ernest, 39, 62n4, 84, 118n18, 132, 137
Woodward, Kenneth, 8
World War I, 24
World War II, 3, 10, 30, 72, 85

Young, Brigham, 159, 162, 163, 223
Young, Milton, 35
Young Men's Mutual Improvement Association, 40

Zion, 70, 73, 74

The University of Illinois Press
is a founding member of the
Association of University Presses.

University of Illinois Press
1325 South Oak Street
Champaign, IL 61820-6903
www.press.uillinois.edu